ALTOGETHER AMERICAN

Robert and Eliza Mills, tintype (1851).

ALTOGETHER AMERICAN

Robert Mills, Architect and Engineer,
1781–1855

Rhodri Windsor Liscombe

New York · *Oxford*
OXFORD UNIVERSITY PRESS
1994

Oxford University Press

Oxford   New York   Toronto
Delhi   Bombay   Calcutta   Madras   Karachi
Kuala Lumpur   Singapore   Hong Kong   Tokyo
Nairobi   Dar es Salaam   Cape Town
Melbourne   Auckland   Madrid

and associated companies in
Berlin   Ibadan

Published by Oxford University Press, Inc.,
200 Madison Avenue, New York, New York   10016

Oxford is a registered trademark of Oxford University Press

Library of Congress Cataloging-in-Publication Data
Liscombe, R. W., 1946–
    Altogether American : Robert Mills, architect and engineer,
1781–1855 / Rhodri Windsor Liscombe.
        p.   cm.
    Includes bibliographical references and index.
    ISBN 0-19-508019-X
    1. Mills, Robert, 1781–1855.   2. Architects—United States—
Biography.   I. Mills, Robert, 1781–1855.   II. Title.
    NA737.M5L58   1993
720'.92—dc20   92-40045
[B]

Printing (last digit): 9 8 7 6 5 4 3 2 1

Printed in the United States of America
on acid-free paper

To Suzanne Windsor-Liscombe

Preface

This book has been written on the basis of three underlying assumptions. First, that the study of the life and career of the individual architect remains an efficacious means of illuminating both the contemporary historical period and the creative process. Second, that personal factors inevitably exert a significant influence on professional practice and even design. Third, that preconceived theoretical or ideological stances can obtrude upon the rediscovery of the present of the past.

The author owes a considerable debt of gratitude to the staff of the public and private archives, libraries, and historical or cultural institutions cited in the text, notes, and photographic credits. Their invaluable aid was reinforced by the interest and assistance of other scholars working in the field, most especially Gene Waddell, and Professors Damie Stillman, William Pierson, Robert Alexander, and John M. Bryan. The research was supported by grants from the Social Sciences and Humanities Research Council of Canada and undertaken with the help of Philippa Windsor Liscombe, who also typed the early drafts of the text. During that stage Florian H. Thayn, then of the Art and Reference Division of the Architect of the United States Capitol, answered a host of questions about Mills's contribution to the architecture of the Federal capital. The transformation of the text into book form was greatly facilitated by Joyce Berry, senior editor at Oxford University Press, her associate Irene Pavitt, and copy-editor Susan Denny; the design work was completed in collaboration with Cindy Reid of Typeworks in Vancouver, British Columbia.

Throughout the final, arduous process of editing and refinement, my wife, Suzanne Windsor-Liscombe, provided not only unstinting help, but also astute criticism and constant encouragement.

Vancouver   R.W.L.
April 1993

Contents

ALTOGETHER AMERICAN

Artists are but tender plants, although they are sometimes able among weeds, briars and thorns to raise their heads, and for a while to enjoy the sunshine of public favor and patronage; yet it more frequently happens that they are destroyed by the insects of an hour, or nipped by the chilling wind of poverty, they languish, wither and die.

Robert Mills, "The Art of Painting"

1

Upbringing and Training, 1781–1808
"the ardent thirst after knowledge"[1]

Robert Mills, preeminent among the first generation of native-born American architects, was born on 12 August 1781 in the architecturally handsome and thriving port city of Charles Town, South Carolina. He was the fourth child and third son of Ann Taylor, descendant of the first landgrave of the Carolinas, and William Mills, an emigrant from Dundee, Scotland, who had prospered as a tailor and was serving as a captain in the Loyalist Militia—an episode Robert would expunge through his own intense patriotism.[2] The family then lived on Tradd Street, moving after his mother's death in 1790 to a larger house at 105 Church Street, in the middle of the isthmus, tangy with the Atlantic breeze, between the Ashley and Cooper rivers, upon which the city had developed. In this community, reincorporated as Charleston in 1783 to celebrate the defeat of the British, William Mills plied his craft. A devout Presbyterian, he established in his children a profound Christian conviction and encouraged their powers of intellect.

The elder Mills's earnings, augmented by several valuable real-estate purchases, enabled him to send his eldest sons, Henry and Thomas, to Scotland to finish their studies.[3] Robert, however, remained at home and was either taught by his brother Thomas, who in 1795 opened an academy (that offered some architectural instruction), or attended the College of Charleston.[4] Thomas advertised a curriculum comparable with that provided by the college, which embraced Classical history and literature, English, French, arithmetic, and geography. Thereby Mills acquired mathematical competence, a liking for history, and an appreciation of literature beyond the sonorous language and ethic of the Bible, which he had read from childhood and which resounds through

a

1.   (a) Miles Brewton House, Charleston
(1765–1769).
(b) St. Michael's Church, Charleston
(1752–1761).   b

his mature writings. His studies stimulated a desire to acquire information that would be demonstrated most amply in the *Statistics of South Carolina*, published in his forty-fifth year during a second period of extended residence in the state. Yet his education was neither truly academic nor technical, resulting in the uncertain grasp of scientific theory and technology that, years after, would contribute to his failure to finish books on architecture and steam locomotion. Equally undeveloped were his powers of critical analysis, especially concerning his own schemes, helping to explain his later adherence to a relatively limited series of structural systems and loyalty to the Palladian style architecture that graced his birthplace.

"No other American city," the Hessian officer Johann Hinrichs fairly decided during the British occupation, "can compare with Charles Town in the beauty of its houses and the splendour and taste displayed therein."[5] Those houses and the major buildings in the city had been Robert Mills's mute companions from boyhood. The handsome facade of the Miles Brewton House (1a) at 27 King Street (1765–1769), divided into three sections by a two-story portico capped by a pediment, etched an ideal of dignity and beauty into his mind.[6] Its ultimate inspiration lay in the architecture of Andrea Palladio, whose brilliant interpretations of Classical design had become standard models. Elsewhere in Charleston, builders had intermixed the heavier ornament of the Baroque style, a blend popularized through the much-used books of the Scots architect James Gibbs. These had, for example, inspired the magnificent stone and brick mansion the planter John Drayton built (1738–1742), overlooking his expansive rice fields abutting the Ashley River near Charleston, and St. Michael's Church (1b) on Meeting Street, which Mills came to cherish as "one of the greatest ornaments to the city."[7] The Gibbs–Palladian style also influenced civic buildings such as the Exchange and Customs House (1766–1767) constructed on East Bay, which Mills described in the *Statistics* as "venerable" and as "a fine building" that "shows how faithfully public work was executed in olden times."[8] The Exchange and earlier Powder Magazine on Cumberland Street (ca. 1713) had fire-resistant brick vaulting—in the magazine having the bricks interwoven along the ribs as in Mills's New England custom houses of the mid-1830s—of which he would learn a more advanced version during his training. Each had survived the disastrous fires that periodically afflicted Charleston, as on 13 June 1796 when the flames, missing his home, destroyed some five hundred houses, kindling an abiding concern with fireproof structure and urban water supply. The functional advantages of the typical local "single" house were obvious in the Charleston climate. The colonnaded piazza, or verandah, shaded the main rooms placed in line behind the narrow one-room-wide street front, allowed ample ventilation, and provided sheltered recreation space. Mills would design hospitals and prisons to incorporate the verandah and its benefits. He would also adapt the characteristic raised portico of Southern Palladian architecture to afford two entirely separate entrances in his public buildings, as well as to endow the structures with architectural significance.

Robert Mills's later adaptation of the raised portico and associated motifs evince his abiding respect for the Palladian architecture. Obviously he regarded it as essentially American despite its origins in the Colonial Georgian period and the architecture put up during his schooling, when his intellect and artistic talent were forming, evolved from pre-Revolutionary conventions instead of expunging them. The heavier forms and richer ornament of the Gibbs–Palladian style were simplified in tune with the transatlantic Neoclassical taste admired in the Federal period. Such was the Bank of the United States (later City Hall) (1799–1800), built prominently at the crossing of Meeting and Broad streets, to the design of the gentleman architect Gabriel Manigault II, scion of a celebrated Huguenot Charleston family. Manigault graced the bank with a raised portico fronted by curving steps (2), another feature to be adapted by Mills.

Charleston thus provided the foundation of Robert Mills's architectural conception. But what motivated his decision to become an architect? Besides his brother Thomas's interest, William Mills might have recognized Robert's artistic bent and recalled the financial and social success of the Adam family. William Adam had designed the Dundee Town House in 1734 and won the acco-

2.   City hall, Charleston (1799–1800), with the courthouse to its left and Mills's
Fireproof Building to its right.

lade of "Scots Vitruvius" while his architect sons Robert and James Adam had
scaled the heights of English society.[9] And he would have known that members
of the great South Carolina families, some his clients, regarded a knowledge of
architecture as an attribute of gentility, being both an intellectual accomplishment and of practical use to the property owner. One such person in Charleston was Manigault, who had toured Britain and collected architectural books.
Then the currency of architectural design, many such books were available to
Robert Mills at the Library Society of Charleston.[10] The 1770 catalog lists G.
Leoni's celebrated illustrated translation of Palladio's *Four Books of Architecture*
(1715–1720), Gibbs's *Rules for Drawing* (1732) and *Book of Architecture* (1728),
the last being widely used in America, notably by William Thornton when
designing the Capitol, plus William Chambers's *Treatise on Civil Architecture*
(1759), which proclaimed the exalted status of the architect as an intellectual,
technician, and artist. Local booksellers advertised some of these titles in the
South Carolina Gazette, together with others, from Isaac Ware's 1738 translation of Palladio to the handbook of British Palladian design, Colen Campbell's
Vitruvius Britannicus (1715). Courses of architectural instruction had also been
offered in Charleston: on 3 May 1790 the *Charleston City Gazette and Daily Advertiser* announced that James Hoban would conduct an "evening school for the
instruction of young men in Architecture" at the beginning of a two-year residence in the city.[11] If Mills enrolled in one of the courses advertised later in
the decade, it is possible that he learned the rudiments of architectural draw-

b

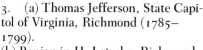
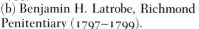

3.   (a) Thomas Jefferson, State Capitol of Virginia, Richmond (1785–1799).
(b) Benjamin H. Latrobe, Richmond Penitentiary (1797–1799).

ing and surveying with Colonel John Christian Senf, whose memory Mills would declare "should be cherished by Carolinians."[12]

Nonetheless, Mills's main architectural education was to commence outside Charleston, albeit with Hoban, who after leaving South Carolina had achieved success at the newly founded national capital by winning the competition for the President's House in 1792 and being appointed superintendent of the Capitol the next year. So in 1800 Robert Mills was "sent by his father to the City of Washington" in order to enter Hoban's office as a fee-paying pupil.[13] Thus William Mills gave his son a valuable start, although Hoban was neither the most influential nor the most talented architect practicing in Washington. Besides the physician Dr. William Thornton, designer of the partly erected Capitol, George Hadfield was completing the modest brick and stucco Treasury and Navy Departments (1798–1800), the mirror image of his earlier Treasury Building (1796–1797). The new capital thus seemed to promise considerable scope for architectural work when Mills set out for Washington via Richmond.

Just two years before his death, Mills could still vividly recall first seeing Thomas Jefferson's Virginia State Capitol (3a): "It gave me an idea of the effect of those Greek Temples, similarly situated, which are the admiration of the world."[14] He also admired Latrobe's semicircular-ended Richmond Penitentiary (1797–1799) (3b), as the "best constructed and arranged prison then in the Union." By comparison, Washington must have been disappointing. For in 1800 it still looked more like an unkempt rural settlement than a capital city, especially when compared with the substantial and gracious towns of Alexandria to the southwest and Georgetown to the west. Atop the only eminence, Jenkins Hill, stood the recently finished brick and stucco north wing of the

Capitol, containing the Senate and Supreme Court. The foundations of the south wing for the House of Representatives were under way, to be completed in 1807. But in between, where Thornton intended a grand portico and domed rotunda, was a gaping space. Its effect as a symbolic beacon of Republicanism and Freedom was also tarnished by the slave stockade and market at the western base of Capitol Hill. Only the handsome Gibbs–Palladian style President's House, together with the two satellite Executive Buildings, were of any consequence architecturally. Otherwise, excepting the incomplete Octagon House a little farther to the west, which was designed by Thornton in 1798 for Colonel John Tayloe III, the major buildings were the hotels and boardinghouses frequented by the 34 senators and 140 congressmen, transients among a permanent population of about 6,000, who were living in clusters of wood and brick houses.

Mills lodged at the more salubrious Georgetown across the Potomac in the home of Joseph Nourse, first register (or registrar) of the United States Treasury.[15] The Nourse family was possibly distantly related to his own; on his mother's side, Landgrave Smith's descendants had, for example, married into the Adams dynasty. Nourse introduced him to his circle of friends, including his kinsman Brigadier General John Smith of Hackwood near Winchester, Virginia, who had a residence at Georgetown. Nourse was godfather to the general's daughter Eliza Barnwell Smith. Perhaps at the Nourse's the impressionable and idealistic Mills first met Eliza, his future wife, three years his junior. But while apprenticed to Hoban, Mills's energies were purposefully directed toward mastering the art and science of architecture.

Hoban introduced him to the practical aspects of architecture: how to delineate three-dimensional structure, the way to select and estimate the quantity of materials required, the basic types of construction, the compilation of specifications and possibly working drawings for contractors, and the process of building. "When I was a student at Washington," Mills was to recall, "the room, called the *Oven,* being of an Oval form was built on the *original foundations* of the *South* Wing of the *Capitol* for the occupation of the House of Representatives in which this body sat for several years, with great satisfaction, being found a most excellent speaking room."[16] Hoban also developed his pupil's draftsmanship and skill at combining design motifs by reference to standard eighteenth-century copybooks and lent new meaning to the copybooks by initiating Mills to the symbolism that the Freemasons attached to architectural form. Inspired by the mason–builders of history, this secret society was dedicated to personal improvement and social good in the service of the "great *Architect* and *Governor* of the Universe."[17] Mills, who enrolled in a lodge after he moved to Baltimore in 1814,[18] learned that the elements of architecture served ideological as well as structural purposes, the three main types of Classical column—Doric, Ionic, and Corinthian—being held to represent Strength, Grace, and Intellect. In addition, the working tools of architect and mason enshrined moral values—as Benjamin French would remind Mills at the laying of the cornerstone of the Washington National Monument in 1848: "The plumb admonishes us to walk uprightly in our several stations before God and man, squaring our actions by the square of virtue, and remembering that we are traveling upon the level of time to that 'undiscovered country from whose bourne no traveler returns.' "[19] Even Mills's later interest in the Gothic style had a Masonic perspective, its fifteen degrees of membership being based on the rules given to the stonemasons working on York and Canterbury cathedrals.

Mills was a willing apprentice, absorbing all aspects of Hoban's working methods, even the use of colored washes to denote different building materials and the combination of one thick and one thin rule to outline presentation drawings. These lines appear on the drawings Mills made in response to an advertisement in the *Washington National Intelligencer* on 8 March 1802 that was placed by the building committee of the newly founded South Carolina College at Columbia. The committee invited proposals for a stone or brick building to cost less than $500,000, and to accommodate professors and students. There was a prize of $300. Mills mailed two drawings. One showed the rear elevation and ground plan, and the other crammed elevations of the front and sides with a plan of the first floor and a section of the building (4).[20] The tall, three-story front gathered about the pedimented center he obviously derived from the American collegiate tradition typified by Nassau Hall at the College of New Jersey (now Princeton), dating from 1754, from which several of the South Carolina College trustees had graduated. But he tried to vary the convention with reference to the Palladian publications. He advanced the side sections, quite likely inspired by the engraving of John Webb's scheme for the King Charles Block of the Royal Naval Hospital at Greenwich, London (1664–1669), in the first volume of Campbell's *Vitruvius Britannicus* and linked them across the front by an arcade, possibly suggested by the engraving of the Villa Emo in the second volume of Palladio's *Four Books*. On the rear he introduced a polygonal projection, cousin to those illustrated in English books such as Isaac Ware's *A Complete Body of Architecture* (1756) but also a distinguishing feature of the mansion that recently had been built for Francis Middleton at Charleston (1797–1801). Looking back over his career in the 1840s, when drafting his unpublished "The Architectural Works of Rt. Mills," he tacitly acknowledged their educational value while claiming that he had "made it a rule never to consult books" when actually designing specific buildings.[21] This denial of direct borrowing is corroborated by the deficiencies of his plan for the college. The awkward, narrow corridors and poor provision for heating prove

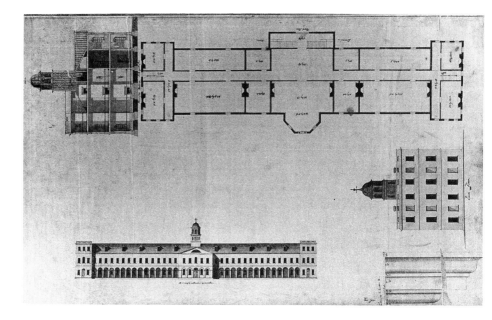

4.   Mills, design for South Carolina College, Columbia (1802), elevation with plan.

that Mills could not yet analyze functional requirements nor establish more than a rudimentary relationship between plan and facade. Still, his proficiency was sufficient to win him the premium jointly with Richard Clark, and his design later influenced Rutledge Hall, the first building on the college campus at Columbia.

Confidently styling himself "Architect," Mills drafted an essay on the "Tuscan Order."[22] Written in the Old English script, it purported to comment knowledgeably on what some still considered to be the earliest form of the Classical Doric column. But the text merely repeats conventional arguments, the recommendation of the Tuscan order for buildings of "Strength and Plainness" copying a passage from Ware's 1738 translation of Palladio.[23] Therein lay the source of Mills's censure of the Greek orders, imported into the United States by Latrobe and Hadfield. Subsequently he would praise Hadfield as an "architect of fine taste, and a beautiful draftsman" and Latrobe as a "man of the first talents of superior genius."[24] Yet in 1802 his other role model besides Hoban would have been the equally conservative Thornton, "a gentleman amateur of considerable taste; a man of genius and public spirit."[25]

Mills's declaration of professional independence may have been presumptuous, but it was a reflection of his entering a new phase of life after the death of his father on 23 April 1802. He inherited valuable property in Charleston, two blacks, 637 English pounds, and all William's "ummade up cloathing," which freed him from immediate financial need.[26] Either on his own initiative or through Hoban, he secured the patronage of the most powerful architectural authority in the nation, President Thomas Jefferson. However, Jefferson could not spare him much time amid his first arduous term of office, a period that Mills would aptly characterize as "the palmy days of our republic."[27] Nevertheless, that summer Jefferson gave Mills letters of introduction preparatory to his "professional visit to all the principal cities and towns in the United States."[28] One to Bulfinch, dated 1 July, remains: "He is now setting out on a journey through the States to see what is worth seeing in that line in each State. . . . I take the liberty of recommending him to your notice, and asking for him whatever information on the subject may be useful to this view while in Boston."[29] Jefferson's kindly endorsement led to new contacts like Jedidiah Morse, who in turn recommended Mills to seventeen ministers and lawyers in the New England states, and the Reverend Robert Wetmore of New York, who assured the Reverend Hasgill at the Episcopal Church in Boston, "Every curiosity of Art and Nature would be highly gratifying to this young Gentn.'s taste."[30]

Such a tour required enterprise and was arguably the earliest undertaken in the United States. Sadly, no record of Mills's impressions has yet been found, apart from scarce retrospective passages in later correspondence, as when he wrote to Jefferson on 13 June 1808 lamenting "buildings public and private, erected and erecting without either taste or design."[31] Mills was to tell the pioneering American art historian William Dunlap that he had completed drawings of "all the principal buildings then erected in the major cities" on his itinerary.[32] Only two of those drawings survive, both of which he presented to the president.[33] One is a signed elevation of the front of Latrobe's Bank of Pennsylvania in Philadelphia (5a), opened but two years before Mills's tour. This small but arresting image anticipates the profound reconstitution of Mills's taste under the influence of Latrobe, for, looking at the bank, he again glimpsed ancient design, forty years later remembering "a beautiful marble structure; of the temple form" if mistakenly attributing its six Ionic columns to the Theseion rather than Erechtheion at Athens."[34] The other drawing, also signed and even more sensitively rendered, shows the rear portico of St. Paul's Chapel facing onto Broadway in New York (5b). It confirms his growing interest in Classicism, since in 1794 Thomas McBean, who had trained with James Gibbs, added not only a steeple but also a four column portico almost spanning the building temple fashion.

Everywhere he traveled, Mills was surely learning: from such advanced structures as the triple-arched Permanent Bridge over the Schuylkill River at Market Street in Philadelphia, begun in 1798, to L'Enfant's 1788 reconstruction of the Federal Hall in New York (where Washington had sworn the presidential oath in April 1789), which demonstrated how the Palladian style could

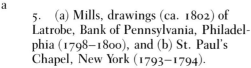

a

5.   (a) Mills, drawings (ca. 1802) of
Latrobe, Bank of Pennsylvania, Philadel-
phia (1798–1800), and (b) St. Paul's
Chapel, New York (1793–1794).

b

be transposed into a more Classical mode. Mills must also have observed how
the social and economic order in the North differed from that with which he
was familiar. With his inclination for the technical, he would have been especially interested in the homespun but effective engineering of the grist and
cloth mills, which were capable of producing greater wealth more efficiently
than the bondage of slavery. Once in Boston, Mills was in the hands of an excellent guide and mentor. Charles Bulfinch had designed its finest architecture, from the elegantly simple first Harrison Grey Otis House (1795–1796),
to the monumental but graceful Massachusetts State House (1795–1798).
The state house was a happy blend of eighteenth-century American Palladianism with the disciplined Neoclassicism that Bulfinch had seen on his tour of
Britain and Europe during 1785 to 1787. The welding of arcaded basement,
raised portico, and dome etched an image of sophisticated nobility into Mills's
visual memory. In fact, when Mills proposed an extension to the vestry of St.
Michael's Church in Charleston in October 1804, he averred: "Of the success
with which this [the elimination of a 'buzz' that was a result of poor acoustics]
may be effected there is a grand specimen at Boston which you have seen in
the Representatives Chamber in the state house, to remedy which they have
lowered a large sounding board."[35] Evidently Mills's enthusiasm made a lasting

impression on Bulfinch, who, twenty years later, was to consult him about the acoustical problems existing in the Hall of Representatives at the Capitol.[36]

When Mills returned to Washington in 1803 from this secular pilgrimage through American history and architecture, he must have been keener still to practice his vocation and to incorporate the best of what he had studied. But he was forced to embark upon a further stage of preparation. "As there were no architectural works to be had . . . Jefferson kindly offered me the use of his library, where I found several works, principally Palladio, of whom Mr. Jefferson was a great admirer."[37] Monticello was still unfinished and Jefferson's library was almost certainly at Washington, so that access to his complete collection of architectural books enlarged Mills's aesthetic and technical perspective. Possibly Mills began by reading the standard works written in his own language such as Robert Morris's *Select Architecture* (1757), which contained several central plan designs, an architectural form Jefferson had always found interesting. Among the English titles was also Ware's *Complete Body of Architecture* (1756), which included an elevation of Wrotham Park (1754), the polygonal drummed dome of which probably influenced the final version of Monticello, notwithstanding Jefferson's professed contempt for British architecture. Unable to read Italian, Mills can have gained only a visual introduction to the compositional motifs of Classical and Renaissance architecture, which may have been adequate to convey a fuller appreciation of the Palladian tradition that Jefferson revered. Jefferson's copies of Philibert de L'Orme's *Nouvelles inventions pour bien bâtir* (1576) and J. B. Rondelet's *Traité théorique et pratique de l'art de bâtir,* issued in France from 1802, helped Mills increase his proficiency in the knowledge of structure by illustrating a system of roofing composed of laminated ribs formed from small sections of wood pegged together and named for de l'Orme, or Delorme. Likewise, engravings in A. G. Kersaint's *Discours sur les monumens publics* (1792) excited Mills's imagination and, melded with other Classical motifs, were to appear in his designs for monuments to Washington. J. K. Krafft's *Plans, coupes, élèvations des plus belles maisons et des hôtels construit à Paris* (1801–1802) contained a number of oval rooms that figure in Mills's early work. It also included examples of the complex but convenient planning that characterized modern French domestic architecture, as Jefferson could have indicated with reference to Monticello.

Perhaps recognizing Mills's lack of facility in this vital aspect of design, Jefferson involved him in the process of completing Monticello. "During this period, I also made some plans and elevations for his mansion at Monticello," Mills later recalled, "to his view of interior arrangements which were of the French character."[38] Rather than preparing working drawings, Jefferson apparently proposed that he come up with an alternative design for the main facade

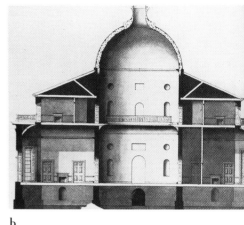

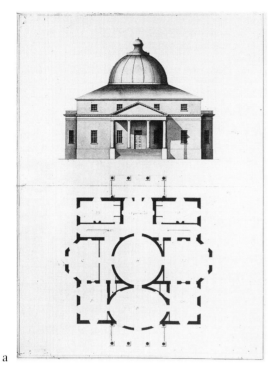

a

b

6. Mills and Jefferson, design for a "Building [for] a Public Officer" (1803): (a) elevation and plan, and (b) section.

and plan. This exercise, combining an elevation for the west front and a plan, is inscribed in his neat, handwriting, "Design for remodelling Monticello," signed "R. Mills" but somewhat coarsely drawn. The Old English inscriptions correspond with the conservatism of some of the detailing, such as the thick guttae plates under the cornice of the pediment, while the interior arrangement was still clumsy, as in the division of the library into four awkward sections. More refined if typically somewhat two-dimensional is an elevation of the west front as erected, almost certainly made at the instigation of the president about the time the outer fabric was at last completed in 1803–1804. Whether at Monticello (a scrap of writing in Mills's youthful hand describing the estate survives)[39] or in the President's House, it is fascinating to imagine those remarkably different figures in company. Using pencil, pen and watercolor brush, sometimes aided by a compass, Mills tried to emulate Jefferson's logical and sober Classicism and evidently considered the drawing sufficiently accomplished to show at the second annual exhibition of the Society of Artists of the United States in Philadelphia in 1812.[40] The importance of this association with Jefferson is indicated by Mills's later comment, many "useful hints are now to be gathered from French works on architecture."[41]

Jefferson apparently enjoyed encouraging Mills's bent, who on 14 October 1805 would gratefully acknowledge the president's "unwarranted attentions

...and instruction."[42] The warmth of that phrase evokes something closer to collaboration, as occurred with "A Building suited to a Public Officer as de-sign'd by Thomas Jefferson—President of the U. Sts——." Probably intended as a residence for the governor of Virginia (6), this precisely follows a "Bill of Particulars" written in Mills's hand, listing the sizes of the rooms shown in the plans and the schedule of work for the contractors, from the foundation la-borer to the ironmonger.[43] Under Jefferson's direction, Mills simplified Pal-ladio's Villa Rotunda, retaining its central dome and lantern but substituting a single portico on the entrance front.[44] The effect is more Classical, even if the portico does not rise to the full height of the attic and the side facades have the polygonal bays favored by British Palladian architects. Similarly, on the inte-rior Palladio's rigorously mathematical planning is relaxed to accord with con-venience. The structure of the dome follows the de l'Orme system, the pegged planks of the ribs being clearly indicated on the section.

Jefferson did his protégé an even greater service. In the spring of 1803, he advised Mills to "enter as a pupil" in the office of Latrobe, whom he had ap-pointed surveyor of the public buildings charged with completing the Capitol. Latrobe would correct the limitations of Mills's previous training and direct him toward a more intellectual and practical comprehension of the process and purpose of design. "The day that you honored me with an introduction and recommendation to Mr. Latrobe," Mills would confide to Jefferson on 3 Octo-ber 1806, "I shall ever have cause to remember with the most heartfelt satis-faction. Then, I may truly say, I began first to imbibe the true and correct principles of architecture, and to throw off the shackles which ignorance, hab-its of education, and prejudice had imposed on my mind."[45] Obviously he meant no disrespect to Jefferson or to his Palladian Classicism; rather, he intended sincere gratitude.

Latrobe was teaching him what he subsequently called a "purely Greek" style that thanks to its "economy and correct taste...[was] exactly suited to the character of our political institutions and pecuniary means."[46] In fact Latrobe's style, which was developed before he emigrated in 1796, synthesized the Greek orders with the simplified Neoclassicism generated mainly in pre-Revolutionary France. This Rational Classical style sought to use ancient ar-chitectural features in order to reveal their underlying geometry and to express the function and structure of each building. Latrobe had absorbed such tenets of the Enlightenment through his travels in Europe in 1783 and 1784 and his training in London. He had apprenticed under S. P. Cockerell, architect to the powerful East India Company, and trained with John Smeaton, one of the most talented civil engineers of the Georgian era. Smeaton had built the Ed-dystone Lighthouse in the English Channel using "hydraulic cement" to seal the dovetailed masonry blocks. The material was quick drying and, when employed in brick vaults, ensured structural integrity. The use of the mortar was to prove one of the most valuable techniques Latrobe imparted to Mills. Latrobe also introduced him to the technologies that powered the British Industrial Revolution, particularly the steam engine and canal, and progressive concepts of institutional design.

At their first interview, apparently in June 1803, Latrobe explained that he charged 200 guineas (English sterling was still in use) to impart his expertise, essentially by on-the-job training.[47] Mills was in harness by 2 July, when he noted in his diary, "Finish'd the pencil drawing of the lock that is to [be] built in the Tiber, as design'd by Mr. L."[48] The Tiber Creek had been canalized to facilitate the carriage of building materials for the Capitol, and preparing the drawing helped trigger Mills's enthusiasm for this new system of transportation. He had completed the drawing by 10 July, when he left it with William Strickland, who was already working for Latrobe, rather contradicting Mills's persistent claim of "being the first American citizen that entered upon the study of architecture as a profession," albeit beginning in 1800.[49] Soon after, Mills collaborated with another of Latrobe's assistants on drawings of a shallow draft commercial barge for the inland "Western Waters."[50] Mills did not mention this job in the 1803 diary, which tells of continuing study of architecture in and around the District of Columbia and fascination with contemporary events, if tinged with his occasionally humorless moralizing. "Alas!" he penned on Independence Day, "instead of rendering thanks to the Almighty Giver of every good thing, they are trespassing His command by getting drunk, fighting, and every detestable passion." The entries also hint at the lack of confidence that dogged his association with Latrobe. "Alas!" he had bewailed on the previous day, "how dull and miserable is my heart. Oh Lord I beseech thee to renew my spirit."

At the beginning of their association it was Mills's diligence, not his talent, that impressed Latrobe. Writing to Jefferson on 2 October 1803, Latrobe commented that Mills "possesses that very valuable substitute for Genius, laborious precision, in a very high degree; and is therefore very useful to me, though his professional education has been hitherto much misdirected."[51] Six months in the office had not altered Latrobe's opinion. On 30 April 1804 he informed his assistant John Lenthall that Mills had drawn a plan of the cellar in the southwest corner of the south wing of the Capitol, referring to it again on 6 May: "The sketch in my letter which was made by Mills in my absence under what I had written, and was I daresay erroneous."[52] Gradually, he recognized that Mills needed encouragement. For he wrote on 3 November 1804 regarding surveys for the canal and town of New Castle, Delaware, "I will only add, that not withstanding the apparent neglect of which I had appeared to have been guilty, no one more sincerely values and respects your many excellent

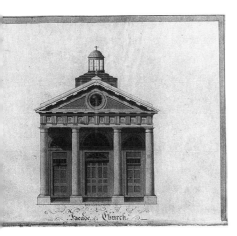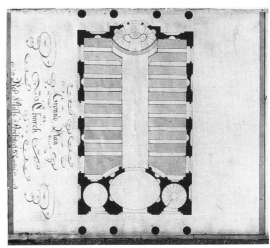

b

7.   Mills, design for the Johns Island Church (1804): (a) front elevation and (b) plan.

qualities or feels more friendship towards you than faithfully B. Henry Latrobe."[53]

By then Latrobe could see that Mills had been able to master a more thorough technical and philosophical understanding of design. When he had returned home to Charleston during the winter break in the building season, Mills eagerly prepared designs for three pending church commissions. The first were outlined in specifications bound, following Latrobe's practice, with six attractive drawings, inscribed in the Old English script, "Designs for an Episcopal church to be erected on Johns Island near Charleston S.C. by Robert Mills Architect."[54] The drawings illustrate how Mills was already seeking to create a distinctive American Classical style by welding Palladian with Neoclassical compositional conventions and decorative motifs. Thus the front (7a) and rear are not only enclosed by four-column porticos, temple-fashion, similar to Latrobe's Bank of Pennsylvania, but also echo the temple-fronted Prince William's Parish Church at Beaufort in his native state (ca. 1751). He adopted the more conservative Tuscan order and heavily proportioned entablature and pediment, yet widened the space between the central columns of the front portico following the Propylaea entrance to the Athenian Acropolis. More directly Latrobean is the diminutive central dome, introduced "both for the distinguishing of the building and for beauty externally and internally." The layout of the interior betrays a comparable mixture of sources and intention (7b). The oval entrance vestibule and circular staircases, rising either side to a gallery reserved for blacks, reverses the plan of the first design for a "Round Church" in Gibbs's *Book of Architecture,* while the pulpit is placed in a recess that breaks Classical convention by thrusting into the rear portico. The prominence of the pulpit reflects Mills's Presbyterian enthusiasm for the "Preaching of the Word" as well as local Episcopalian convention typified by the similar arrangement in St. James at Goose Creek near Charleston in 1711. Latrobe, too, was greatly interested in the subject of acoustics and about 1798 had made drawings for rebuilding St. John's Church at Richmond, Virginia, situating the pulpit and reading desk in the position customarily reserved for the altar, backed by a semicircular apse.[55] Seeking to ensure audibility from the twenty pews ranked within the 42- by 26-foot nave, Mills also introduced a coved ceiling.

Mills intended that his Christian temple should be built of stuccoed brick with marble floors and plaster ceiling. He estimated that it would cost $6,400, based on "Enquiries and proposed Queries to the different Master Workmen relative to the prices," not including a further figure of $800 for "Risk in Carriage, Time expended." The members of the vestry apparently decided that they could not afford to proceed. Eventually in January 1816, work began on a plainer wooden structure, apparently designed by the vicar, that was completed in 1817 for about $3,000.[56]

Mills's initiative was better rewarded by the members of the Congregational, or Circular, Church in Charleston, although he acted principally as technical assistant to Dr. David Ramsay—local physician (a pioneer in the use of Dr. Edward Jenner's smallpox vaccination), abolitionist, politician and historian—who led the congregation in the construction project.[57] Ramsay favored a circular plan influenced, as he acknowledged in his *History of the Independent Congregational Church in Charleston* (1815), by his mathematically inclined third wife, Martha Laurens, daughter of the celebrated republican family that, as Huguenots, reputedly worshipped in a circular building in Charleston. He recommended the form at the meeting on 19 December 1803 when the project was set in motion.[58] On 13 February 1804 the church building committee thanked "Mr. Mills for his ingenious and elegant drawings which have essentially assisted the members and supporters thereof in forming a correct opinion of the form and plans of their proposed building."[59] His drawings traced out a circular auditorium having an internal diameter of 88 feet. Within its 30-foot-high walls would be up to 171 pews on the main floor and 52 in a gallery reserved for the poorer members, with segregated space for blacks, every seat being easily accessible through the 7 doors and amply illuminated by 26 windows on two levels. The capacious fabric, covered by a coffered domical roof, would be embellished by a six-column portico crowned by a 60-foot steeple rising from its vestibule to reach 182 feet. Mills estimated that completion of the structure would cost $21,000. That figure was entered in the minutes, which were signed by Ramsay and by the amateur architect and contractor Thomas Bennett, Sr., indicating that the amount was a result of careful computation.

It is clear that Latrobe also looked over the drawings, writing to his young assistant on 12 July 1806, "You remember the faults I pointed out to you at an early period of your studies in my office especially in the round church—You corrected them—Your design had besides very great and intrinsic merits of its own."[60]

This is not to underplay Mills's primary role in the creation of this advanced building—an American Evangelical version of the Roman Pantheon (8a). He had studied from engravings in the *Four Books* (8b, 8c), including Ware's 1738 translation, which in the second chapter of the last book likened the circular temple to the "infinite essence, the uniformity, and the justice of God."[61] Latrobe may also have commended its acoustical properties in his unpublished draft essay on the subject written about 1803.[62] In his *Book of Architecture,* Gibbs included two superb designs for round churches (8d) that had influenced British circular plan churches Latrobe admired.[63] Each was graced by a steeple soaring above the entrance portico, as imitated in the Gibbsian St. Michael's located lower on Meeting Street. Deferring to another local covention, Mills marked the edges of the front wall of the Circular Church with quoins and topped it with curved gables. Only in the portico columns did he match the Latrobean austerity of the auditorium wall and its recessed windows, although the congregation insisted on the "modern [Renaissance rather than Greek] Doric style."[64] Inside a "light gallery," he proudly wrote in *Statistics,* "sweeps nearly a complete circle round the room, and presents the appearance of a great settee the [tapered] columns supporting it being of a character suited to convey an idea of this kind." Seated in pews on the main floor or in the gallery located in the arc of the amphitheater facing the elevated pulpit opposite the entrance, the congregation occupied a light and airy space wholly suited to their concept of the enlightening truth of the Word of God. Above them the ceiling extended in a shallow curve, symbolically pierced at the center by a lantern, which increased the illumination as well as acting as a ventilator. The ceiling itself was supported by laminated wooden ribs and intervening beams that Mills adapted from the de l'Orme system and defined in a letter of 15 October 1804: "The ribs may be of inch boards doubled, cross jointed and nailed together."[65]

Despite his major role in the design, the Congregationalists would not grant Mills full authority, and Latrobe expressed his dissatisfaction with the final product, "It is therefore with sincere regret," Latrobe lamented in his letter of 12 July 1806, "that I have observed your talents thrown into a sort of scramble between the two parties [the 'Building Mechanic' and the *Gentleman architect*'] in the designs of the churches you have given to the congregations at Charleston." Latrobe was probably referring to the Congregationalists' insistence that the vestibule be enlarged into the auditorium and that its ceiling be raised.

a

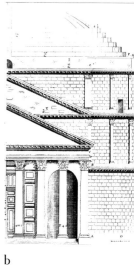

b

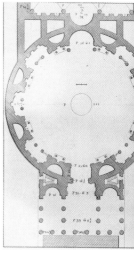

c

8.   (a) Mills, Congregational Church,
Charleston (1804–1806).
(b and c) Pantheon, Rome, from Palladio,
Four Books of Architecture, book 4.
(d) James Gibbs, design for a "round church,"
from *A Book of Architecture*.

The result was an annoying echo initially discovered at the sale of pews on 25 June 1806, when Mills's brother Thomas bought No. 36 for $240.[66] Ramsay in his history identified the vestibule wall as the perpetrator, while the *Charleston Courier* of 16 July 1823 faulted the "lowness of the floor," the opinion Mills was to endorse when he wrote to Senator Jefferson Davis on 1 May 1850, "Contrary to my instructions, the *height* of the dome was increased beyond the maximum point."[67] The changes resulted from Mills's youth and inaccurate estimates. Costs escalated alarmingly so that, despite the substitution of wooden shingles for copper sheathing on the roof and deletion of the spire, the total reached $60,000 by April 1806, leaving the congregation with a debt of almost $42,000.

Insufficient funding also thwarted Mills's third proposal: a 28-foot extension to St. Michael's church accommodating forty-two new pews in the nave and gallery. Early in March 1804 he had assembled four drawings (using the engineer's scale of 10 feet to 1 inch) and a specification titled "Contemplated Addition to St. Michael's Church."[68] On 11 March it was "resolved unanimously that the thanks of the Vestry and Wardens be presented to Mr. Robert Mills for the handsome drawings done by him" plus a payment of $60 as "a further mark of approbation." Those renting pews voted in favor of the extension on 5 May and the vestry advertised for tenders in the *Charleston Times* on 20 June 1804, only to have second thoughts upon receiving estimates from contractors well above Mills's figure of $10,000. Nonetheless, his scheme passed muster with their consultant Thomas Bennett, Sr. It entailed the installation of a pulpit, delicately elevated above a reading desk, in a shallow altar apse at the center of the new east wall, and a curved vault between the side coves of the existing flat ceiling. Only the curved vault troubled Bennett because it would necessitate removing the central sections of the main beams. He liked Mills's suggestion for raising the wall above the exterior cornice to the base level of the steeple and, with the parishioners, accepted his views regarding the pulpit. The apse would be a better "receiver and augmenter of Sound" than the traditional pulpit canopy. Anxious that building operations should begin, Mills accepted Bennett's criticism but opposed the retention of the flat ceiling in a letter of 15 October 1804, which the vestry superscribed "on the Doctrine of Sounds." Instead, he advocated an elliptical vault to replace the cove. Drawn in section at the top of his letter, it was to spring some 16 to 18 inches above the windows, the ribs being of the de l'Orme type, "inch boards double jointed and nailed together." But the vestry stalled mainly due to rumors that a new Episcopal church was to be established at Charleston, which eventuated with the construction of St. Paul's Radcliffeboro in 1811.

Mills therefore had to be content with his part in the flawed Congregational Church (9a), which yet served adequately from the summer of 1806 until

a

b

9.   Mills, Congregational Church, Charleston: (a) after the 1861 fire and (b) front elevation, drawn by E. C. Jones (ca. 1853).

burned in the disastrous fire that engulfed Charleston in 1861. Long before the addition of the spire by C. F. Reichardt in 1838 and the substitution of richer Corinthian columns in the portico during renovation (1852–1853) (9b), the church stood testament to the Christian religion Mills so cherished. The auditorium admirably suited what became an increasingly popular interest in sermons, fostered by the Great Revival that spread from Kentucky in 1801 to the southern states.[69] How gratifying to hear from his sister, Sarah Lusher, on 29 April 1812: "This evening went to the Circular [Church] very full."[70] Altogether more original than the gabled hall-type Congregational churches with central pedimented entrances and low steeples built at Pittsfield and Taunton, Massachusetts, by Bulfinch (1790–1793), it was "the first attempt in this country," as Mills would boast to Dunlap "to execute such an immense spread of roof without any intermediate support."[71] While regretting that "its portico is heavy and of wretched proportions," the author of an article in the June 1857 issue of *Harper's Magazine* praised "the effect" of the interior as "very striking, particularly with a full house." The burned-out shell collapsed in the 1886 earthquake, to be replaced six years later by another circular building, this time designed in the Romanesque style by Stephenson and Greene of New York.

The Congregational Church did not bring Mills any other commissions in Charleston despite current prosperity.[72] Before returning northward, he determined to seize the opportunity to explore South Carolina. It became another kind of learning experience, judging from the three letters he addressed to a Quaker friend, Sarah Mather.[73] He was shocked by the poverty of the interior of the state, which the Episcopal bishop of Charleston would call, even in 1821, "the fag end of creation."[74] The farther he traveled from the wealthy coastal strip, the more he encountered impoverished homesteads "mostly built of logs plast'd with clay," and everywhere the "want of schools." In the lowland, the higher living standards were based on slavery, a socioeconomic structure that fostered "ideas of pride and superiority" and a disinclination to improve the land for farming. Interwoven are passages that read like admonitions to himself as he struggled to win his place in the world: "Religion," he wrote, "is the only support and stay through all the storms of life." Occasionally he waxed poetical as evoking the shallow wood-embowered Pee Dee River, scintillatingly suffused by "the mild Queen of Night [which] shone in all the splendor of her beauty."

Through that fall and winter, Mills worked for Latrobe chiefly on the survey of New Castle, lodging at Wilmington and Iron Hill, Maryland.[75] After he and Strickland had finished the survey, Latrobe began to entrust Mills with more important jobs. On 3 February 1805 he was asked to prepare a "complete set of drawings for the [Roman Catholic] Cathedral" in Baltimore, probably according to Latrobe's initial Neo-Gothic proposal. Bishop Daniel Carroll, however, preferred the Classical style, which Latrobe developed in designs conceived between March 1806 and March 1808, successively enlarging the size of the rotunda at the crossing of the nave and transepts, perhaps even prompted by Mills's Congregational Church.[76] Latrobe's correspondence also indicates that Mills was assisting with building operations at the Washington Navy Yard, the Capitol, the President's House, and possibly the segmental brick vaulted Treasury "fireproof" addition. Amid this activity Mills found time to correspond with Catherine Hall of Wilmington from July 1804 through October 1807, when he frequently stayed at Burlington, New Jersey, on the farm owned by his brother Thomas.[77] Of gentle English birth, Catherine had been both financially ruined and physically assaulted by her husband, arousing Mills's sympathy and chivalry. The amorous dimension of those characteristics was more evident in his relationship with "A.M.A." of New Castle, which waned after he moved to Philadelphia in the winter of 1805/1806 in order to supervise the construction of Latrobe's stylish Neoclassical town house for the china merchant William Waln (begun in June 1805).

Mills had now become more of a junior partner than an apprentice. Latrobe laid down to him the realities of contemporary practice in a letter started on 12 July 1806, recalling the corrections recommended for the Congregational Church. He counseled Mills to resist interference from amateurs and contractors, to insist on controlling the execution of his designs, to charge a fee of at least 5 percent on the estimated total, and, above all, to be quite clear about the requirements of his client. Lastly, he must retain his drawings. What prompted Latrobe, busy with widely dispersed commissions, to compose such a full and valuable statement? Perhaps, as with Dr. Ramsay and the Congregationalists, because Mills was being too obliging, in this instance to the entrepreneur, amateur architect, and dilettante John Dorsey, whom Latrobe despised.[78] Dorsey is credited with the Pennsylvania Academy of the Fine Arts built on Chestnut Street in Philadelphia (1805–1806), but, when it was rebuilt in 1847, item number 7 inserted in the cornerstone was a "View of the Academy Building, as originally constructed in 1806, from designs believed to be by Robert Mills."[79] The facade composition of two in antis columns framed by simple pavilions and capped by a dome obviously imitated Latrobe's Center Square Pump House (1799–1800), but would recur with greater acumen in Mills's later work. Mills left himself open to exploitation by his very urgency to secure independent commissions. Over the spring and summer of 1806, and beyond, he strove to capture the commission for the South Carolina Penitentiary. The scheme had been proposed in 1803 by a progressive caucus within the state legislature but resisted until the following June. Then the new governor, Paul Hamilton, liking Mills, corresponded with the governors of those states having penitentiaries—New York, New Jersey, Massachusetts, and Virginia.[80] They all stressed the advantages of a healthy site, adequate water supply, sanitation and security, together with the provision of solitary cells and religious instruction. Indeed they corroborated the humane specifications entreated by John Howard, especially in *The State of Prisons in England and Wales* (1777) and *Account of the Principal Lazarettos in Europe* (1789), to which Latrobe and Jefferson had drawn Mills's attention. The State Committee on the Judiciary of South Carolina, when reporting the scheme on 27 November 1806, was clearly influenced by Mills's association with "the celebrated Latrobe" and by his "utmost pains . . . in ascertaining the probable expense of the Building of which he has furnished the state with an elegant draft which is on a large scale and as far as the committee are able to judge of the subject, an excellent plan."[81]

Unfortunately, this plan and a book of drawings, mentioned by his brother

Thomas in a letter of 24 June 1806 to Governor Hamilton, are lost. Nonetheless, some of their features can be gleaned from Mills's correspondence with Hamilton and Latrobe. The "arrangement of my plan," he informed the governor on 7 July, "was such as favored its gradual extension without disturbing the whole," further explaining on 6 November that the main building would be fronted by a gate house containing baths, privies, and a laundry. Latrobe's negative reference eleven days later to the absolute segregation of the sexes imposed at Sing Sing prison in New York, implies that Mills planned cell blocks for male and female prisoners linked to a communal facility for supervised work, eating and worship.[82] The letters suggest a polygon of cell blocks behind the main building, plus a washhouse akin to the 1791 addition on the Walnut Street Jail in Philadelphia; or cell blocks radiating from a central facility; or a version of Latrobe's semicircular Virginia Penitentiary, which Mills was to reproduce in 1831 for a prison in Washington, D.C. In 1806, however, he had not mastered the full compass of Latrobe's expertise. Although the walls were to be of brick, as Hamilton learned on 2 September, the floors would be composed of flammable oak beams covered with pine planks, the only incombustible materials being the wrought-iron window and door bars. Furthermore, the first estimate, for $200,000, that Mills sent Hamilton from Philadelphia on 7 July was calculated on the "common detail method." Not until 2 September could he apply Latrobe's more accurate "regular detail'd method," of assessing the expense per square foot, which reduced the figure to $184,984 (comparing well with the $166,000 spent on the smaller stone Massachusetts Penitentiary).

When writing on 7 July, Mills had tried to direct the committee's attention away from cost to the social and economic advantages of his penitentiary: "A man who has been publicly whipped or branded is, both in a moral and political view, lost to himself and society, but it is not so with him who unknown and unabused suffers the punishment and acquires the industry of a confinement in a Penitentiary house." Neither his idealism nor his revised estimate could overcome the reactionary rump within the legislature. By December, they battled the proposed site near Charleston, which Mills considered necessary for the employment and social welfare of the inmates. Their strength gathered as Hamilton's term ran out.

Although Hamilton could not secure him the penitentiary commission, he did help Mills in one vital respect. In December, he composed an admirable letter of recommendation to General Smith of Hackwood in support of Mills's proposal of marriage with Smith's beautiful, vivacious, yet serious-minded daughter Eliza.[83] Besides her qualities of character and appearance, Eliza was undoubtedly a good match. Her father, son of John Smith of Shooter's Hill in Middlesex County and Mary Jacqueline of Jamestown, had served with the colonial militia in Lord Dunmore's War against the Indians in 1774 and with the Virginia Line during the Revolution, commanding the Winchester District and eventually being promoted brigadier general. He had moved with his brother in 1773 to Frederick County amid the beautiful uplands of Virginia, a combination of forest wooded and stony clearings, and established an estate on the highest ground but close to spring water. Smith had designed and built Hackwood between 1776 and 1777, a large house that stands mainly unchanged to this day. Five bays long and three deep, the flanks had three-sided projections of the type found in the British Palladian copybooks. To this handsome home, faced with rough-cut local stone, John had in February 1781 carried his bride, Mary Animus, second daughter of General John Bull of Berkeley County. A member of the house of delegates, subsequently to be elected state senator for two terms and justice of the court and lieutenant for Frederick County, Smith was able to live in some style thanks to a yearly pension of $600 for his Revolutionary service and the income from his farm and estate, reckoned by some to be 4,000 acres. Anna bore him eight children, the first in January 1782 (Martha Maria, who married William Davison, who became a friend and patron of Mills). Eliza, her second child, was born at midnight on 10 February 1784.

General Smith, sitting as a Democrat in the House of Representatives (1801–1805), might have been inclined to overlook Mills's somewhat inferior social status. They shared an interest in architecture, since in addition to designing Hackwood, Smith was made a trustee in 1790 for building the Tobacco Warehouse on Water Street in Winchester. In about 1796 he laid out the town of Middleway (originally named Smithfield), northeast of Winchester. The general also valued intellectual pursuits—his third son, Augustine Charles, became principal of the Old Winchester Academy and later took charge of the Female Seminary in Columbia, South Carolina, paralleling Eliza's activities as an educator—sharing Mills's nationalistic chauvinism: "Few men who have not witnessed the revolutionary contest have a proper idea of the perseverance of an American, or his ingenuity in supplying his wants."[84]

The major obstacle to their marriage, apart from unfounded rumors that Mills had attempted to elope with a Miss Stroud, was his lack of financial security.[85] He had hoped to establish that security with the commission for the South Carolina Penitentiary. Awaiting a final decision, Mills diligently studied penitentiary design, on 30 October 1806 commending the "principal" of the Philadelphia prison, Caleb Loundes, for the policy, "Wisdom, which while it punishes, would reform the criminal."[86] A majority in the South Carolina legislature disagreed, and on 30 November it defeated a bill to erect a penitentiary at Columbia, although Mills did not inform Eliza, to whom he was now engaged, until March 1808.[87] Their marriage was deferred, requiring each to ease their longing through religious ardour. "Yes! My beloved, my valued brother,"

10.   Latrobe, Bank of Philadelphia, Philadelphia (1807–1809), engraving by
W. Bush (1828).

Eliza wrote, "unworthy, consciously so of your friendship yet I would not re-
sign it for any temporal enjoyment I know of. . . . Jesus is ever the watchful
guardian of the sons and daughters of affliction, it is the sweet consolations He
gives, that can alone support us under the craving wants of nature, the temp-
tations of Satan, and the despondency of mourning in bitterness of soul."

Mills had tried to hasten their union by selling the Charleston property inherited from his father to augment the fees for supervising the construction of
Latrobe's Waln and Markoe houses and the Neo-Gothic Bank of Philadelphia
at Fourth and Chestnut streets (10).[88] The experience did much to increase his
grasp of construction. The interior of the bank had a fireproof vaulted ceiling
of thin, brick, cross-arched ribs bonded with quick-drying hydraulic cement,
"the first fireproof building," Mills later stated "erected by me."[89] Like the
pointed and flat Tudor arches of the doors and windows, the vault represented
Latrobe's rationalized interpretation of the Gothic style. By way of aid Latrobe
on 13 February 1809, sent him the "1st pt of Britton's Gothic Antiquities," the
first volume of the handsomely illustrated *Architectural Antiquities of Great
Britain* (1807).[90] The efficient plan of the Markoe House, including an indoor
bathroom, was finished in December 1810 and also became a recurrent model

for Mills. Throughout this period, Latrobe fired off letters frequently peppered with sarcastic expostulations in response to Mills's ignorance about technical points. Thus on 12 July 1807 he wrote testily with reference to the Gothic arches in the bank, "*all of them* intersections of elliptical lines," which "*must be all struck with a trammel* [an instrument for drawing ellipses]," and more so on 18 September, "I find, that you have not only not used a Trammel in describing the ribs of the Arch, but that you absolutely appear ignorant of what I meant by the term."[91] After inspecting the bank, Latrobe revised his opinion and would next April assure Mills, "I shall undoubtedly always keep you in mind and one way or another find employment for you."[92]

Fortified by Eliza's love, Mills had turned Latrobe's condescension to good effect. In July 1807, while scanning the Philadelphia papers, he had noticed an advertisement circulated by the Presbyterian congregation in Augusta on the Georgia bank of the Savannah River. The members wanted designs for a steepled church to accommodate at least 100 pews with additional seating in galleries. By 22 July he had written out a meticulous specification inscribed, "Designs for Augusta Church, State of Georgia, by Robert Mills of South Carolina, Architect, Philadelphia," and bound it with eleven crisply rendered drawings that demonstrate the tutelage of Latrobe.[93] More experienced in the financial realities of building programs, Mills opened the densely scribed "General Observations" pragmatically, "As *economy* is a material object recommended, I began, and finished the following designs with this in view," adding, "I did not, at the same time lose sight of convenience, strength and beauty: As it is false oeconomy to construct a building *weak,* so it is a disgrace to the institution and country to disregard *grace* and *proportion,* in the arrangement of the details." The first four drawings outline the floor plans and roof. The nave, measuring approximately 70 feet by 54 feet, could seat 1,100 worshippers in 135 pews on the main floor and a three-sided gallery 15 feet deep (11); an upper gallery at the entrance end was reserved for blacks. The main gallery was to be supported on twelve tapered columns, having palmlike capitals based on those in the Congregational Church. Again, the chief feature was the pulpit, poised on a graceful elliptical arch against the rear wall. The acoustical properties were to be augmented by the segmental ceiling obviously based on the de l'Orme system, since the supporting ribs were to be "formed out of short lengths of inch plank cross jointed and nailed together in two thicknesses."

Now he could conceive the clever counterpoint between the semicircular upper windows and the three imposing arches framing the main entrance doors, or integrate the steeple with the Rational Classical facade (12b), harmonizing the technical and imaginative polarities of design so that the practical elements are expressed in appropriate ornamental features that define func-

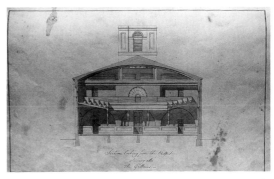

11.   Mills, drawings for the Presbyterian Church, Augusta (1807):
(a) plan and (b) section.

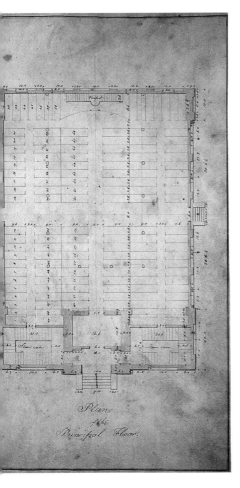

12.   Mills, drawings for the Presbyterian
Church, Augusta (1807): (a) side and (b)
front.

b

tion. Thus the front exhibits a subtler handling of the utilitarian requirements and symbolic features, managed by adapting the Roman triumphal arch. One arch pierces the shallow central projection that forms the porch and the base of the steeple. On either hand others create frames for the recessed rectangular windows and fanlights that illuminate the gallery staircases. The ascending triangular pattern described by those fanlights is then repeated in inverse order by the three louvered bell openings in the tower and sustained by the changing form of the steeple terminating in the conical spire. Equally assured are the harmonious variations between the nicely balanced front, side and rear facades, the blind arcading surrounding the windows along the side walls extending to the rear in a rhythmic progression (12a).

The congregation, impressed by his care and swayed by his southern origins, chose his designs, even if its building committee took two years to collect enough money to execute his lucid plans with "a few slight modifications." On the broad, tree-lined Telfair Street, Mills's capacious, well-lighted and well-ventilated church with excellent sound and sight of the preacher was dedicated for worship on 17 May 1812, when the Reverend Dr. Keith of Charleston delivered the sermon. Six years later, the galleries and steeple were finally installed. Neither letters nor records have been found to tell us if Mills ever had the satisfaction of inspecting, or worshipping in, this early but lasting achievement, the dignified proportions of which survive despite the Neo-Norman refacing of the exterior in 1847 by a local architect.

The efficient exploitation of space permeated another design from this period for the villa of Joseph Hand (13). This was to have been erected at Bristol, downstream from Philadelphia on the Delaware River, but never progressed further than the drawing board. Mills crammed three views, one section and three plans, together with various details onto a single sheet; perhaps the client found this presentation confusing, and that system seldom reappears in Mills's subsequent work.[94] By making it of one story at the front and three at the rear he skillfully used the descending site. The "piazza" and broad windows on the upper floors of the rear facade and the three-sided projections, reminiscent of Hackwood and the Markoe House, would have enjoyed fine views over the river. Only the colonnaded piazza of the Hand villa recalls Mills's South Carolina origin, the articulation of the design being thoroughly Latrobean in its simplicity.

That quality was entirely appropriate to the first of Mills's completed secular buildings, the "Debtor's Gaol and Work-House for Felons" at Mount Holly commissioned for Burlington County in New Jersey. The commission was some consolation for the disappointment over the South Carolina Penitentiary, and the prospect of marriage no doubt speeded his assembly of the presentation material. That comprised four plans, three elevations, two sections, and four

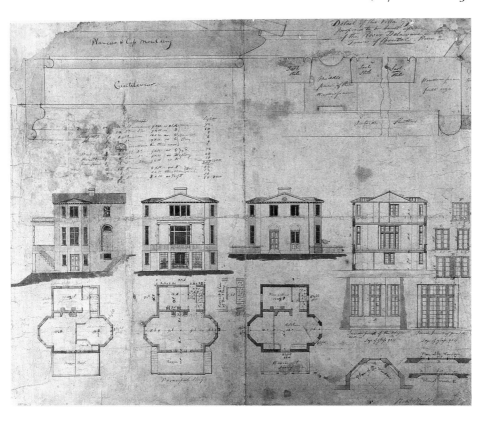

13.   Mills, design for the Joseph Hand villa (1807).

pages arguing his principles of prison design, all bound into a volume signed "Robert Mills, Architect, Philadelphia, May 1808."[95] The drawings display increased facility in rendering architectural form (14). The blind arcading of the front, for instance, is etched with strong shadow that denotes secure construction in the manner of the Frenchman Claude-Nicolas Ledoux's "architecture parlante."[96] That impression is reinforced by the word "Prison," intended to be carved over the entrance and by the flanking festoons of chains, reminiscent of those on George Dance Junior's Newgate Gaol at London, begun in 1769. The expressive austerity is heightened by the thin channeled rustication and exposed roof beams along the cornice.

The tripartite arrangement of the central section, slightly recessed between two side pavilions fronting the cell blocks, reflects the sophisticated simplicity of the internal plan. Behind the single narrow entrance is a small vestibule overlooked by the keeper's office and apartment. Leading off the vestibule, corridors, a mere 3 feet wide for security, extend outward to the brick, vaulted cell blocks. At their intersection are staircases to the upper arcaded passages that run along the inner wall of the cells, thereby ensuring adequate ventila-

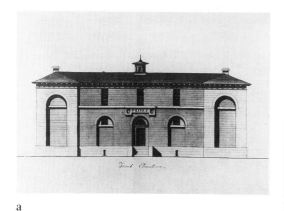
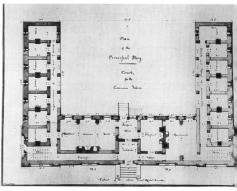

a   b

14.   Mills, drawings for the Burlington County Jail, Mount Holly (1808): (a) front elevation and (b) plan.

tion without detriment to the hot-air heating system. The debtors and less dangerous inmates are accommodated in the central block. In the basement are the furnace, kitchens, and a washhouse served by a well in the enclosed rear court, together with a refectory and workshops for the felons.

Such humane and intelligent planning was still a rarity in the United States, particularly for rural prisons, as Mills stressed in his written report. Not that he confused humanity with sentimentality, since he considered the primary requirements to be "strength and permanency." Consequently, he wanted all the cells, rooms, and corridors "vaulted or arched with brick" and paved with brick, while, as a further fire precaution, the staircases should be of stone. He pointed out how his plan allowed for separation of the sexes, supervision, and workshops to teach "*Industry,*" the social palliative of early-nineteenth-century reformers and an inspiration in Mills's own life. Architecture, he was convinced, could be a positive factor in social reform when motivated by idealism tempered by practicality. Thus, besides recommending the installation of an infirmary, on 4 June 1808, he enjoined the building committee, "Encouragement should be given to the *religious* visits of *Gospel Ministers.*" Operating by 1811, it was among the earliest fireproof institutions in the United States and remarkable for the implementation of advanced concepts on a restricted scale.

The Burlington County and Augusta commissions had emboldened Mills to write to Jefferson on 13 June 1808, "I have . . . made such progress in the study of architecture as make it necessary to think of establishing myself in the practice of my profession."[97] Naturally he was angling for patronage because he confronted a decline in "private business in my profession." The sluggish economy was due in no small measure to the cumulative effect of the president's recent embargo on British commerce. Yet Mills implied no criticism, surely sharing the widespread frustration with the British naval blockade of American trade with Napoleonic Europe and the impressment of sailors from U.S. vessels to serve in the Royal Navy; in explaining his decision to remain in the North, he did not cite the crippling loss of trade suffered by his home state, which halved the revenues collected in the Charleston District.

Instead, knowing the president's longstanding fascination with agricultural implements, he enclosed a design for a reaping machine, consisting of scythes attached to the wheels of a small cart, and invoked patriotism: "For the honour and benefit of my country I would desire to realize and would run the risk of trusting the execution of my designs to a stranger. . . . My wish is to endeavour to show to the European who visits us from the metropolis of his country, that the *American* talent for *architecture* is not a whit inferior to the European under the same advantages."

2

Philadelphia, 1808–1814 *"The Genius of the American Talent"*

Jefferson, regretfully, declined to intervene, and faulted Mills's reaping machine by pointing out that the scythes would cause drag. Against that disappointment were the Augusta and Mount Holly commissions, plus the increasing assurance that the Smiths would sanction his marriage to Eliza. They recited their vows at Winchester on 15 October 1808 and seem to have spent the first days of married life at Hackwood.[1] Here began a second new era in Mills's life, heralding a profoundly rewarding emotional and spiritual relationship. Eliza became the lodestone of his existence, sharing his religious idealism, quickening his creative aspiration, and founding the home life that would sustain him through the vagaries of his professional career. Their first home was an unpretentious house at 229 Mulberry Street in Philadelphia, made comfortable by her servant from Hackwood and, apparently, the two blacks whom Mills had inherited.

Fortunately, within six months, Latrobe's erstwhile patron naval captain John Meany commissioned Mills to design a row of eleven houses. This placed him on a par with Strickland, friend as well as rival, who that year began his Neo-Gothic Philadelphia Masonic Hall. By 1 May 1809, Mills had finished at least one sheet of designs to show to Meany and his partner John Savage (15). It offered a choice between two designs for a row of eleven three-and-a-half-story houses between Ninth and Locust streets called Franklin Row.[2] The most carefully drawn design occupies the lower half, each house being tied into the whole row by the arches that run along the front at main-floor level. These alternately enclose paired doorways and Neoclassically styled triple windows. The bonding of disciplined ornament to functional features transposes

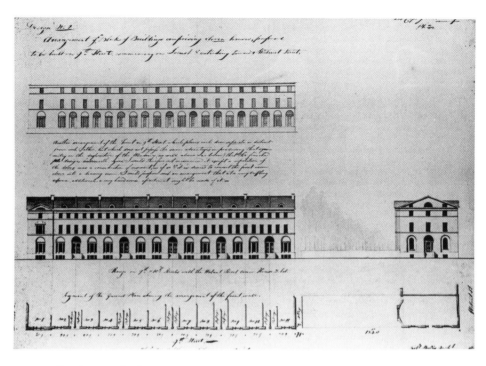

15.   Mills, design of a housing development for John Meany, Philadelphia (1809).

the facade of Latrobe's Waln House, especially in the pedimented end house fronting on Walnut Street. Meany, however, was more interested in profit than in such urbane Classical allusions. So he asked Mills to delete the end house and modify the plainer design sketched on the upper part of the sheet. Besides promising to be cheaper, Meany probably thought buyers would prefer entirely separate entrances. These led into a side through-hall, adjacent to the living rooms, and staircases to the basement kitchen and bedrooms. Lavatory facilities were situated in the yard, while the brick structure, having raised party walls, reduced the risk of fire so prevalent in the closely packed streets.

The row of ten houses, built under Mills's supervision, would be ready for occupation by the winter of 1810, thereby boosting his reputation. Franklin Row was a cut above its surroundings and emulated, albeit on a smaller scale, the elegant terraced housing popularized in Britain by the Woods of Bath and Robert Adam. In that sense, Mills was already fulfilling his stated ambition to compete with European architects, an aim to be even more apparent in the aggrandized version he would exhibit at the first annual show of the Society of Artists of the United States in 1811: "Arrangement of A Square Lot of Ground situate in Walnut Street and Locust Street, between Ninth and Tenth Sts. with the Designs of four blocks of buildings comprising forty-two houses, proposed to be erected thereon."[3] Now the arched and rectangular doors and windows, together with the continuous cornice, integrated each unit into the overall facade. Possibly to be financed by Meany, this project coincided with a recession precipitated by the cessation until 1816 of the charter of the locally based First Bank of the United States. Nonetheless, the success of Franklin Row might just have secured him the commission for Carolina Row (now part of the 900 block of Spruce Street), completed sometime between about 1812 and 1815, although the clumsily placed circular windows suggest that the contractor departed from Mills's plans. Consequently, Franklin Row stood unrivaled in Philadelphia before the erection in 1830 of John Haviland's grander Colonnade Row.

While the bricklayers labored on Franklin Row, Mills became involved in efforts to renovate the venerable Pennsylvania State House, where the Second Continental Congress had on 15 June 1775 appointed George Washington commander-in-chief and on 4 July 1776 summoned his nation into being with the Declaration of Independence.[4] Since 1799 when the state capital moved to Harrisburg, the hall (including the blocks on Fifth and Sixth streets), which had been used by the Supreme Court and Congress from 1790 to 1800, had been offered to the city and county of Philadelphia. Only the upper floor had been leased from 1802 to Charles Wilson Peale for his portrait gallery of Heroes of the Revolution and Museum of Curiosities.[5] Peale was among the leading exponents of Rationalist Thought in America and from the mid-1790s he had promoted the Columbian Academy, forerunner of the more successful Academy of Fine Arts.

In a letter of 28 October 1809 Peale wrote of "drawings made by Mr. Mills of the additions proposed to accommodate the museum in the State House."[6] His program initially embraced four rooms 40 feet square above "fifteen rooms fireproof for public offices" in new wings, attached to but not communicating with the main building.[7] He could have finalized these plans by October, or before the death on 1 December of Eliza's brother Peyton in a duel, perhaps causing her to miscarry since their first child was not born until the winter of 1811.[8] By February 1810, he had apparently simplified his design for the additions, though still satisfying two distinct purposes: judicial offices below and museum above. No official action was taken until 24 March 1812, when Mills was paid $200 for his drawings, a boon to celebrate the recent birth of Sarah Jane. Work began in 1812, and he proudly exhibited an elevation at the Society of Artists of the United States' second show.[9] It survives, showing the whole Chestnut Street front, stretched across a long sheet framed by thin painted outlines and signed April 1812 (16).[10] Somewhat brittle in the sharpness of line and flatness of the wall planes, Mills varied the articulation of the main windows: arched like those of the Augusta Church on the left side of the sheet and flatheaded with panels on the right. Old photographs confirm

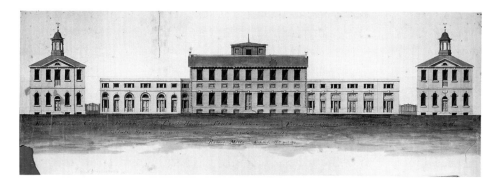

16.   Mills, drawing for extending the Old State House, Philadelphia (1809).

that the Chestnut Street side had the flat variety, while the theme of arched windows, echoing the large central arch of the Venetian window below the steeple, ran along the south front.[11] In notes accompanying the exhibit, he strongly recommended the reconstruction of the "ancient steeple," amputated in 1781 due to dry rot, which was finally accomplished in 1828 by his rival, Strickland. Lack of funds would also prevent him from building a balustraded portico beneath the Venetian window, to be decorated with niches sheltering statues for Wisdom and Justice and supporting "a rostrum for public speaking." Mills did succeed in harnessing the terse Latrobean Neoclassicism of the wings to the more florid Georgian original and providing practical accommodation. In addition to the museum, there was a series of 17-foot-square brick vaulted offices served by a 10-foot-wide corridor communicating with staircases, which was described as "the essence of solidity."[12] Finished by December 1812, the wings were demolished in 1912–1913 (Peale's Museum had closed in 1827) as part of the restoration of the State House to its colonial appearance.

Mills regarded the state house commission as among his most important early works. In his draft autobiography he mused, "In 1810 the author entered upon the practice of his profession at Philadelphia."[13] By that time, his professional ability was beginning to be recognized. There is circumstantial evidence that he was offered the presidency of the Philadelphia Water Works, but, perhaps because he was insufficiently qualified as an engineer, the expansion of Latrobe's system (1799–1801) was instead entrusted to Frederick Graff.[14] Other evidence of Mills's work at this time is an unclear sketch dated 30 May 1810 marked only "Mr. Kraumbar's" and a note reading "Recd of Mr. Isaac Harvey [a local merchant] for Dec. 22nd 1810. Ten dollars for drawings of his establishment on High Street," possibly stylistically akin to the pair of houses he designed that spring for two other merchants, Gideon Fairmen and Richard Willcocks. Above shops on either side of a central doorway rose three floors of domestic accommodations, each marked by string courses and arched and rectangular windows diminishing on the upper stories.[15]

Yet Mills's eager pursuit of commissions could backfire. In late March 1810, the wealthy lawyer Benjamin Chew asked him "to delineate & color the Division of certain Lots advertised by me for public Sale" on the family property along Fourth Street.[16] But because Chew had been assembling building materials for a house, Mills opportunistically sent several drawings made (in their new home at 43 Sansom Street) between 5 and 26 April, two alternative plans for the "Principal story" and an elevation of the "Front answering to either Plan," each carefully rendered in pen and colored washes. The first shows an attractive Latrobean Neoclassical building three bays wide and three stories high above the basement, distinguished by triple windows arced by moldings (17). For the interior, he offered Chew a nice choice. He could have either a central passage through an apsidal-ended hall to the staircase, very like the barbell-shaped layout of the Markoe House, or a staircase at right angles. The first shows a second semicircular-ended "Office or Library" on the left side, but both plans are otherwise similar. Right of the hall are interconnected dining and drawing rooms (respectively measuring 26 feet by 18 feet and 25 feet by 18 feet) while, behind the office, a housekeeper's room was to have communicated with a service stair and kitchen. The sheet also has a pencil plan for the upper story, placing two bedrooms separated by closets on either side of the central staircase landing.

The next day he made a more carefully rendered version, omitting the semicircular wall and office but including a bathroom adjoining the service stair between the house and kitchen block, modeled upon the one in the Markoe House. More in the manner of Jefferson are the ample walk-in closets, one for china adjoining the housekeeper's room and another "Fire-proof" fitted into the angle of the office. The plan might have been handed to Chew on 26 April, together with Neoclassical "Designs for coach house and stables of Benjamin Chew Esqr." Chew was impressed by the quality of Mills's proposals, but irked by his bill "amounting to $160—[which] is so far beyond all Idea that I could have entertained."

The issue for Chew was not merely one of cost or presumption but of Mills's assumption of professional status equal to his own. Here was the very core of the difficulty facing Mills and the new generation of purpose-trained American architects, a problem he would confront as late as 1842.[17] Irked, Mills sharpened his quill on the morning of 2 August, undaunted by Chew's power in Philadelphia. He had charged only 1 percent of the estimated cost, $16,000,

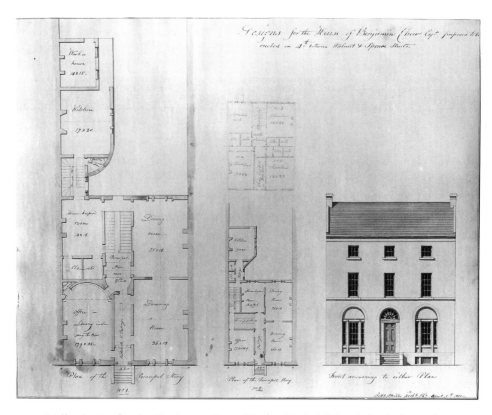

17.   Mills, design for the Benjamin Chew House, Philadelphia (1810), front elevation with plan.

whereas "Architects in England [charge] 1st On the whole expense incurred in executing their designs is 5 and ½ per cent. 2nd—For furnishing drawings & descriptions alone, without any further direction of the work either personally or by letter—2.5 per cent upon the estimate whether the work be executed or not." All the "English architects of eminence," he remonstrated, ironically revealing how Britain remained the chief fount of ideas and taste for most Americans, "charge 5 guineas per day, no surveyor or measurer less than one guinea per day." He was quite willing to refer the settlement to competent judges, although this brought him right back to the essential issue: "But as my profession is *novel* in this Country, and there are no cases that can be referred to for decision, it is impossible that a correct view can be taken of the subject to found a correct opinion." That was a weak argument, especially since Chew had not commissioned any design. Within two days Mills had settled for $100, while Chew built his house for $25,000, evidently letting his contractor consult, and partially alter, Mills's designs. Its construction from 1810 to 1813

must have been a reproach to Mills, for he had antagonized the kind of powerful patron mentioned in his 1808 letter to Jefferson.

The Chew fiasco coincided with another effort to foster the artistic profes-
sions in the United States. "The author," Mills recalled in his autobiography,
was "one of the founders of the Society of Artists [of the United States] in
Philadelphia, being elected a Fellow on 11 July 1810 and appointed Secretary
soon thereafter," a sign of popularity reinforced by acceptance into the ranks
of the influential Scottish St. Andrew's Society.[18] The Society of Artists' goals
of accelerated national cultural development and professional recognition were
especially congenial to Mills, who, as he wrote to Jefferson on 4 June 1810 enclosing its constitution, was experiencing "much difficulty in receiving such
pecuniary returns as suffice reasonable to remunerate me for my trouble."[19]
The society—restyled the Columbian Society of Artists in 1813, the year
Thomas Pope advertised his short-lived Philadelphia Architectural Academy—was among the earliest attempts in the United States to match the educational and exhibition facilities available to European artists through institutions such as the Royal Academy of Arts in London, still under the presidency
of Benjamin West, who had been born at Springfield township near Philadelphia.[20] West's presence in London and the absence of comparable American institutions had attracted the best young American artists to London over the
preceding decade, including Mills's fellow Charlestonian, Washington Allston,
and friend Charles Bird King.[21] Beyond the cultural and intellectual advantages
to be found in London, those talented and chauvinistic Americans also admired
the greater appreciation afforded the arts in Britain and Europe.

By contrast, many Americans mistrusted the fine arts as decadent, tainted
by aristocratic privilege. That antipathy was addressed by Latrobe in the oration he delivered on 8 May 1811 to the society, after Mills had organized his
election as vice president.[22] "Many of our citizens who do not fear that they
[the fine arts] will enervate our minds and corrupt the simple and republican
character of our pursuits and enjoyments, consider the actual state of society
unfit for their introduction: more dread a high grade of perfection in the fine
arts as the certain indication of the loss of personal liberty, and the concentration of wealth and power in the hands of a few." Latrobe spoke from a frustration that Mills increasingly shared, although his contemporary correspondence
is interspersed with optimistic prognostications, as the prediction to Jefferson
on 8 June 1812 that the population growth would result in an "increasing demand for the production of the Fine Arts," ensuring "to our country the means
of being furnished within ourselves with what we have hitherto sought in distant countries."[23]

This letter reflected Mills's contribution between November 1811 and April
1812 to the report of the committee appointed by the society to examine the

Rise, Progress and Present State of the Society of Artists of the United States. Its main recommendation was unification with the Pennsylvania Academy, but toward the end of the document, and doubtless to secure support while relations with Britain worsened, the committee optimistically suggested that the isolation of the United States would encourage the fine arts. Within a few weeks President Madison indirectly put its theory to the test by declaring war against Britain on 18 June 1812. Two years into that conflict, Mills, ever fervently patriotic, was to detect positive signs when writing to Jefferson on 7 June 1814: "We are gaining that purity of taste, which if combined with knowledge, will advance us to the honour of becoming rivals to European artists."

Mills had earlier hoped to earn that honor in the design of the projected new Pennsylvania State Capitol at Harrisburg on the Susquehanna River. In February 1810 Governor Simon Snyder had ordered it completed by 1812 and appointed three commissioners to select a suitable site and design.[24] One, John Dorsey, was Mills's acquaintance and he had surely alerted Mills to prepare a scheme. For by 16 April 1810 Mills had signed a beautiful pen, pencil, and colored-wash drawing inscribed "DESIGNS for the PUBLIC BUILDINGS Proposed to be Erected at Harrisburg—State of Pennsylvania," combining an impressive perspective view and main floor plan of the complex (18).[25] He conceived five buildings arranged in an arc at the center of a large, formally landscaped enclosure. At either end are two-story structures, each having entrance porticoes of four baseless Greek Doric columns sandwiched between slightly projected side sections. Reminiscent of Latrobe's Chestnut Street Theater (1801), the left structure was planned as the governor's house and the right as public offices. The offices contained two circular "rooms thrown into one Fireproof," a more Roman Classical version of the curved rooms in the governor's house. Mindful of the rigors of the Harrisburg winters, both buildings were linked by Greek Doric colonnades, first to the single-story "public offices" (again planned with the remarkable conjoined circular "fire proof" apartments of 30-foot diameter) and then to the commanding three-story state house.

The state house was Mills's most original design to date. V-shaped to match the axes of the wing buildings, the composition also clearly differentiated the two legislative chambers. The House of Representatives, measuring 60 feet by 40 feet, would have been on the left of the central circular hall and staircase, and the Senate, measuring 40 feet square, on the right. The house follows the oval plan that Latrobe had contemplated for the federal Hall of Representatives, while the Senate copies its half auditorium plan that was actually built. Each was to be lit by large triple openings enclosed by a single arch and divided by a broad entablature so that the upper section simulated the Roman thermal window. Mills used another Roman theme, the circular peristyle, for the main portico, which resolves the two angled facades and, together with the

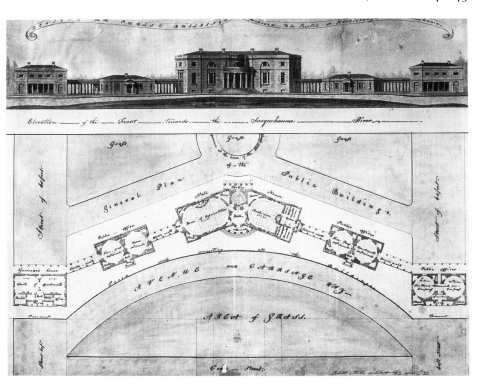

18.   Mills, design for the Pennsylvania State Capitol, Harrisburg (1810).

wider rear portico, monumentalizes the Greek order that extends across the whole complex. If those abstractions of ancient Classical form and unifying geometrical articulation imitate his mentor, the plan of the state house could owe in part to Thornton's Octagon House in Washington and Dorsey's unexecuted design for a V-plan house of 1809 with an elliptical four-column portico at its acute angle.[26]

Dorsey seems to have pushed for the unofficial acceptance of Mills's "striking" design in 1810, when the state legislature authorized the construction of roads to the designated site on the eminence between the present Commonwealth Avenue and Third Street.[27] However, the history of the commission over the next few years was complicated and frustrating for Mills. By the summer of 1810, the architectural initiative had already passed to Stephen Hills, an immigrant builder who was, ironically, from Britain.[28] Hills drew up a master plan between that summer and the fall of 1812, receiving an annual payment of $100 for the "carpenters work & directing" the erection of two fireproof buildings 325 feet apart for the chief state administrative offices.[29] The design of the rectangular two-story fireproof offices, replete with semicircular porticoes at the center of their Main Street facades, suggests that Hills consulted Mills or examined his scheme; he was to become an architect, but his major work dates from the 1830s, exemplified by the Missouri State Capitol at Jefferson City (1836–1837). At the 1811 Society of Artists' show, Mills exhibited "No. 331. Design of the public Buildings now erecting at Harrisburg." Whether this was his 1810 design or an elevation of the two fireproof buildings erected by Hills is not clear. Not by nature dishonest, Mills perhaps believed that Hills had used enough of his ideas to justify the claim and hoped that the Pennsylvania legislators would be able to raise sufficient funds to complete at least the main building according to his conception.

Fortunately, other projects progressed. Mills's papers include sketch plans for improvements to the seating in the Chestnut Street Theater, originally built between 1791 and 1794 and remodeled by Latrobe in 1801, and a "Plan of the Circus of Messrs Piper & Fox as it now stands Pha Nov 1810."[30] Early in 1811, the 100-foot facade of the circus on Ninth Street was extended by 40 feet, enabling a corresponding increase in the central circular space to an extreme diameter of nearly 140 feet. The expansion permitted a series of boxes and a refreshment room to be introduced above the level of the circus ring, with more boxes and galleries on the upper floor. According to Dr. John Mease in a *Picture of Philadelphia* (1811), to which Mills subscribed, the "new arrangements will render the exhibitions more interesting and diversified."[31] Although Mease did not attribute the alterations to him, Mills had the expertise to cover this large space using the de l'Orme principle. Quite different from the essentially technical character of those drawings is his vigorous sketch, "Mr. Dorsey's Floor Cloth manufactory 60 ft." This hybrid "Gothic Mansion" was built in 1809 and 1810 with advice about structure and stylistic details from Mills, on Chestnut between Eleventh and Twelfth Streets. The sketch must date from this period, since it formed the basis for the engraving published in the February 1811 issue of *Port Folio.*[32] This journal, an important source of political, cultural, and scientific news, was controlled by Joseph Dennie and, of great significance for Mills's future career, Asbury Dickins, later a leading figure in the Columbian Society of Washington, D.C., and secretary of the Senate. Also in 1811, Mills forged a more immediate link with the federal capital when Dr. Thornton, as commissioner of the Patent Office, placed him, and Strickland, on the list of draftsmen qualified to produce technical drawings for patent applications.

Nor had Mills been forgotten in Charleston. Some months earlier, the newly founded Protestant Episcopal Society for the Advancement of Christianity in South Carolina commissioned him to design a seal, possibly on the advice of the Reverend Nathaniel Brown, until 1809 rector of St. Michael's, Charleston.[33] Neatly embodying the society's purpose, he drew an open Book of Common Prayer resting on a Bible and encircled by the society's title. By June

1812, a thousand copies of the seal had been printed in Philadelphia by B. Tanner (whose son, H. S. Tanner, was to engrave Mills's *Atlas of South Carolina* in 1825) and dispatched to Charleston.[34]

The popular enthusiasm for evangelism and his competence in large-span buildings brought another commission. Late in January 1811, Dr. William Staughton asked Mills to draft plans for a church to accommodate the substantial breakaway group he had recently led from the First Baptist congregation. Many were also of British descent and adversely affected by the "heated condition of politics" in Philadelphia just prior to the War of 1812, although to prove their loyalty, Staughton recruited sixty of his flock to join the citizens who volunteered to build earth fortifications on the west side of the town.[35] Besides then being Mills's near neighbor, Staughton had from 1793 served the church in South Carolina and New York before moving to Philadelphia in 1805; their friendship held into the 1820s when Mills visited Staughton in Washington.[36] Triumphantly, Mills included an elevation, since lost, of "the New Baptist Church Building in George Street [Sansom Street] between 8th and 9th [No. 339]" in his exhibit at the 1811 Society of Artists' show. Mease referred to the church as "now erecting" and fortunately, since it was altered during construction, supplied "a particular description."[37] "The plan of this church within is a rotunda, ninety feet in diameter, surmounted by a dome, crowned with a lanthorn or cupola, upwards of twenty feet in diameter. The walls, with the dome are elevated upwards of fifty feet above the ground, built of brick and the dome constructed of short pieces of plank, upon the principle adopted in that of the Halle de Bled at Paris" (though Mills probably also read the "Essay towards a History of Temples and Round Churches" in his copy of Britton's *Architectural Antiquities of Great Britain*). The entrance facade of the Baptist Church had "square projections" capped by octagonal "belfries or cupolas" rising above but parallel to the adjacent buildings, while also emphasizing the inviting recession created behind the two elegant Ionic in antis columns of the portico (19a). The composition dignified the aspirations of the Baptists and provided separate entrances to the nave and to the gallery via staircases in the projections. Those seated on the main floor proceeded up the marble steps through the Ionic columns—spanned by a more Doric-looking frieze—and through a "great Venetian door" into the "grand aisle." This passed between rows of boxed pews leading toward the sunken baptismal pool at the center, which could be "closed over by a floor to accommodate the choir," and the pulpit prominently raised against the rear wall. Initially, Mills had contemplated elevating the pulpit to the level of the gallery on columns providing a vestibule to the vestry rooms in a single-story story rear projection closed off by folding doors. But because of cost and capacity, Mills deleted the cross aisle and lowered the pulpit. As a result the gallery, supported on tapered

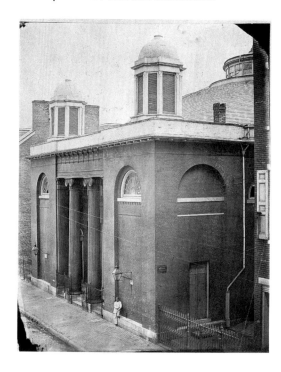

19. Mills, Dr. Staughton Baptist Church, Philadelphia (1811): (a) facade and (b) interior (ca. 1815).

a

columns, was changed to a horseshoe shape in order to leave space for a rectangular window above and behind the pulpit.

The completed interior is illustrated in a print (19b) that strikingly conveys how admirably Mills's auditorium satisfied the requirements of Staughton's services, which were compounded of highly charged teaching from the Bible and vivid baptismal rites.[38] Despite the squash of men, women, and children in their Sunday best, the auditorium seems spacious, fulfilling Mease's prediction that it would "seat with comfort upwards of two thousand people," the "whole church being encircled with sashes [the square windows below and semicircular ones above the gallery] that open and shut at pleasure." The effect of airy lightness was augmented by the dome gracefully curving up to the "lanthorn" from which sunlight and fresh air were suffused over the rotunda, warmed in the winter by a hot-air furnace installed by Mills.

Dedicated on 16 August 1812 and completed for some $40,000, including the purchase of the lot, the Baptist church was a spectacular success, attracting what one local minister reported as "the largest church gatherings I have ever seen under one roof . . . and regularly for many years," boosting the annual income from pew rentals and collections to between $4,000 and $5,000 over the first period of its sixty-odd years of use.[39] Mills took particular pride in the functional qualities of the design. On 26 April 1815 he wrote to Daniel Pettibone in Washington, D.C., whom he had met as manufacturer of the hot-air furnace for the Bank of Philadelphia and from whom he would purchase a license to install heating systems, "I have on all occasions (when the furnace was in use) found the room comfortable in the coldest days."[40] Since he had exercised sole control over the commission, Mills regarded the Baptist Church as his first major achievement in acoustical design. On 6 August 1830, when actually outlining a proposal to improve the acoustics in the federal Hall of Representatives, he described the church to his friend Robert Gilmor as

> the *first circular room* for *public speaking* which I constructed. I based
> the design upon what I conceived *the true principle* of accoustics. . . .
> [T]he room held 4,000 people and the voice of the speaker, whether
> the room was full or empty, was distinct & clear to the most distant
> hearer, and the speaker made no uncommon effort to speak. . . . I
> hold nothing upon *theory,* but all on matter *fact,* certain of a given
> effect resulting from a given cause.[41]

On 24 September 1811 a greater challenge to his pretensions as a structural engineer was advertised in the local press. The board of managers of the Lancaster-Schuylkill, or Upper Ferry, Bridge Company invited designs for a new bridge on a recently purchased site at Sheridan's Ferry some 200 feet north of an existing floating bridge. They wanted it to stand as high above the river (20 feet) as the Market Street or "Permanent Bridge."[42] Competitors were required to submit designs for a roadway 36 feet wide "in the clear with footways," preferably having a "single Arch" to reduce damage from debris washed down river. In fact, Mills did not submit his proposals until 26 October 1811, enclosing a formal letter describing two plans, neither extant. He estimated that his first scheme, presumably having a single arch but no roof, would cost $36,674 including a separate tollhouse. An alternative version with a roof and small rental building "at each angle of the bridge . . . one reserved as a toll house" would require $44,174. His speculation that savings could be effected if the company purchased a quarry suggests that he specified stone seatings on each bank; secure construction was to be in the public mind that winter when the New Madrid earthquakes destroyed property throughout southeast Missouri, redirected the mighty Mississippi, and even rang church bells in Boston.

On 14 November the board of managers voted for a 350-foot-long bridge supported on "two equal arches with one pier," further agreeing on 6 December to appoint three of their number to "give general instructions to Lewis Wernwag with whom the Managers have contracted to build a bridge," only two days later to decide that the bridge be "constructed with one arch, the cord of which shall be 330 feet and that Mr. Wernwag's plan of a Bridge of one arch with 330 cord be adopted." Born at Reidlingen near Würtemburg,

20.   Lewis Wernwag and Mills, Upper Ferry Bridge, Philadelphia (1811), aquatint by Duborg after Bushby (ca. 1820).

Wernwag had emigrated to Philadelphia in 1796 and had become associated with various manufacturing ventures. In 1810, he had designed his first bridge, which was wooden, across Neshaminy Creek on the road from Philadelphia to New York, followed by an innovative cantilevered drawbridge at Frankford Creek, nicknamed the "Economy."[43] The scale and technology of the Upper Ferry Bridge, soon to be known as the Colossus of Fairmount, was remarkably advanced (20). Its total length of 340 feet, 4 inches exceeded any other wooden span bridge, being almost 98 feet longer than the one at Wettingen in Switzerland of 1764 by the famous Grubenmann brothers.[44] The double carriageway and footpath were supported on five parallel laminated ribs formed of seven thicknesses of timber and strengthened by zigzag trusses (invented by Palladio) along either edge. While the lamination bears some relation to Mills's version of the de l'Orme system, the bonding of the main timbers was achieved in a novel manner that he later explained to Dunlap: "All the timbers are sawed through the heart, and no two pieces touch each other, being separated by iron plates, securing by this means the works from the attack of dry rot."[45]

In that account, Mills described Wernwag as merely "the builder" and implied that he had been the designer.[46] But the first reference to Mills in the company minutes does not appear until March 1813, by which time the Upper Ferry Bridge had been almost completed. It recorded his contract to enclose the carriageway and to build a separate circular tollhouse on the Philadelphia bank. Yet at the Society of Artists' 1812 show in the Pennsylvania Academy, he exhibited "Designs for the bridge now erecting at the Upper Ferry, Schuylkill River. Span 330 feet" and next year another drawing carrying an equally equivocal caption, "No. 122. Design of the Upper Ferry Bridge, over the Schuylkill River as it is now finishing."[47] He would stake a direct claim to this bold engineering feat in his *Statistics,* to be repeated almost verbatim in Dunlap: "The greatest span of arch that ever was attempted in any country and executed in this, over the River Schuylkill near Philadelphia, was designed by Mr. M."[48]

One explanation might be that his entry in the 1811 competition anticipated the chief constituents of the single-arch design that Wernwag contracted to erect or that, more enthusiastic than prudent, Mills allowed Wernwag to use his idea. The two were to cooperate on schemes for the improvement and bridging of Jones' Falls at Baltimore in 1818 and 1830; indeed, Wernwag would call Mills his "friend" when corresponding in 1819. Moreover, in mid-March the managers of the Upper Ferry Bridge recorded in the minutes "a verbal agreement with Robert Mills for covering and enclosing the Bridge and building a Toll house to be completed within six months" for $5,520.[49] Once the contract was under way, Mills warned the managers on 4 June of the danger "from the frequent thunder gusts we are subject to," in vain recommending the installation of conductors from 60 to 80 feet apart.[50] Then, and indicative of their confidence in Mills's technical competence, they urgently requested him on 13 July to "examine into the cause of the defect in the Bridge." A crack in the northern abutment had continued to expand despite reinforcement. Mills's solution was to substitute two brick arches, significantly paid for by Wernwag, who then altered the stone footings for the arches. The remedy proved effectual but pushed the total cost to more than $70,000. By August, Mills was able to continue his contract for the superstructure, receiving a final payment of $600 on 4 November. The bridge was opened in December. All seemed satisfactory until June, when faults appeared in the roofing and weatherboarding and were initially blamed on Mills. He seems to have successfully countered that charge, for on 28 January 1815, he proposed among other repairs that "a fascia or band should be run fore and aft on both sides of the interior of the bridge." Notes in his 1816 pocket memorandum book indicate that a further $1,100 was spent, some unwisely contributed from his own resources, for which he was not fully reimbursed.[51] The "Colossus" remained in profitable service for the next twenty-two years, long after the board had dismissed Wernwag in April 1819 because "the Abutment of one of the dams has fallen down and that other damages have been done to the works in consequence of your negligence in their construction."[52]

Mills's part in the Upper Ferry Bridge commission reflects not only a laudable ambition but also a corresponding lack of acuity or caution in professional and financial dealings, reflected in the investments he made with mixed success in Philadelphia real estate between May 1812 and 1814.[53] Yet in the

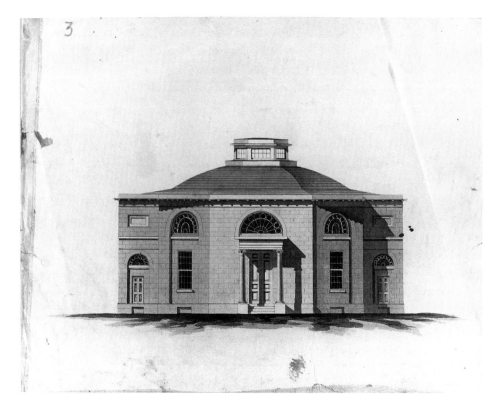

21.   Mills, drawing (ca. 1828) of the Unitarian Church, Philadelphia (1812).

spring of 1812, Mills had reason for satisfaction: happily married with one child, solvent, and acquiring respect as an innovative and functional designer. Hence at the second annual exhibition of the Society of Artists in May, he exhibited designs for two churches, one about to be erected in Richmond and the other already under construction, "No. 36. The Unitarian Church, now building at the corner of Tenth and Locust Streets."[54]

The Unitarians had hitherto held services in the main hall of the University of Maryland, although they had acquired the site for a church and cemetery in 1808.[55] For them, Mills selected an octagonal plan, perhaps to symbolize a central tenet of their faith—the diverse unity of creation—or to exhibit his knowledge of Renaissance church design as illustrated in Jefferson's library, not forgetting Latrobe's reference in his essay on acoustics to the "Octagon chapel, Bath" (1767) by Thomas Lightoler.[56] The actual design that Mills exhibited in 1812 has disappeared. It is probably represented in the pen-and-wash drawing he made on a sheet of paper watermarked 1828, the year his small church was replaced by a more conventional rectangular building with a four-column Greek Doric portico designed by Strickland (21).[57] However, the relative size of the central domed section and the two side projections seems somewhat smaller than the 70-foot diameter that Mills later ascribed to the church. There are also other inconsistencies. The round-headed windows impart a Classical nobility reinforced by the scoring of the stucco finish on the brick walls. Yet neither the low base nor the continuous bracketed cornice entirely controls the diverse formal constituents.

The church was built between March 1812 and 14 February 1813; a few weeks later, Mills reexhibited his elevation at the Society of Artists, by then restyled the Columbian Society of Artists. Unfortunately, no reliable information remains about the contractor, the cost, or Mills's fee, and the only contemporary description is the brief reference in T. Wilson's 1824 edition of *A Picture of Philadelphia*. Deeming it to be "a neat brick building nearly of an octagon form," Wilson did not mention the delicate two-column Ionic portico or describe the interior, which apparently had a seating capacity of 300. The seating may have radiated from a pulpit standing opposite the front entrance and spread into the side projections, without the doorways in Mills's 1828 drawing. Wilson was equally vague about the roof structure, probably built on the de l'Orme system, but noticed one feature missing from Mills's drawing, "a cupola and bell" above the entrance.

Mills's second design, "No. 60. The Monumental Church, about to be erected at Richmond, Virginia," later to be engraved by W. Goodacre and printed in the second volume of J. H. Hinton's *The History and Topography of the United States of North America* (1846), published in London and Boston (22), became the most celebrated of his ecclesiastical buildings.[58] The commission also arose out of a widely publicized event, the disastrous fire in the Richmond Theater on 26 December 1811 in which seventy-one people had perished.[59] A committee of leading citizens organized a competition for a monument under the unofficial direction of the wealthy local physician and banker Dr. John Brockenbrough. Latrobe and an obscure local contractor, Henry Hiort, each entered designs, of an octagonal domed and of a pyramidal structure, respectively. Mills apparently worked up two schemes for a monument, unaware that his revered mentor already considered himself the chosen architect. Then in February 1812, the committee decided to combine the monument with a church to be erected on the site of the theater about half way up the steeply inclined Broad Street from the lower town and James River. Latrobe complied, drawing a solemn, square, domed church framed by two corner towers and fronted by a lower vestibule surmounted by a stepped pyramid, a traditional symbol of both death and eternity.

Latrobe might have refused had he known that Mills was also asked to submit a new design. Worse, his former pupil came up with a comparable arrangement. At the entrance to a domed church would stand a deep commem-

22.   Mills, design for the Monumental Church, Richmond (1812), engraved by
W. Goodacre.

orative portico, entered through two in antis columns and supporting an
allegorical sculpture. However, Mills's church was octagonal in plan, anchored
by three projections: two for staircases to the gallery and one to contain the
pulpit, altar recess, and vestry room capped by a tall steeple. Deeply offended
that his "professional child" had been included, Latrobe wrote to Brockenbrough on 22 March 1812. He was "exceedingly reluctant" to compete further, "especially when the principle on which Mr. Mills has made his design,
is my own idea communicated to him; though much modified." Specifically he
accused Mills of having stolen the manner of combining the church with the
monument and of lettering the inscription with granite set in aquia marble,
despite admitting that Mills was "a man of the strictest integrity and virtue
and talents which close study have much improved."[60] Latrobe withdrew and
the commission, together with a prize of $500, was awarded to Mills, just be-
fore the Society of Artists exhibition was opened and a few weeks prior to the
declaration of war against Britain.

Mills's success did depend to some extent on information communicated to him by his father-in-law about the committee's wishes. General Smith had written from Washington on 25 February 1812 confirming the arrival of "your second design—both specimens of your talents are admired, and have been sent on to Richmond."[61] More important than the inference that Mills had already made at least two designs for a monument, Smith went on to tell him that the committee envisaged its integration with a church, adding, "It is the wish of Mr. Clay that you would design a monument so as to meet the wishes of the committee & to occupy the space formerly mentioned—You will do this with all convenient speed, and detail the minutiae of expense." Naturally, the general's standing in Virginia was of advantage to Mills. The letter reveals his privileged position, Smith confiding that Napoleon (whose Milan Decree of 1807 had declared American ships searched by the British to be liable for confiscation) was "in good temper with us at present but I rely not on any of his acts." Mills received further encouragement from another influential Richmond resident and later patron, Colonel John Ambler. A member of the grand jury that indicted Aaron Burr for treason in 1799, he had married Catherine, daughter of Philip Bush of Winchester. He was to be one of the first pew holders of the Monumental Church and a lay deputy from 1817, while his wife became the director of the Sunday school.[62]

However helpful such links, Mills won the commission because he best interpreted the requirements of the committee. First, his design seemed more capacious yet less costly than that of Latrobe; indeed, he hazarded an optimistic estimate of $35,000, perhaps including the use of iron sheets for the roof about which he corresponded with Latrobe in September 1812.[63] Second, Mills's church looked more like a traditional Episcopalian building thanks to the arresting steeple, symbolically appropriate for this the first erected by the Virginia Episcopalians since the Revolution. Third, that steeple, climbing to a conical spire, promised to counteract the adverse effect of the relatively low height of the church on its sloping site. And, as he likely pointed out, the erection of the steeple could be delayed pending sufficient funds without impeding the function of the church.

The steeple embodied Mills's desire to fashion a modern American style. The sharply defined ornament, including the spiral fluting, was in the current Neoclassical mode, but its ancestry was Georgian Colonial, reversing the arrangement of Gibbs's two influential schemes for a "Round Church."[64] Significantly, in Gibbs's first scheme, single-story two-column porticoes are at each side of the auditorium, as on the Monumental Church. The porticoes as built had a modified version of the partially fluted Greek Doric columns from the Temple of Apollo on the Island of Delos, much admired by Latrobe, who projected their use, alike in antis, in his unexecuted design for St. John's in Richmond. Originally designed to be surmounted by mourning figures, Mills's monumental portico was more directly integrated with the church in the completed building. As constructed between 4 August 1812 and its dedication on 4 May 1814, the Monumental Church is severely Neoclassical, as in the acute angled, rather than arched, centers of the Venetian triple windows lighting the nave. Limited funds necessitated the permanent postponement of the steeple as well as simplification of the monumental portico. If more concise in effect, those changes diminished the imaginative and dramatic architectonic expression of the different purposes of the edifice. Yet Mills had, as he later wrote, created "a temple for divine worship."[65]

Very probably he had traveled to Richmond in the summer of 1812 with the revised working drawings for the contractor, Isaac Sturdevant of Boston.[66] Thereafter, he periodically left Eliza and little Sarah in order to check progress on the brick and stucco fabric, staying with the Brockenbroughs; perhaps concerned for the safety of his family, Mills did not enlist in the American forces, unlike Alexander Parris, who gained useful technical experience in the Army Corps of Engineers.[67] Thus on the evening of 5 December 1812 he assured Eliza that "Mrs. Brockenbrough and the Doctor have been as usual very kind," and he was to dine with Colonel Ambler. Yet he found that "I have a great many drawings to make, . . . as most of the work will be going on this winter. . . . [T]he building is nearly ready for the roof—I have a complete command of the building from the window of my chamber."[68] In fact, the de l'Orme system dome was not finished until the next spring, concurrently with the costly aquia stone monumental portico eventually capped by a triangular attic in 1816 and hence more like a conventional frontispiece (23a). By 20 May 1813 Brockenbrough wrote to Mills at Philadelphia, reporting that the dome was about to be shingled and its interior painted by "Mr. Bridport," while the use of "sheet iron" to cover the monumental portico was under discussion.[69] But his main purpose was to warn Mills that the building committee was beginning "to feel great anxiety on the subject of expense which they fear will exceed their means." Lack of money delayed the installation of the commemorative monument for more than two years beyond the signing of the Treaty of Ghent on 25 December 1814, which ended hostilities with Britain. For it, Mills designed a funerary urn atop a tapered base that blended the Roman cippus and Egyptian form, anticipating the style of several of his subsequent monuments. The Richmond monument was cut by the immigrant Italian sculptor Antonio Capellano, whose bills might be among the receipts from the contractors, Douglas and Huddleston, amounting to some $7,800, noted in Mills's 1816 pocket memorandum book; on 11 August 1817 Capellano received a further payment of $150 for the frieze of funerary urns that replaced the triglyphs shown in the original design.[70]

By then, the Monumental Church had been in use for almost two years,

23.   Mills, Monumental Church, Richmond (1812–1814): (a) facade, (b) interior, and (c) plan.

b

c

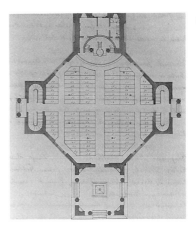

much to the chagrin of Latrobe, who on 10 October 1814 wrote to the French immigrant architect Maximillian Godefroy that "Mills is a wretched designer."[71] The intelligent arrangement of the auditorium alone disproves Latrobe's outburst (23b, 23c). The ranks of pews in the nave and polygonal gallery were easily accessible through the three entrances and adequately lit and ventilated by the broad windows in the angle walls and the 20-foot-diameter lantern. The pews faced toward the semicircular recess, which acted as a sounding board for the altar and raised pulpit, arrestingly lit by windows in the base of the rear projection. The recess was screened by two in antis columns adapted from the graceful Erechtheion Ionic order, but with American pentagonal stars and flaming tapers in the necking band below each capital—an ongoing process of modification of the ancient orders for aesthetic, economic, and practical reasons. The most intellectual of Mills's religious auditoriums, he was to be excessively modest when, in his 1853 article "Architecture in Virginia" he described the church as "somewhat original in its plan."[72] That very originality prevented it from setting a pattern, with the possible exception of the octagonal plan and steepled New South Church, which Bulfinch built at Boston in 1814.[73] Interestingly, the church that most resembled it was the Albion Chapel in Moorfields, London (1815), by William Jay, who later worked in Georgia and South Carolina.[74] It also had a domed auditorium, but fronted by a more Classical rectangular facade pierced by a modest two-column in antis portico. The distinctive cast of Mills's increasingly assured American Classicism becomes obvious if the Monumental Church is compared with the next major church to be built at Richmond. Thomas U. Walter's First Baptist Church (1841), higher up on Broad Street, has a rectangular plan and two-column in antis portico similar to the smaller Neo-Greek churches first popularized by the New York architects Town and Davis in the 1820s and subsequently copied in the Deep South by their former assistants, James Dakin and James Gallier, Sr. That members of this generation of American architects considered Mills's design to be too idiosyncratic is condensed in the dismissive comment that Isaiah Rogers entered in his diary on 16 May 1841: "The interior is bad."[75]

Nonetheless, the Monumental Church, and his friendship with Brockenbrough and Ambler, had won Mills other commissions in Richmond. One appears to have been for a shot tower, 30 feet in diameter and 160 feet to "the top of the battlement," according to the caption he wrote under the design exhibited at the Columbian Society of Artists in May 1813.[76] The shot-tower commission figured in the correspondence between Eliza and Mills during his absences from Philadelphia, which helps chart their relationship and disclose their personalities and attitudes.[77] In a letter Eliza mailed on 25 April 1813 from Philadelphia to Richmond transmitting a message about the timber for the Upper Ferry Bridge, she reported the visit of a man who claimed to be "qualified to superintend the manufactory of shot: says he understood you wished to engage a man of this description to go on to Richmond."

The constant refrain of her letters was longing for his return. Four days earlier she had written, "My dear Husband will perceive that I think much of him, from the frequency of my communications. . . . I cannot tell my better half how much I already long to see him, but he is fully sensible my fondest affections are all his own and that in the enjoyment of his society I derive my summum Bonum of all Earthly good." Mills's fewer replies usually include an indirect homily, "I went to church at the Capitol today and found a very large assembly. . . . I am glad to learn that you are able to go and hear our excellent Dr. Staughton—there is more edification in one of his discourses than in that of half of most of the clergy put together." But he also made much of "the pleasures she [Eliza] heaps upon me," and alluded to current news "that the frigate Essex has been taken by a British seventy four [gun ship of the line] and carried into some port in England. I hope it is not true, tho' nothing dishonorable attaches to an American 32 gun frigate being conquered by a British 74." Evidently he did not think that Eliza would be unduly worried, especially since she could retreat to Hackwood, as she did periodically during the fever months of high summer. Her response was to chide him on 5 May that he "must recollect what a Family I have at present to attend to, and use all *possible* industry in order to take your share of domestick cares off my shoulders," yet ending "and *another* thing you don't write me often enough in return, but I am not angry, I love you as dearly as ever." On 19 May she tried a different tack, coincidentally indicating an idea on the education of children she would later implement in her school projects:

> Little Sarah has not forgott you she often turns an enquiring eye towards the door when hearing a rap and calls out peet papa see peet Papa—dear little Babe we should feel grateful my dear Robert for this interesting pledge of your love, given us by our heavenly Father, I trust to comfort our declining years if properly instructed and brought up in the fear of the Lord. Train up a child in the way that he should go, as the wise man says, and when he is old he will not depart from it. This I hope and trust we shall be enabled to perform through the blessing of God.

During a reunion, Eliza conceived their second child, Jacqueline, who was born in 1814.

Their love comforted him during the trials that attended the pursuit of his other love, architecture. When staying at Hackwood en route for Richmond on

8 September, he wrote that Eliza was his "closest friend, and the sweet balm of known affection soothes the pain occasioned by absence." On 24 May, she wrote again after having been interrupted by "the rejoicing and illumination tonight in honour of our victories...and I mean to make some display of my patriotism." Still she yearned to assume a larger part in his career: "I wish you were more explicit with me on matters of business often times, not that impertinent curiosity prompts the desire, I would agree to relinquish a great many indulgences willingly before you should be harassed in the smallest degree, and it is *right* that I should be acquainted with every particular concerning you." Wishing to be her protector or already conscious of his own lack of financial acumen, Mills was loathe to expose Eliza to money worries. The problem was then a relatively minor irritation, since property investments proved profitable as in the development between May 1812 and December 1814 of two tenements on a 38-foot lot at South Eighth and Locust streets.[78] Yet in her next letter, dated 27 September, she ended on a prophetic note: "All your cash will be too little I fear to meet demand."

The search for new income had, of course, imposed these separations. Beyond checking on the Monumental Church and the shot tower (which was delayed until the next summer, since it was not until 10 July that the *Virginia Patriot* carried his advertisement for bricks), he secured at least four commissions for dwellings before 1815.[79] Two came in either late 1813 or early 1814 from the merchant Joseph Marx, each for two-story houses on raised basements. The simpler of the two was for Marx's mother, while he required the other for his family. Named Hanover House, it was distinguished by a balustraded portico with coupled columns of a hybrid Ionic order and a full-height colonnaded loggia on the south facade, anticipating the giant order columns Mills placed across the center of the villa he designed for Carter B. Page on the same bank of the James River in 1815. References to all three appear in Mills's 1816 diary, including the purchase of marble for Hanover House, insured from October 1817 at $23,000. Mills imitated its entrance portico, but capped by a pediment, on the Edward Cunningham (Archer) House at Franklin and Fifth streets (24). A handsome two-and-a-half-story building, the center bay was slightly projected, the corners defined by vertical mouldings, and the windows elegantly varied in shape and scale. More conservative was the stepping of the side walls up to two chimney stacks, prefiguring one of his standard designs for district jails in South Carolina. While these were in the vanguard of more sophisticated architecture in Richmond, other projects came to naught. Back in May 1813, for instance, Brockenbrough had asked him for the "relative *expense* of such a bridge [Upper Ferry Bridge] as you have constructed over the Schuylkill compared with ordinary bridges."

The completion of the Upper Ferry Bridge indicates how hostilities with the

24.   Mills, Edward Cunningham House, Richmond (1815–1816).

British stimulated rather than depressed the economy. Another consequence was the intensification of patriotism, which, while genuinely shared by Mills, he turned to his own advantage. At the spring 1814 show of the Columbian Society of Artists, he exhibited two designs that each recalled the supreme importance of Washington's contribution to the now threatened new republic. One showed the front of a hall commissioned to be built in Philadelphia by the Washington Benevolent Society of Pennsylvania; the other depicted his winning entry in the competition organized by the board of managers of the Baltimore Washington Monument Society, whose membership included many supporters of the Philadelphia Benevolent Society.

Dedicated to the "Free Republican Principles and to those which regarded the public conduct of George Washington," the Benevolent Society had contacted Mills in September 1813 to draw up plans for a two-story building.[80] The membership asked him to provide a large lecture hall and several meeting rooms on a site adjacent to the former Bingham Mansion on the west side of Third Street above Spruce, which he had recently converted into the Washington Hotel.[81] He devised some ten designs from which the society's building committee selected one that cleverly satisfied its functional requirements and, on the facade, its patriotic motivation. The "principal feature," he noted in the caption to his perspective view exhibited in 1814, "is a great niche, which sweeps into the front to make room for a statue of the illustrious Washington."[82] The soldier–statesman was to stand between Mills's in antis columns,

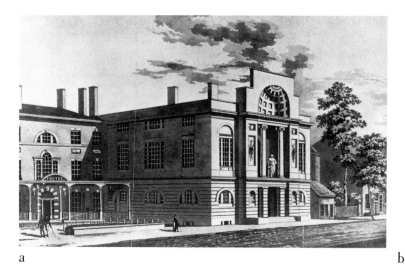

a   b

25.   Mills, Washington Hall, Philadelphia (1813): (a) aquatint by W. Strickland (ca. 1816) and (b) plan.

here of the simpler Ionic order of the Temple of Ilissus at Athens (25).[83] These columns carried a full entablature on which he perched the American eagle against the background of the coffered semidome of the "great niche." On either side were to be "civic wreaths encircling the names of *Penn* and *Franklin*," busts of whom would be placed in smaller niches on each side of the two square pillars framing the entrance. But Washington's military prowess was uppermost in his mind, since the composition elevated the in antis portico in order to simulate the Roman triumphal arch.[84] The rectangular recesses flanking the main niche were to display "trophies, emblematic of the military and civil glory achieved by the Father of his Country." Only the eagle was deleted before the hall was dedicated on 1 October 1816 at a cost, probably including his fee, of about $120,000.

The expense was due largely to the size and ornamentation of the building. Its arched and flat-headed windows, echoing those on the adjoining hotel as well as reinforcing the Roman triumphal theme that was continued, as were the stucco channeled rustication and moldings, around the side walls enclosing the varied accommodations within. On the first floor was a large dining room, measuring 130 feet long by 30 feet wide (presumably served from the hotel kitchen) together with small committee rooms and, to the right side of the entrance, a two-flight staircase to the upper level. Ascending to a vestibule, situated behind the statue of Washington, off which lay another committee room, this stairway also communicated directly with the aptly named "grand Saloon." An "elongated ellipsis," measuring 120 feet long by almost 70 feet wide, it was "encircled by a colonnade supporting the gallery" reached by a further flight of steps. The saloon and its gallery could comfortably seat up to 4,000 people, and another 1,000 if necessary. Those on the main floor were assured sight of the patriotic orators by the thinness of the pillars, apparently of cast iron, which supported the gallery. The "acoustical" ceiling, "a dome elevated about thirty feet above the floor crowned by a lanthorn skylight," enabled all to hear the rousing speeches in a well-ventilated atmosphere. One functional feature specified by Mills was omitted—the brick vaulting on the first floor. The lamentable result was a damaging fire in 1823, though the hall was repaired and purchased in 1835 by the Freemasons.[85] Meantime, Mills was deservedly proud of the building and in 1816 asked George Strickland to make a drawing of the front, which was engraved for public distribution by a "Mr. Hill."[86] He had checked this engraving by 11 December, awaiting the final payment of his fee by the society of $220.

The completion of Washington Hall likely held special significance for Mills because the first months of building coincided with the brief but devastating British invasion of the Chesapeake basin commanded by Vice Admiral Sir Alexander Cochrane. His subordinates, Rear Admiral Sir George Cockburn and Major General Robert Ross, had, in the sweltering heat of late August 1814, moved against the city of Washington, routing the American army at Bladensburg on 24 August and then occupying the federal capital. In retaliation for the burning of York (later to be renamed Toronto) in Upper Canada, the British had torched the major federal buildings, which must have roused Mills's indignation, if also the aspiration to participate in their reconstruction. The arson was soon avenged, General Ross being killed on 12 September during a skirmish at North Point—an incident Mills would seek to commemorate—and, a day later, Fort McHenry, nearer to Baltimore, valiantly defended.

Just returned from Baltimore on 22 September, Mills had sat down in his house at 114 South Eighth Street in Philadelphia to write to a family friend, Sarah Zane, in Winchester and then to Eliza at Hackwood, where she had gone for safety and the country air, since she was pregnant with their second child.[87] At Baltimore, Sarah learned, he "found the gloom that prevailed but a little time before, entirely dispelled, and the people in high spirits at their success in repeling the invaders—they acknowledge the protecting hand of Providence, as they were sensible of their weakness—and when we consider the little damage done by the enemy, they may truly say that 'God fought on our side.' " As for Philadelphia, "the city seems settling down a little, and some few are doing business—but generally speaking business is at a stand." To Eliza he wrote, as in earlier correspondence with Jefferson, on the possibility of securing the post of architect of the public buildings, fueled by his professional success in Philadelphia and the exciting prospect of executing the first truly impressive architectural monument to George Washington.[88]

3

Baltimore, 1814–1820
"directing their building"

Mills delayed entering the $500 competition announced in March 1813 by the Baltimore Washington Monument Society until the last moment, after, possibly, toying with several allegorically complex schemes.[1] He sought the maximum impact, especially drawn to a comment in the managers' advertisement "that the American artists will evince by their production that there will be no occasion to resort to any other country for a monument to the memory of their illustrious Fellow citizen" (a phrase he later copied into his 1816 pocket memorandum book). On 30 December 1813 he applied for an extension of the 1 January 1814 deadline to 15 April. In fact, he submitted his final set of designs with a letter dated 12 January 1814, paying close attention to the description in the advertisement of the proposed site in the center of Calvert Street. A massive pedestal pierced by a vault, so that the lower part of the monument simulated a triumphal arch, was to support a huge Greek Doric column surmounted by a Roman quadriga (26). The vault followed the axis of the "principal street," while the column immortalized Washington's achievements through both its very size, 140 feet high, and its applied sculptural reliefs and inscriptions, reinforced by the dramatic crowning quadriga "in which is represented the immortal Washington in military costume, guided by Victory." The monument "develops the character of those great men who were his compatriots in arms and dear to the heart of the generous Washington," he explained in the inscription appended to his design when it was shown in the Columbian Society exhibition of 1814.[2] That intention motivated his choice of the "Doric proportions" for the column, which, "from its solidity and simplicity of charac-

ELEVATION
OF THE PRINCIPAL FRONTS.

26. Mills, design for the
Washington Monument,
Baltimore (1814).

ter, harmonizes with the spirit of our government, and is emblematic of the
illustrious personage to whose memory it is dedicated."

The managers were obviously greatly impressed by the size and grandeur of
Mills's proposal. Consequently, they overlooked the problem of raising such a
huge column on a pedestal 50 feet square and 20 feet high, cut through by a
broad arch, and the cost of the decorations on its shaft, including the "six iron
railed galleries" to "accommodate the reading of those historical inscriptions
recorded on the face of the column" and relating "the eventful years of the

American revolution," from 1776 to 1781. Unlike many of his fellow artists in Philadelphia who, according to Rembrandt Peale, judged that his scheme had bordered on the ridiculous, the managers were swayed by Mills's beautifully finished presentation drawings and the enthusiastically persuasive letter that accompanied them.[3]

He appealed to their patriotism, heading his submission "Designs for a Monument proposed to be erected in the City of Baltimore to the Memory of General George Washington submitted to the honorable the Board of Managers by Robert Mills of South Carolina, Architect, Philadelphia 1814." Then followed seven drawings, each with explanatory captions, handsomely depicting the main and subsidiary elevations, the plans of the pedestal, shaft, and capital levels, together with a section of the column revealing the internal circular staircase. Framed by colored lined borders, each was drawn with a firm hand that, enhanced by a skillful use of watercolor washes, lent the impression of reality—although he would hire Hugh Bridport to make perspective drawings. The monument's great height was set off by the small trees painted picturesquely around the pedestal, illustrating a sentence in his letter. Monuments on open sites "should be *towering,* and commanding in their elevation, especially when they are encircled by a City, otherwise its popular intention may be frustrated."

The managers appreciated that Mills's splendid supercharged column far outstripped previous American examples, such as Bulfinch's Beacon Hill Revolutionary Monument in Boston (1790–1791). They probably recognized its unique adaptation of the established types, contrary to Latrobe's unconvincing accusation that Mills had copied William Wilkins's dissimilar Nelson Pillar in Dublin (1809).[4] Rather, Mills was stimulated by compositional ideas he found from books in Jefferson's library, such as the illustrations in Charles Francois Lubersac de Livron's *Discours sur les monumens Public* (1795) and in Ledoux's Barrière du Tron, Paris (1785–1789), the two outer gates of which had fluted columns standing on arched pedestals.[5] Indeed, Mills wrote justifiably to Jefferson on 16 June 1820 that neither his original design for the monument nor the much simplified version actually completed was copied directly from any one source, differing "intirely in the style of its design from either Trajan, Antoninus, Pompey's, the National Column at Paris [to the Grand Armée in the Place Vendôme (1810)] or the London Monument [to the Great Fire of 1666 by Sir Christopher Wren]. In making the design originally I had reference rather to the character of a Monument than simply to a Column."[6]

That assertion is corroborated not only in the convincing argument in his letter to the managers for the different elements of his design, but also in the stress he laid on his own American artistic independence and expression of patriotism through architecture. An "American by Birth" and training, his architectural concepts were "altogether American and unmixed with foreign habits," unlike his competitors the French émigrés Maximilian Godefroy and Joseph Jacques Ramée, adding the pointed caution: "For the honor of our country, my sincere wish is that it may not be said: To foreign Genius and to foreign hands we are indebted for a Monument to perpetuate the glory of our beloved Chief." On a more practical level, he asserted that it could be built within their budget (some $113,000), implying that the decoration might be simplified. But his appeal to their chauvinism clinched the issue, since, when relaying their decision in his favor on 2 May 1814, Robert Gilmor, son of a wealthy Baltimore merchant and one of the managers, wrote, "It is gratifying to me that a native American artist should have bourne the palm away from foreigners whose designs certainly did them credit."[7]

Mills and Eliza must have been elated by this news, for by winning the most publicized contemporary competition he was catapulted into the forefront of American architecture. By the beginning of May 1815, he was at Baltimore house hunting, on 3 May sending Eliza a sketch plan of a "small but comfortable" four-room house on Calvert Street set in and alongside shady gardens, a dwelling they temporarily moved into a week later.[8] By mid-July, they were sufficiently settled for Eliza to have coached to Hackwood for a respite from the city's heat. Returning from a "camp Meeting near Charles Town," she wrote on 1 August to assure him that "nothing in the world can contribute so much to my happiness—when absent—as your frequent communications" and that the health of the children "alone reconciles me to a separation from my best Friend." She stayed there through the month of August, sending him instructions for minor improvements to the Baltimore house and counting the days until he could join the family in the country with its late-summer fragrance instead of the disagreeable odors of contemporary city life. On the last day of October, Mills brought the family to Baltimore after clearing up their affairs in Philadelphia, possibly including the sale of property on George Street and the rental of their home at 114 South Eighth Street.[9]

The significance of the Washington Monument commission aside, Mills may have found Philadelphia steadily less conducive to the practice of his profession. He had been denied membership of the prestigious American Philosophical Society, despite the earnest letter of application he had written to its secretary, John Vaughan, on 16 December 1814.[10] "No institution," he had pleaded, could better gratify his "ardent thirst after knowledge," adding, "The extensive field of science which necessarily connects itself with my professional pursuits may present to me some means by which I might advance the progress of the Arts of sciences, and it will prove a source of pleasure to me, to contribute my mite to the comfort of mankind by communicating the results of such discoveries to the Society." Worse, the Columbian Society of Artists had encountered the kind of public indifference that later afflicted the New York–based Academy of Fine Arts and Charleston's Academy of Fine Arts.[11] As secretary, he informed the local press (reprinted in the *National Intelligencer* on 1 April 1815) that a dearth of good exhibits had forced the society to postpone its annual show. Although egalitarian republicanism left American artists "little to expect from individual patronage" and hampered the society's appeal for funds to erect teaching and exhibition facilities, he nonetheless expressed the "hope that a new era is about to commence in the fine arts in America."

In Baltimore, however, he had the opportunity to exercise his architectural ability; the managers rejected Godefroy's appeal for reconsideration of their decision, although the Frenchman would dub Mills "Bob the small."[12] The importance of his taking direct charge of the commission would be underscored when, in the last week of May 1815, John McNulty, the contractor charged with digging the 40-foot-wide foundation, consulted the local architect Robert Cary Long, Sr.[13] The jealousy of peers paled against the exciting prospect of transforming the drawings into reality, which was temporarily delayed by the decision to relocate the monument advantageously atop the hill north of the city on land, now known as Mount Vernon Place, donated by Colonel John Eager Howard, a hero of the American Revolution and of recent hostilities. Then, on 3 January 1815 he joined J. A. Buchanan, president of the board of managers, in Baltimore to sign the first contracts for the foundation work. What a propitious event with which to celebrate the christening of his second daughter, Jacqueline Smith, named after Eliza's great-aunt, Martha Jacqueline.[14]

Mills's jubilation, though, was soon to be tested as the unrealistic estimates for his competition design became apparent. On 21 January, Gilmor asked him for "the final precise plan," wondering "whether a solid pedestal will not be better."[15] Mills hurried to pare down the whole scheme, and, following Gilmor's advice, he replaced the structurally problematical arched pedestal with a more solid base, having a vaulted vestibule, providing for the display of artworks depicting Revolutionary leaders and events and access to the spiral staircase ascending within the 178-foot-high column. Fifteen feet taller than Trajan's Column in Rome, the column was also simplified. The iron galleries and much of the ornamentation were eliminated. Chosen from at least three variants, according to Rembrandt Peale, the revised design was depicted by the theatrical scene painter Henry Warren, for exhibition at the cornerstone ceremony held at the site on 4 July 1815.[16] Warren's painting shows the shaft decorated with only bands of stars and shields and wreaths intersected by spears, rising to a more austere capital and abacus capped by a plinth supporting a statue of Washington in contemporary dress (27a).

The changes were more than likely made before the contracts for the next

a   b

27.   Mills, Washington Monument, Baltimore: (a) revised design as painted by Henry
Warren (1815), and (b) as completed (1816–1842).

stage in the foundations were signed on 11 May, including those with the
haulers who were to bring the stone from the quarries of General Carnac
Ridgley, recently elected governor of Maryland. This task and the completion
of the working drawings probably caused Mills to set aside the preparation of a
handbook of architecture he seems to have begun when still resident at Philadelphia. To be entitled "The Principles of Architecture," Mills's book was to
have been financed by subscriptions according to a printed advertisement
distributed on 5 October 1817 by the Philadelphia stationer and publisher
Joseph Delaplaine, who had solicited manuscripts on architecture from, among
others, Latrobe.[17] Delaplaine described Mills as "of Philadelphia, Architect"
and claimed that the "plan" of this single-volume work would "be entirely original." The only extant related document, a printed outline, stated that it was
intended to be "popular and useful, and peculiarly adapted to the mechanic
and gentleman in the interior parts of the United States"—a tacit admission
that American architecture was still dominated by the two essentially amateur

groups that Latrobe despised. By inference, Mills dismissed as "neither satisfactory for the mechanic nor suited to the local habits of the United States"
such publications as Owen Biddle's *Young Carpenter's Assistant* (1805) and
Asher Benjamin's *American Builder's Companion* (1806), which combined basic
geometry, ornamental details, and stock plans. Benjamin's book (subtitled *A
New System of Architecture: particularly adapted to the present style of building in
the United States of America*) exemplified the deficiencies of the genre by the
omission of the base of the Tuscan order.[18] In fact, Mills envisaged a comparable approach, the advertisement stating that the section on geometry, for
example, would explain "the practical utility in every branch of mechanics."
Its scope might have been quite broad. The single volume was envisaged to
enclose between its bound covers at least 100 pages and 50 plates and to cost
$5. The scheme never materialized; it was superseded by the three-volume
Builders Assistant (1818–1821), published in Philadelphia by John Haviland
and Hugh Bridport. But Mills may have used some of the drafts in the notes
for a book and lectures on architecture that he was to assemble in Abbeville,
South Carolina.

Mills needed all his energies to organize the cornerstone ceremony for the
Washington Monument, slated for Independence Day 1815. Well before the
100-gun salute at noon on Tuesday, the Fourth of July, Mills had likely escorted Eliza up to the house close to the excavations where he had an office
(shared with Robert Tuxworth, a general carpenter and laborer) and introduced her to the state and civic dignitaries and board of managers, influential
people who could promote his career.[19] Chief among them were the governor,
General Ridgeley; Colonel Howard; and Levin Winder, worshipful grand master of the Baltimore Freemasons, who was to lay the stone and under whose
aegis Mills became a member of Cassia Lodge Number 45. Besides the president of the board, Colonel James A. Buchanan, a director of the Baltimore
Water Company (on which Mills later served), and the mayors of Baltimore
and Boston, there were the wealthy shipowner and trader Robert Gilmor, Sr.,
and his son Robert, who befriended the Mills family; David Winchester, the
board's treasurer; and Fielding Lucas, the bookseller who, in 1820, was to
publish Mills's *Treatise on Inland Navigation*.[20] With them were other board
members, leaders of the then vibrant business community, several of whom
were to patronize Mills, such as Isaac McKim, a notable philanthropist (particularly in the field of education), James Williams, Edward J. Coale, Nicholas
C. Ridgely, and William H. Winder. They were probably joined by other
worthies such as the lawyer Charles Carroll Jr., whose son-in-law, the attorney Robert Goodloe Harper, was surely present to congratulate his fellow
South Carolinian. A prime mover in the Exchange and the Library Company
of Baltimore, for each of which Mills made designs, Harper later involved him

in the erection of seven houses on property he owned on the west side of Courtland Street, Mills's two being mortgaged and then surrendered to Robert Oliver following the 1819 recession.[21]

The dignitaries gathered around the cornerstone, flanked by the ranks of the Third Brigade of the Maryland Militia under the command of Brigadier Samuel Sterret and watched by nearly 30,000 citizens. As the reverberation of the gunfire died away, Mills, assisted by Stewart and Towson, supervised the placing of the stone, while final adjustments were made by the chief stone-mason, Sator Stevenson. Thereupon, Winder invoked "the Grand Architect of the Universe" to bless the event, after which the throng was reminded of the achievements of Washington. To that eulogy Mills replied with a brief address shot through by his patriotism, idealistic sense of history, and unabashed pride: "I feel a double inducement to use my best exertions to execute faithfully, and with ability, the important duty entrusted to me, from the recollection that the work performed is the execution of a monument to perpetuate our country's gratitude to the *Father of her Liberty;* and that you have given a preference to native talent in the choice of a design for the work."[22] Following a prayer by Dr. Inglis, the crowd, after straining to catch snatches of the speeches, could at last participate by singing "Yankee Doodle." The soldiers then fired three volleys, echoed by rockets let off from Fort McHenry. The celebration ended with fireworks. That evening, it may be imagined, Mills believed that his fame and career were assured.[23] His monument would be the first to this American hero, looking down on the work of all his potential rivals, including Latrobe's cathedral and Godefroy's more distant and diminutive Battle Monument on Court Square.

After the ceremony, Mills took direct control of the building operations, the backbone of his work over the next four years. The society's account books record that both the contractors and the suppliers were paid through him and that he received his first fee payment on 17 July 1815, a sum of $500.[24] Besides those duties, he still had working drawings to prepare for the masons, a lengthy process including the presentation in May of alternative schemes for the decoration of the shaft alluded to in an entry for 5 June in his 1816 pocket memorandum book: "Drawings in prospect to be made: Washington Monument as altered." The foundations were to be "laid out" by 28 October 1816 and the gray marble pedestal finished by the fall of 1817, while the lighter colored shaft had risen perceptibly before the year's end. Terminating the vista northward from the city along Charles Street, it became an object in the public eye, promising to express the heady patriotism of a rousing ballad sung at a concert reported in the *Baltimore American* on 29 October 1817:

> When first infant liberty dropped upon earth,
> The Mountains and forests then cradled her birth...

But banished and spurn'd by profligate race
Long time she conceal'd both her grief and disgrace,
Till beaming forth glory, great Washington's star,
Recall'd the bright goddess from regions afar,
Columbia hail'd her, delighted to see
Men firm to their land, and resolv'd to be free

Such patriotic sentiments, however, could not restore the dwindling funds of the society or counter the recession that afflicted the Baltimore economy in 1819. Still, Mills could report substantial progress to the managers on 12 January 1818 that, for an average cost per foot of $500, the monument would reach 137 feet by year's end.[25] The recession confined the next season's progress to a mere 3 feet and, despite vain attempts to initiate work on the decorations from early April 1818, caused the managers, reluctantly, to cease his employ. The eventual completion of Mills's monument spanned the ensuing two decades, necessitating brief sojourns to Baltimore. Another section of 25 feet was added after Mills moved to South Carolina in 1820 and before he corresponded with Robert Gilmor in March and May 1826 about the ornamentation of the pedestal and shaft.[26] Mills contemplated bronze tripods on each side of the entrance with the pedestal, stars and wreaths in the frieze as well as trophies at each corner, bronze shields and flags around the lower part of the shaft (recalling the sheet with four alternative elevations probably drawn in 1816),[27] and, atop the capital, a marble statue of Washington. Mills's advocacy of an idealized statue of Washington proffering his sword proved to be more acceptable than bronze decorations to "change in some degree the simple idea of the *column* into a Monument."[28] On 10 October he was paid $167 for providing the plans for the basement and pavement, as well as for returning to Baltimore in order to draft the advertisement published in *Niles' Weekly Register* for a "colossal marble statue of Washington" together with "bronze or marble *trophies* . . . civic *wreaths* and *stars* in the frieze . . . and *inscriptions*" for the pedestal and "*tripods* on each front of the blockings of the steps to the entrance, all of bronze."[29]

The competition for the statue was won by the Italian immigrant sculptor Enrico Causici. As Causici finished the cutting of the four-section marble figure during the summer of 1829, Mills started to jot notes in his journal on the optimum method lifing it into place. Late that September he visited Washington to consult Commodore Isaac Hull, commandant of the Navy Yard, and by 19 October "commenced operations at the Washington Monument to raise the Statue."[30] He deployed wooden beams placed on the abacus to support a system of naval blocks and tackles (sketched in his journal on 1 September and 24 October) operated under the direction of his friend Captain James D. Woodside. Anxious to forward this partial completion of his original concept, and hence to raise his own profile, Mills was even prepared to accept deferred payment of his expenses, totaling more than $501.43 after the final block of the statue was installed amid considerable ceremony on 25 November.[31] Just over a week later, in some desparation to recoup his indebtedness, he sent Gilmor an "appeal to the liberality of the citizens of Baltimore" to repay those debts, but was still owed $152.77 as late as 7 May 1830 when he again wrote to Gilmor, hoping in vain to shame the managers into ornamenting the pedestal and column.[32]

The decoration of the pedestal, including the installation of a cast-iron railing, represented the last phase of the Baltimore Washington Monument commission and would involve Mills periodically until 1842. In fact, Mills had just sent drawings for the railing before 3 November 1828, when he wrote to Gilmor of his wish "to combine simplicity with beauty" in its design and that of the pedestal ornamentation.[33] The railing then combined canon, the Roman fasces, and spears, interspersed with the arms of Maryland, the last motif proving efficacious in the board's search for funding, since the state legislature voted an appropriation of $10,300, matching Mills's estimate, on 3 December 1830. Mills was paid $50, but the casting was stalled, despite his steady dispatch of letters—one mailed on 21 November 1831 arguing that American and not Italian marble be ordered as the paving—forlornly reintroducing the trophies on the pedestal, for models of which he was paid $100 on 17 May 1833. Before the managers eventually accepted a simplified design for the iron railing and gates alone, Mills had persuaded them to approve a revised plan for the development of Washington (now Monument) Place with a prospect of increasing the funds available to ornament the monument. In all likelihood, this scheme appears on a plan showing two facing blocks of ten house lots, on average 30 feet wide by 160 feet deep, on either side of St. Paul's Street to the east, and of eight to the west on Cathedral Street, with two additional blocks of three and four smaller lots each to the north on Madison Street and south on Center Street.[34] Negotiations with the city council proceeded to the point that on 11 July 1830 the clerk of the First Branch appointed a committee to inquire into the practicality of "enlarging the square at the Washington Monument."[35] As a consequence, the peripheral streets were widened between December 1830 and March 1831 to the advantage of the monument, but the housing development was not activated.[36] The proposal for the railing and gates fared better. Mills was paid $80 for design work and visits in June 1834 and February 1835. A contract for their casting was finally signed on 26 June 1836 with Amos A. Williams, president of the Savage Manufacturing Company, which began casting in August.[37] Before this operation ceased in 1842, Mills had further simplified the design of the gates, but not to the detriment of the ensemble, which remains one of the finest examples of large-scale Neoclassical ironwork in the United States.

Mills would ever regret that the society could not afford the bronze trophies and shaft ornamentation he believed essential to the symbolic and aesthetic distinction of the monument. Yet shorn of those features, and of the more novel elements of his original design, the Baltimore Washington Monument assumed greater solemnity and modernity (27b). Thereby Mills better expressed the republican ideals and stoical character of Washington. Atop the nobly austere shaft, the statue mimicks the commander-in-chief's magnanimous act of resigning his military commission and potential dictatorial power, truly "First among Equals." The monument was to become an enduring American symbol, some 125 years later inspiring J.R. Pope's American Battle Monument dedicated in July 1937 at Montfaucon in France to American soldiers killed during the closing months of the First World War.

The early phases of the monument commission had coincided with Eliza's third pregnancy. On 11 January 1816 she gave birth to another daughter, christened Mary Powell. Mills's delight in and concern for their children is especially manifest his letters to Eliza that summer, when, at his urging, she took the children to Hackwood to avoid the heat and infections of the city. "Oh may we my dearest Eliza appreciate the blessings we enjoy," he wrote on 15 September, his thoughts perhaps affected by memories of the death in April of his stepmother in Charleston, "and improve the privileges which we are favoured with, in striving through faith in the blessed promises of the Gospel to enter in at the straight gate, and realize the bliss in store for all the redeemed of the Lord."[38]

Appropriately one of the material "blessings" of 1816 was a commission from the Baptist congregation of Baltimore. On 18 February, he noted in his pocket memorandum book that their committee, chaired by the prosperous merchant William Wilson, "agreed to give me for directing their building 600$" based on drawings prepared ten days earlier.[39] This was the first of $5,201 in fees on projects in Baltimore and Richmond that he would enter under "Monies to be collected" on 28 December 1816. Together with property deals, at least one with Joshua Fort involving lots on Cathedral Street and the "exchange of property in Charleston," it enabled Mills to acquire land on St. Paul's Lane, some blocks north of the Baltimore downtown core.[40] On one plot, he was to extend an existing house into which he "moved the family" between 6 and 10 May 1816. The tax records for the tenth ward of the city listed his holdings in 1816 as "Calvert Lot 125 improvements unfinished $400. Lot 225 St. Paul's Lane furniture $300 House 25 Cow 5 Male Slave—Peter—207 Female Slave—Eliza—207," yielding a total assessment of $1,264.[41]

The Baptist Church commission was attractive to Mills not merely for the fee and the chance to evolve his ideas on ecclesiastical design, but also because

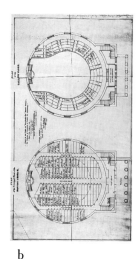

b

a

28.   Mills, Baptist Church, Baltimore (1816): (a) facade and (b) seating plan.

the building committee had purchased a prominent site.[42] It overlooked the intersection of Lombard and Sharp streets, east of the harbor yet close to the best residential area, the entrance portico being placed on the fashionable Sharp Street (28a). His design was influenced by but not governed by the Roman Pantheon, since as he assured the church committee on 8 February, "The experience I have had in these structures lead me to hope that I will be able to distinguish between what is really necessary to the strength and durability of the building without resorting to the useless expense which is often lavished upon buildings of this nature either from a want of this experience or want of knowledge of design."[43] Consequently, he reduced the number of columns in his portico from the eight of the Pantheon to six and substituted the Ionic order published by Scamozzi. The vestibule behind the portico of the church was broader to make space for an entrance into the auditorium and the staircases up to the horseshoe gallery with separate seating for "colored persons" (28b). All this was fitted within a rotunda nearly 77 feet in diameter, about half that of the Pantheon. To ensure audibility, Mills lowered the height of his dome relative to the portico, while externally and for aesthetic reasons he welded together the portico, vestibule, and rotunda with a continuous entablature.

The progress of the Baptist Church commission is recorded in Mills's 1816 pocket memorandum book, which also provides an invaluable picture of building practice in early-nineteenth-century America. Between 23 and 25 February 1816 he met with the church building committee to review the contractor's tenders. The entry for 25 February proves how Mills had taken to heart Latrobe's caution that the architect should supervise all aspects of the commission: "Had Mr. Milliman the carpenter to ask some questions relative to his proposal." Milliman, working with another contractor named Booth, wanted reimbursement for the materials used at the customary local prices, with wages of $2 per day plus 25 cents each for their assistants; but they also offered to make a substantial donation to the church. Among the other proposals was one from Mr. Batchelor, who would charge 14 cents a pound for iron bolts. With those under consideration "Mr. Walker began digging foundations" on 26 February. The bricklayers commenced the footings on 9 April, so that on 22 April, Mills was "engaged in laying out [the] circle of Church" and again on 3 May when he also marked out the portico and vestibule. Evidently he made the detailed working drawings as the pace of construction demanded, continuing up to at least 6 June; a later reference to "Drawings in perspective" suggests that he continued to be interested in advertising his work. One of the church would possibly be used for the engraving of an 1823 illustrated map of Baltimore to be published by T. H. Poppleton. The portico was being erected in July, as indicated by the offer of the sculptor "Chevalier" to cut the Ionic capitals for 25 cents "per piece [foot?]," although Mills actually gave a drawing of the flattened spirals of the Scamozzi Ionic to a "Mr. Mountain." By 8 December the contractors started to shingle his de l'Orme structure dome. Within two days, the plasterers were at work and the carpenters were beginning to install the four blocks of seating ranked before the raised pulpit and beneath the tiers in the curving gallery. The results of their labors were detailed on a copy of the original 1818 pew rental plan, which notes that Wilson chose number 27, and his son, numbers 38 and 39.[44] That document confirms that the church was dedicated in March 1818 and, by way of explanation for the delay in fitting up the structure for use, states that the total expenditure was $56,000, rather than the $50,000 printed by Poppleton. The debt nearly caused its closure in 1822 and was outstanding until 1852, twenty-five years before its demolition.[45] Nonetheless, the church earned for Mills the accolade of Latrobe's commendation of the portico as "a beautiful thing" when writing on 20 November 1817 announcing his impending resignation from the post of architect of the public buildings "as a former friend and pupil in confidence, that you may act as you please."[46] Mills's suave design certainly won local acclaim. His friend Fielding Lucas, writing in A Picture of Baltimore (1832), commented, "It altogether forms quite an ornament to that part of the city."

Concurrently, Mills fulfilled an assortment of lesser commissions, also

29.   Mills, (a) William Gwynn House, Baltimore (1816), and (b) sketch design for the Baltimore Exchange (1816).

a

logged in his memorandum book. Before Wilson personally visited him on 15 February with advance notice of the acceptance of his plans for the church, Mills was installing a Pettibone patent furnace in the Patapsco Cotton Factory and, on 13 February, arranging minor alterations for Fielding Lucas's store.[47] More than twenty other furnace jobs are logged, such as those in June for Colonel Buchanan's house and Long's St. Paul's Episcopal Church (1812). He undertook various improvements to private houses, such as the drawings he presented on 25 November for "Mr. Winchester's front door" and the refronting of Tusculum, the five-bay, three-story Baltimore house owned by William Gwynn, editor of the *Federal Gazette* (29a).[48] He inserted an in antis portico of two tall, hybrid Ionic columns between the stuccoed outer bays and unified the ensemble with a spare Rational Classical cornice. Several apparently unexecuted schemes appear sporadically throughout his memorandum book, such as the sketch design on page 13 (29b) for the Baltimore Exchange (won in January by Latrobe) and the entry for 11 November, "Began design of a house for Mr. T. Chase," for which he claimed $100, and a dispatch in mid-August to Winchester of "drawings of a monument for Mr. Davison," likely for the husband of Eliza's elder sister, Martha Maria. Interspersed are jottings on technical matters for possible future use, such as those on blasting screws taken from "[Peter] Nicholson's Philosophical Journal Vol. 5th, page 31," on methods of rust prevention, fuel conservation, and, marking the onset of his interest in railroad technology, information that wooden rails plated with cast-iron rims might cost about $4,150 a mile.

Nor were Mills's responsibilities confined to Baltimore. In March 1816 he had journeyed to Richmond with high expectations to prepare designs for the city council on which his close friends, Brockenbrough and Ambler, sat. Mills had been corresponding with Ambler about the extension of his house at Twelfth and Clay streets, which coincided with the commission for the pedimented but compact Brander House (1816–1817).[49] On 2 February 1816 he had acknowledged news of "the safe arrival" of Ambler's "marble mantels and your being pleased with them—It gives me much pleasure to hear that the finish of the [scored stucco] exterior of your house gives so much satisfaction to yourself & others." He went on to assure Ambler that he would forward information respecting the construction of a steam engine and to thank him "for your attention to my interest in the Court house."

Thus after a three-day journey, Mills was welcomed on 8 March 1816 by "Col. Ambler's family and took up my residence there."[50] Between his arrival and 23 March, he rapidly produced several schemes, the largest being for a new city hall and courthouse to be north of Jefferson's capitol on Capitol Street between Tenth and Eleventh streets. He presented the outline plans to the city commissioners on 13 March, followed by a drawing of larger scale, which was approved on 18 March. All of them have disappeared, the only remaining record being the thumbnail sketch plan and elevation on page 20 of his memorandum book (30).[51] Neither sketch is precisely related to the building, but both depict an impressive Neoclassical edifice having a tripartite composition both in facade and layout. Commanding the approximately 64-foot-wide main front is a portico of six Doric columns, apparently of the Greek order.[52] The pediment is framed by the attic superstructure, which encloses a central domed courtroom, itself flanked by lower sections pierced by double-story windows recessed within tall arches containing jury rooms and staircases to the gallery opposite. The arrangement recalls Latrobe's unexecuted 1802 proposal for New York City Hall.[53] But Mills contemplated a more graduated composition and authentic Classicism by lowering the portico onto a shallow platform corresponding with the ancient stylobate base. In allowing the domed centerpiece greater prominence, he also effectively bonded the subsidiary facades, geared to the disparate purposes of the building but within the tripartite pattern: on the 100-foot sides created by the projections formed by the jury rooms on the northwest and in antis portico leading into the court opposite, and on the rear or southeast by the positioning of the separate city hall, measuring 50 feet by almost 25 feet and intended to be cross-vaulted. As a result, he proposed a diverse yet integrated succession of facades that would have imaginatively exploited the open site. In recognition, the commissioners paid

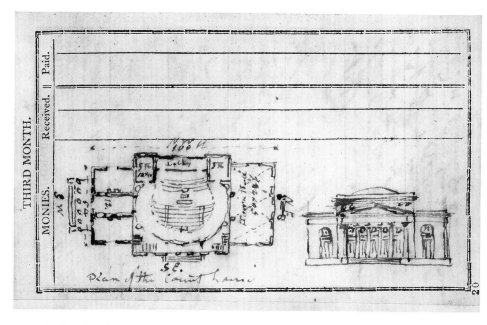

30.   Mills, sketch design for the city hall and courthouse, Richmond (1816).

him $200 on 21 March, and two days after agreed "to give me $400 for my designs," probably for supervising their construction.

Although he proceeded with the detailed working drawings in early June, the commission for the actual city hall and courthouse was passed on to Godefroy in September. Upon reflection the commissioners must have decided that Mills had not included sufficient office space and disliked the diversity of his composition, since they asked Godefroy to transform it into "a regular edifice." He contracted the side projections but increased their height to accommodate the extra offices and also raised the main portico so that its entablature could continue around the whole building. In Godefroy's design, the portico rather than the dome became the dominant feature. He heightened its columns, reduced their number to four, and eradicated the pediment. As a consequence, his dome, having the de l'Orme structure likely intended by Mills but adding an octagonal lantern, looked more like an appendage. The overall effect was less refined and somewhat dull in comparison with Mills's scheme, although the building remained in use until 1870. That Mills fell foul of local politics is indicated by the fact that Godefroy also improved the Capitol Square, for which he had made sketches on 19 March 1816 amid tracing the course of a canal between Richmond and its port at Rocketts on a backwater of the James River at the foot of Eighth Street.[54]

The one commission he did achieve during his sojourn at Richmond in March 1816 would be of considerable historical interest. Dr. Brockenbrough

31. Mills, Brockenbrough House, Richmond (1816–1818), after the addition of the third floor in 1857.

asked Mills to design a house for him to be built on the crest of Shockoe Hill at 1201 East Clay Street.[55] Although childless, Brockenbrough and his sociable wife, Gabriella, desired a grander residence than their existing house at Clay and Eleventh streets, in which Mills had earlier been a guest. He designed a charming house originally of two stories lifted up on a low basement, five bays wide and entered through a small, central two-column portico (31). The simple flat-headed windows, horizontal moldings, cornice, and attic lent Neoclassical chasteness to the Federal tradition. Across the rear and facing south are triple windows lighting three interconnected living rooms also of Latrobean pedigree.[56] Separated by fireplaces and doorways, the en-suite arrangement could accommodate large social gatherings while providing more intimate spaces. These and two smaller front rooms are served by a staircase situated on the left side of the entrance vestibule that connects with the basement. This contained the ordinary dining room, the meals being prepared in an outside kitchen within a separate building at the rear to keep cooking smells and the danger of fire at bay. The family and guest bedrooms on the second floor are reached by an elegant cantilevered wooden stair curving up the semicircular-ended space to the right of the vestibule. The external fabric of brick covered by stucco, the rear colonnade of coupled Greek Doric columns, and the slate roof appear to have been completed in 1818, since the insurance rose from

32.   Mills, design for the Henry Didier House, Baltimore (1816), drawn ca. 1828.

$7,000 to $20,000 by year's end. Altered in 1844, and again in 1857 when Lewis D. Crenshaw added a third story and dressed the building in an Italianate style, the house served as the official residence of Jefferson Davis during the Civil War; since 1896, it has commemorated that tragic period as the Museum of the Confederacy.

Mills continued to experiment with the giant order during the construction of the Brockenbrough House. The Baltimore merchant Henry Didier, Jr., commissioned a house, probably for his property at the northeast corner of Franklin and Cathedral streets.[57] In a stylish pen-and-wash drawing, Mills pictured a two-and-a-half-story facade fronted by an imposing colonnade (32).[58] The six columns were adapted from the Delos Doric, having the fluting restricted to the capitals. Otherwise, the detailing recalls the Brockenbrough House, but the effect is more monumental, a Classical revision of General Washington's Mount Vernon, likely often in Mills's thoughts when building the Washington Monument at Baltimore. Sadly, however, Didier decided to sell his property rather than to realize Mills's handsome design.

The winter of 1816 had brought other more modest domestic commissions. On 16 November he noted in his memorandum book, "Went out with Mr. [Samuel] Sterret [a notary public, auctioneer, commission merchant, and militia officer], to his country seat [and] examined it." Presumably an addition was to be built for an estimated $3,500. Nothing more can be established beyond two further entries, one for 27 November stating that Sterret had "adopted [the] plan of his country house & placed the business of carrying it into execution to me," and the other on the back of page 63 indicating that Sterret owed him $300. A great deal more information exists about the "range of houses for [the] water Company," for which he made drawings between 12 and 20 November, concurrently with a "drawing of Col. Buchanan Hse." The range was erected between 1817 and 1818 on North Calvert Street, below and two blocks southeast of his Washington Monument. Later numbered 606–628 and named Waterloo Row, supposedly to mark Wellington's final defeat of Napoleon in 1815, it was to be the cause of a harrowing legal battle for Mills.[59]

This speculative development grew out of his post of "Engineer" to the Baltimore Water Company, which he held from early August 1816 until October 1817.[60] During this period Mills was also tempted into unwise property and stock investments. It was not just a matter of improving his house on St. Paul's Lane—he petitioned the commissioners of the Western Precinct of the city on 21 October 1817 for a gravel alley—but the purchase on 27 December 1817 of some 24,000 acres of land in Bath County, Virginia, for $2,880.[61] Bounded by the Jackson River and by Back and Cedar creeks, these "Bath Lands" were in the spectacularly beautiful western fringe of the state, over the Blue Ridge almost into present-day West Virginia. His Allegheny estate was described on 7 July 1818 by one Charles Francisco to John Morris, a local surveyor known to Mills, as "altogether mountain land, no one living on it, nor never can live on it."[62] With less funds, Mills could not have plunged into such a speculation, even if it had superficially elevated him into the ranks of Virginia landowners and promised profit consequent upon the state and federal programs of internal improvements launched in 1816.[63] For by October 1820 Mills was to be forced to take out a mortgage on it with John Morris for $691.11. No less disastrously in 1818 he purchased $500 of 6 percent Baltimore City Stock (a loan for the Belvidere Street improvements), which he renewed in 1819 at the height of the yellow fever epidemic and financial crisis that resulted in the cancellation of the bonds in 1823.[64] Already overextended before he made that altruistic but misguided investment, Mills owed the city $105.23 in back taxes.[65]

With the very different economic conditions in the fall of 1816 Mills planned a terrace of twelve houses worthy of comparison with contemporary British and European urban design.[66] Measuring on average 23 feet wide by 40 feet deep and of four and a half stories, including the basement and attic, each house had an arched doorway at first-floor level reached by a staircase parallel to the sidewalk (33a). Next to the door was a large rectangular window framed by a relieving arch. Above were a narrow and a wide window on the upper floors, together with a centrally placed dormer in the pitched roof. If the win-

a

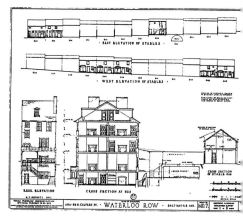

33.   Mills, Waterloo Row, Baltimore (1817–1818): (a) facade with altered steps and (b) section.

dows were rather crammed, the detailing of the doors and iron balustrades on the staircases exhibited a refined Classicism, particularly the flattened Greek key motif along the upper part of the railings. The Greek idiom spread inside to the Doric mantlepieces and elegant Neoclassical ornament in the main living rooms on the basement and first floors. At the front of the basement, Mills placed the dining room with the kitchen behind. On the first floor were two interconnected parlors alongside the through-hall and staircase communicating with the bedrooms, those in the attic presumably being for servants. Across the 66-foot-long yard, each house was also provided with a privy, built into the approximately 22-foot-deep stable and carriage house raised over a brick storage vault (33b). The row was fairly described as "handsome" by T. W. Griffiths in the *Annals of Baltimore* of 1824. Yet the development fell victim to the collapse of the Baltimore economy as well as being "considered too distant for men of business."[67] None of the houses now remains to demonstrate how gracious high-density row housing can be.

The sorry fate of this the grandest housing development in early-nineteenth-century Baltimore would have seemed unthinkable when the contracts were witnessed on 22 January 1817. A fascinating example of contemporary commercial and architectural speculation in the United States, its history would be recounted during the trial of "the President & Board of Directors of the Baltimore Water Company versus James C. Neilson & others," heard before Judge William Kiety, chancellor of Maryland, in the chancery court in Annapolis during the September term of 1821.[68] The records contain the story of how Mills, as an executive of the company and "Architect & Treasurer" for the "Calvert Street building Company," had transacted a viable agreement with a diverse group of local businessmen. Judged by modern commercial ethics, it might have transgressed the rules concerning conflict of interest. In 1817, however, the pursuit of profit was barely controlled by municipal or state legislation, and the development would have been regarded as an asset to the city and a source of employment.

Mills's associates, with the exception of Samuel Sterret, were all local tradesman or building contractors. They were later joined by the stonemasons working on the Washington Monument, Thomas Towson and William Stuart. The Water Company "agreed to execute leases at the rate of Six dollars per foot on Calvert Street to the other contracting partners for Ten of the said lots of ground," to "erect and build two houses on two of the said twelve lots," and to advance "their full portion of the estimates required for the erection of . . . the said houses." Mills and the other investors were to be entitled to one property each, with the exception of Charles Hammell, a plasterer who expected to receive a half interest in one house, and James C. Dew and James Grimes, partners in a feed and flour store; James Barnard, a seedsman; and Charles Williams, a drayman, who were each to have title on one-fourth part. However, the final distribution depended on a process of bidding that would begin once the terrace was roofed, those successful being "at liberty to finish the interiors." The contract further stated that the individual investors had together contributed $23,112 in the form of "cash & notes of reserve," but looked to raise another $14,900, since Mills estimated the total cost at about $105,200. In the meantime, they vested the right of the whole property in the Water Company until they could repay the money it had advanced but added the further rider "at the same time we do not consider that such of us as may have a balance due to us respectively should have houses or concerns in houses held responsible for others that are in arrears," adding optimistically "as those houses that are in arrears will at all times sell for more money than has or will be advanced." The contractors and tradesmen among the investors were, of course, attracted by the fact that the houses would be built with their materials, "of the best kind," and labor.

Apparently untroubled by his irregular position, Mills distributed the funds to the supplier–contractor–investors, as can be verified in a batch of check stubs that he signed between 24 December 1817 and 28 October 1818.[69] He also valued the ongoing work, based on "customary rates" and "market prices."

The roof structure was up by November 1817, when the division of houses was decided, numbers 4 and 6 going to the Water Company and number 12 to Mills. The fabric was entirely finished in the spring of 1818 for the much increased total of $141,141.29. Yet three of the contractor–investors had outstanding claims and contended that the two company houses should be sold to satisfy their claims, although it was agreed on 9 May 1818 that all the houses should be regarded as security. This dispute led to the initial legal proceedings in the July term of 1820. The court ruled that William Cole, David Winchester, and David Williamson should act as arbitrators and that the interests of the company and various groupings of investors, not including the now virtually bankrupt Mills, should be represented by lawyers. The investigation disclosed that the company had advanced almost $24,900, including some $1,724 directly to Mills, in the form of loans, in addition to the $26,000 put up for its two houses.

The arbitrators found that the investors owed the company $22,355.51, plus back interest from May 1818 to May 1819 and legal costs. If unpaid before 29 October 1821, their ten houses would revert to the company and be sold at auction on 12 November, starting with Mills's number 12. Only Hugh Bonner, a coppersmith, escaped on the grounds that he had never signed the articles of contract and had merely been employed by Mills, who still owed him $940.68. Not surprisingly, only three of the original investors could comply and acquired their houses for greatly discounted prices at the auction in September 1821. In his absence, Mills's number 12 went to Talbot Jones for only $3,000. The total proceeds from the auction were but $27,650.

Almost three weeks after signing the contracts in January 1817 to begin Waterloo Row, Mills had returned to Charleston via Washington in order to settle family business after his stepmother's death. In Washington, while he was exploring the prospects of employment, he had met Eliza's "friend" Major Lane, superintendent of the public buildings, and also Thornton, who obligingly offered him a horse to carry him overland through Fredericksburg to Richmond.[70] Apart from checking work in hand there, his purpose was likely to pick up a boat for Charleston. Having arrived there on 27 February, he wrote to Eliza of finding "the improvements or I may say additions made to Charleston so extensive that it was with difficulty I could distinguish places I was formerly familiar with." The spate of building was the harvest of the cotton boom of 1816, which had also caused the local population to swell "amazingly, & with good reason as it ranks now the 3rd city in the Union and (would you believe it) is more healthy than either Baltimore, Pha or New York." His regret at "the absence of her I love" was mollified by having "received invitations for every day this week if I remain here," including one for the Race Ball, which had given him "an opportunity of seeing and knowing more of my fellow citizens and particularly to see the standing of my fair countrywomen in point of good taste & beauty."[71] The sparkling evening lead him to conclude, "Compared with that of the north, there is none of those high flights and displays of agility brought into fashion to the north of Baltimore. There was a grace and modesty of movement which made the whole scene agreeable to the eye." Mills's remarks suggest that the sense of distinction across the Mason-Dixon line during the contemporary Era of Good Feelings centered on matters of taste. The deeper economic and political differences were as yet masked by policies of national development.[72] South Carolina's rising federal politician, John Calhoun, had, for example, promoted the establishment in 1816 of the Second Bank of the United States under the presidency of a fellow South Carolinian, Langdon Cheeves, and supported the bonus bill, which would have allowed the bank to fund schemes for internal improvements. Inspired by the road and canal construction proposed by Jefferson's treasury secretary, Albert Gallatin, this bill was vetoed by President John Quincy Adams. So the internal improvements went ahead on a state-by-state basis that was to excerbate rather than eradicate regional rivalry. Before the inherent divisions resurfaced, Calhoun voiced a widespread optimism, "Let us bind the republic together with roads and canals."[73]

One reason for the current sense of national purpose lay in the still vivid memories of the conflict with Britain and actions like that fought at North Point near Baltimore in September 1814. At the request of the local militia company, the First Mechanical Volunteers, Mills in April 1817 apparently designed a monument to commemorate its major incident, the shooting by Aquila Randal of the British General Ross.[74] On a single sheet, he drew two elevations and a plan that, though neither signed nor dated, display the economy of line and combination of simple Classical motifs—a squat plinth supporting in turn an obelisk, a tripod, and an urn—typical of his contemporary style. Enclosed by iron railings interspersed with small canon, the plinth was to have carried large bas-reliefs illustrating the battle and the death of Ross. The volunteers, however, in July 1817 raised a plainer monument on the spot where Ross was killed—a plinth topped by an undecorated pointed obelisk.[75]

By that time, Mills was preparing a design for the Baltimore Library Company, incorporated in 1797. Its directors had in 1816 acquired a lot at the intersection of Church Street with Washington Square and by April 1817 were contemplating a building with a library and reading room above offices for a budget of $30,000. After rejecting a domed design submitted by Latrobe on 3 June 1817, Mills was invited to compete through "the politness of Mr. Sterret" and his fellow directors, Robert Gilmor, David Winchester, and John Hoffman.[76] On the first floor, atop leaseable cellars, Mills planned twelve offices, all with adequate lighting and access, plus the use of six privies in a rear courtyard (34a).[77] The court would also illuminate and ventilate the 38-foot-diameter library room above the central section of the building. Reached from street level by staircases on either side of a two column in antis portico, the library communicated with a large reading room and accommodations for the librarian flanked by others for the trustees and a small museum of natural history. "Hanging Galleries," presumably of wrought or cast iron and served by two small stairs, increased the shelving space. The plans prove Mills's claim in a letter to Hoffman of 19 July 1817 that he had sought "economy both in space and cost having occupied all the ground appropriated except what is absolutely necessary for light & air, and laid down simplicity as the ground work of the design." Whether or not Mills's plan won general favor, the company had raised a mere $4,500 by late 1818, was forced to sell the lot a year later, and eventually in 1855 to merge with the Maryland Historical Society.

In the summer of 1817, Mills designed a house for another friend of longer standing, Richard Potts, who lived in the charming rural town of Frederick, Maryland. He and Eliza often visited the Potts family on their way to and from Hackwood.[78] Mills's design is preserved in a letter to Potts dated 23 July 1817, accompanying two elevations and three plans outlining an L-shaped two-and-a-half-story house to be built at the intersection of Church and Court streets for $7,000.[79] The warm red brick house that was finally erected in 1819 alongside the courthouse was symmetrical, with nicely proportioned Neoclassical detailing, although retaining old-fashioned crow-stepped gables at either end. Although a third story was added in 1894 and the interior divided into apartments in 1946, the fabric survives as testimony to his refined taste.

A more substantial commission came soon after, from the vestry of St. John's Evangelical Episcopal Church. Founded in 1816 under the leadership of the Reverend George Dashield, the congregation had acquired a site on the east side of North Liberty Street south of Conewago Street and quite close to St. Paul's Lane.[80] Because the funds were restricted, Mills relied on the more usual American church type, a rectangular hall, and concentrated the architectural resources on the main facade (34b). Framed by slightly recessed side sections (possibly housing staircases up to a gallery behind the front) stood the centerpiece having one large central and two smaller arched doorways crowned by an attic with an incised panel. The three openings nicely blended the Roman triumphal arch theme with the symbolism of the Trinity. Together with the Doric entablature binding the whole facade, the composition shows that Mills was edging toward a more specific Roman Classicism than he had learned from Latrobe; Mills was never so dogmatic as Alexander Jackson Davis, the New York architect who in a draft for a lecture on architecture was to assert: "*Egypt* invented, *Greece* brought Architecture to its extreme perfection and *Rome* disfigured it by gaudy and tasteless decorations, and ominous

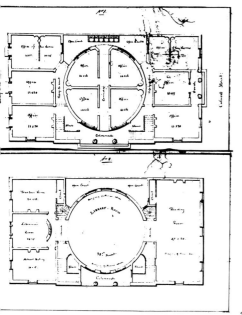

34.   Mills, plans for (a) the Baltimore Library Company (1817), and (b) St. John's Evangelical Episcopal Church, Baltimore (1817), engraved in 1823.

spoilation of its purity and beauty of outline."[81] No plans survive, but the pews surely flanked a central aisle leading to a pulpit, a lectern, and the altar, all lit by the three tall round-headed windows along the sides. The church was consecrated in 1818 and, according to Poppleton's 1823 plat, cost $30,000, possibly including Mills's 5 percent fee. Some time after the church was acquired in 1832 by the Methodist Protestant Church, the front was altered adversely by the enlargement of the arched entrances and attic, as illustrated on the 1851 edition of the Poppleton plat. The brick and stucco building remained in the charge of the Methodists until it was destroyed in a 1904 fire.

    In order to go forward with the church commission and work on the Water Company system, Mills did not travel with Eliza and the children to Hackwood that summer.[82] On 14 August 1817 he wrote to her, lamenting the "great devastation made in the lower part of Baltimore by the great flood down the Jones Falls." The freshet had damaged the company's system as well as sweeping away the wooden bridges spanning the falls near their house, "one of them lodged in a garden just below."[83] In consequence, Mills prepared proposals that he delivered to the mayor and council later that month and eventually published in the *Baltimore American and Commercial and Daily Advertiser* on 25 and 29 September 1817.[84] The major recommendation was that the bed of Jones' Falls should be cleared and rendered navigable up to Madison Street and that roads be created on either side that would be "planted with trees and provided with seats." The irregular course of the falls (now covered by the Jones Falls Expressway) should be straightened between Bath and Gay streets, walled, and protected against blockage by "reservoirs or pits" dug at intervals. Together with new bridges of 80-foot single spans estimated at $20,000 in wood or $30,000 in stone, he reckoned the total cost at $126,757.

The council, meeting on 29 September, acknowledged the "considerable importance" of his plan, resolved only to repair the bridge on Pratt Street and temporarily span Bath and Center streets. But the council did not abandon a permanent solution, and its succeeding actions deserve to be considered here. These can be retraced in two later documents, beginning with a letter that Wernwag wrote to the incumbent mayor on 15 July 1837, following yet another disastrous flood.[85] Wernwag maintained that he had advised Mills, "who was a noted character at that time in Baltimore, and with whom I unfortunately got acquainted in Phila and requested him to copy my report, & hand it to Mr. Stiles [the mayor, George Stiles]." The earlier document is an 1830 council report concerning a request from the "Representative of the late B. H. Latrobe" for payment for a plan to upgrade the falls. It states that on 28 May 1818 the council had ranked Wernwag's submission as the best, followed by Mills's, with that by Latrobe as number five of eleven.[86] Clearly, Mills had passed on Wernwag's proposal as well as entering a version of his own published scheme. For by 2 June 1818 the council had reconsidered and now "of opinion that the plan No. 2 in Mr. Robert Mills' map, is under all circumstances . . . that which is most suitable to their views." Then, on 30 June, the council apparently decided on another joint plan submitted by Mills and Wernwag on 24 June, limited to a budget of no more than $140,000.[87] Enlarging on Mills's 1817 proposal and another by John C. White, the council recommended covering the bed of the falls "with two inch plank laid upon sleepers about ten inches square four feet apart from center to center forty-six feet long to extend to the upper end of the lock and the dam [above Center Street], with dry rough stone walls, three feet thick at the foundations, on either side of its forty feet width." While the solution ignored the problem of wood rot, the estimate was within the stipulated amount, at $138,400. Formal estimates were invited but not proceeded upon, apart from some improvements executed under Mills's supervision, including the "laying out and grading of the extension of South Street."[88] And in the summer of 1819, Mills was to be "appointed by the Legislature of Maryland for opening and extending and improving Belvidere St. from Baltimore St. to York Road [Calvert Street, actually using Wernwag's designs for a 60-foot span bridge at Belvidere Street], and he, having been charged with the engineering and fiscal concerns of the work, completed the same."[89] His fee is not indicated, but, needing funds, he was quite prepared to supervise the construction of Wernwag's bridge.[90] Even after the "calamitous" July 1837 flood, the falls were not tamed until 1868–1869, when the essentials of Mills's 1817 scheme were at last executed.

Meantime, in the fall of 1817 Mills had found time to reactivate his proposed book entitled "Principles of Architecture," for which Joseph Delaplaine circulated a flyer from 5 October. He also addressed Mayor Stiles on 12 October about the urgent need for a more secure powder magazine.[91] More than five years earlier, the Second Branch of the Council had suggested replacing the old magazine on Federal Hill, its fifty-cask capacity being insufficient to meet the rising demand for explosives required for excavation and land clearance. Warning that the recent explosion in the powder room at Messrs Levering and Company, 8 miles from Baltimore, had been felt "by many citizens," Mills proposed erecting "*separate* buildings to contain the powder in prudent quantities," circular in plan as being the "strongest & most capable of resisting high winds or any other violent effort to overthrow." The explosion elicited other projects, including a two-story "Plan of the Powder Magazine," but Mayor Stiles chose only those by Mills and Latrobe: pupil and teacher once again were in competition.[92] Apparently built according to Mills's scheme some miles from the city on the Patapsco River, the powder magazine, the council would complain in January 1820, was "so remote from navigation owing to the shallowness of the River as to render it entirely useless to the city."[93]

Fortunately, Mills's contacts in the then more prosperous South brought a most gratifying commission. Two weeks after engaging Henry Huber to paint and glaze the "new building [mill] of Robert Oliver on the Gun Powder river,"[94] Mills sent his admired friend, the Reverend Richard Furman, the firmly drawn "Elevation of the Front of the 1st Baptist Church in Charleston, South Carolina," dated "Baltimore Jany 2[2] 1818" (35).[95] Its origin is apparently recorded in a letter written to Eliza on 5 March 1817 in which Mills reported that he was expecting to remain at Charleston for "a day or two longer" to "make a design for one or two churches which are contemplated to be built here."[96] The Baptists were fired by the dynamic Furman, formerly a medical doctor and Revolutionary leader who had been called to the ministry in 1786 and moved to Charleston the following year.[97] But they could not invite contractors' bids on Mills's scheme until late April 1819, and then for a structure 84 feet long by 60 feet wide instead of for the completed building with dimensions of 110 feet by 60 feet. The cornerstone was laid on 16 September 1819, but the actual building (inspected by Mills in spring 1820) by the contractor, E. M. Curtis, was to drag on beyond its dedication on 17 January 1822 into the next year, by which time almost $29,500, apparently not including Mills's fee, had been expended. Furman's biographer lauded Mills's "uniting amplitude of space with durability, simplicity and neatness, and affording one of the

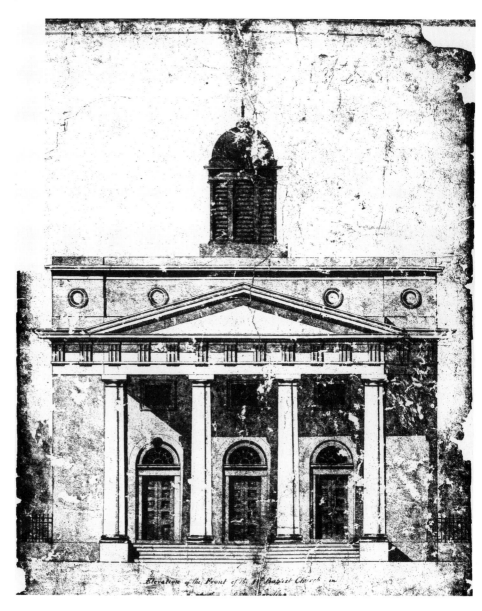

35.   Mills, drawing for the First Baptist Church, Charleston (1818), front elevation.

most correct specimens in the city of sacred architecture."[98] Fortunately, it stands largely unaltered, apart from the dismantling of the belfry, which is not represented in J. W. Hill's 1850 aerial view of Charleston. The font was subsequently removed, and the center section of the rear wall extended to form a shallow recess behind the raised pulpit, an alteration that was not detrimental to the serene and quietly noble interior. Repaired in 1883, the fabric survived the hurricane of 1885 and the earthquake of 1886, to be restored in 1966 under the direction of Albert Simons, a keen admirer of Mills's architecture.

The First Baptist Church confirms the emergence of a new phase in Mills's American Classicism intimated in St. John's Episcopal Church in Baltimore. The dignified four-column portico, plain stuccoed front wall, and delicate circular belfry develop the sober expression of Jefferson's Romano-Palladian style (36). Indeed, the three arched openings of equal height behind the portico echo the entrance front of Jefferson's Monticello. And the overall composition recalls that time Mills had spent leafing through Jefferson's books on contemporary French architecture, there being a resemblance to an engraving of Jean Francois Thérèse Chalgrin's more substantial stone-faced Sainte-Philippe-du-Roule in Paris (1775). However, Mills was bound neither by any one source nor by a partisan view of archaeological precedent. In the *Statistics of South Carolina,* he would have no hesitation in describing the First Baptist Church as "the best specimen of correct taste in architecture of the modern buildings in this city. It is purely Greek in its style, simply grand in its proportions, and beautiful in its detail."[99] While the claim might seem self-congratulatory, it played on the stirrings of local antiquarianism among the privileged typified by John Izard Middleton's privately published *Greecian Remains in Italy . . . and Roman Antiquities* (1812). By "style," Mills clearly meant aesthetic principle rather than archaeological accuracy. For if the belfry could just have been inspired by the circular Choragic Monument of Lysicrates at Athens, the columns have bases but no flutes after the Roman manner, and the centralizing of the triglyphs in the entablature over the columns follow the Palladian system.

In that respect, the First Baptist Church prefigured the subtle re-creation of South Carolinan Palladianism he was to achieve in those public and domestic commissions he completed after returning to the state in 1820. He thus retained some of the local architectural conventions. The four "massy [portico] columns" are boldly projected, mirrored by pilasters on the wall behind, and flanked by side bays, all as on the not far distant St. Michael's Church. Furthermore, the width of its nave is also 60 feet and displays an intriguing synthesis of traditional American design and Neoclassical details (37). The relatively confined site and the fact that many of the congregation reputedly had New England origins could explain why he chose the rectangular hall plan in place of the round configuration of his earlier Baptist churches. The three-sided gallery, reached by circular staircases on each hand of the vestibule behind the portico, summons up a long Colonial Georgian ancestry, even if the supporting columns are fluted Greek Doric and Scamozzi Ionic columns, "each with their regular entablature." Opposite the entrance, he placed "the baptismal font [partly sunk into the floor] and pulpit [made of West Indian mahog-

36.   Mills, First Baptist Church, Charleston (1819–1822).

37.   Mills, First Baptist Church, Charleston (1819–1822), interior.

any costing nearly $1,000]" lighted by a large vaulted window, "flanked by doors to the vestry rooms." He thought the church "finished in a rich chaste style" that produced "from the unity of the design a very pleasing effect." Surely his judgment holds good for most visitors to this very day.

Searching for new opportunities back in 1818, Mills learned that the Baltimore city council, in response to rising unemployment and vagrancy, was reconsidering the construction of a workhouse. A committee for the euphemistically styled House of Industry had been established in December 1814, and all fines received by the city treasurer directed into a building fund from February 1815 (aided by a lottery organized by the state legislature in March 1815).[100] Yet the council dallied, fearing that it could "encourage Indolence rather than Industry." Such harsh sentiments conflicted with Mills's awareness of humanitarian proposals for institutions to shelter the homeless poor.[101] Nevertheless, he did not think out a plan until the council decided that the accumulated funds earmarked for the project, some $26,190, merited the striking of a committee with a separate budget of $30,000 for the purchase of a suitable plot.[102] On 26 February, Mills addressed a letter to the members, together with drawings of three different schemes.[103]

Only the letter and one drawing for the "Asylum or House of Industry proposed to be built on Forrest Street" survive. Inscribed "Half Plan of Design No. 3," this depicts the rear elevation onto East Street and a ground plan for one part of his three-sided complex (38).[104] In the letter he explained that the third design kept the major features of the other two, being "spacious—airy and well situated" with good illumination for the "roomy and well ventilated" working halls, public rooms, and dormitories. He further stated that his first design had a longer main block and porticoes at the center as well as on each wing. The simplest was the "Half Plan of Design No. 3," having only a central eight-column portico, and the wing corridors placed centrally rather than to one side, which, as he acknowledged in his letter, reduced the cross-ventilation and thus the healthfulness of the communal halls and washrooms but improved good communication. His chief aim was to erradicate "the gloom of a prison." Consequently, he had added features such as the Venetian windows to simulate domestic architecture and to give the inmates a sense of dignity while "suitable to the funds of the institution." Mills need not have been so obliging, for the scheme foundered with the Baltimore economy, which, ironically, intensified the need for a poorhouse.[105]

The issue of taste, not of budget, confounded his next attempt to secure a valuable commission. In the *Philadelphia Gazette* of 13 May 1818, the directors of the Second Bank of the United States advertised a competition for new headquarters.[106] It was to be built on a site in Philadelphia, still the financial heart of the Union, bounded by Chestnut and Library between Fourth

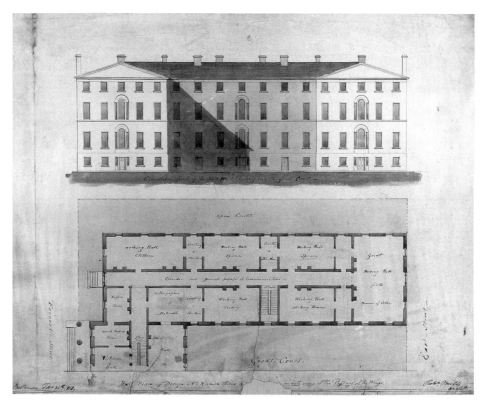

38.   Mills, design for the "House of Industry," Baltimore (1818).

and Fifth streets. "In the edifice," Mills surely read with mounting excitement, "the directors," including, as he knew, the South Carolinian Langdon
Cheeves, "are desirous of exhibiting a chaste imitation of Grecian Architecture, in its simplest and least expensive form." He finished one set of drawings
by 30 July, when he drafted a letter to the board of directors. Only the rough
version survives.[107] Evidently, it accompanied a plan, two sections, and three
related elevations. In the first elevation, the entrance facade on Chestnut
Street was to have been spanned by eight Greek Ionic columns carrying only
an entablature and enframed by lower "watch boxes." In the second, the front
and rear (on Library Street) had pedimented eight-column Ionic porticoes,
while the third substituted narrower six-column Doric pedimented porticoes
with pilasters along the flanking bays of the building. After he had mailed his
entry, Mills seems to have concluded that it offered too many alternatives or
lacked sufficient ancient Greek austerity, perhaps having learned that Latrobe
and Strickland had submitted more severe temple-fronted designs. So, on 31
August, he sent eight more drawings (listed on the verso of the draft for another explanatory letter), the elevations of which clearly aggrandized the third

elevation sent in July. He pictured monumental pedimented six-column Greek Doric porticoes guarding the main and rear facades. The front portico would have been reinforced by lower colonnaded wings for the watchmen, and above the apex of the pediment "a cupola encircled with attic columns forming if necessary an additional watch tower." Underlining the "altogether Greek Doric character" of the facades, he remarked that this scheme embraced "more extent of accommodation," the building alone measuring 76 feet wide by 138 feet deep. The central banking hall was again reached through a columned vestibule, although the space was not treated as a complete rotunda: "The east & west ends are thrown into a semi-circular form providing in the angles very convenient spaces for the daily cash vaults and notes." The directors' room and offices for the president, stockholders, and clerks were placed beyond at the rear, together with bureaus for loans and the cashier, as well as a staircase up to accommodations for the "engraver & printer," who produced the bank's paper currency.

Analyzed independently, Mills's August entry was intelligently planned and inventively composed. But he faced potent competition from at least two architects with better local credentials and prestige. First there was Latrobe's imaginative welding of a massive cubic banking hall to eight-column Greek Doric porticoes front and rear, creating a kind of Rationalist Attic Temple to Mammon. Then came Strickland's much less intellectual but unabashedly archaeological Neo-Greek Acropolis of Commerce. Not surprisingly, given the wording of their advertisement and the forceful presence of Nicholas Biddle, who had visited Athens in 1806, the five directors and President Cheeves (succeeded by "Czar Nick" Biddle in January 1823) picked Strickland's design followed by that of Latrobe. Their decision, printed in the *Philadelphia Gazette* on 12 September 1818, was a dire blow to Mills.[108] It bode poorly for his more synthetic and subtle idea of design, since Strickland's bank heralded the popularity of the copyist Greek Revival for institutional architecture in the United States. Moreover, it established the association between a stricter Neo-Greek style and Americanism, despite the popularity of the revival in Britain and its North American colonies.[109]

Nor did Mills profit from two other major public competitions decided in 1819. In his draft autobiography, he claimed that he had been invited to present a design for the city hall at Washington, D.C., which had been "approved by one branch of the council, and the premium was accordingly awarded to him," only for the other branch to insist on the adoption of a plan by another architect.[110] To break the stalemate, all the proposals were sent to George Hadfield, who, Mills freely admitted, was "an eminent architect residing in Washington," to "report a new arrangement," which resulted in Hadfield's undertaking the commission. Mills contended, with more pride than bitterness, that

Hadfield had copied his composition for the south front facing toward Pennsylvania Avenue. This facade, built in stages beginning with the east wing from 1820 to 1823, certainly has some characteristics of Mills's work: an E plan, marked out by a six-column Ionic portico at the middle and two embracing pavilions faced with in antis two-column porticoes. However, that was not untypical of Hadfield's work, and Mills failed to record that Hadfield wished to cover the main block with a large dome, though insufficient funding later forced its omission.

After that disappointment came the disheartening announcement that Stephen Hills had won the premium of $400 in the second and binding competition for the Pennsylvania State Capitol in Harrisburg.[111] This competition had been advertised in newspapers from Boston to Washington, since, after three years of stalling, the legislature had allocated $120,000 for its construction. In fact, a competition had been called prematurely in 1816 (the state Senate, but not the House, having voted funds), to which Mills had responded, as did Strickland and another Harrisburg resident, Joseph C. Laveille.[112] Waiting for a decision then, Strickland had written sarcastically on 24 February 1817 to Nicholas Biddle:

> Mr. Mills . . . proposes to superintend the erection of the building for *Three dollars* per day provided an *assistant* be appointed to make the necessary contracts for materials etc. Your good sense will discover at once that this is a mere *trick,* for the assistant must be paid for his services, so that the State will gain nothing by the scheme- his proposals are 20,000 dollars for the whole cost.[113]

A fascinating insight upon the maneuvering of some architects in pursuit of the relatively few well-funded commissions, this letter discloses how Strickland had nurtured a friendship with Biddle, which paid dividends in the commission for the Second Bank. Unfortunately, Strickland wrote no description of Mills's lost submission; busy with several jobs in Baltimore and Richmond, Mills might have merely reworked the center building of his 1810 scheme.

In 1819 Mills had the time to conceive anew, anxious to secure the commission now that Eliza was about to give birth to their fourth child. He wrote on 22 February 1819 to George Bryan, residing at Harrisburg and brother of a Charleston merchant, seeking information about the competition to be relayed via "my friend Mr. Wernwag from Pha (the bridge builder)."[114] Toward the end of the letter, Mills sketched what he supposed to be the appearance of the two extant offices. Nonetheless, the sketch (39a), showing a lucidly proportioned rectangular building commanded by a four-column Ionic portico that stretches the full height of the front up to the unifying cornice, could reflect his current

39. Mills, (a) sketch design for the Pennsylvania State Capitol, Harrisburg (1818), and (b) John Hoffman House, Baltimore (ca. 1821).

b

proposal for the capitol. "The experience I have had," he declared to Bryan, "since I made that design [in 1810] will I hope enable me to exhibit something more worthy of attention." Whatever its precise composition, the Pennsylvania legislators chose Hills's design over Mills's 1819 scheme. Chiefly memorable for the high drummed dome over the central rotunda, the semi-circular Ionic main portico could have been inspired, like those on the office blocks, by Mills's 1810 drawing.[115] Still, Mills was awarded second prize, the most welcome sum of $200.

That money was especially welcome after the birth of another daughter, Anna. On some days that summer he must have felt frantic, confronting the "pecuniary pressure of 1819."[116] His one consolation was that Eliza and the children had escaped the yellow fever epidemic that persisted beyond mid-September when, supervising the Belvidere Street improvements, he assured Eliza that "our side of the Falls still remains healthy."[117] Facing the end of work on those improvements and the Washington Monument, he was forced to swallow his pride and trudge around the city in search of jobs. He had little success, although the mayor consulted him in November 1819 about "the damages that may be sustained by opening Brandy Alley" and "extending Sharpe St."[118]

In the long winter evenings, he sought to profit by his pen. His earliest project was probably the "Essay on Architectural Monuments," which was to be published in the April 1820 issue of the *Analectic Magazine*.[119] Signed only "M," the mixture of rather superficial philosophizing and lengthy but imprecise historical allusions was typical of Mills's thought and lumbering style of writing. Nevertheless, by way of quoting Cicero, he effectively summarized the purposes of monumental art: "It perpetuates the name and virtues of the deceased, it fills the bosom of the living with generous and noble sentiments... and not infrequently gives rise to useful and serious reflection." Several of those purposes were fulfilled in the monument he probably designed about this time for Captain Charles Ross of the First Troop of the Philadelphia City Cavalry, whose honorary muster roll included Dr. James Mease.[120] The plain Neoclassical design, although not executed, was reproduced in the same April issue of the *Analectic Magazine* with a caption expressing Mills's ideal, untarnished by recent reverses: "It has the merit of being entirely American in design, materials and execution."[121]

Mills then turned his energetic mind to a much more significant project aimed at halting the continued diversion of trade from Baltimore, and other northeastern ports, down the Mississippi to New Orleans—a legacy of the Louisiana Purchase unforeseen by Jefferson. Entitled *A Treatise on Inland Navigation accompanied by a Map by Robert Mills, PA. Engineer and Architect*, it was published in August 1820 by Fielding Lucas.[122] Capitalizing on his survey expertise, he had explored the country south and north of Baltimore for the route of a potential canal system linking it to the city with the Potomac and Susquehanna rivers, possibly financed by Lucas and other concerned merchants. Just about every influential, and commercially stricken, Baltimore resident subscribed—from Mayor Edward Johnson, members of the Washington Monument Board of Managers, merchants such as McKim, Rembrandt Peale, and even Asbury Dickins. Most would have responded to the advertisement Mills placed in the *American and Commercial Daily Advertiser* on the morning of Thursday, 24 August 1820, announcing that the "Plan of Proposed Canals" accompanying the *Treatise* could be inspected in the reading room of the Exchange. The map and *Treatise* outlined the construction of a canal from Shepherds Town, Virginia, where the Potomac pushed through the Allegheny Mountains, northeast to join the Susquehanna River at Conewego Falls, intersecting at the summit by Middleton, Pennsylvania, between Westminster and Gettysburg, with a branch running from near Emmitsburg, Maryland, along the ridge dividing the Gunpowder and Patapsco rivers into Baltimore. It was much more ambitious than the typical existing canals, such as the system set up in 1815 by the Schuylkill Navigation Company to tap the coal and ore deposits and limestone and marble from the environs of Reading, Pennsylvania, a route that essentially followed the river.[123] Marshaling corroborative evidence from ancient and modern history, Mills's chief purpose was to show the "practicality and importance" of his transportation network, to link Baltimore via the Potomac and Susquehanna "with the country west of the Allegheny." That region contained great agricultural wealth vital for the commercial survival of Baltimore, and once settled promised "great political interests."

About a third of the way through the 103 pages of the *Treatise,* he posed two perspicacious questions, coincidentally exposing the ceaseless battle between sectional interests and national policies:

> Shall we remain passive spectators of the grand preparations making upon the western waters, which, in the course of a few years, will sweep every article of produce west of the Allegheny mountains by way of the Mississippi, down to the great emporium of the western world? Or shall our energies sleep, whilst another powerful competitor, is laboring to secure the interests of the lakes, and all the country lying north of the Ohio River; the trade of which properly belongs to Baltimore, if she will but do her duty to secure it.[124]

The "powerful competitor" was most likely the New York–financed Erie Canal opened in 1825; another contender was the Pennsylvania Canal Company, set up by the state legislature in 1826 to consolidate and extend the canals thrusting north and west. Mills blithely assured his readers that for an investment of $2,025,000, his plan would restore the Baltimore economy and generate an annual income of approximately $758,000.

Yet, and this was typical of Mills, at once ambitious and altruistic, the *Treatise* also sought to realize the ideal in Secretary Gallatin's 1808 report on public roads (republished through August and September 1818 in *Niles' Weekly Register*): "external independence, domestic peace and internal liberty."[125] He actually quoted two less partisan authorities. One was John E. Howard, who predicted that "the day which connects the western waters with the Atlantic, by means of an uninterrupted canal navigation, puts a seal to the bond of union, which these states will never break"; the other was portrait painter turned engineer Robert Fulton, who expressed the hope that "every intelligent American will, in a few years, be fully convinced of the necessity of roads and canals, to promote the national wealth, and his individual interest."[126]

Mills's scheme, described by the most recent historian of Baltimore as "brilliantly integrated," asked more than the "individual interest" would provide, so city authorities forwarded it to the Maryland legislators. They effectively weakened the plan by appointing two commissions to study the feasibility of building separate canals between Baltimore and the Susquehanna and Potomac rivers, their respective reports not being published until 1821. Not before 1825 did the Baltimore council appoint yet another commission to formulate a less expensive scheme in the face of further competition from the Chesapeake and Delaware Canal. That same year, the legislature invested $500,000 in the Chesapeake and Ohio Canal with a link to Baltimore. At last in 1827, the merchants of Baltimore, led by William Patterson and Robert Oliver—quite possibly aware of the "series of Papers" Mills had written to promote the construction of a railroad between Baltimore and York Haven—assembled $500,000 to begin the laying of tracks for the Baltimore and Ohio Railroad. That, surely to Mills's disappointment, was to be surveyed in 1828 by the U.S. Army Corps of Engineers. The railroad achieved what he had envisioned for his canal, a transportation web to fuel the Baltimore economy and to preserve the political power of the northeastern states.

Only one commission may have stemmed from the publication of his *Treatise*. This was for a house at the corner of Franklin and Cathedral streets, built around 1821 for one of the subscribers, John Hoffman (39b). In the *Annals of Baltimore* (1824), T. W. Griffiths described it as the "first private house of extent, beauty or cost erected afterwards [the completion of Waterloo Row]. . . on a plan of Mr. Mills, of common quarry stone, stuccoed."[127] The particular feature Griffiths chose to detail was the recessed entrance at the center of the three-bay, plain Neoclassical facade. It was "raised several steps" and later extended by a canopy leading up to a doorway guarded by two fluted Greek Doric columns standing unarchaeologically on plinths.[128] The house rose two stories above a low rusticated basement and was topped off by a steeply pitched roof with two dormer windows. A curved staircase on the left side, decorated with an elegant iron railing, ascended to an arched doorway in a semicircular recess. Until 1824, this commodious house was occupied by Hoffman—merchant, dilettante, and reformer—who, although a slaveholder, had at a public meeting in 1819, perhaps attended by Mills, moved a resolution against the institution of slavery west of the Mississippi. It passed into the ownership of the Maryland Club in 1858, being acquired in 1892 by Enoch Pratt, the famous local philanthropist who donated it to the Maryland Academy of Science, but was demolished in 1908.

Before the Hoffman House was begun, Mills was forced to send a desperate letter to the Washington Monument Board of Managers on 8 April 1820, requesting a "small sum from your Treasurer in anticipation of compensation for professional services—I have no claim for any compensation, and it is only from a matter of necessity that I am compelled to solicit this favor—I have no business bringing me in anything, and should you deny me this favor I shall know not how to obtain the means to go to market."[129] His torment reflected the discovery that Eliza was again pregnant. "I have nearly completed my engagements here," he wrote euphemistically to Jefferson on 16 June 1820, seeking a recommendation for the post of state engineer in Virginia, only to learn two days after that Thomas Moore and Isaac Briggs had been appointed.[130] Then in July came the trauma of the first legal proceedings concerning Waterloo Row. Sympathetic toward the plight of Mills and his family, the managers of the Washington Monument ordered the addition of a small section of the column.[131] The meager salary eased them through the last stage of Eliza's pregnancy and the birth of their only son, John Smith, on 13 September. But on 30 October, Mills felt impelled to write again to Gilmor, "The state of business in my profession have put it entirely out of my power to support my family—and I therefore shall be compelled to look elsewhere for those means of support."[132] More than a month later, on 14 December, he made one last attempt to keep the commission by sending Gilmor an unexecuted proposal for a housing development on Mount Vernon Place, speciously claiming that the leases could yield over $30,000 annually.[133]

The abortive Mount Vernon Place scheme recalled the intelligently planned and aesthetically pleasing architecture that Mills had executed in cities north and south of the Mason-Dixon line. Its fate demonstrated no less clearly that Mills's attainment of creative maturity offered scant protection against the unpredictable fluctuation of the American economy. Then came salvation when, just before Christmas, he was enabled to escape the dread of the debtors' prison by the invitation from the South Carolina legislature "to enter into her service, in prosecuting a system of internal improvement there."[134]

4

Columbia, 1820–1830
"to advance the interests and honor of his native state"

On 20 December 1820 the South Carolina legislature appointed Mills as one of two acting commissioners of the Board of Public Works charged with supervising the state internal improvements; the news reached Wernwag, who wrote archly on 13 January 1821, "I believe that I am right of putting you in mind, that you should let no opportunity slip to get me some [canal] contract."[1] Mills's success was not entirely fortuitous. Apart from his friends and work in Charleston, he had written the *Treatise on Inland Navigation*. With the excess revenues accumulated from the cotton boom, the legislature in December 1818 had appropriated $1 million for internal improvements and the next year established a five-man Board of Public Works.[2] Two members of the board were full-time paid executives: the Camden lawyer Abram Blanding, who overlooked the Department of Roads, Rivers, and Canals; and Thomas Baker, a surveyor and architect, who had charge of public buildings.[3] As expenditure rose to $24,608 in 1820, the board engaged one of its unpaid members, the gifted British Neoclassical architect William Jay, to aid in the architectural commissions, specifically for the design of standard courthouses and jails. However, he failed to win the confidence of the board.[4] For in December 1820, after supplying six sets of drawings for the courthouses and jails that although not without fault, were quite adequate, he and Baker were dismissed in favor of Mills.

Mills certainly had powerful backers. Besides influential Presbyterians such as Blanding, he was endorsed by Thomas Bennett, Sr., and his son, who served as governor of South Carolina from 1820 to 1822. Together they stood bond on 1 January 1821 for $25,000 that "the said Robert Mills shall faithfully discharge the duties of his said office."[5] By then, he had been at work for nearly two weeks under the executive direction of Joel Roberts Poinsett.[6] Discerning and purposeful in visage, Poinsett on 21 December 1820 noted in his journal an order "on the contingent fund for $200 to Robt. Mills acting commissioner," a desperately needed advance on his salary.[7] The entry coincided with the communication of his duties. These were primarily architectural—drawing up plans and specifications, assessing builders' proposals, drafting contracts, and occasional supervising—with a mandate to offer professional assistance to Blanding on canal and road construction by checking the work of masons and contractors such as Robert Leckie and the local superintendents managing the small armies of "navigators" around the state.[8] The magnitude of the program emerges from other entries in Poinsett's journal as when, on 27 January 1821, he "wrote to Col. Burn [at] Frankfort, Pennsylvania, to apply to Mr. Thomas a Master Mason to engage and send to Charleston 100 workmen in stone."[9] Such large requirements for men and materials in competition with other states inevitably drained available resources in a nation with a population of less than 10 million and resulted in inflated costs.

Impatient to play his part, and now aided by a loan from Gilmor, Mills settled the family in a rented house in Columbia before 6 March 1821, when he wrote affectionately to Eliza from Charleston, where he was engaged on state business.[10] Having a regular salary and an important position, Mills took out a mortgage on a frame house on an acre lot, which was held by another of Scots ancestry, Robert McKie.[11] It overlooked the intersection of Sumter and Pendleton streets in the fashionable central district opposite the campus of the South Carolina College and close to the state capitol. By 27 February 1824, at the beginning of sharp reductions in state expenditures, Mills owed McKie $7,000 and the mortgage was to be foreclosed on 1 August 1825, although the family managed to remain at Columbia until September 1828, when they moved to Abbeville. Throughout this period from October 1821, his name appears irregularly in the session book of the First Presbyterian Church in Columbia.[12] Within three years, Mills, obviously respected and well liked, was elected an elder. In 1824 he would serve on the committee that, on 28 May, handled the sale of land to the incumbent minister, the Reverend Robert Means.[13] The support of their fellow Presbyterians must have been especially appreciated when the Millses son died on 13 July 1822. "Our dear little John," Eliza had written in anguish to him at Camden on 8 July, "is again attacked by disease. He now has a bilious fever, Doct. Davis is attending him & I hope for the best."[14] Within five days he was dead, perhaps before Mills could return home.[15] On 19 November 1826, he and Eliza would carry their last child, Eliza Virginia, to be baptized in the church, although she, too, died in infancy, apparently before they left Columbia.

Mills began work for the board before Christmas 1820, suspending work on

Jay's unfinished Colleton and Fairfield district courthouses pending revision, a situation that calls into question three private commissions during this period that have been attributed to him.[16] The Jesse De Bruhl House at Marion and Laurel streets in Columbia, dated 1820 on one gutter pipe, is uncharacteristically dull in plan and articulation.[17] Equally at odds is the positioning of the six-column Doric portico one quarter-bay short of each side of the facade of Edgewater, built about 1820 to 1821 at Barryton on the Hudson River in New York State for Margaret Mary Livingstone upon her marriage to Lowndes Brown of Charleston.[18] The Doric columns are of the Roman rather than the Greek order that Mills preferred during the 1820s. While it is possible that Mills sent a design to Brown, recently discovered documents prove that he did not, as formerly believed, design another house, Mulberry Plantation. Located beside the Wateree River near Camden, it was constructed for Colonel James Chesnut by the same master builder that Mills engaged for the Bethesda Presbyterian Church in that town.[19]

The Bethesda Church was, in fact, Mills's earliest major commission once resident at Columbia. The Camden Presbyterians, including Abram Blanding, had convened a three-man building committee in July 1820 headed by Alexander Young.[20] Young reportedly favored Mills, whose candidacy was probably also promoted by Blanding and the minister, the Reverend John Joyce, appointed in the spring of 1820 after serving for three years at Mills's Augusta church. The cotton and grain grown on the surrounding plantations along the Wateree was shipped to Charleston, where, as many Camden citizens knew, the now quite celebrated architect had been raised among them as a Presbyterian. Mills must have felt honored to add a substantial building in the community where, as recounted in the *Statistics,* Baron De Kalb, although mortally wounded, had valiantly attacked the British on 16 August 1780, and the local militia commanded by the Polish colonel Kosciuszko had forced their retreat on 10 May 1781.[21] Mills may have considered the church to be a lasting memorial to those who had endured the onslaught of the British troops, "marked with blood, and with deeds of atrocity."

Mills was to make an attractive, if perspectively faulty, colored rendering of the church in 1826 (transposed into an engraving by John Hill in 1827),[22] showing his 1826 monument to De Kalb with, to the right, two brick buildings that the session used for meetings and schooling (40). The portico—originally, as the engraving shows, to have had modified Greek Doric columns without the present bases—is gracefully dignified or, in the words of his description in the *Statistics,* "handsome."[23] Deftly proportioned, it continues to illustrate the distinction he would define in his draft essay "Progress of Architecture in Virginia" between the "servile copying of the buildings of antiquity" and the use of the "*orders* in columns as established by the ancients."[24] Behind the widely

THE MONUMENT TO DE KALB, WHO FELL FIGHTING BRAVELY IN DEFENCE OF THE RIGHTS OF MAN ON THE PLAINS OF CAMDEN, STATE OF SOUTH CAROLINA, AUGUST 16TH 1780.
ERECTD IN THE TOWN OF CAMDEN, FRONTI THE PRESBYTERIAN CHURCH : THE CORNER STONE LAID BY GENL LA FAYETTE MARCH 9TH 1825; IN PRESENCE OF A LARGE CONCOURSE OF CITIZENS OF THE STATE.

40.   Mills, drawing of the Bethesda Presbyterian Church, Camden (1820–1821), showing the De Kalb Monument (1826), engraved by J. Hill (1827).

spaced columns are arches, patterned after the triple Roman triumphal arch, the two outer ones having delicately curved fanlights. The purity of the sharply raked pediment is not compromised by a lantern, as in his design for the Johns Island church, the belfry being installed in the "neat spire in the rear," a miniature echo of the steeple envisaged for the Richmond Monumental Church.

   The interior of the Bethesda Church is an equally inventive development of the Johns Island design. The ceiling is coved and the elevated pulpit placed behind the front wall, between the outer arched front entrances. The pulpit faces the pews, which, he wrote in *Statistics,* "rise as they recede" to the back of the nave, "giving every advantage to the audience both in seeing and hearing." Formerly at the rear was an "organ loft and gallery, one side of which was reserved for negroes," entered through doors reached from external staircases. Those doors were incorporated into "the 'five porches of Bethesda,' " which Joyce directed Mills to include "on the outside in the rear."[25] Not mentioned in *Statistics,* the porches were "ruthlessly altered" in 1890. The rear wall presently has four doors—two leading into the nave and above, two more into the gallery—while the brickwork has been altered in various places. The upper doors are served by an awkward scissor staircase enclosed by a portico of three Doric columns perched on tall plinths each too crude to be attributable to Mills.[26]

Before the two-year building program on the Bethesda Church began in the summer of 1820, Mills had finished the working drawings for reconstructing the partly built Colleton and Fairfield courthouses.[27] He endeavored to improve the Jay's plan since local grand juries had frequently complained of disturbance by noise from the street. Contrary to conventional practice, he followed the style of Bulfinch at the Worcester County Courthouse (1801–1803) (and of Benjamin in his *American Builder's Companion* [1806]) in elevating the courtroom over the offices.[28] Consequently, he reversed the relative height of the floors and windows to position the courtroom above the now more convenient offices. Unable to introduce fireproof-brick vaulting over the offices, since the upper floor joists had been stepped in, he simplified the facade by removing Jay's four pilasters and enclosing the whole front with an elegantly low-pitched pediment pierced by a fanlight. At Colleton, he further distinguished its offical purpose by adding a single-story portico with two pairs of Roman Doric columns.[29] The result was quite as architecturally effective as Jay's more ornamental design and presaged Mills's preparation of entirely new prototypes for both the district courthouses and jails.

Mills began that process the next summer, amid a busy schedule checking progress on the state road being laid from Charleston via Columbia, Camden, and Cheraw into North Carolina, the various canal projects along the upper reaches of the rivers, and the work on the courthouses.[30] A hint of Mills's peripatetic life comes in the letter that Blanding sent to Poinsett on 5 June 1821: "Mr. Mills will attend to the Goose Neck Road [north of Charleston] and give Mr. Bee all the necessary instruction."[31] Other momentos of his lonely rides can be found in the extant scraps of family correspondence. On 19 September, Eliza addressed a note to him at Pinckneyville and eleven days later at Greenville.[32] He tried to capture the appearance and atmosphere of the unfolding scenery in speedily stroked pencil-and-wash drawings.[33] On 20 September, he inscribed one "A View of the Mountains descending the hill to North Tiger on the Road from Spartanburg & Greenville 5 miles from S. and in a direct line 22 miles from the mountain." The drawings vividly depict the settlements and landmarks, while the inscriptions bespeak the geographical definition of the civil or military surveyor—"View of the country seat of W. Gibb[es] Esq. in Chester District entering from the S.E. by the Road"—or revert to his patriotic sense of history—"Battle ground of Fishing Creek." He probably showed them to his family, surely describing the countryside and weather—his sketch in Columbia on 1 July 1823 of a double rainbow "of a perfect segment," a phenomenon possessing of religious and scientific significance for him—the meals he had eaten, the places he had stayed, and the people he had met.

Those journeys across the state inspired him to make an exhaustive topographical and statistical study that would provide the framework for two major improvement schemes published in 1821 and 1822, but especially his *Atlas of the State of South Carolina* (1825), and associated *Statistics of South Carolina, Including a View of its Natural, civil and Military History, General and Particular* (1826). In *Statistics* he was to evoke the remarkable geographical variety of the state, from the flat coast fringed with islands etched by the interaction of the Atlantic swell and outflowing rivers, coniferous forested sandhills, lowland rice and cotton plantations, and chain of lakes, to the crags and deciduous wooded clefts of the Allegheny Mountains. His imagination was particularly stirred by those romantic heights: "The scenery in this section of the state is sublime and beautiful in the extreme;... the landscape is for every varying, and every variation affords matter to interest or to delight."[34] The mystery and untamed grandeur excited his intuitive response to the romantic sensibility already defined in British literature and art and beginning to be appreciated as a uniquely American experience by members of the Hudson River school. The "painter of American scenery," Thomas Cole, would in 1835 declare of the Catskills on the northern fringe of the Alleghenies, had "indeed privileges superior to any other. All nature here is new to art."[35]

Mills's post, however, required that he direct his expertise to the taming of nature toward the state's goal of establishing upward of 2,000 miles of navigable waterways. To that end he delivered a report on 13 December 1821 to Jacob Bond, chairman of the legislative Committee on Internal Improvements, examining the feasibility of digging a canal from the coast via Bee's Creek to Hamburg on the South Carolina bank of the Savannah River to wrest trade from Augusta on the Georgia side of the fast-flowing river.[36] High water levels had rendered it impossible to make a direct survey of the general route on Mills's visit to the area in 1820. On a second visit, he surveyed the tidewater of Bee's Creek up toward the valley of the Great Swamp, which convinced him that a canal on the contemplated line "would be attended with an expense that no advantage calculated to arise from it to the State would justify." If really "*expedient*" he counseled in his report, other routes would have to be followed: from the Savannah to the Broad River, or along the Yazoo freshet. Each should conserve the topsoil by providing an overflow for the Savannah, but at a cost of at least $300,000. However, he advocated a canal linking the Savannah and South Edisto rivers, and to order the opening "of what is called *Walls cut*" between the Savannah and Broad rivers to "secure [the] interests of the lower part of the State." Indeed, the uncertain utility of such a competitive development surely determined Mills to compile his two major reports, on inland navi-

gation and on internal improvement, in order to offer a more effective use of
state revenues, even as he investigated other options as when writing to Eliza
from Charleston on 12 May 1822 about to "embark on the examination with
Mr. Shultz of the inland navigation between this [city] & Savannah."[37]

Mills's responsibilities for the canal program were advisory. One exception
was the construction of the complicated series of locks on the Broad and Congaree rivers, intended to be completed by 1822 as the hub of the canal system,
and extending 2 miles above and 1 mile below Columbia. Various difficulties,
including damage from freshets, delayed the opening of the lock system until
16 February 1824, lending validity to Mills's claim in the manuscript of his
autobiography that he had "designed and directed a series of locks between the
canal river at the foot of the hill on which the city of Columbia was built."[38] In
the *Statistics,* he was to explain that four locks alone had to be constructed "to
overcome the great falls of the Congaree river, opposite the town. Those were
of considerable importance to the country trade, as well as to that of Columbia. These locks are the largest in the state, being 16 feet wide and 100 feet
long in their chamber, with a lift of each of about 9 feet."[39] A guard lock and
dam across the Broad River at the upper edge of the town provided access for
the vessels trading up into the Piedmont via the Saluda River system.

Mills was keen to improve the network, already in 1821 sensing the excessive concentration of funds on works in the upstate regions. Before the fall he
had sent to printers in Charleston his text of *Inland Navigation. Plan for a
Great Canal between Charleston and Columbia and for connecting our waters with
those of the Western Country.* The ninety-three-page pamphlet and explanatory
map tacitly criticized the existing policy of piecemeal canalization. Instead, he
proposed the construction of a canal from Columbia at the center of the northern river system (with potential extension into the barely tapped resources
beyond the Alleghenies) to the port of Charleston. Cousin to his Baltimore
scheme, the Great Canal was to run predominantly along the high ground between the Santee and Cooper, and Edisto and Ashley rivers, being carried by
aqueducts across the Congaree River and Congaree and Beaver creeks. Estimated at $1 million, it would enable steamboats to travel the 110 miles
between Charleston and Columbia in twelve hours. Aware that the South Carolina legislators would be as timorous as those in Baltimore, despite the current enthusiasm for internal improvements, he detailed the advantages of his
system.[40] It would boost commerce, reviving the ailing Santee Canal, and also
provide water for Charleston irrigation, resource development, settlement, and
much-needed manufacturing. In the 1820s there were cotton mills only at
Greenville and Spartanburg and iron furnaces at Spartanburg and York, which
also had a nail factory, but their future was threatened by the tariff that
favored northern industry to the detriment, as Mills understood, of southern

economic growth.[41] To those arguments he added some of the supporting material assembled for his Baltimore proposals and quoted the injunctions of American statesmen, including the revered Washington, who believed that canals could bind the western territories into "the chain of the Federal Union."[42] Undeniably farsighted, Mills's plans were yet unrealistically optimistic, overlooking the geographical problems in his enthusiastic advocacy of the Great Canal, epitomized by one sentence on page 7: "Our swamps we may convert, if we will, into so many gold mines."[43]

The economic and societal advantages of land reclamation were reiterated in his *Internal Improvement of South Carolina particularly adapted to the Low Country* (1822). It opened with a subtle appeal to profit and racism: a "*general system of embanking, draining and reclaiming our river and swamp lands, rendering them fit for cultivation and capable of becoming the permanent residence of a white population.*" For $18 an acre, areas presently "solitary as the grave" could be transformed by clearing, ditching, and embankment into farmlands "resounding with the cheerful voice of the labourer, and enlivened by groups of cottages, and the grazing of herds." Another clever image this, inspired by Jefferson's idea of an agrarian republic and popular prints of picturesque or romanticized rural scenes such as those painted by Thomas Gainsborough and George Morland.[44]

Again reflecting Jefferson but remarkably brave for a man in the employ of a legislature dominated by slaveholding planters and their professional advisers, Mills rated the greatest benefit as the diminishment of slavery. Admittedly in a footnote, he condemned the "bad cultivation, the indolent and destructive habits generated by slavery," if blaming the "evil" on "our progenitors without our consent," softening the point by noting "that our country is originally guiltless of the crime of slavery, which was legalized by Great Britain under our colonial government and consummated by commercial avarice, at a time when our powerless legislators vainly implored the mother country to abolish a trade so impious in its character, and dreadful in its consequences."[45] Actually many of his fellow citizens participated in the trade, and the British had outlawed it in 1807 and in 1833 were to abolish slavery throughout their colonies. He might have fared better by appealing to renewed fears of slave insurrection in the South following the violent Vesey revolt and by omitting his observation that the diminution in slavery "would induce a degree of moral improvement in the country, which would elevate us high in the scale of the Union, and of the whole world; and would remove the stigma which has unjustly been attached to Southern States on account of the existence of slavery amongst us."[46] Nevertheless, he continued to own slaves,[47] like Jefferson, to whom he sent a copy on 28 August 1822, explaining, "If I shall appear to be too sanguine, attribute the warmth to the best of motives, the love of country."[48]

41.　Mills, Union Courthouse (1821–1822), based on the Marlborough prototype designed in 1821.

Fortunately, Mills's patriotism found more lasting expression in the buildings he erected throughout South Carolina for the better governance of his native state. From the summer of 1821, he prepared entirely new prototypes for the courthouses and jails, beginning with those for the Marlborough District at Bennettsville, situated in the wooded uplands near the border with North Carolina, and later copied in Union (41); the plans may have been finished before 1 July 1821, when he received a payment of $600 toward his salary.[49] In order to provide separate entrances to the offices and court, as well as to manifest the authority of the state and judiciary, he adapted the Southern Palladian two-story portico. At street level, the central opening within a projected triple arcade afforded direct access into the barrel-vaulted corridor intersecting fireproof-brick- and hydraulic-cement-vaulted offices, while curved steps ascended to the four-column pedimented portico fronting the accommodation for the

42.   Mills, Union Jail (1821–1822).

judge, and the jury and court (also available for those "Town-meetings," which Tocqueville described as being "to liberty what primary schools are to science; they bring it within the peoples' reach, they teach men how to use and how to enjoy it").[50] The pediment was welded onto the front by parallel raked cornices edging the low pitched roof. The composition, aside from its functional advantages and despite its relatively small size, being on average 40 feet wide by 50 feet deep, was obviously intended to evoke such well-known South Carolina edifices as the Charleston City Hall and the District Courthouse, and entirely deserving of his epithet "handsome" in the *Statistics*.[52] Inside, the courtroom described "a semi-circle with its diameter elongated & bounded by a straight wall," as Mills wrote Judge William Cranch, chief justice of the Washington District Circuit in about 1838, and "were found to prove good speaking and hearing rooms,—their ceilings also were curved."[52]

The Marlborough jail, necessarily more austere and again copied at Union (42), was not less representative of Mills's Vitruvian philosophy of design: "utility and economy will be found to have entered into most of the studies of the author, and little sacrificed to display, at the same time his endeavors were to produce as much harmony and beauty of arrangement as was practicable."[53] He sought to make an aesthetic virtue in the design of the incarcerating two-story walls—"brick, rough-cast to imitate stone," as he explained in the *Statis-*

tics—and to establish a sense of architectural consequence by the shape and arrangement of windows and doors. On the "neat, characteristic front," he indicated its civic purpose by a triple-arcaded entrance. More expressive and impressive than the jail that Jay built at Pendleton, it also provided light and air for the inmates, together with the three arched windows above and the flanking square and rectangular barred openings.[54] Where Jay divided the two floors of his 45- by 35-foot building into four nearly equal rooms around a central staircase hall, Mills introduced more diverse facilities within a slightly larger structure of 48 feet by 37 feet, as described in the extant specification for the similar Edgefield Jail of 1825.[55] The first floor accommodated the jailer, minor offenders, and prisoners awaiting trial: "Three rooms on one side, one in the centre & two on the other side with the stairway with substantial & neatly made door shutters & thirteen glass windows of fifteen lights each." The cells for criminals and blacks were on the upper floor, 10 feet high, lined with "two inch oak plank spiked to the walls by three courses of iron spikes driven into solid pieces of timber let into the wall at proper intervals," lighted and ventilated by barred windows and entered through heavy 4-inch oak-plank doors strengthened by iron nails. The plan thus afforded a high level of security, the corridors being narrow and the wider main entrance being directly watched over by the jailor. But it also reflected Mills's enlightened views on penal reform, since malefactors could be safely imprisoned, thus rendering "chaining, handcuffing, &c. unnecessary."[56] Finally, to reduce the risk of fire, the interior had brick vaulting, although the hipped roof was built of wood and slate.[57]

Approval of the Marlborough jail design probably spurred him to enter the competition for the Louisiana State Penitentiary, with a $500 prize for the best plan received by the 1 January 1822.[58] Initially, the penitentiary was to hold 200 convicts and to provide quarters for the warden and guards, solitary cells, a separate ward for women prisoners, a chapel, and a kitchen, together with dining halls and workshops. The legislators, goaded into action by the terrible conditions prevailing in the old New Orleans Jail, selected Mills's design with a budget of $250,000 and a site 1 league from the city hall on the north bank of the Mississippi. But not until 1834 was a reduced version of his plan, comprising a three-story main building and cell wing for 100 convicts, erected at Baton Rouge, although not under his supervision. In 1834 Mills listed this smaller penitentiary among his works in the biography he sent to Dunlap and two years later offered it as proof of his qualification for federal patronage when writing to President Andrew Jackson on Independence Day 1836.[59] To Dunlap he further boasted that the "principle" on which his "design was founded has been adopted in other penitentiaries." His allusion is vague unless he meant the provision of separate cells, because the main American type followed the radial plan of Eastern Penitentiary, built in Cherry Hill,

Philadelphia (1821–1837), by the British immigrant architect John Haviland; Mills's daughter Sarah Jane Evans was to write to Dr. Charles T. Jackson on 28 June 1861 about his "brother Architect, Mr. Haviland of Philadelphia, one who knew and loved him well, and would have delighted to have done justice to his memory."[60]

In Marlborough, Mills had begun to create his architectural legacy for South Carolina.[61] Enshrining the southern heritage, it was also founded on the ideal of practical and durable design outlined in the report he had addressed to the Board of Public Works in December 1821. The "false economy" of the "minimum of expenditures, without regarding the permanency of the object" had left the state with dilapidated courthouses and jails, exposing the local communities to the risk of escaping criminals. Those problems were compounded by the inefficiencies perpetuated in the contracting process, which he proposed to remedy by the practice common "in several of our Northern cities" of hiring disinterested "mechanics" and obtain separate agreements for each trade instead of leaving that responsibility with the contractor. Mills's advocacy impressed the board, which persuaded the legislature to implement those reforms and to accept his argument that "there is no fact in political economy more obvious than this, that money laid out in the execution of *temporary works* for *public purposes* is so much loss to the state."

On this basis, one that entrenched the concept of posterity in public patronage, Mills would proceed with his most important architectural commissions in South Carolina. Sixteen courthouses and twelve jails erected to his plans during the decade, while the most distinguished architecturally were the Fireproof Office Building in Charleston and the State Lunatic Asylum in Columbia. The Fireproof Building and the Lunatic Asylum were commissioned on 20 December 1821, together with four district courthouses and three jails—each with boosted appropriations of $10,000 and $8,000 respectively—as well as a four-story fireproof-brick-vaulted cell block for Charleston Jail.

Three of the courthouses, those for the northerly Districts of Greenville, Newberry, and York, repeated the Marlborough pattern, their unpretentious Southern Palladian facades introducing a higher quality of design and construction. From the *Statistics* we learn that at York, Mills was even able to use stone for the outer walls and somewhat enlarge the courtroom to become "spacious, convenient and airy, amphitheatrical in its form, with a segment spherical ceiling," and add galleries over the jury rooms on either side of the entrance.[62] For the fourth courthouse in Kingstree in the Williamsburg District on the Black River, he tested an alternative design for the front, reflecting his thoroughly American, experimental concept of building types (43). As can still be seen, he covered the whole width of its front by a six-column Roman Doric portico elevated above a blind arcade and crowned by a pediment

43.   Mills, Williamsburg District Courthouse (1821–1822).

angled to the pitch of the roof. He was revising Jay's temple-fronted court-house in Sumter (1820–1822), restoring Roman monumentality by the substitution of a more solid base, addition of two columns to the portico, and closer integration of roof and pediment. Thereby he coincidentally simulated Jefferson's Virginia State Capitol, and more so Pavilion 7 recently built at his University of Virginia in Charlottesville to the design of William Thornton.[63] Nonetheless, due to the larger pediment, the effect was less graceful than his first, more Palladian, courthouse type. The single archway also contradicted the sense of easy but separate access to the offices and court, now by way of side steps. Beyond lay the usual barrel-vaulted corridor, but flanked by two rooms on one side and three on the other. The offices were, in addition, segmental and not cross-vaulted.

He also experimented with the design of the three new district jails, searching for the best type. All three were located in the Piedmont. Two, in towns

44. Mills, Lancaster Jail (1822–1823).

established by veterans of the War of Independence under the patriotic names of Union and Spartanburg (after the famous Spartan Regiment), copied the Marlborough plan. The third, east of the Catawba River at Lancaster, enclosed the facilities in a more fortified-looking fabric (44). The interlocked corner quoins, moldings, and gabled end walls weighted down by flat attics expressed the function of imprisonment. Still the origins of those features, even including the semicircular recess in the attic, were ultimately domestic and Colonial Georgian; indeed, the three molded arches on the first floor recall a house design in James Gibbs's A Book of Architecture (1728). Under Mills's practiced hand, though, such compositional sources had been transformed into a somber image of authority.

His mastery of design had fuller play in the commissions for the remarkable Fireproof Building and Lunatic Asylum, for which the legislators voted initial appropriations of $25,000 and $30,000. Some of them might have been influenced by the draft scheme for the Fireproof Building that Mills had drawn in October 1821, which probably compared closely with the accomplished elevation of the commissioned design he later pictured on paper watermarked 1828 (45).[64] The design was all but decided before he wrote to the Charleston City Council on 18 February, proposing that the Fireproof Building be part of a

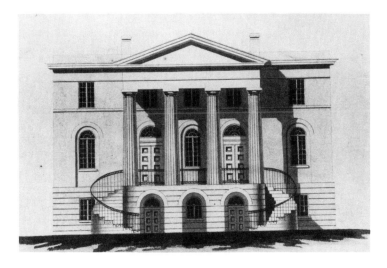

45.   Mills, design for the Fireproof Building, Charleston (1821), front elevation.

general development of the city square. Although his suggestions for the adjacent street frontages were not implemented, partly due to ominous local signs of the declining state economy (the revenues paid to the federal government from Charleston dropped from $549,866 in 1820 to $511,852 in 1821), he was paid $200 for the "several designs which he has drafted for the improvement of the City Square," including parks on two sides (the present tree-shaded Washington Square) and to widen Beresford Alley (now the charming, cobbled Chalmers Street).[65] The cornerstone was laid with Masonic ceremony in January 1823, and construction by the contractor Frederick Wesner (who had built the Williamsburg courthouse)[66] was completed by December 1826.

Mills exploited the open site, alternating the two Southern Palladian porticoed facades with the Neoclassical flanks, a contrast heightened by that between the Greek order of the former and the Roman triumphal-arch motif of the latter but neatly resolved by the semicircular relieving arches enframing the first-floor front and rear windows, the repeated rectangular upper windows, and the continuous entablature (46b). He aligned the north portico to face onto Beresford Alley, the proposed location of the Federal Courthouse, and the south portico toward the rear of the city hall. The porticoes, moreover, identified the entrances into the two parallel stone-flagged and barrel-vaulted corridors connected with the central hall and cantilevered staircase rising through its three floors (46a). There are four doors, one placed at either side of the arcaded basements, and two next to the head of the steps that originally curved gracefully up to the porticoes. These entrances permitted direct access to the twenty-four separate offices assigned to the ten state agencies disposed through the three floors, a solution Mills understandably lauded in the *Statistics*, not forgetting that the "offices are vaulted with brick [the partition walls

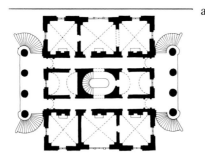

a

46.   Mills, Fireproof Building, Charleston
(1821–1827): (a) plan and (b) as photographed
in 1883.

b

being of masonry] and the roof covered with copper so as to render the building
secure from fire. As a further guard the sashes and frames are all of iron with
the shutters."[67] Actually only four offices were entirely fireproof, since the remainder were built with fireplaces, and the upper floor was originally enclosed, like the roof, with wooden beams. The whole interior, and particularly
the larger groin-vaulted rooms on the first floor, share a simple graciousness.

In the *Statistics,* Mills indicated his pride in satisfying such diverse functional requirements, only briefly describing the exterior as "designed in a
simple Greek Doric style, without any ornament, except that afforded by the
porticos which face each front." That reticence also resulted from the changes
made by the on-site supervisor John G. Spidle. Without consultation, he dis-

pensed with the fluting on the columns (albeit anticipating Mills's further modification of the Greek order in later public architecture), although their capitals have the requisite recesses for flutes, enlarged the third-floor windows, and omitted the molding intended to link their sills. Spidle also incorrectly laid the brownstone of the channelled rusticated basement, hence exposing the grain and causing surface deterioration, and placed the iron balusters on the curved steps randomly rather than alternately. The combined effect of these alterations was to impose a harsher classicism than Mills had conceived. The elegant purification of the Southern Palladian tradition he had envisaged in 1822 was further compromised when, after the 1886 earthquake, the damaged pedimental cornices were replaced by a triangulated attic and the curved steps were rebuilt in straight flights. The pediments were restored to their original state in 1983 by the South Carolina Historical Society, which had already opened its cool, well-lit interior to the public with relics of Mills displayed in the rotunda-like stairwell.

Neither natural disaster nor Spidle's meddling could detract from Mills's beautifully proportioned forms, subtle interplay of planes, circular and square motifs, and color differentiation between the brownstone basement and yellowish hue of the Roman-inspired stucco finish. The Fireproof Building marked a new zenith in his interpretation of the Palladian heritage: more monumental by virtue of the Greek and Roman elements yet no less refined than the best of its eighteenth-century legacy in British Neoclassical design.[68] But any comparisons serve only to emphasize the innovation and beauty of Mills's creation.[69] Fortunately, the state legislature, conscious of the political importance of Charleston, was prepared to absorb the sharply inflated cost of the Fireproof Building, which, upon final accounting in 1828, was to reach $74,416.61 (including $10,000 to the city for the site).

The legislators were not so generous when dealing with the escalating expenditure on the Lunatic Asylum in Columbia. Not only was it larger, but it was also regarded as more expendable in the face of the recession that afflicted the economy in the mid-1820s. It was still an institution that many thought unnecessary, the first asylum in the United States having been erected in 1773 at Williamsburg under colonial authority. Mills's original estimate of $28,932.30 was supposed to cover the completion of four sets of partially fireproof wings, measuring 45 feet by 25 feet, staggered back on either side of a central block, and terminated by halls for the male and female patients.[70] The appropriations were alike too low restricting construction to the main block on Bull Street between 22 July 1822, when the cornerstone was laid under the auspices of the Columbia Masonic Lodge, and 1828.[71] Until March 1827, Mills supervised the contractor Charles Beck, walking down to the site from his house on Sumter Street.

The Southern Palladian raised portico, 60 feet high and extended to six un-

47. Mills, drawing for the South Carolina Insane Asylum, Columbia (1821), front elevation.

fluted Greek Doric columns, commands the middle, drawing together the mass of the wings through the continuous moldings and repeated openings. The coalescing movement is, as shown in the strongly delineated pen-and-wash elevation of about 1828 (47), reinforced by the thicker pilasters enframing the center block and by the rhythmic ascent from the lower basement, through the steps arcing up the rounded base of the portico, to the columns, pediment, and, by way of the attic, the tall circular lantern.[72] The design was, as he wrote in the *Statistics,* "both novel and convenient," combining "elegance with permanence, economy, and security from fire. The rooms are vaulted with brick and the roof covered with copper. The building is large enough to accommodate the upwards of 120 patients, besides furnishing spacious corridors, hospital, refectories, a medical hall, several parlors, keepers' apartments, kitchens, and sundry offices. The whole is surrounded by a lofty enclosure."[73] He was justified in commenting that the "cost of the whole [as completed, including the purchase of the site] is considerably within $100,000" and that "similar buildings executed at the north and in England, of equal accommodation, yet not made fireproof, have exceeded this sum."

The allusion to northern and British asylums was apposite. For both he and several of the liberal-minded South Carolinians who promoted the asylum, which originally was also to have been a "school for the deaf and dumb," who were then classified with the insane, were inspired by the British example. What Mills terms as "the liberality of the State" in voting the asylum appropriation was, too, an expression of the partial acceptance in the South during the Era of Good Feeling of progressive northern policy.[74] The strands of transatlantic reforms had come together in the Friends Asylum constructed in Frankfort,

Pennsylvania (1817), under the direct inspiration of the English Quaker reformer William Tuke, author of the *Description of the Retreat* (1813), advocating the dignified treatment of the insane, a rural site, small cross-ventilated wards, broad corridors and staircases, and supervised exercise yards. Mills also looked to the angled wings of Bulfinch's Asylum for the Insane (McLean's Asylum) in Boston (1817–1818).[75] By staggering the wings of his asylum, Mills achieved ample cross-ventilation and illumination, with the main front facing north. Moreover, the composition afforded varied vistas for all the inmates, a large area for supervised recreation, and, for both staff and patients, a sense of expansiveness in place of the cramped, dark, and depressing quarters heretofore generally parceled out for their care. There was not "the smallest appearance of a prison," the *Charleston Courier* for 21 February 1824 enthusiastically commented; "security is agreeably disguised under appearances familiar to the eye in every private house. The iron bars take the similitude of sashes; the hinges and locks of the doors are all secret; so every temptation is put out of the way to make an escape." Even from the rear, it was "strikingly interesting," while the "massy and grave character of this front, [and] the magnificence of its portico" complimented the enlightenment of the state and its architect. The correspondent was alike fascinated by the statistics of its structure, such as the 1.5 million bricks laid in the walls—not stuccoed and patterned to simulate masonry, as Mills had wanted—in the barrel-vaulted corridors and the groin-vaulted apartments, or the large quantity of granite cut for the sills and lintels of the 260 windows.

Other details are explained in a set of drawings copied from Mills's originals by John Gray, who assumed the conduct of the commission in 1827.[76] Their later date is implied by the inscription on the elevation of the main front: "Total extent of the Building already completed 186 feet." This and other floor plans demonstrate the intelligence that Mills brought to his task (48). On either side of the 12-foot hall on the "principal story" entered through the portico were, to left and right, capacious groin-vaulted rooms for the keeper and his family, each measuring 39 feet by 20 feet. Ahead lay the cross-axial 10-foot-wide corridors, broken into less monotonous sections by projected wooden pilasters and beyond the rear entrance beneath the semicircular ended cantilevered stone staircase linking all the floors. Thereby he centralized the internal communication and divided the female (on the left) from the male inmates while introducing healthy circulation of air. The corridors led past accommodations for patients requiring special supervision and for storage, into the wings housing smaller staircases and on each floor five separate 10- by 6-foot cells lit by individual windows. The corridors could also be used for exercising dangerous patients or when bad weather prevented the other inmates from walking in the enclosed rear courtyard. In winter the corridors were warmed by hot air ducted from two heat chambers served by furnaces installed in the

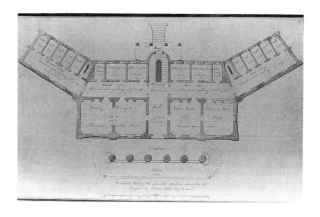

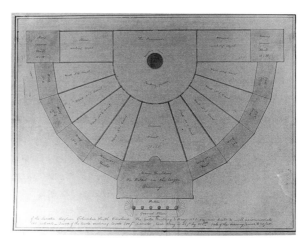

48.   Mills, plans for the South Carolina Insane Asylum, Columbia (1821).

refectories abutting the kitchen and side staircases to ten cells in the semibasement for wholly unmanageable patients. On the third floor, the right side of the main block was assigned to the trustees board room, with dormitories for the less troublesome inmates on the left. The fourth floor had more dormitories, while the attic housed the hospital, lighted and ventilated by the circular windows and cupola. The main lavatory and bathing facilities, being dependent on earth drains, were in the courtyard, isolated from the major accommodations. Movable baths and chamber pots were provided, and by contemporary standards of hygiene the asylum was advanced. When funds became available, Mills's original scheme was implemented by the addition of successive pairs of wings in 1835, 1843, and 1859 to 1861. The building later became part of the Columbia Hospital and has been restored recently for commercial use. Thereby the main fabric of this finest example of Mills's inspired blend of social idealism with architectural excellence has been conserved.

A more modest expression was the Columbia Female Academy built close to the city center at the intersection of Washington and Marion streets as an off-shoot of the impetus to improve education within the state.[77] Its three-story rectangular brick structure was fronted by a four-column Doric portico elevated on a triple-arcaded basement flanked by curved staircases. Characteristic of his flexible composition, the pediment was sliced off to provide a balcony and repositioned above the cornice of the slightly projected center bay behind the portico. The simpler flanks were also given Classical character by pilasters and pediments angled to fit the roof pitch. Contemporary documents prove that it was erected in 1822 and 1823 at a total cost of $18,201.14.[78] In 1824 the first principal, Dr. E. Marks, had 110 pupils. The day students each paid annual fees of between $24 and $48, while the charges for the 45 boarders ranged from $175 to $200, according to Mills in the *Statistics*. "The building is so arranged as to afford," Mills continued, "besides two large rooms for school exercises, a spacious refectory and three parlors; it provides also for a number of dormitories, sufficient to accommodate 70 ladies [some from as far away as Alabama]; additional buildings have been lately erected for the teachers &c. [perhaps to his designs]." A later advertisement boasted that the academy taught "a judicious selection of the cardinal branches of education, adapted to the age and capacity of the pupils, systematically pursued, thoroughly studied and well digested."[79] Mills would have approved those educational aims, which Eliza labored to implement in the schools she was to open at Abbeville and later in Washington.[80]

Mills further developed his harmonious blend of Palladian with Neoclassical idiom in the new courthouse prototypes and private architecture he conceived before 1825. The third courthouse prototype was designed early in 1823 for Georgetown (49), a thriving rice port at the junction of the Sampit River and Winyah Bay. In place of the blind arcade (or aqueduct motif) and single entrance of Williamsburg, the Georgetown Courthouse has a stuccoed channeled rustication and three openings, arched on either hand, but in the middle being flat headed and ornamented with two Tuscan columns.[81] Thereby he reestablished separate access to the courtroom by staircases rising from the outer openings and created a more impressive underpinning for the six-column Tuscan portico and pediment enclosing the upper part of the front.

Mills essentially extended the portico downward in arriving at his fourth prototype after experimenting with a more overtly Palladian scheme. Depicted in a handsome pen-and-wash elevation (50a), the portico he initially planned in late 1824 or early 1825 for the Kershaw District Courthouse in Camden was neither so dominant nor so severe as his final solution.[82] Of four Ionic columns, admittedly copied from the Erechtheion, it projects from the central bays and is capped by a separate pediment fitted within the broader triangle of

49.   Mills, Georgetown Courthouse (1823–1824).

the one spanning the full width of the front, more similar to the Palladian villa than to the ancient temple, if also classicizing his first prototype. Upon reflection, he recognized the imbalance between the thin columns and wide front wall, quite heavy in appearance despite the square and arched windows. So, possibly in tune with his not far distant Bethesda Church, he decided to front the courthouse in Camden with six Greek Ionic columns "spreading," as he would write in the *Statistics*, "the whole extent of the building, and rising so high that the main roof will cover it, and constitute its pediment."[83] More graceful than massive, and looking to the Virginia Capitol as much as to ancient Greek architecture, the portico matched the refined classicism of the courthouses Jefferson had designed two years before for Botetourt and Birmingham counties in Virginia.[84] By concentrating the architectural effect on the columns while retaining the single, central entrance, Mills produced a less convenient internal layout since the inside staircase robbed the courtroom of space. But let Mills explain his own intentions writing in the *Statistics* shortly after the contractor William Robinson had finished the courthouse:

> The offices (six in number) occupy the lower or basement storey, arched with brick and made fireproof; a double flight of stairs rises within the vestibule to the court-room storey, which occupies most of the second floor; the jury-rooms on this floor are so disposed as to admit galleries to extend over them. Four columns rise in this court-room, carrying their imposts, between which springs a grand arched ceiling, the whole width of the room, and extending its entire length.

b

a

50.   Mills, designs for the (a) Kershaw District Courthouse, Camden (ca. 1824), and (b) Chesterfield Courthouse (1825).

He went on to give the dimensions, including the portico, 62 feet long by 43 feet wide, and to note that the as yet incomplete roof would be "covered with metal (copper or zinc), so as a permanency and security from fire will be given to the whole edifice: the walls were of brick." He judged it to be his best courthouse, being "superior in its design to any in the state both for convenience of accomodation, beauty and permanency." His opinion was endorsed by the Honorable Thornton Niven, the Scottish immigrant architect who in 1841 copied its facade and double-flight internal staircase for the Goshen Courthouse in New York State.[85] Unfortunately, the Camden courthouse was reconstructed in 1845; Mills's splendid portico was torn down and replaced by four lumbering Greek Doric columns penetrated by an ugly staircase.[86]

Notwithstanding his pride in the Camden temple of justice, Mills reverted to the Georgian tradition when commissioned a few weeks later in 1825 to design the Chesterfield District Courthouse. The plans and specifications for this, his fifth prototype, were finished on 7 March but earned him a scanty $25.[87] Of three stories, with gabled rather than pedimented ends, the raised portico was latched onto one of the longer facades and flanked by two straight flights of steps (50b). These led into a barrel-vaulted hall separating two cross-vaulted rooms from the court. Above were four jury rooms served by two internal staircases, and below, at street level, were offices and storage. The arrangement was serviceable but, like the bluff exterior, less sophisticated than his other state buildings. A major factor in this outcome was the scarcity of able workmen at this "very neat and rural" village close to the border with North Carolina, which Mills recorded in the *Statistics* as having only "100 inhabitants, 12 houses, and 2 stores." In the specifications he required the contractor, John Chapman, Jr., to build the brick vault 2 feet thick and reinforced with "six [iron] bars, one and one fourth inch square, to extend across the building under the court room floor, headed at each end with axe bar iron eighteen inches in length five d[itto], crossing lengthways in the same manner, all of which are to be concealed within the work."

Mills's most direct yet subtle transposition of the Southern Palladian legacy was finishing about the time work began at Chesterfield. In January 1823 the Columbia merchant Ainsley Hall asked Mills to design and supervise the construction of a new house on Blanding Street.[88] It was to be erected opposite the house he had just sold to General Wade Hampton.[89] Built five years before, possibly to the designs of William Jay, Hall's vacated house was tall and bluff looking, with Neoclassical and heavier Georgian motifs. Hampton had offered Hall $35,000 for the house, providing he could take possession the same month. Mills perforce had to produce a design rapidly, and Hall might have initially suggested that he conceive a version of his first house. Mills's refined wash elevation could be the response to that request (51), hitherto identified as a scheme for altering the Hampton–Hall house.[90] Although on paper watermarked 1827, it forms one of the series of drawings he made during that period illustrating earlier projects. The facade is more ornamented than the house Hall sold to Hampton—for example, echoing the Scamozzi Ionic columns of its portico in pilasters on the upper story. The proportions are somewhat different, but the design would have mirrored Hall's first house, including the deep corner quoins and the balustraded attic, both of which were untypical of Mills. In any event, by April he had won Hall's approval for a much finer design: a beautiful restatement of the great South Carolina Palladian houses.

The process of transposing concept into contract took several weeks, the major agreements being signed on 6 May 1823; an estimate for one of the two separate block dependencies standing on either side of the garden behind the

51.   Mills, design for the Ainsley Hall House, Columbia (1823), drawn in 1827.

house was not presented until 3 July, after Hall's death. How tragic that Hall could not enjoy Mills's modern southern mansion (52). Quietly commanding the tree-lined streetscape, the four slender stuccoed Scamozzi Ionic columns of the portico are elevated on an arcaded basement, originally embraced by curving steps. The frieze of the portico continues smoothly as the cornice of the house, echoed by the molding that links the sills of the upper windows to seal a tighter, more suave bond than at the Fireproof Building. The house was substantially finished when 27 June 1825 lawyers compiled a list of "articles had for [the] New Buildings previous to the death" of Hall to the amount of $19,414.36.[91]

The harmonious manipulation of the Palladian system owes to the example of both Jefferson and Latrobe. Latrobean are the semicircular headed windows set within relieving arches, the impressive entrance doorway, the flat-headed triple windows, and the layout of the music and drawing rooms at the rear. Each flows toward inner semicircular walls, with retractable sliding doors, similar to the arrangement of the living rooms in Latrobe's Commandant's House at the Pittsburgh Arsenal (1814).[92] Mills repeated the apsidal theme in the adjoining lobbies into the hall and piazza that shades the rear. The spacious hall extends past the dining room on the right, with, opposite, the library

52.   Mills, Ainsley Hall House, Columbia (1823–1825).

and a separate staircase. Only the awkward position of the landing halfway up
the side window intrudes upon the atmosphere of gracious urbanity. The living rooms and bedrooms are simply decorated (although the chaste Neoclassical mantles and moldings are replacements), being light and airy thanks to the
large windows. Mills's adept fulfillment of practical needs by aesthetic means
is deftly reversed in the simulated Classical entablature of the two dependencies. For the traditional architrave, frieze, and cornice are mimicked by the
slightly projected bricks laid horizontally, vertically, then horizontally in
courses.[93]

Despite his distinguished reputation, Mills was not protected from economic
and political realities. As early as 21 May 1822 a member of the Board of Public Works, W. J. Middleton, scion of one of the leading South Carolina dynas-
ties, warned him that the state fund for "Internal Improvements is very low."[94]
Thus in December 1822 the level of appropriations was reduced and the Board
of Public Works replaced by a superintendent of public works and a superintendent of public buildings, under strict budgetary control in tune with the reforms Mills had instituted.[95] For, in his final report to the board (printed in
1823), he recalled that detailed drawings and specifications were supplied to
competing contractors who were selected by "the lowest price for the work,"
resulting in "a reduction of expense exceeding eleven per cent" on buildings
begun under his supervision.[96] This record probably secured his appointment as
superintendent of public buildings (Blanding also survived as superintendent
of public works), although for only one year.

Mills's first task as superintendent was to build five new district courthouses for Darlington, Georgetown, Horry, Marion, and Union districts, plus jails for Marion and Williamsburg. The budget for each jail was $8,000 and for each of four of the courthouses, $10,000. The legislature voted $12,000 for the courthouse at Georgetown.[97] The remainder of the construction reverted to his more economical prototype, as for the Marlborough District courthouse and jail. He was also to "complete" the contract "entered last year," for nine circular magazines and a rectangular barracks, advertising for bids on the foundations in the May 1824 *Charleston Courier.*[98] The next year, the legislature voted $17,380 for the complex, which was described in the *Statistics* as "now erecting" at Charleston Neck, 2 miles from the city and thus accessible but beyond risk of damage from accidental explosions.[99] Based on his 1817 Baltimore facility, the nine magazines were "of brick, rough cast [stuccoed] and made fireproof. . . circular form, with conical roofs, and disposed in three ranges 130 feet apart. The centre building is the largest, and intended exclusively for the public powder. It will contain, upon an emergency, four thousand kegs." The roof was "made bomb-proof" by curving the vault inward from the wall to rest on a central brick pier, remarkably like such medieval market crosses as that at Malmesbury, Wiltshire, illustrated in Britton's *Architectural Antiquities of Great Britain,* which Latrobe had adapted for the directors' room of the Bank of Philadalphia.[100] By way of additional protection, the magazines were surrounded by an embankment that doubled as a "walk for a sentinel" drawn from the Charleston Neck Militia Detachment for which Mills provided new quarters in the two-story barracks on the east side of the enclosure. Stylishly austere, this sandwiched a broad pedimented center containing an arched entrance between slightly recessed three-bay wings. It was demolished with the magazines in 1940.

Before construction on the magazine started, Mills's fortunes collapsed once again. Late in December 1823, the legislature replaced him by Evander R. McIver, brother of a prominent state senator, and a contractor rather than an architect, later building Sumter Jail in 1826 to Mills's design.[101] Beyond nepotism and adverse reaction to his statements on slavery, Mills evidently fell victim to the legislators' exasperation with internal improvements. The canal network in particular had proved to be a costly failure, especially since drought had rendered the rivers unnavigable. Compounding the situation was the drastic fall in state revenues hastened by the development of new plantations in the Deep South. In a larger perspective, the seeds of the nullification movement were being sown, evinced by articles in such publications as the *Southern Review,* which in 1828 protested that internal improvements, tariffs, and attacks on slavery were "threatening even to prostrate the fair fabric of our hopes and of our prosperity, and to obscure the lustre of that example which the United States were expected to exhibit for the instruction of mankind."[102]

Thus Mills, a reforming Unionist, was affected by the early stirrings of the sectional forces that were to blight the future of the republic he loved so dearly.

Disappointed and distracted by the ogre of unemployment, he hurried in the first days of 1824 to apply for the newly vacant post of surveyor of the state of Virginia. He was able to marshal two powerful references.[103] On 17 January his father-in-law wrote from Winchester to the governor, James Pleasants, commending his "diligence and integrity," while three days later Nicholas Herbemont, formerly on the South Carolina Board of Public Works, took "much pleasure in testifying that your talents as an architect and civil engineer have been eminently useful to the State of South Carolina." Eliza warned against overoptimism in the letter she mailed on 29 January to Richmond, where Mills had speeded to lobby on his own behalf.[104] It was her *"father's opinion, that you have applied too late for the Engineer's office, Mr. Briggs* [the successful candidate] *having been engaged in* electioneering," continuing: "And the fond hope that providence may prosper your present exertions in behalf of your family sometimes steals in to gild the prospect darkened by uncertainty and doubt. But if so order'd, that you do not succeed, we must rest satisfied, all is right & good."

Through the ensuing months, Mills learned over again that ability, like virtue, frequently had no material reward. What must have anguished him most was the impact upon Eliza and the girls. Eliza was badgered by tradesmen over unpaid bills, as she disclosed when writing to him at Charleston on 24 January 1824:

> I sometimes feels as if I could not bear up under the difficulties that
> still appear to pursue us, and my heart almost desponds, we have
> been toiling for years, & still meet with trials of every description,
> poverty and harship still keep in view, as if willing to humble our
> pride & vain glory, whilst the substantial good things of this life,
> like tempting baits have only allured us to follow them, only to end
> the chase in disappointment, fear and mistrust, thus it has been.[105]

Her main solace was their relationship: "But then my beloved husband, your image rises to my view and I feel resolved with you to live & die, for without your society existence itself could have no charm, ungrateful that I am to repine a moment at my lot, if ever misfortune be my lot with such a friend as I have in my dear husband." Brave, devoted, and a deeply responsible woman, Eliza yet endeavored to maintain the society she had established with Mrs. Blanding and other ladies of Columbia for the relief of the local poor. He steeled himself again to petition friends for help, as when he wrote on 2 September 1824 to Robert Gilmor, whose loan was still outstanding.[106] "But alas one disappointment and another has deprived me of this pleasure and I am still left in *hope* that the time will come when I shall as far as money will do it return you the obligation I am under to you." He appealed to Gilmor's sympathy by outlining the circumstances leading up to his dismissal:

> You no doubt have long known how the Legislature of my native state served me—first by the intrigue of a few who were enemies to internal improvement in the State. These individuals gathered strength, and induced their colleagues to abolish the Board of public work altogether, thus was I thrown suddenly out of employment— out of the means of support and in a place where but little call for the exercise of my profession existed. . . . I could not have expected such treatment as I have rec'd from the Legislature of my own small state, but the imprudent expenditure in the internal improvement system of the state previous to my coming into office occasioned the abolishment of the office, and I believe that if they could have done it the whole system would have been also abandoned—Tho' I was able to economize in the public works during my time to the amt. of 30 thousand dollars—this was but a drop in the bucket.

Fortunately, Mills's competence was not entirely overlooked. About this time Father Dennis Corkery asked him to design a church that would be dedicated to St. Peter and serve Columbia's small Roman Catholic congregation.[107] A substantial number of the members of the church hailed from among the Irish navigators brought into the state to labor on the canal and road system.[108] Mills responded with his first independent and noteworthy design in the Gothic style. The motivation for this significant change from his previous church architecture, however, could have originated with Corkery. Recently emigrated from Ireland in the vanguard of an increasing number of Irish immigrants, he surely reminded Mills of the historical association between the Roman Catholic church and the Gothic style, which was being reactivated in North America as for Notre Dame Cathedral in Montreal (1824–1828), designed by the Irish-born New York architect Father James O'Donnell.[109] Mills nevertheless genuinely appreciated the stylistic and religious attributes of medieval architecture. In September 1824 he sent the *Charleston Courier* an article, published anonymously on 22 September, describing this first "Essay" in South Carolina of that "peculiar style of Architecture, denominated (but improperly) Gothic." The remarks on the Gothic style were clearly inspired by the section on King's College Chapel, Cambridge (1512–1515), in Britton's *Architectural Antiquities of Great Britain* and would recur in his 1846 proposal for the Smithsonian Institution. He followed Britton in preferring the more regular Tudor Gothic of fifteenth-century Britain, while enthusiastically supporting the Picturesque detailing and religious symbolism of medieval design:

> Its lofty towers,—its turrets—its buttresses and battlements, crowned with enriched finials,—its high pointed arches—its clustered and banded columns . . . its "cloud capt" spires, crowned with the sublime emblem of the Christian's hope—all, all tend to produce an effect upon the mind that may be *imagined* but cannot be *described.*

The exalted phraseology hardly found expression in the modest fabric of St. Peter's (53a), fortunately fully recorded in Mills's article. Still, besides economies such as the substitution of stuccoed brick for stone and a spire merely 80 feet tall, he was creating a simplified adaptation of the style, suited to contemporary American conditions ultimately deriving from his supervision of Latrobe's "modern Gothic" Bank of Philadelphia. And the buttressed facade of St. Peter's, with its broad central arch, sharply pointed side niches, circular window, and pinnacles, echoed the Gothic design for Baltimore Cathedral he had traced for Latrobe. The "lofty vaulted porch" contained circular stone stairs on either hand rising to the galleries and an entrance into the nave (53b). Based on the Greek-cross plan, it measured 80 feet long by 44 feet wide (60 feet across the transepts) with a "double range of *four clustered* columns . . . carrying a light impost, from which springs a vaulted roof or ceiling, intersected with groined arches," probably constructed of wood. The organ and choir were situated in a gallery over the entrance, itself surmounted by another reserved for the black congregation. The "grand altar" was set in a "spacious and lofty niche, thirty feet high, crowned by a semi-dome, and lighted by a skylight." If the top lighting followed his earlier practice, the pulpit was not "placed centrally but at one angle of the grand altar niche and . . . crowned with an enriched canopy."

The article failed to attract sufficient donations to commence building. St. Peter's was only "now erecting" when he wrote the *Statistics* in 1826 and called it a "handsome brick church in the form of a cross."[110] The fabric was repaired in 1844 and again in 1857, when the interior was likely altered to the appearance illustrated in the remaining nineteenth-century photographs.[111] A more thorough reconstruction was required in about 1866, but the church continued to function until its demolition in 1905. St. Peter's was no less convincing in style than other Neo-Gothic churches of the period and remained unique in South Carolina until E. B. White built a new Huguenot church on

53.   Mills, St. Peter's Church,
Columbia (1824): (a) facade and (b)
interior in ca. 1900.

b

a

Church Street in Charleston (1844–1845). Not before 1850 did another Columbia congregation opt for the Gothic, when the congregation of the First
Presbyterian Church, among whom Mills and his family had worshipped, began its new church on Marion Street, to be graced by a more soaring spire
than the funds of the Roman Catholic community had allowed him to attempt.

The delay in beginning St. Peter's was symptomatic of Mills's predicament,
only relieved by the sporadic judicial building program and tasks for the state
government. One noted in the *Statistics,* concerned their attempt in December
1823 to establish a U.S. Navy depot in Charleston Harbor when John C. Calhoun was secretary of war.[112] To many South Carolinians, the issue also represented a test of the Union. Mills was given the important task of drawing the
plans for presentation to Calhoun and the U.S. Army Corps of Engineers and
invited to join the delegation to Washington in September 1824. Glimpses of
his participation are recorded in a letter he began to Eliza on 4 September and
finally posted from the capital on 28 September.[113] He reveled in returning to
the center of power and, although not directly mentioned, exploring the possibility of securing a post with the corps. Before the lobbying began in earnest,
he had visited the navy yard to determine what facilities would be required and
the Capitol, nearing completion under the direction of Bulfinch, whom he ap-

parently did not meet again. "Everything," he assured Eliza, "is finished in the best style," although he had reservations about the octagonal stepped drum encasing the footings of the dome over the Capitol rotunda. More to his taste was the west wing of the city hall, for which he claimed some responsibility, and the "*model*" of the entire building that he inspected, perhaps with Hadfield, "beautiful both in design and execution." Certainly he visited another artist friend of at least ten years' standing, Charles Bird King (1785–1862), the portrait painter with whom he had probably first become acquainted at Richmond in 1814. "He is here in great eclat—he has a handsome gallery [at 486 Twelfth Street, on the east side between E and F streets] & well filled with paintings mostly portraits—I visited him this morning [25 September] and was much pleased with the display—particularly with the portraits [commissioned by the superintendent of Indian trade] of the [twenty-five] Indian Chiefs who were here."[114] King excelled in "dead subjects—fruit, fish, fowl etc.," but Mills most admired a picture that combined King's talent for realistic illusionism with religious morality, depicting "the trial of Joseph's virtue by Potiphar's wife, which has a thin gauze curtain painted before it which is so natural that you are much inclined to go & pull it aside." Religious duty, even as he tried to promote his own interests, was ever present. On Sunday 27 September he heard two sermons, one by his friend Dr. Staughton, now principal of Columbian College, forerunner of George Washington University, and the other by the Reverend William Hawley in the elegant St. John's Lafayette Square (designed by Latrobe), where he had sat beside Major Charles Nourse, son of Eliza's godfather. "Religion is no fable, it is a delightful reality, constituted of the love of God,—Oh how great are the privileges granted us by our gracious creator, and how unworthy are we of their enjoyment but God is merciful." Those beliefs were very real to him and explain his tendency to hope the best from his fellows. Hence the glowing report he gave of Calhoun, who had invited him to dine at Oakly, his fine mansion on Georgetown Heights (later Dumbarton Oaks) on 27 September: "one of your easy affable men, of vigorous mind, quick in perception, free in conversation, and always a smile upon his countenance, nothing affected, but the natural impulse of a heart uncontaminated by the folly of the world, and full of kindness."

Mills's ingenuous enthusiasm led him to assure Eliza that the administration had "approved" his plan and that the Corps of Engineers had "recommended what manner I should proceed to bring the subject before Congress." Evidently he did not recognize bureaucratic evasion and, confident of success, returned home via Baltimore, where he met Lafayette, then on his triumphant tour of the United States (1824–1825), officially escorted by Calhoun.[115] Mills's blithe expectations were to be swept away the next year. With Calhoun by then safely off the scene, Captain Hartman Bache of the U.S. Navy blockaded Mills's attempts to obtain a copy of the official survey of Charleston Harbor, claiming the "impractibility of his project" for its improvement but aware that the South Atlantic Naval Base would be sited in Key West, Florida. "The Government," Mills complained in the *Statistics,* "takes from us all they can get, and do not spend a cent among us."

The one bulwark against such adversity was Eliza's strength of character, as Mills acknowledged in a letter he mailed from Charleston on 16 January 1825, shortly before she conceived their last child, Eliza Virginia.[116] He grieved that he could not pay Eliza an income of $10,000 "to carry your domestic and benevolent objects into effect" (in the *Statistics* he commented, "Females have always been advocates in the great works of benevolence")[117] before confiding:

> Your letters as I have often repeated to you, act as a balm to my
> heart, and it is no small pleasure to me to know mine convey equal
> delight to the bosom of her I love best of all created beings, for in
> this knowledge I feel how much I am beloved by her—I reciprocate
> all that you have expressed of the blessings flowing out of this bond
> of union which the marriage state affords. It is that which was orig-
> inally designed by a kind of providence to constitute the highest of
> bliss to human nature—"It is not good for man to be alone" said the
> divine author of creation, and a help mate was given, and a help
> mate was not man but *woman* peculiarly formed in disposition, body
> and delicacy of expression of countenance, exactly fitted to be the
> bosom companion of man, and he to be beloved by her.

Thus fortified by his "bosom companion," Mills had pushed ahead with his cartographic and literary projects. The *Atlas of the State of South Carolina* had originated in his proposal that he should revise and reprint the district maps compiled between 1816 and 1821 by several surveyors (chiefly Stephen H. Boykin and John Wilson).[118] Through Blanding it was approved on 19 December 1823, since about $2,000 in appropriations for the maps remained unspent and because the sale of the books promised to be a means of recovering the printing losses incurred. The legislators concluded that Mills's *Atlas* could be profitable and enable the local commissioners, especially those responsible for the roads, "to make correct decisions." So, from Christmas 1823 to January 1825 he conscientiously revised the twenty-eight district maps into a uniform and notable work. He imposed a scale of 2 miles to 1 inch, corrected the inscriptions, introduced standard symbols to delineate topographical features such as swamps and waterways, and inserted the bearings of each district courthouse to Columbia. Those revisions added about one-third more information and necessitated that he traverse the state again, mainly on horseback and

often in considerable discomfort. Those long rides evidently quickened his conviction about the potential of steam locomotion.

Mills discussed the new technology with Dr. Wallace of South Carolina
College, who had assembled the Boulton and Watt steam pump imported from
Britain to serve Blanding's Columbia Water Company. Consequently, when
the *Atlas* was well in train, Mills scribed "Improvements in the Rotatory Engine: or several modes by which a Direct Circular Motion may be obtained, using either as an Agent, Steam, Air, Water, Gunpowder or any other Propelling
Power" and "Sketches of Designs for Rotory engines. Several inventions or
modes by which a *Rotatory* motion may be given to all Engines now subject to a
previous *Rectilinear* motion."[119] The text is handwritten on twenty-two sheets
of stiff quarto paper, while the illustrations are delineated in ten pencil and
color-wash drawings on twelve quarto sheets. Seeking to overcome the power
loss in reciprocating engines, and thus simplify their more complex construction, he conceived two types of rotary engine that anticipated aspects of the
practical application of the principle in twentieth-century technology. In one,
two to four pistons mounted within a square steam case attached to the drive
shaft would induce motion by pushing against fixed curvilinear frames (54a).
In the other, a movable circular wheel would be propelled within a stationary
hollow wheel by the periodic injection of steam through valves (54b), for
which he provided two alternative systems. The explanation of his ideas is engaging, like the fascinating illustrations, but lacks an empirical, scientific, or
engineering basis. Thus the fixed frame in his first engine is too thin to sustain the thrust of the pistons from the central steam case, while the steam
pipes in the axle and piston block could have been subject to excessive pressure and corrosion. Similarly, the second system courts failure because the
valves controlling the bursts of steam turning the axle, paddle-wheel fashion,
would be liable to jam or excessive wear. Either because of Wallace's more ex-
pert criticism or because difficulties encountered in attempting to transform
the drawings into the working models required by the Federal Patent Office to
register his invention, Mills decided to abandon the scheme. More than
twenty years later, he was to retrieve it in one of his memorials addressed to
Congress promoting a transcontinental railroad.

So Mills returned to the completion of the *Atlas* during the winter of 1824.
The thoroughness of the revised maps, engraved by H. S. Tanner of Philadelphia in 1825, took an extra appropriation of $12,200 that December, and a
price increase ($16) for the expenditures "by which the work has been en-
larged and more permanency and beauty has been given to it."[120] His achievement was widely acknowledged, most gratifyingly by Jefferson in March 1826
and Andrew Jackson, who wrote on 8 July 1827 to thank the author warmly
for a map of his native Lancaster District.[121] However, the *Atlas* was to leave

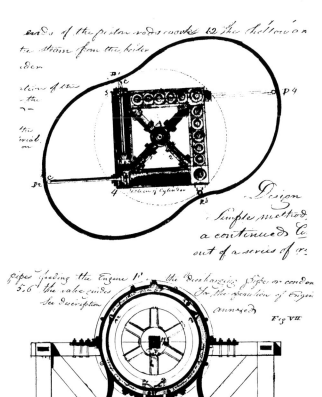

54.   Mills, sketch designs for "Rotatory" engine (1824).

Mills with a dismal legacy. He received a payment of only $600 on 20 January 1826, which was not as generous as it might appear since he had been responsible for his expenses and, initially, Tanner's fees. By December, therefore, after the publication of the *Statistics* he petitioned the state senate for a further $1,000.[122] The senators meanly dismissed that plea on 5 December, yet fifteen days later accepted a copy of the *Atlas* as "a fine specimen of American science and art" and proof of his "zeal, industry, enterprise and skill."[123] Intermittently over the next three decades, Mills forlornly sought restitution.[124] Nonetheless, his industry yielded some profit through what he called its "appendix" in the letter accompanying his gift of the *Atlas* to Jefferson on 15 February 1826 (endpiece).

The *Statistics of South Carolina including a view of its Natural, Civil, and Military History, General and Particular,* printed that summer at Charleston and copyrighted in the District of Columbia on 28 November, remains a monumental and engrossing account of the physical, economic, and social makeup of the state at its zenith. The 782 pages of text and 30 of appendices were gleaned from a "circular" addressed from 1823 to "those gentlemen in this state, who had either leisure or inclination to answer the various queries" on the "natural, geographical, political, agricultural and literary history of their section of the country," culled from the writings of David Ramsay, F. D. Dalcho, and Alexander Heurat, and based on his peripatetic observations.[125] Opening with a review of the primordial origins of the state, he assembled the mass of information thematically, chiefly economic and historical, and then district by district, subdivided under such headings as topography, climate, soil, products, district towns, waterways, population, minerals, education, literature, religious sects, eminent men, and "improvements wanting." Thus it is a huge compendium of facts, an exemplar of the empiricism fostered by the Enlightenment. But statistics, such as the nearly twenty carpenters and sixty painters resident at Charleston, are interwoven with the poetic, anecdotal, trivial, and even moralistic: ball playing at Spartanburg being "productive of some evil." Within a mere three pages from the section on Columbia, we learn of the active religious denominations, charities, and societies; the location of the strangers' burial ground; the weekly charges for hotel accommodations; the chief edifices (including the abandoned theater); and commerce.[126]

Behind his tireless research lay love for South Carolina and its citizens, to whom he dedicated the book. If the cynic might accuse Mills of insincerely playing upon the chauvinism of his fellow citizens—and as he recalled in his journal for 1 February 1829 he had enlisted the aid of influential citizens such as Thomas Bennett to generate subscription sales—Mills's words in the preface ring true: "To advance the interests and honor of his native state, has been with him always paramount." The contents, he further averred in the preface, would contribute to the realization of South Carolina's "glorious destiny" by advertising its preeminent natural, political, and social "advantages" and by disclosing its untapped resources. Those he believed to lie chiefly in the reclamation of the state's "numerous deltas," the "rich and inexhaustible tracts that border her rivers, the cultivation of one of which would exceed, in the value of its products, the agricultural wealth of a whole state." He was deliberately optimistic in the face of economic decline (the state debt in 1826 reached $1,509,332), predicting that if the *Statistics* were used to boost development "South Carolina must increase rapidly in population, wealth and political power."[127] But such prosperity depended on reform of federal taxation. Out of the nearly $7 million accruing from the export in 1824 of rice, cotton, indigo, and other raw materials, federal tariffs had swallowed almost $1 million, the majority of which had been "laid out to the advantage of the Northern States, in accomplishing objects, which could be equally as well effected in the place from whence this vast sum is drawn."[128] But he was no nullifier, adding that with "a little exertion, and a proper representation of the facts" the southern states would be assigned greater federal funding for such projects as the naval depot at Charleston; wishful thinking, as has been told, although Robert Leckie of the War Department was named among the Washington subscribers.[129]

Mills also argued for social reforms, avoiding outright condemnation of slavery, but pleading that the legislature "nobly resolve to seize the last remaining opportunity offered us, of redeeming the honor of the state, by taking the shattered remains of this once powerful tribe [the Catawba] under its special care."[130] Where public opinion clamored for their removal, even elimination, in order to release land, Mills acknowledged the "native dignity in the Indian character, that deserves consideration, and gives a promise of success to any efforts that might be made (on proper principles) to civilize and enlighten them." If paternalistic, his empathetic view anticipated George Washington Parke Custis, whose play *Pocahontas* sentimentalized the life of an Indian princess, and the artist George Catlin, who depicted the vanishing life-styles of the indigenous peoples.[131] As a humanitarian, Mills was also offended by the persistence of capital punishment and harsh treatment of prisoners. The "proper object of human punishment," he counselled, "is the reformation of the offender," citing Charles G. Haynes of New York, author of an 1822 report on the penitentiary system, as well as the British and French propagandists, including Sir Samuel Romilly.[132] Neither should the lunatic be spurned as worthless, nor the poor be despised as feckless. The care of the poor, often victims like his family of uncontrollable economic and political forces, was "one of the most sacred duties imposed upon men in a state of civil society; one of those enjoined immediately by God himself."[133] Decent employment, not paternalistic charity or the loveless workhouse, was "the only correct and effectual" solution, "enabling them by that means not only to contribute to their own support, but to acquire habits of industry, which will prove a benefit to society at large." Further distancing himself from the American myth of beneficient individualism, he stressed the need for government intervention, as in the provision of local educational and cultural facilities, "reduction of the number of licensed taverns and dram shops, which proved so ruinous to our youth and servants," or legislation requiring brick construction in urban architecture: "Where we are blind to our social obligations, public authority should intervene to compel us to the performance of what is right."[134]

His language was modest and spare only in the description of his own architecture: "handsome," "neat," and "elegant." That last he justly applied to the courthouse erected in 1826 on the center square of Orangeburg, then sufficiently prosperous to support two coach makers.[135] For it he reverted to his first prototype, the most influential of his five designs being imitated, for example, in the courthouses at Camden, North Carolina (1827), and Troy, Alabama (ca. 1862). The contractors, Gray and Dane, also used Mills's designs for an enlarged version of his first jail type. In addition, he sent similar drawings and specifications of that type to the contractor Campbell Humphries at Newberry and probably to the Horry commissioners for jails finished in 1827, all demolished.

While finalizing those plans, Mills delved deeper into the Classical heritage, seeking the most appropriate symbolic form for three monuments. His quest led him, once again, to the Egyptian obelisk, by then associated with American history, as in the Battle Monument at Lexington, Massachusetts (1799);[136] from French scholars, countrymen of soldiers and politicians who helped defeat the British in the War of Independence, came the earliest significant publications on Egyptian architecture, notably Denon's *Voyage dans la basse et la haute Egypte* (1802), which Jefferson owned. The first honored General Johann De Kalb, comprising, as he wrote in the *Statistics,* "the obelisk form, raised on a pedestal, all of white marble, and resting on a granite base composed of several expanding blocks, in the character of steps, and surrounded by an iron balustrade."[137] Ironically, the arrangement bears some resemblance to the engravings in Gibbs's *Book of Architecture* (plates 85–86) and in Ware's *Designs of Inigo Jones* (plate 42) also having a wreath, but not Mills's American pentagonal star. Its nationalist purpose was confirmed when, on 9 March 1825, General Lafayette laid the cornerstone, praising Mills's "talent and zeal in the direction of the work."[138] Soon after assisting his "Illustrious brother [Freemason]" Lafayette, Mills finished two designs in response to an advertisement distributed by the Bunker Hill Monument Association. As early as 4 April 1776 the Massachusetts Grand Lodge Freemasons had petitioned the state council for a monument to the battle that said, in the words of the address sent to the selectmen of the Massachusetts towns by the association in 1824, "to change, and to improve the condition of mankind." Their eloquence had, at last in 1825, generated enough money to proceed. Although one of Mills's designs was a simplified version of his columnar Baltimore Washington Monument, his preference now lay with the obelisk for symbolic and aesthetic reasons. As he wrote in a letter accompanying his proposals dated 20 March 1825, the obelisk was "peculiarly adapted to commemorate *great transactions,* for its lofty character, [its] great strength, and furnishing a fine surface for inscriptions—There is a degree of lightness and beauty in it that affords a finer relief to the eye than can be obtained in the regular proportioned column."[139] Both his obelisk and column designs, Mills later informed Richard Wallack writing from Washington, D.C., on 1 July 1832, were "on a large scale and finished in oil colors, with a distant view of Boston in the back-ground."[140] In the possession of the association but inaccessible, only two pen sketches for the obelisk on blue-lined letter paper survive (55a, 55b).[141] Mills included a more precise de-

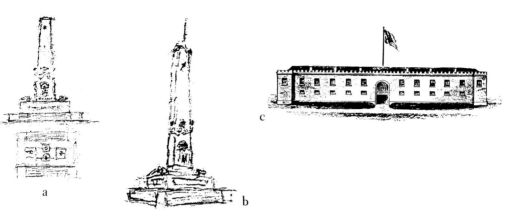

55.   Mills, sketch designs for (a, b) Bunker Hill Monument, Charlestown, Massachusetts (1832), and (c) Arsenal [Citadel], Charleston (1826).

scription in his letter to Wallack, frustrated that the "design now carrying into execution bears all the proportions of that I sent." Twenty-four feet square at the base and 15 feet at the top, 220 feet high, this obelisk with an internal showcase was to be decorated with four "great compartments" carrying inscriptions and other "appropriate ornaments" separated by "oversailing platforms, enclosed by balustrades, supported as it were by winged globes (symbols of immortality peculiarly of a monumental character)," surmounted by a great star and at its apex a tripod, the "classic emblem of immortality," fitted with a gaslight to "serve as a *beacon* for marine purposes." If the association eventually did chose the obelisk form that Mills favored, his Greek Doric columnar design would have alluded more directly to the engagement that had taken place on Breed's Hill (a little beyond the better known Bunker Hill) on 17 June 1775, being decorated with Neoclassical military symbols and the words "To Warren and his brave associates."[142] After vacillating for some months, on 5 July the members of the association, including the great Republican orator Daniel Webster and Charleston-born painter Washington Allston, appointed the Bostonian Solomon Willard architect and superintendent to erect an obelisk monument of Quincy granite with a budget of $100,000.

Doubtless a consolation in 1825, the Clariosophic Society of the College of South Carolina approached Mills through Congressman McDuffie to conceive a marble monument to its founding president (1804–1820), Dr. Jonathan Maxcy.[143] In recognition of Maxcy's academic leadership, Mills reworked his De Kalb monument. Above the larger stepped plinth, he placed a taller obelisk encircled by an Egyptian cavetto cornice ornamented with the winged orb, denoting divine wisdom, and a broad band alternating the initial *M* and American star surmounted by a bronze tripod and globe. The monument to Maxcy's "highly cherished" memory still stands in the middle of the tree-shaded grass campus, between the college buildings, at a cost of $200,000, that he had brought into being, including the one based on Mills's 1802 project.[144] Mills expressed his pride in immortalizing Maxcy, and De Kalb, in a letter posted to Robert Gilmor at Baltimore on 1 March 1825. In it he mentioned two other monuments, not executed but quite possibly in the Egyptian manner, to Kosciuszko, the Polish patriot who had served under General Nathanial Greene during the War of Independence, and to "the Worthies of the Revolution belonging to this state."[145] This last he conceived following Lafayette's visit and exhibited his design at the St. Andrews Society Hall at Charleston and in the office of the *Mercury,* which on 18 April 1825 printed a description intended to encourage subscriptions.[146] His design was for a 50-foot-high obelisk atop a marble base, 20 feet high and 25 square, fronted on each side by "four massy columns" surmounted by the wreathed "escutcheons" of founding states. The solid shaft, 10 feet square at the base, was to be divided into two registers by bronze decorations: the lower would carry life-size busts of Lafayette and Washington with a frieze of the "symbols of immortality," and the upper would be emblazoned with the names of the heroes and the state military and civil leaders, all "crowned by an eagle with expanded wings" holding a wreath.

Rebuffed, Mills turned his attention to civic issues. On 27 April 1825 the *Charleston Courier* reported the passage by the city council of an ordinance to establish a company to furnish a "full supply of pure fresh water—for which purpose Mr. Robert Mills, and other such persons as may be associated with him are incorporated into a company with full powers to lay down pipes, etc. through the respective streets, lanes and alleys of the city." He was on the point of surveying the "streams contiguous to the city preparatory to commencing the undertaking." Shortly thereafter, he drafted a petition to the state house of representatives for a charter based on the city ordinance, and an outline plan of the system that included two reservoirs having a capacity of 2 million gallons.[147] The scheme was in abeyance by the time Mills sent the manuscript of the *Statistics* to the printers and so remained, apart from a brief mention in his correspondence with General Gratiot in March 1836, until he revived the idea in a series of letters addressed to the editor of the *Charleston Mercury* in 1850.[148]

One important commission in Charleston apparently benefited by Mills's advice. Shaken by yet another slave rebellion in 1825, the Municipal Board of Charleston determined to go forward with the building of an arsenal and barracks for the city guard on the site of the old Tobacco Inspection Building (the present Marion Square). Joseph Johnson, chairman of the municipal board, reported to the state legislature on 25 November 1825 that the workmen had already completed part of the exterior, although "not finished as contemplated by Col. Gadsden in his plan [estimated at $34,500] submitted to you."[149] From a prominent Charleston family, Gadsden had constructed the Pentagon Barracks near Baton Rouge (1819–1823), with a two-story colonnaded court but in a Neoclassical style. By contrast, the arsenal, as originally finished in 1830, parallels Mills's concepts and classicized Gothic style (55c). As he wrote in the *Statistics,* indicating a close knowledge of the design when the structure was only partially begun, the plan imitated the Gothic quadrangle "guarded by bastions at the four angles on which canon will be mounted—the whole surrounded by a high wall."[150] Before the addition of a third story in 1849 (now occupied by the South Carolina Military Academy), the overall composition and placing of the two rows of austere windows matched the accomplished proportioning of Mills's public buildings. Equally sophisticated yet practical was the interior of the quadrangle, surrounded on three sides by semicircular arches springing from Delos Doric columns, massive cousins of the order he had chosen for the Monumental Church at Richmond. Moreover, on 20 January 1826, Mills was paid $1,200 by the upper division of the South Carolina's treasury, too large a sum to be his fees for the district and other state buildings still in progress; only later in the year did he send drawings of his first jail type, built in 1827 to 1828, to the commissioners at Laurens.[151] The arsenal— marked in on the "Plan of the City of Charleston and Suburbs Lithographic By Robert Mills Engineer and Architect 1826" entered at the U.S. Copyright Office—might well have been among those projects. Mills wrote to Gilmor on 26 May 1826 of having "just returned home [to Columbia] after an absence of upwards of two months in the low country where I have been constantly occupied in looking after the public buildings executing in that part of the state, and collecting information for my *statistical* work on the state."[152]

The main purpose behind his letter was to reactivate the Baltimore Washington Monument commission. He was only partially successful, as noted, and so tried to obtain a commission from the federal government, as he was to recall in correspondence next spring with Calhoun and John N. Nourse, clerk in the Treasury.[153] Calhoun had earlier forwarded Mills's 12 September 1826 plea for appointment to the Federal Board of Internal Improvements, though the answer was a summary rejection by Major General Alexander Macomb, chief engineer of the Army Corps of Engineers.[154] Undaunted, Mills personally presented a memorial to the secretary of state in which he suggested means of ameliorating the troublesome acoustics in the House of Representatives. Dated 22 October, he had three main recommendations: the retention of the present domical ceiling, the erection of a screen behind the columns fronting the gallery on the north side, and the raising of the floor to the level of the bases of the main columns in the House. Neither the secretary nor a majority of congressmen was then willing to proceed, so Mills was once again in want of employment, if convinced that the best opportunity for stable employment lay at Washington, D.C. In March 1827 Colonel Michael Nourse, another son of Eliza's godfather, was appointed clerk in the War Department. So on the last day of the month Mills wrote that he "would rather accept a salary of only $1,000 a year in Washington than double the sum here where I have no field for the exercise of what talents I have." However, rather than await a reply, he traveled to Baltimore to resume work on the monument and from there wrote to Calhoun on 5 May asking for a recommendation to work as a surveyor with the newly founded Baltimore and Ohio Railroad.[155]

Mills recognized the tremendous potential of the railroad, avidly reading the publications from Great Britain, where the Stockton to Darlington Railway had opened on 27 September 1825. He had already composed the "Plan of a Rail Road," dated Columbia, 16 December 1826, and printed on 27 June 1827 in the Washington National Intelligencer, American Farmer on 6 July, and in the Baltimore Gazette on 7 July, with a woodblock illustrating his horse-drawn railroad carriage.[156] The illustration resembled a print of the British horse-drawn mail coach Union published in the Intelligencer on 16 October 1826 and the "Elevated railway" engraved as the frontispiece of H. R. Palmer's Description of a Railway on a New Principle (1824). Addressed to Postmaster General John McLean, Mills's system would speed the mail between Washington, D.C., and New Orleans via Richmond, Raleigh, Columbia, and Tallapoosa and, in a confused political allusion like the Roman roads and British railways, "result in the consolidation of the interests of the Union, and establishing on an imperishable basis the freedom of our political institutions."[157] Running on a single rail raised 3 feet on posts set 9 feet apart constructed of iron or 15 feet apart if of wood (developing an idea presented by the Hoboken, New Jersey, businessman John Stevens in Documents Tending to Prove the Superior Advantages of Railways and Steam Carriages [1812]),[158] the coaches would consist "of 2 receptacles or boxes suspended on each side of the rail by an iron or wood frame; the wheels about 30 inches in diameter and placed in the same line or plane on the rail, and the face of the rims made concave and fitted to the convex surface of the rail." The motive power, however, remained the horse, although Mills naively suggested that propulsion might even be supplied by oars levered against the ground—summoning up an extraordinary picture of the U.S. mail being rowed across the country! If he could marshal good reasons for the overall concept, he underestimated both the cost and the practical difficulties. While his system might have halved the time required for the passage of mails between the two cities to eight days, it is most unlikely that the monorail could have been constructed for $2,310,007 (or without the iron rim

$1,305,000), let alone yield an annual revenue of $156,000. But then Mills was a man of imagination outreaching current technical expertise, as evinced by his prescient closing comment that the carriages should have "*track wheels*" for independent movement in the cities along the track.

He developed the plan in "Timber Rail-Ways," an article printed in a Baltimore journal, *The American Farmer,* on 20 July 1827, soon after reprinting his "Plan of a Rail Road."[159] Now recommending an elevated double track, he amplified his earlier distaste for the "quantity of animal torture" by opting for steam locomotion, as illustrated in a delightful scene of a 10-horsepower steam locomotive drawing three kinds of carriage, plus two sections of the rail bed and carriages. In response to criticisms of his preference for wood, he paraphrased the analysis of types of fire-seasoned timber as tabulated by Sir Humphrey Davy, the British scientist celebrated as inventor of the miner's safety lamp, opining that when the wood was properly seasoned, the track could survive up to fifty years if "the cap or wheel rails [are raised] entirely *above* the *ground* (one foot or more) supporting them at every ten or twelve feet by piles or posts of wood driven into the ground, and well secured there with stone or gravel." Indeed, he estimated that his wooden track would cost some $7,000 a mile, fully $13,000 less than iron, and could be financed by first building a single line according to his "Plan." Moreover, besides being less subject to snowdrift and consequent loss of income, it could in urban areas be built over rentable storage.

Publication coincided with the completion of the "papers I wrote on the Rail road to the Susquehanna," mentioned in a letter to Eliza on 4 August 1827.[160] This railroad equivalent of his 1820 canal scheme was directed to the newly established Baltimore and Ohio Railroad Company, for, as he told Dunlap, a "rail road between Baltimore and York Haven," Pennsylvania, on the Susquehanna River.[161] The prospects looked good when he wrote Eliza that "a deputation of the Road companies has been held in the Exchange, which has agreed to enter upon surveys of the route. The Committee have spoken to me on the subject and I have promised to meet them on Monday to confer with them on the business." At last, it seemed, they might prosper, Mills yearning "to see my beloved E and family settled here [at Baltimore] early next spring,—and I humbly trust that it will be in my power to render you comfortable dearest love, and that we shall be enabled to enjoy each other's society more frequently." In vain, underinvested and confronting opposition within the Legislature to grant a right-of-way, the survey languished and was in any case entrusted to the Corps of Engineers. He stayed in Baltimore should the situation improve and because he had a better chance of picking up commissions than in Columbia.

Separated from Eliza, and often alone, he brooded, questioning his dedication to architecture. "Innumerable cares occupy my bosom," he confided to her on 4 September,

> and harass my mind in consequence of being out of business—We must all get wise by sad experience, and in the meantime suffer for our folly—I was too ambitious in past days to be useful in the world, when my means were totally inadequate to support it—neglected too much our pecuniary interests or ventured imprudently into speculations which a change of times in business [at Baltimore] totally destroyed. . . . Oh better is it to be in the cottage retired from the world with those we love than dwelling in the splendid mansion of a city, and be deprived of their society.[162]

He admitted to Eliza that he felt crushed by the "selfish world—every one is pursuing his own interest, and not disposed to [? forward others'] except he can at the same time advance his own." Yet in expressing his sense of desolation, of putting his perplexities on paper, he reasserted his faith and determination "O yes—the christian principle is implanted in many a human bosom, and works good to its fellow men." He would tour South Carolina selling his district maps, settle in one of "our large cities" with the "prospect of doing something in the school way," or seek employment in Washington, where the postmaster general and secretary of state were "both friendly disposed towards me." That mood prevailed when he wrote on 30 September.[163] He had been "doing a little business both for Mr. Oliver and Mr. Buchanan," the latter entailing the installation of an "air furnace" in part of his factory. The Washington Monument Board had promised him "a certain annual sum," $200, once building commenced again, and he had applied for a position with the Washington Canal Company, sent his former patron Joseph Marx a plan for a railroad between his coal mines on the James River and Richmond, and had "made some designs for the Masonic Hall Augusta." His self-confidence and ambition were returning—"God will bless some one of my efforts to procure professional employment"—so that he resisted Eliza's wish to move upstate to Abbeville.

The change of heart also depended to some extent on renewed interest in "my writings on Rail roads" in Baltimore, which the advent of the railroad could turn into "one of the grandest cities in the Union." (On 4 July 1828 Charles Carroll of Carrollton turned the first sod for the Baltimore and Ohio Railroad, almost at the same time as President John Quincy Adams inaugurated the Chesapeake and Ohio Canal: the former system of transport soon to triumph over the latter.) Chief among them was the "Manual on Rail Roads with numerous Tables (containing the theory and Practice of these Roads under all circumstances—whether connected with their plan of construction, operation of the carriages running upon them or motive powers used").[164] Finished before 8 November 1827 when, back at Columbia, he mailed one handwritten draft of 101 pages to General Macomb in another attempt to secure a post with the Corps of Engineers.[165] Mills had first contemplated a "professional" manual, but opted for a "more popular" work, having received requests for technical advice from correspondents such as Joseph Catswell of Chapel Hill, North Carolina. Bound in with the remaining draft is a letter addressed on 24 January 1829 to the Philadelphia printers Carey, Lea, and Carey, soliciting a contract for publication and answering, unspecified, criticisms of his statements on friction and accompanying tables "grounded on English data."[166] The text is certainly filled with references to the parliamentary reports and the books of Thomas Tredgold, including *Strength of Cast Iron and other Metals* (1822), *Treatise on Railroads* (1825), and *Steam Engines* (1827). No doubt Mills had also read Strickland's *Report on Canals, railways and roads* (1826), undertaken for the Pennsylvania Society for the Promotion of Internal Improvements.[167] But Mills's text exudes enthusiasm of eighteenth-century Rationalism rather than the precision of nineteenth-century scientific method: "Wherever our attention is directed Man is rapidly emerging out of the thick mists of ignorance, superstition and prejudice.—Enlightened by science Man now proceeds in the march of improvement with fearless confidence." Similarly the arrangement of the table of contents appears random. The section entitled "Practical results of Railways" is placed tenth out of forty, while others on the size, weight, and cost of carriages and locomotive engines are widely separated. Nevertheless, there are imaginative glimpses of developments in transportation, including a three-page review of the application of "Atmospheric [compressed] air" to different types of motive power.

It is not unreasonable to suppose that Mills showed the manuscript and copies of his printed articles to friends in South Carolina. Among them, Abram Blanding and Thomas Bennett, Jr., were directors of the newly constituted South Carolina Canal and Rail Road Company.[168] With the approval of the legislature, the company proposed to construct a railroad between Charleston and Hamburg, again to counter the flow of Low Country produce toward Augusta and Savannah. In their first report, printed in Charleston on 11 November 1828, Blanding as president reviewed the proposed route (surveyed by William Howard) and the construction costs. "Mr. R. Mills's estimate of the wood and workmanship, is but $126,000," based on a system of piles "firmly driven into the earth, at a distance from each other of from eight to ten feet." Iron-capped wooden rails with an optimum size of 8 inches square were to be "longitudinally placed on these at an elevation of from six to twelve inches above the surface of the ground, to prevent *premature decay*." According to Blanding, Mills calculated that the company would have to lay 140 miles of track, including "turn-out places," and expend a total of $405,000 allowing for 5 locomotives and tenders, 100 wagons, 10 (six-passenger) carriages, and various structures such as engine houses. But Blanding had consulted other engineers and, as a result, concluded that although his estimates were too low, Mills's system was viable. In 1829, however, the directors were to appoint as their chief engineer the New Yorker Horatio Allen, who had married into a prominent Charleston family and had been engineer of the Delaware and Hudson Canal. Allen expended $4,300 a mile of track as against Mills's estimate of $3,250, but the yellow-pine frame quickly rotted, being replaced with graded wooden sleepers by 1839. Before that costly process Mills in his pamphlet *Substitute for Railroads and Canals* (1834) would aver, "This plan of road was designed by Mr. Mills, late engineer of that State."[169]

A comparable confusion arose over his part in the design of the west wing of the Maryland Penitentiary in Baltimore (1828–1829). The 1828 report of its directors named the architect as William F. Small.[170] However, Mills could have given technical advice on brick vaulting, justifying its inclusion among those fireproof structures that, he was to write to President Jackson on 4 July 1836, qualified him for the post of federal architect. In fact, his only ongoing commission was the capping of the Baltimore Washington Monument in preparation for the statue of the general.

To occupy his time, Mills began to draw a series of almost uniformly sized pen-and-wash elevations of his major public buildings and domestic designs, each measuring approximately 9 by 11.5 inches. The earliest of the surviving six is on paper watermarked 1827 and may, as has been posited, represent the original scheme for the second Ainsley Hall House at Columbia.[171] The remainder are equally refined in style, if still demonstrating limited powers of spatial and pictorial rendering: the unexecuted schemes for the Didier House and Camden courthouse, together with elevations of the State Lunatic Asylum in Columbia, Fireproof Building in Charleston, and Unitarian Church in Philadelphia, the two last on paper watermarked 1828. Since his purpose might have been publication, he could have intended to add drawings of his other work in the state, which would explain their virtual absence from the archives.

The exercise was overtaken by temporary retirement to Abbeville in the southwestern Piedmont region of the state about the time Campbell Humphries contracted on 13 May to build a new district courthouse using Mills's first standard design; a day later the contractor, J. Bennie, began a jail according to his first type at the not far distant Greenville.[172] By contrast, the College of Charleston had recently commissioned William Strickland to design an extension and Mills could no longer afford the mortgage on his Columbia house; indeed, that debt would still be unpaid on 16 January 1830 when he was to offer part payment if he could raise $2,000 from its sale.[173]

If relocation eased his finances, Mills won almost no new commissions except the addition in late 1828 or early 1829 of a raised portico for the house of his friend Thomas Pinckney, Jr., on Broad Street in Charleston.[174] Flanked on the lower level by curved steps, the portico proper had four columns of the Tuscan order, topped by a flat entablature akin to the Columbia Female Academy. On 27 December 1828 he sent "Mr. Daniel" a design for a monument to commemorate the defeat of the British in Eutaw Springs on 8 September 1781 by General Nathaniel Greene, but to no effect.[175] A later entry from his journal, for 18 April 1829, notes another fruitless effort, the "Designs for Masonic Hall Charleston 100 ft front 45 feet deep main building with two wings in the rear each 70 feet by 27 feet whole cost $38,700 one *Gothic* & one *Greek* design."[176] Sketched under the entry for 25 April (56a), the "Gothic front" is studded with buttresses crowned by battlements and finials as well as a central turret, while the "Greek front" is an enriched adaptation of his Southern Palladian style, the run of pilasters and the four columns forming the portico being raised on a channeled rusticated basement. The design differs markedly from the typical revivalist solution of Thomas U. Walter in his temple-fronted Hibernian Hall on Meeting Street, Charleston (1835–1839), a competition in

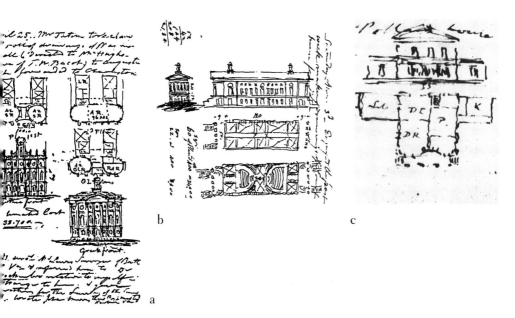

56.   Mills, sketch designs for (a) Masonic Hall, Charleston (1829), (b) Savannah Courthouse (1830), and (c) the Pollard villa (1830).

1835 in which Mills's design, since lost, placed second.[177] For the interior, he envisaged circular and semicircular ended apartments on the first and two upper floors and cross-vaulted rooms in the two rear wings.

Thus, bereft of commissions, Mills concentrated his energies on new literary projects, all nugatory. In February or March 1829, he had started to prepare "Works for the Use of Schools" on the "Geography of South Carolina, Epitome of Natural Philosophy, Ditto of Chymestry, Ditto of Rhetoric, Ditto of History of the United States, Ditto of Arithmetic, Ditto of the Bible. All in questions and answers."[178] It is interesting that he should choose not learning by rote but the Socratic method of teaching through query. In early June, he drew up a prospectus for a weekly paper to be entitled "the Abbeville Journal and People's Friend, price 2$ per annum" and divided into four parts: domestic issues ranging from politics to religion and internal improvements, foreign news on similar matters, poetry, and advertisements, all "treated in a summary way." Battling frustration, he revived an objective for which he had already assembled material. Jotted in reverse order through his journal notes variously titled "Heads of a Work on Architecture" and "Heads of Work" (surely associated his 1 September 1829 entry: "Engaged in arranging the heads of an Architectural Work"), "Plan of a Course of Lectures on the Practice of Architecture & Engineering," and "Memoranda. Origin of Architecture."[179] The first recalled his 1817 proposal for a book, while the second, tracing the evolution of architectural styles by nation and culture, anticipated Louisa Tuthill's pioneering *History of Architecture from the Earliest Time; its present condition in Europe and the United States* (1848). The section on the origin of architecture, explored more fully in his "Memoranda," offered an intriguing religious variant on the theory propounded most fully in 1753 by the Abbé Laugier, which pictured the earliest human habitation as a quasi-templar wooden hut.[180] Looking beyond that myth, likely told him by Jefferson or Latrobe, Mills saw the ultimate inspiration in the endowment of mankind by "the great Architect divine" of the power to surmount "the exigencies of his nature," echoing his contemporary theological ruminations, for on the end papers of his journal are written ideas concerning a "Plan of a Religious Manual—the title *Pearl of Great Price*," comprising selections from the New Testament beginning with "God" and ending with "Charity." Practical issues would have predominated in his projected "Course of Lectures," the first sixteen elucidating geometry and mathematics for "Mechanics," and the next twenty defining the use of the orders with special reference to the United States, the thirtieth being listed as "American." Part of the reason was the urgent need to produce a saleable book, but part also reflected his relative disinterest in aesthetics and current architectural theory. There is, for example, no indication that he had read the functional philosophy and systematic classification of building types propounded two decades before by J. N. L. Durand, or of other European theorists who sought to define principles by which architecture could express the modern times. Although in his "Memoranda" Mills advanced the idea of progressive evolution in design—thus presaging antirevivalist views of architect/writers such as Gottfried Semper and James Fergusson—he did not delve into the intellectual issues connected with the design process or attempt to codify doctrines for planning or aesthetic in architecture. Furthermore, and notwithstanding their cursory nature, none of the notes suggest that Mills's lectures would have reinforced the tenuous status of the architect in contemporary American society.

In any event his attention was diverted by the resumption of work on the Baltimore Washington Monument, and the hope of quitting the nonetheless congenial Abbeville: on 9 September 1829 he was elected president of the Temperance Society assisted by the local grandee John Calhoun, who had been appointed U.S. vice president by Andrew Jackson in March 1829. The bond with the Calhouns was further strengthened that fall when their three children joined Eliza's school. She was yet troubled by his wish to practice again in Baltimore as well as by their debts, but especially by uncertainty. "To speak candidly I am not in favor of your Northern plans," she wrote on 27 December 1829. "It appears to me, following the shadow and losing the substance . . . I would by no means depend on the visionary prospect of a little business which may occasionally offer." Nor was she any longer convinced that their problems were caused by fate, writing "dear husband, I have but one objection to make to you—and that is that you *want decision,* and keep me in a wandering state of mind, I love practical minds and trust that you will fall on some plan that may be realized soon." A miserable Robert replied from Baltimore on 17 January 1830: "I am sensible that I am defective in this Virtue [decision], but under present circumstances I do not wish to decide upon the subject of a removal too hastily."[181]

Yet he had already, in the second week of January 1830, persuaded the board to approve a revised plan for the development of Mount Vernon (now Monument) Place with a prospect of increasing the funds available for ornamenting the column. His ambition to move north was intensified by the renewed activity in canal and railroad construction. Beginning on 15 December 1829, his journal records short excursions to the Susquehanna with a Mr. Colt "to make surveys of the Maryland Canal," meetings with the commissioners, and the drawing of plats or plans, finished by 8 January 1830, prior to a fuller survey between the 21 January and 5 February for which he charged almost $400. In fact, he received only $230, after having offered on 16 January to repay Blanding his $300 mortgage. Other of his contemporary railroad proposals never materialized. One would run a line from Baltimore northeast to

Lackawanna on Lake Erie, and thence to New York; later that year, Mills corresponded with Governor Clinton of New York regarding the operation of ice boats through the winter on the Erie Canal.[182] He also gave further thought to technical developments, on 17 January 1829 corresponding with Dr. Jones of the Patent Office about his "Revolving Steam Engine." Probably before he wrote on 24 April 1830 to Colt about unspecified "improvements in the Baltimore Railroad," he sketched an impractical arrangement of vertical double tracking (one rail below and one above the drive wheels) supposed to increase the friction on the inclines that would be confronted in the eastern and western mountain ranges.

His architectural career was also reviving. Whether by invitation or on his own initiative, he finished a "large drawing of [the] front of Christ Church" in Baltimore for the "Reverend Mr. Johns pastor (Gothic)" by 19 January 1830.[183] But he had to be content with a less prestigious expression of his skill in the Gothic, then nearing completion in Winchester, Virginia. This was Christ Church, on Boscawen Street, where his father-in-law was a vestryman. "Returned to Winchester," Mills scribbled in his diary for St. Valentine's Day. "The Gothic church which I designed built [by John Bruce] at Winchester, 40 × 60, cost, 5300$."[184] From the end of March until 24 April, he was working periodically on a superb but ultimately abortive scheme for a courthouse at Savannah, Georgia. Even these roughly drawn elevations and plans summon up a magnificent melding of his second, third, and fourth courthouse types (56b). Standing on a full basement, raised 12 feet, were to have been six 24-foot-high columns, apparently of the Greek Doric order and embracing the width of the building so that the pediment established the pitch of the roof. Adopting the composition of straight flights of steps up to the spaces between the side columns of the portico that Bulfinch had used for the Massachusetts General Hospital, in Boston (1818–1823), Mills not only maintained the intelligent multilevel access employed in his district courthouses, but also offered a more visually attractive and functionally sophisticated solution to the problems of transferring ancient Greek models to modern American conditions.[185] Mills drew a corridor through the 120-foot-deep building, intersected at the center by a cross hall lighted by broad arched windows, thereby affording each of the eight cross-vaulted fireproof offices two doors, and each of the two pairs of back-to-back semicircular courtrooms separate entrances. The remarkably low estimate of $24,000 implies that he intended that it should be of brick construction faced with stucco, as also designs for two modest houses.[186] The larger was for an Abbeville neighbor who asked him to make "changes for [the] portico" and received a bill for $50 on 24 April. By contrast, he charged Benjamin Pollard only $20 for an attractive villa design conceived between 17 April and 3 May (56c). Both its plan and its elevation were broken into three parts, formed by a two-stage central pedimented block arising from an in antis portico be-tween single-story wings containing a library and kitchen.

Amid the entries concerning those projects, he wrote on 10 April, "Engaged a house on the New York Avenue of Mr. McClennan [McClelland] rent 220$ per annum from 1st May." Mills had stayed with Nourse in January, armed with his proposal for the improvement of the poor acoustics within the House of Representatives. Confident of its acceptance, he had sent Eliza on 17 Janu-ary a brief letter together with a welcome $20,[187] and a harassed but resigned Eliza wrote to him from Abbeville on 6 February, "My corn is almost out, and my bacon quite gone, I shall be delighted to labor with you & am certain I can assist, perhaps it would be as well to try a boarding establishment, but I would wish to make it an object by getting as many boarders as I can.... Please send me some money. I am striving to extricate you here—so that we can get away honorably and I and the children are kept bare in consequence."[188] When he re-plied on 19 February to his "Beloved Friend," the Committee on Public Build-ings and Grounds wanted him to start on altering the House of Representatives and the Susquehannah Canal Company to "finish this [survey] work begun there."[189] Then came instructions for the final removal of their possessions—his "trunk of books" already on its way north, although bereft of some hundred copies of the now lost "Phylosophical Remarks on the Christian Religion." Finishing the letter two days later from Baltimore, he had snippets of news about old friends and a fascinating if pompous account of his attendance at President Jackson's New Year levée, "which was crowded to excess with the fashionable, the gay, and many of the plebian cast—I saw here the republican principle carried into effect, the heads of government mingling with the sover-eign people—It was an amusing scene—The room was splendidly furnished & lighted and all appeared pleased." Thanks to an order for an *Atlas* for the trea-sury, he could send the $10 and was "laying by what money I can to meet our expenses & provide for house keeping here." And, to assure Eliza that her talents could be exercised to the public good in Washington, he summarized a sermon he had heard on "Christian Liberality" commending the "interests of infant schools, particularly for the children of the poor—these are admirable institutions; and promise important results to society—I hope they may be en-couraged."

By 10 May, Eliza and the girls, although not all their chattels, had arrived at Savannah en route from Charleston heading for Washington, D.C. Their departure "from the place in which we have made an important figure for the last two years, and productive of some good in the Village I humbly believe" was quite an event. With the aid of their friends Colonel and Mrs. Noble, she had been able to pay the passage downriver to Augusta, while another local no-table, General Hodges, had bought Eliza's old slave Nanny for $75, sufficient to repay their debt and leave them with $25. "Heaven grant that we may all be preserved in health," she closed her letter, "and may the God of all our mercies provide for us & bless us & strengthen our faith in the precious promises held out in the Gosple of his dear son our lord & saviour."

Awaiting their arrival, Mills may have thought back over the decade spent in his native state. He could take pride in having instilled a much higher standard of public architecture, appropriately based on the best of its historical traditions. He had also improved the standards of construction and contracting, recorded the physical and social topography of South Carolina, and proposed enlightened schemes for its reform and development. If those remained fallow, to the detriment of its future, his handsome and practical Classical adaptations of the Southern Palladian heritage not only dignified towns across the state but also established a pattern adapted within and beyond its borders up to the mid-century, epitomized by the elegant architecture that Edward Brickell White completed in the 1840s and 1850s.[190] He could, as he had predicted when writing to Eliza on 30 September 1827, truly "have the satisfaction to think that I have in some measure paid the debt of gratitude to the State that gave me birth by the execution of the works I have done."[191]

5

Washington, 1830 – 1842
"engaged in the service of the general government"

By the end of May 1830, Mills and his family were settled in Washington, D.C. It was a courageous move, since the renovations of the House of Representatives were delayed, even if the District and federal government were expanding. "On one hand a rising city," he would write in the otherwise prosaic Introduction to his *Guide to the Capitol* (1834), "with its numerous avenues... its splendid public buildings, and hum of active life, on the other... the noble Potomac, rolling its ample tide to the ocean," rich, he might have added, with tasty shad that was salted and barreled for distribution throughout the United States. To the north lay the "range of high lands, with a varied scenery of groves and buildings"; to the southeast, the navy yard and marine barracks; to the south, the arsenal and penitentiary, while to the west lay Georgetown, "with its cluster of buildings rising in bold relief," and beyond the city of Alexandria stood General Washington's Mount Vernon, a "spot endeared to every American bosom."

The house Mills had rented from McClelland on the south side of New York Avenue between Thirteenth and Fourteenth streets placed him in sight of the President's House.[1] Not far distant was the Second Presbyterian Church, where the family would worship until 9 September 1835, when Mills and Eliza were "received as members of" the First Church under Moderator Reuben Post.[2] They lived amid a bustling community of nearly 9,000 people, including the transient politicians whose deliberations, recorded by Joseph Gales and William Seaton in the *Register of Debates in Congress* and thrice weekly *National Intelligencer and Washington Advertiser,* formed the sometimes intrusive background to Mills's permanent residence in the District. The most controversial was the nullification crisis, which had dominated public debate during his last years in South Carolina.[3] Although President Jackson had adopted Calhoun as his vice president before taking office in March 1829, he increasingly veered away from Calhoun's theory of free Union, ultimately in 1832 enforcing a new tariff bill that imposed higher duties on southern exports and imported manufactured goods. The rift that would precipitate Calhoun's resignation in December 1832 was growing in the months following Mills's move to Washington. With deep regret and divided allegiance, Mills must have observed the souring of President Madison's boast (inscribed on the vestibule wall of the Madison Building of the Library of Congress): "The happy union of the states is a wonder, their constitution a miracle, their example the hope of liberty throughout the world." That vision was being eroded by sectional concerns, the divisive aims of which were adeptly coated with pacific jargon. "Nullification," the South Carolina congressman Warren Davis had assured one correspondent in 1829, "*is* the rightful and peaceable remedy for federal usurption," while Senator Robert Y. Hayne in 1830 called it "a peaceable redress of our grievance."[4] If Mills admired Calhoun, and had lauded the leading nullifier, McDuffie, in the *Statistics* as a "distinguished Statesman and orator," his ultimate political sympathies lay with the unionism of Jackson.[5]

Mills's earliest architectural employment took him to the main political arena. Since the reopening of the reconstructed House in 1821 (now the Statuary Hall), the debates had suffered nearly as much from inaudibility as from partisanship or the vulgarities observed by Tocqueville during his 1834 tour of the United States.[6] Congressmen had chivied Charles Bulfinch, architect of the Capitol, who had erected a partition behind the speaker's chair and proposed installing a ceiling below the dome, believing the main problem to be the height of the chamber.[7] Alterations were made before Bulfinch's office was terminated, so Mills's intervention in January 1830 seemed particularly timely. Several congressmen had direct knowledge of his acoustical expertise, and he enjoyed the patronage of some powerful Southerners whom northern members of the first session of the Twenty-first Congress might have wished to propitiate in this less contentious manner. McDuffie, as Eliza learned in a letter he mailed from Washington on 17 January, had advised him to compose a "memorial addressed to the Speaker," Andrew Stevenson of Virginia, and declaring it the "most feasible plan that had yet been offered," arranged an interview with Mr. Clark of the Office of the Superintendent of Public Buildings.[8] As a result, Mills compiled a fuller version of his 1826 proposal: besides enclosing the colonnade screening the gallery, raising the floor to the level of the bases of the columns, and constructing a new gallery on the south wall, he recommended opening windows into the library and document room flanking the existing speaker's chair and adding two more doorways from the lobby off the rotunda.[9]

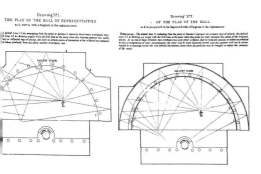

57.   Mills, (a) acoustical diagram of the
Hall of Representatives (1830), and (b)
sketch design of a Washington Monument
for the United States Capitol (1830).

b

But Mills's most radical suggestion was the removal of the speaker's chair from
the south wall to the middle of the inner curved wall next to the entrance of
the rotunda (57a).[11] Estimated at $7,000, these proposed alterations were pub-
lished in House Report 83 on 18 March 1830.

Mills's initiative paid dividends. Within the year he would be appointed a
draftsman of public surveys in the General Land Office (a bureau of the Treasury) at an annual salary of $1,150, $350 below the highest earnings then paid
to senior government clerks.[10] Awaiting the decision of the House and the arrival of his family, Mills on 17 March sent the Maryland Democrat George E.
Mitchell, chairman of the House Committee on the Centennial Birthday of
General Washington, the idea for a monument to be installed in the Capitol,
reviving a proposal presented before Congress just over sixteen years earlier by
a fellow South Carolinian, Benjamin Huger.[11] This and a succession of others
had withered, apart from the excavation of a vault beneath the center of the
crypt that Bulfinch had created under the rotunda. Mills wanted to install a
tomb surmounted by a statue of Washington extending into the rotunda (57b).
About 9 feet high, following the example of the great Italian sculptor Antonio
Canova's Neoclassical pyramidal monument of Pope Clement X in St. Peter's
at Rome—indicating knowledge of contemporary European art—the figure of
the general would be in "*Modern costume,* so managed as to produce a *classic effect.*" He proposed a brilliant synthesis of Classical and biblical allegory, with
contemporary dress and naturalistic appearance in the statue cut for the Virginia capitol by the French sculptor, J. A. Houdon: "All other statues fall into
the shade before this beautiful & correct representation."[12]

The committee declined to proceed in 1830, but Mills would revise the
scheme almost two years later when Congress again applied for entombment of

Washington's remains in the Capitol upon the centennial of his birth. On 9 February 1832 he addressed the Committee on Public Buildings, then chaired by Leonard Jarvis, a Democratic congressman from Maine, recommending the cutting of a circular aperture "so as to admit a light from the skylight of the Rotunda into the tomb below [in the Crypt] where the sarcophagus would be deposited, with which a flight of steps would communicate & upon the pillar around which the steps would wind to place a suitable monumental symbol."[13] Sketched on the back of a contemporary draft for a letter, he estimated their weight at between 10 and 15 tons but did not attempt to estimate costs for construction.[14] That same day he also delivered a general letter to the Centennial Committee (shortly to commission a marble statue from Horatio Greenough) stating the Unionist idealism that inspired his design: "The will of our political Father would be again brought in full force before his children . . . to heal all our political bickerings, and make us like a band of brothers united in love, and determined to preserve the integrity of the Union."[15] Mills was clearly convinced that art could nurture the ideological as well as the cultural growth of the nation.

He had been equally sure that his talents could improve the Capitol. His journal entry for 20 March 1830 records drawing "alterations of the center dome of Capitol, also in examining water courses about the city and proposed plan for supplying the Public buildings with water." Here he was working at the behest of the chairman of the Committee on Public Buildings, Gulian C. Verplanck, former professor of theology at the Protestant Episcopal Seminary in New York who, although a Federalist, had supported the Jackson ticket. In common with most Washington residents, Verplanck was dissatisfied by the dependence on well water, with its attendant danger of pollution or drought (a situation that persisted until Captain Montgomery C. Meigs constructed a piped system from Great Falls [1852–1853]). By 5 April, Verplanck had Mills's opinion that the best solution would be to pipe water to the President's House and public buildings from Rock Creek.[16] Mills's submission contributed to the laying down of pipes in 1832 along North Capitol Street that supplied water to large pools on the east and west fronts of the Capitol; among other benefits would be a reliable supply to the roof tank for periodically flushing the mahogany-seated lavatories that Mills later installed at the Capitol for a fee of $30.[17] Thereafter, he devised upgrading for the Tiber Basin of the newly opened Chesapeake and Ohio Canal and, on 17 April, recorded in his diary "an improvement" of the "entrance into the Capitol," almost certainly an abortive development of his design for "the decoration of the *Tympanum* of the *grand Portico* [East] of the *Capitol*" mentioned in a letter of 1 March 1828 to Gilmor.[18] In place of Luigi Persico's relief of an eagle and allegorical figures of Hope and America (1825–1834), Mills, as he stated in his 1834 *Guide to the*

Capitol, pictured Washington "in a chariot drawn by six horses abreast, coming out of the Capitol, crowned by Liberty and Wisdom; the whole encircled by a glory studded with the thirteen stars." Obviously, it resuscitated his original idea for the crowning feature of the Baltimore Washington Monument, whose board of managers had on 7 April sent him a further $200 for superintending the installation of the statue.[19]

Shortly after, Mills focused on the mandate of another committee, that for the Congressional Cemetery. The cemetery had been established at Eighteenth Street and Pennsylvania Avenue in 1812, since which time the committee commemorated the passing of the republic's legislators by erecting somber Neoclassical cenotaphs of a standard design by Latrobe. This procedure, Mills clearly decided, must soon involve considerable expenditure that could be better spent on one truly impressive edifice containing catacombs. So on 24 April he "Made a design for a Mausoleum" and "Communicated the same to the Chairman of the Committee Judge [Gershom] Powers [a member of Congress from New York]." His colored-wash elevation depicts a 100-foot-diameter and 50-foot-high rotunda enclosing 500 catacombs surmounted by a 76-foot column ornamented with the wreath and sword motif proposed for the Baltimore Washington Monument (58).[20] The forging of the Roman rotunda and column was possibly also influenced by J. Molinos and J. Legrand's unexecuted project for a Bastille monument, the engraving of which he could have seen in Jefferson's copy of the *Discours sur les monumens,* and by Latrobe's similarly constituted scheme for the Frank's Island Lighthouse, near the mouth of the Mississippi (1805–1809).[21]

Therefore, Mills had reason to boast in his 3 June 1830 letter to Gilmor about "the many improvements which I have suggested in the Capitol and approved by the Committees."[22] The Committee on Public Buildings had endorsed his $7,000 plan for altering the House, in part due to the "Experiments in the Hall to satisfy," as he had written to Gilmor on 7 May, "the correctness of the principles of sound advocated by me . . . that *sound* is subject to the same *general laws which govern light*"; on 8 April 1853, when corresponding with Captain Meigs about the extension of the Capitol, he would recall having in 1830 submitted his ideas on acoustics to a "Prof" in New York.[23] Such conscientiousness had impressed the members of the House, but as a disconsolate Mills informed Gilmor on 3 July 1830, the final vote on the appropriation was delayed by the "Indian question." Ironically, in view of Mills's concern for the native peoples, Jackson's Indian Removal Act (1827), ordering the sequestration of the Cherokee lands in northwestern Georgia, had encountered stubborn opposition.[24] Fortunately, by the middle of July the Congress endorsed Mills's plan, and work began immediately on building the partition in the House. Buoyant, he wrote to Gilmor on 6 August that even after the comple-

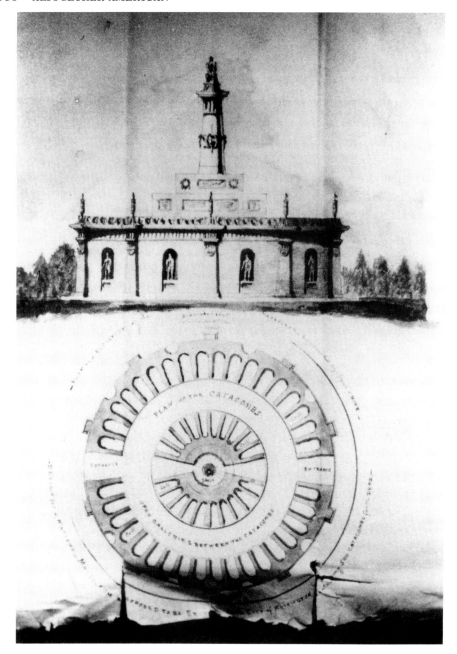

58.   Mills, design for the National Mausoleum, Washington, D.C. (1830).

tion of "but a small section," a "member who previously never could distinguish what was said in the house was astonished by receiving a distinct conveyance of the voice of the speaker to his ear" and "many of the Members agreed unanimously to recommend to the house the adoption of all the improvements which I have suggested."[25] He even pompously boasted that he could transform the rotunda, then "a perfect *Babel*," into one of the "best speaking and hearing rooms in the world."

"I am doing some business," Mills also told Gilmor, "for the Treasury superintendent in the professional way." He was referring to the commission to put up "Privies & engine house" for pumping well water between the Treasury and State departments east of the President's House. These cost some $1,720, exceeding his estimate due. Mills claimed that the excess expense was due to the substitution of tin roofs, a material that must have made use of the privies disconcertingly noisy in the summer thunder and hail storms of Washington.[26] On 16 October, a few days after presenting the final account, he submitted a $21,792 proposal for running a 1500-foot iron railing atop a stone coping around the four executive buildings, the first of several propositions aimed at beautifying the "President's Square." That lay fallow, but the Treasury, through its chief clerk, Asbury Dickins, would ask him to draw plans in December to provide a "vaulted Room under the fireproof building to adapt it for the reception of papers." He complied by 14 March 1831, certain that for about $886 a space 70 feet by 18 feet could be excavated 2.5 feet below ground level under the "Treasury Fireproof" that Latrobe had added in 1805.[27] Lath and plaster partitions divided the room into four compartments that communicated through arched openings, the fireproofing supplied by cement floors, and iron doors and window sash.

Mills's good standing with Congress brought another commission, related to Gilmor on 3 November, to provide additional temporary seating "arrangements in the Senate chamber for the trial of Judge James Hawkins Peck."[28] It came via McDuffie, one of the managers of the trial appointed by the House, and involved installing temporary seating in Latrobe's beautiful but cramped semicircular chamber. The case was an important test of the legitimacy of land grants disbursed by the Spanish and French authorities in upper Louisiana before the territory was admitted into the Union as the state of Missouri. At issue was the 1825 decision of Judge Peck of the U.S. District Court of Missouri to reject one claim and convict Luke Lawless, attorney for the defeated claimant, of contempt. Peck's judgment was upheld, while Mills earned $30.[29]

Equally valuable recognition came in Mills's election on 1 November to the Columbian Institute for the Promotion of Arts and Sciences, chartered by Congress in 1818 to compile a "topographical and statistical history of the different districts of the United States," to establish a museum, library, and

5-acre botanical garden, prefiguring the aims of the Smithsonian Institution.[30] Mills was moved for membership by William Elliot, a senior official in the Patent Office and friend of Asbury Dickins, who, as secretary, had designed its seal—combining the Roman fasces, Christian cross, and American eagle and stars.[31] Meeting in the Capitol basement, members read papers on scientific and philosophical subjects, as well as civic improvements. In January 1826, the members of the institute suggested that the government pipe water from the Tiber Creek to a reservoir in Capitol Square to supply the botanical garden below, to improve local firefighting, and to create such amenities as a 30-foot-high "beautiful jet d'eau"—a phrase that Mills would later employ in describing landscaping schemes for the District. The institute consistently acknowledged the architectural profession by electing to membership Latrobe, Bulfinch, and Hadfield, along with politicians sympathetic to their cause such as Jefferson, Jackson, Calhoun, and Poinsett (a corresponding member since August 1824 and whom Mills was to propose as a resident member on 24 June 1837). Mills would attend regularly from January 1831 to March 1838 and be elected a "Counsellor" on 5 January 1835, perhaps in recognition of voluntary tasks such as the preparation of plans for a large brick, wood, and glass greenhouse, estimated at a mere $300 but beyond the resources of the institute.[32]

Among the members were William Seaton and Joseph Gales, editors of the *National Intelligencer,* in which Mills on Tuesday, 4 January 1831 "respectfully tended his professional services to his fellow citizens generally" and offered to furnish "Gentlemen in any part of the Union" with "designs, drawings, etc upon moderate terms." Although that transgressed Latrobe's 1806 stricture, Mills's main purpose might have won his favor: "Mr. Mills has concluded to take a class of young men into his office, and give them a course of professional instruction." He vaunted the most "favorable opportunities" for study presented by Washington and the now thriving Baltimore, adding the wishful thought, "The rising importance and value of the profession to our country, justifies the hope that no state of the Union will be without its own native Architect and Engineer." In fact, Mills's idea seems to have owed something to Eliza's Abbeville school and to the Washington Female Academy, which she was busy organizing aided by her older daughters. Apart from completing the education of their other children—Anna's record card survives to this day—Eliza was seeking to vie with such well-established secondary schools in the area as the Georgetown Seminary, which attracted pupils from across the United States and Canada.[33] Mills tempted parents of potential students with the assurance "that every attention will be paid to their moral deportment equally with professional advancement."

Yet few, if any, replies appear to have reached him at his temporary office in the north wing of the Capitol. There he was preparing an estimate for enclosing the ground to its west with an iron railing 3,650 feet long, calculated at $26,540 by 7 January, and overseeing minor alterations to the Supreme Court for which he countersigned bills to the sum of $23,380 on 12 January.[34] Then in March, Congress approved an appropriation of $2,100 to "take down, remove, repair, reconstruct, & complete the Naval Mon[ument]. at Navy Yard" agreeably to the "drawings & specifications shown us by Mr. Robt. Mills Architect."[35] The Naval, or Tripoli, Monument had been cut by the Italian sculptor Charles Micali of Leghorn to commemorate "the memory of the officers, seamen and marines of the U.S. Navy who fell in support of the Union and the liberty of the country" while serving with the squadron that Jefferson had sent in 1801 to patrol the coast of Tripoli (present-day Libya).[36] The tiered monument, decorated with allegorical figures and short Roman rostral column, had suffered considerable damage from weathering since its erection in 1808 at the Washington Navy Yard. Consequently, Mills instructed the competing contractors to submit proposals for its repair and reerection on a new marble base in the oval basin on the lower of the two earth berms Bulfinch had created on the west side of the Capitol. Installed before October 1831, it remained there before being removed to the Naval Academy at Annapolis between 1860 and 1862.

Mills was fast becoming unofficial federal architect, in March 1831 being asked by Dickins to prepare specifications for "Alterations of Treasury offices." To accommodate the growth in public business, Mills inserted brick-vaulted rooms at each level of the existing building, sandwiching at the rear a reconstructed semicircular staircase.[37] He signed a certificate for the completed work by 21 September and received a fee of $75. But he still hustled for more important commissions. The unsanitary overcrowding of Bulfinch's city jail, constructed in 1826 at Fourth and P streets Southwest (the modern Fort McNair), probably prompted him about this time to draw the impressively functional "Design for a Prison calculated to hold about 300 Prisoners in separate rooms beside providing for the requisited Offices, Refectories, Hospital, & c " (59). The drawing is inscribed in Old English and plain script, and signed "Robt. Mills Engr. & Archt. city of Washington 1831."[38] It delineates only the main floor of the U-plan prison, clearly inspired by Latrobe's Virginia Penitentiary (1797–1798). Sixty cells on five floors, 8 feet by 12 feet, separated by a 10-foot-wide corridor, extend like curved vertebrae from each side of a central structure accommodating the keeper and wardens, washing and toilet facilities in the basement, and a hospital on the top story. The building is fronted by a six-column portico on the main floor served by two side staircases, recalling his design for the Savannah Courthouse. At the rear, a single staircase provides access from the 70-foot-diameter inner exercise court through a four-column portico bent around the semicircular ended main staircase. Subsidiary stair-

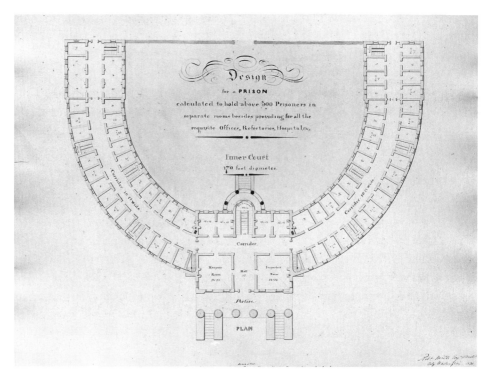

59.   Mills, design for a prison, Washington, D.C. (1831).

ways in the wings link the cells with large, vaulted workrooms and refectories. The city council and alderman could not persuade Congress to release the requisite funding. Thus Mills's concept languished while Bulfinch's jail was enlarged in 1831 and eventually demolished in the 1860s.

The scraps remaining from his 1831 papers indicate that, despite his salary from the Land Office, he was still troubled with debt, if able on 14 March to pay the $10.58 taxes due to the state of Virginia on the 24,000 acres of his Bath Lands property.[39] His finances soon improved, thanks to the commission in April from the Treasury for a marine hospital in his native Charleston. His plan for its main building related to the central block of the prison design, with the semicircular rear staircase and cross-axial corridor leading to short wings set at right angles like his Burlington County Jail. In fact, the marine hospital design might have preceded the prison plan, since Treasury Secretary Ingham wrote on 19 April to the collector at Charleston that having compared drawings by Frederick Wesner with those of Mills, he had "concluded to adopt that of the latter gentleman."[40] For a fee of $300 paid on 10 May 1831, he was required to supply working drawings and specifications, and to seek estimates from a "competent contractor" for a brick structure, two stories above a base-

60.   Mills, Marine Hospital, Charleston (1832–1833).

ment, divided into the main block and two rear wings, each with a piazza to agument cross-ventilation.[41] The main block contained three surgical wards on the first floor, and four medical and one venereal on the second, together with accommodation for the steward. Symbolically appropriate to its function, the outer elongated pointed arches and thin colonettes of the intervening piazza simulate the Gothic style of the medieval hospice (60). Those features might have been inspired by engravings in Britton's *Architectural Antiquities*, presented to him by Latrobe, whose unexecuted 1812 scheme for the Washington Naval Hospital also influenced Mills's plan. Latrobe had been advised by the U.S. Naval Surgeon William Barton, who on a visit to Europe had been particularly impressed by the Royal Naval Hospital at Haslar (1746–1762), near Portsmouth, England, comprising a main block with side wings. This plan afforded good cross-ventilation and, therefore, improved sanitation, effective separation between the different wards, efficient communication between the floors, and semienclosed exercise space. However, the majority of hospitals erected in the United States before the Charleston Marine Hospital, including Strickland's U.S. Naval Asylum in Philadelphia, and Haviland's contemporary U.S. Naval Hospital at Norfolk, Virginia (1827–1832), had impressive Greek-style exteriors but less convenient plans.

Those hospitals were also much more expensive than Mills's hospital, not least because he was keen in scrutizing the contractors' offers. Those from Charleston he thought excessive and so braving the nullifiers, recommended the Washingtonian Daniel Holmans, with whom a contract was signed on 31 May for $12,100. That coincided with an order from the new treasury secretary, Louis McLane, to move the site from Hampstead to a plot at the intersection of the modern Queen and Mazyack streets. Here Mills's attractively simple building was erected and in operation from November 1833, for a mere $263 over the estimate, an unusually good performance at that time. Some nine months later, Mills proudly reminded President Jackson that he had saved the government nearly $8,000 by rejecting the greed and incompetence of the Charleston contractors.[42] The hospital continued in use until the Civil War, successively serving as a school and an orphanage until 1938, when the main building was restored as part of a low-cost housing development, a use that is entirely appropriate to Mills's reforming social views.

Fortune favored Mills's efforts. That summer he saw another opportunity associated with the opening in 1830 of the first section of the Chesapeake and Ohio Canal (reaching Cumberland in 1837 and Baltimore in 1846)—a chance to revive the Washington Canal. Dug from 1810 to 1815 under Latrobe's eye, the canal began at Tiber Creek off the Potomac between the present Lincoln Memorial and Washington Monument. The cut moved east along the line of the modern Constitution Avenue, turning sharply south across the base of Capitol Hill, and thereafter branched into two arms terminating at the harbor and on the Eastern Branch. Apart from facilitating the delivery of materials during the reconstruction of the Capitol after the War of 1812, the canal was too narrow and shallow to be a commercial success. On 3 January 1831, to protect local commercial interests, the city authorized funds for its improvement and completion by the ailing Washington Canal Company.[43] By 1 September he had finished his "plan of the Washington Canal from the mouth of the Tiber Creek to the Eastern Branch with its connection with the Chesapeake & Ohio Canal and the proposed Basins for the two Canals," deftly combining three plans on one sheet.[44] On his second plan, he indicated a pattern of streets radiating around a "Monument," likely the monument to the Revolution desired by President Washington and prophetically close to the site of his own Washington National Monument on what is now the Mall. He delivered the drawings to the Washington Canal Board shortly before 15 September when, to the great sorrow of the family, Eliza's mother died at Hackwood. Her death must have seemed to end an era in his married life.

Although Mills's improvements to the Washington Canal were not implemented, they won for him the post of engineer to the company. In that capacity, in May 1832, he signed a drawing inscribed only "No. 3," a plan for

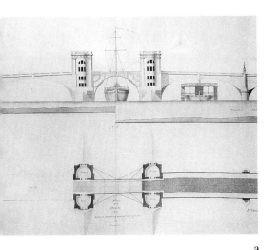

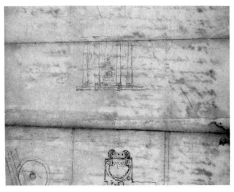

b

a

61.   Mills, designs for (a) a bridge between Washington, D.C., and Arlington (1832), and (b) a new entrance to the Hall of Representatives (1832).

increasing the flow of water in the section from the Tiber Basin to the foot of the Capitol by redirecting the Tiber into the Anacostia River.[45] In August 1832 he labored on two other designs intended to enhance the commerce of the local canal systems in the face of growing competition from the Erie Canal and Baltimore and Ohio Railroad.[46] They illustrate an aqueduct bridge to cross the Potomac and thereby allow the canal boats to bypass the Georgetown wharves and dock in the port of Alexandria. Both designs envisage a wood frame bridge constructed with lattice truss sections braced by two levels of elliptical arches supported on piled stone piers. Neither was adopted, although from 1838 to 1841 an aqueduct was built over the Potomac upriver from the present Key Bridge. Another, and exceptionally long, drawing he made, perhaps in 1832, pictures a bridge to join the city of Washington with Arlington (61a).[47] The roadway rises from each bank on stone piers to towers that were to house machinery for retracting projected spans mounted on semicircular toothed wheels, far ahead of such famous bascular bridges as Tower Bridge in London (1886–1894) by Sir John Barry and Sir Horace Jones. Mills's imagination greatly exceeded federal resources, as did the report he compiled for Commissioner of Public Buildings Joseph Elgar, in collaboration with the engineer J. A. Dumeste, on potential sources of water, including Smith's Spring (which was eventually to be acquired by the government in October 1833).[48] Nothing came of their investigations, but the House did ask Mills to resubmit his remaining proposals for improving their chamber. Restated with some revisions in a paper deliver on 4 February 1832, it was printed in House Report 495 at the end of June.

Again he recommended closing in the gallery, but behind the third row of seats, raising the floor level, and relocating the position of the speaker's chair. Now he cited the French Chamber of Deputies by Bernard Poyet (1806–1807) as corroboration for his belief that the arc of the semicircular north wall would amplify the speaker's voice and clarify the member's speeches (compare with Mills's 1830 diagram [57a]). The "*form*" rather than the "*size*" of the room, he maintained, "constitutes it a good or bad speaking and hearing room," continuing with what many might have accepted as self-confidence but others found arrogant. He could construct "a room which would hold five or ten thousand persons, in which the voice in a common tone, would be distinctly heard at the most distant points in it." His qualifications soundly declared, he proceeded to list extra improvements, including the creation of a much-needed second entrance on the south side (61b).[49] If Mills's boasting failed to sway the politicians, it had already come to the uncharitable notice of at least one of his professional peers. On 4 June, Ithiel Town wrote from Fayetteville, North Carolina, where he was engaged in the construction of one of his patent scissor-truss bridges, to his partner Davis, then in Washington seeking federal commissions for their expanding office.[50] In referring to Davis's contemplated book on "the science & practice of Architecture," Town counseled that under no circumstances "should you talk with Mills about the plan of such a book, he would be very likely to anticipate the plan & say that he had intended it himself."

Actually Mills had been working on a very different literary project, which was published in Washington about the time he received a payment of $100 on 27 August for designing and overseeing the construction of "stairways to [the] Senate Chamber gallery, sheet iron fascial columns for air flues."[51] His book was *The American Pharos or Light House Guide: founded on official reports received at The Treasury Department; also a general view of the coast, from the St. Lawrence to the Sabine. To which is added An Appendix, containing an account of the Light Houses on the gulf and River St. Lawrence, with sailing directions for the St. Lawrence founded on official reports from the Trinity Board of Quebec in 1832.* It was printed by Peter Force, an avid collector of material on American history, editor and publisher of the *National Journal,* and fellow member of the Columbian Institute. The text Mills prefaced with a poetic couplet as applicable to his own aspirations as to a lighthouse:

> It looks lovely as hope;
> That star of life's tremulous ocean.

He had been assembling material since well before 25 November 1830, when he told Gilmor of his desire to "serve commerce & the Mariner's safety," but the original idea resulted from a "commission from Scotland to obtain information on our Lighthouses for a work to be published thereon the light houses of Great Britain, which I sent in; the present work I am engaged in is on an enlarged & more valuable scale." It exhibited Mills's talent for collecting prodigious amounts of detailed information, even if a considerable part of the most thorough material had been supplied by the British authorities in Quebec.[52]

Mills did not neglect daily tasks at the Land Office. His duties included handling correspondence with the registers and receivers in numerous local centers, recording sales of public lands, and the associated updating of the accounts and maps. The office handled a great deal of business, amounting to almost $200,000 between 1828 and 1829.[53] The problems those officials confronted, and on which the federal office had often to rule, revolved around the abuse of the preemption system, which extended the right of ownership to settlers. They were summed up in a letter written on 8 May 1831 by Receiver Gideon Fritz of the Mount Salus, Mississippi, office to Commissioner Elijah Hayward, quite possibly read by Mills. "At present," Fritz complained in the wake of President Jackson's order to sell forfeited and relinquished land, "it is customary for the leader of a party of speculators to agree with a number of dealers, with their witnesses men, women & children, to meet on a certain day, at the Registers office—they come like the locusts of Egypt & darken the office, with clouds of smoke & dust, and an uproar occasioned by Whiskey & avarice, that a Register at least can never forget." The protection of the registers' and receivers' records, as Mills immediately realized, was vital. He seems to have submitted a standard design for the local offices, either to the commissioner or to those registers in need of new accommodations. One of those commissioners might have been Colonel Samuel Gwin in Clinton, Mississippi, who was related to the Mississippi senator to whom Mills would send a transcontinental railroad scheme in 1852. On 9 November 1832, Gwin informed Commissioner Hayward, "We are now building one fire proof which will soon be completed. It will cost about $500." Thus it must have been a small brick structure, perhaps not even vaulted. Gwin went on to present a version of the functional argument Mills frequently made to penny-pinching legislators: "As the Gov. is more deeply interested in the preservation of their records than any other person & as this is a very heavy expense to us who are dependent for every thing, I would ask if it would comport with your ideas to grant the use of 500 dollars to the erection of this building, *holding* the Receiver responsible for the money & I being responsible for my proportion." The office was opened before 22 December when Gwin requested desks to store the all-important maps. By such small means, the fabric of a great nation was created.

Shortly before Gwin wrote for the desks, Mills suffered "an accident in the fall of a bridge [possibly the unstable Long Bridge across the Potomac] I was passing over," as Gilmor learned in a letter dated 2 January 1833.[54] "By a kind [act?] of Providence I had no limb broken, but a severe inward bruise about my ankle." He had been confined to a bed for at least three weeks. Happily, he was sufficiently recovered by 21 January to write to Robert Oliver in Baltimore, upon hearing that Congress had received an application from the city for aid to improve its harbor.[55] Thereupon, he addessed "a few lines to you on the subject," concentrating on methods of removing silt. In the postscript, he also offered to send along a plan for an addition to the exchange, a wing intended for a hotel. This enforced period of recuperation allowed him to catch up on various of his initiatives: three years later, on 4 July 1836, he would remind President Jackson of the plans for extending and landscaping the Capitol grounds that he had submitted to the Committee on Public Buildings at this time; he had probably also submitted designs for a federal Washington Monument.[56]

In the wake of the moves by Congress to mark the centennial of Washington's birth, a group of private citizens under the leadership of George Watterston, librarian of Congress, began to discuss the possibility of erecting a monument in the District. The deliberations resulted in the formation of the Washington National Monument Society at the city hall on 26 September 1833, presided over by the redoubtable Chief Justice John Marshall, assisted by Judge William Cranch, with whom Mills corresponded.[57] The aim of the society was to collect subscriptions of $1 from citizens in every state. Adept at searching out potential architectural prizes, Mills apparently dashed off his "Description of the National Monument to Washington proposed to be Erected by the Citizens of the United States at the City of Washington."[58]

The paper described an extraordinary monument quite different from the one he would erect on the Mall, but redolent with his allegorical imagination and fascination with the sublime. An enormous four-sided rusticated pyramid, 1,000 feet square at the base, and soaring 650 feet, would support "a collossian statue of Washington 1000 feet in full high."[59] At each corner were to be oblelisks 45 feet square and 350 feet tall, while the pyramid was to be divided into seven "grand states or terraces," diminishing in height from 112 feet to 30 feet, buttressed by arches fronting galleries extending through the width of the pyramid. On the first stage would be thirteen arches to symbolize the union of the original states, screened by a "series of Massy pillars" 13 feet in diameter and 76 feet high in order to sustain the architectural allusion to the Revolution. The number of arches diminished proportionally to three on the fifth stage, changing to fluted pilasters enframing historical and biographical inscriptions on the sixth, and wreaths encircling the single word "Washington" on the seventh. The stages were to be linked by an inclined ascending plane "so that carriages may ascend & descend with ease & safety, & the visitor may be conveyed to the top without fatigue," foreshadowing the spiral ramp for automobiles that Frank Lloyd Wright was to plan in 1925 for the unexecuted Gordon Strong Observatory and Auto Object atop Sugar Loaf Mountain in Maryland.[60] Mills's ever fecund if fanciful invention also prefigured a feature of Bartholdi's Statue of Liberty in New York Harbor (1870–1886), since a stairway was to climb "through [the] Washington Statue & into vaulted apartments disposed at intervals terminating in a little observatory in the head of the Statue."

Probably before Mills wrote out that fantastical description, Congress in March 1833 had at last voted funds for altering the House of Representatives according to his 1830 program. Its decision was, incidentally, recorded by the clerk of the House and Washington Monument board member, the Pennsylvanian Matthew St. Clair Clarke, whom he had met in Philadelphia. To Clark's endorsement was added that of the speaker, James K. Polk from Tennessee, who later asked Mills to design a house for him. The appropriation was for $13,000, including the architect's fee of $1,000.[61] He was to alter the position of the speaker's chair, raise the floor level, and upgrade the public galleries. Also he was ordered to supervise the design and rearrangement of the new desks for the members, the repair of the clock above the speaker's chair, and the refurbishment of draperies and spittle-stained carpets.[62] Thus over the summer recess, Mills radically changed the interior of the House from its appearance as reinstated by Latrobe and Bulfinch, which had been arrestingly depicted in 1821–1822 by Samuel F. B. Morse.[63] Most congressmen, Mills was to tell Gilmor on 19 May 1834, expressed a "general satisfaction" that "the alterations made have proved really improvements, the great object, being in the main, accomplished with improving the effect of the voice,—The curve of the dome still makes the room too lofty and those speaking in the line of the semidiameter of the room are subject to a slight reverberation."[64] Although his admission of incomplete acoustical success proved to be true, the immediate reaction was sufficiently positive to further enhance Mills's reputation with the legislators. By dint of hard work and initiative he had founded a federal practice.

Hard upon the House commission, Mills was asked by Treasury Secretary McLane to report on the arson fire that destroyed the Treasury on 31 March 1833.[65] Indirectly promoting his qualifications at fireproof construction, Mills stressed that the fireproof wing and some small vaulted rooms adjoining the center block on the north side alone had escaped damage; his 4 July 1836 letter to President Jackson implies that he may even have appended a design for the new building.[66]

Whether or not Mills sent such a design—the commission remained in limbo for three years—his abilities were recognized. Soon after, McLane hired him to enlarge the courthouse in St. Augustine, Florida, for the the receiver of the public moneys (although he did not receive his $100 fee until February 1836). The commission was well in hand when Mills wrote on 18 September 1833 to the new secretary, William Duane, advising that the local collector advertise for proposals "agreeably to the plans ... [which] embrace every accommodation for the offices required at the least expenditure consistent with decent appearance."[67] These delineated Neoclassical additions to the existing building erected by the Spanish colonial government prior to 1821, when it was acquired for the United States during the governorship of Andrew Jackson.[68] The end walls were stuccoed and divided into three sections, while along the flanks a double colonnade of ten plain columns standing on square piers afforded both shade and architectural consequence, metaphorically marching his work to the Classical rhythm of republican democracy (62).

But this was a modest job compared with the July 1833 commission for four new customhouses in New England and, shortly after, the Appraisers' Stores in Baltimore; as Dunlap would note in 1834, "Mr. Mills is now engaged in the service of the general government."[69] The Federal government initially agreed on appropriations of $9,800 each for the customhouses at Middletown and New London, Connecticut, $15,000 for Newburyport, and $23,000 for New Bedford, Massachusetts, with $50,000 for the Appraisers' Stores in Baltimore, and paid him a handsome $200 for each set of designs with an extra $50 for the stores.[70] To gain five federal commissions was a notable achievement, particularly since 90 percent of the federal revenues right up to the time of the Civil War derived from custom duties.

Mills, keen as in South Carolina to create durable and distinguished buildings, asked for a leave of absence from Treasury Secretary R. B. Taney on 11 October 1833.[71] He was indirectly aided by the collectors, who pointed out the differing local conditions, J. W. Crawford complaining that Mills had not been "accurately informed with respect to the angle of descent from the street to the iver [Thames]" at New London and later that the local masons considered "the outer walls should be of greater thickness."[72] Consequently, Mills assured Duane on 14 August that he could upon personal inspection "reduce their estimates several thousand dollars; and ... reduce the nature of the work down to the standard of the appropriation, retaining as much of the fire proof character ... as practicable."[73] Duane concurred, instructing Mills on 16 September 1833 to visit the four New England towns in order to finalize contracts for the foundations and obtain the proposals, as well as to examine the site selected for the Appraisers' Stores in Baltimore. As a result, revisions were made, in the case of the stores apparently involving an increase in budget and scale. Mills had presented drawings for the stores using an economical brick structure since, on 16 September 1833, the auditor of the United States certified

62.   Mills, enlargement of courthouse, St. Augustine, Florida (1833).

that "the sum of two hundred and fifty dollars is due to him for designs, specifications and estimates, for the custom house stores proposed to be built at the
southeast corner of Gay and Water Streets" submitted in December 1833 and
estimated at $43,000 for a fireproof building encased in granite (noting that
the $50,000 appropriation ignored the $30,000 required to purchase the site).[74]
On 4 October 1833 the Baltimore surveyor and building contractor James
Mosher, who had earlier mailed plans to Secretary McLane, wrote to his successor Taney, "I understand that something more ornamental is now contemplated than a plain brick building."[75] Taney countenanced a fivefold increase in
the budget for the Appraisers' Stores, allowing Mills to conceive a much
grander brick and granite building, which was begun in July 1834.

The delay in the program suited Mills's private agenda. For on 17 September his daughter Jacqueline married Edward Pendleton. Eldest son of a respected family from Culpepper County, Virginia, Edward must have seemed
an excellent match. Within the year and to celebrate the birth of their first
grandchild, Eliza presented him with the deed of a plot (100 feet by 50 feet) at
the southeast corner of F and Ninth streets, which she bought in November
1833.[76] Pendleton would prosper, although not by means that his parents-in-
law could have approved. He opened what became the most fashionable gaming
house in the District, the Palace of Fortune between 4½ and Sixth streets, on

the questionable side of Pennsylvania Avenue, and lent money to many congressmen, thereby acquiring considerable power as a lobbyist.

The delay also allowed Mills to renew his interest in the subject of transportation. In the fall of 1833 he evidently read accounts of the performance of Goldsworthy Gurney's steam carriage between Bath and London from 1827, which had been published in 1831 by a select committee of the British Parliament, and by 1 January 1834 had compiled a twelve-page manuscript, which was to be published that fall by the *American Railroad Journal* under the title "Substitute for Railroads and Canals embracing a New Plan for Roadways; combining with the operation of steam carriages, great economy in carrying into effect a system of Internal Improvement." Once again, his enthusiasm derailed his powers of pragmatic analysis. He underplayed the expense of constructing the necessarily more substantial two-lane roadways required by the heavy steam carriages, and took no real account of the problems of American topography. Contemplating the use of macadam paving, he underestimated the average cost per mile, $13,600 compared with $53,640 for the Baltimore and Ohio Railroad, but inflated the carrying capacity, potential speed, and traction of the steam carriage. He even argued that the mountainous terrain in the United States would suit the "Undulating Roadway" principle of down-grade acceleration discussed by, among others, the famed British engineer Robert Stephenson. In only one respect was his optimism justified—the ability of the steam carriage to "travel in any direction."[77]

Mills was in addition able to work on proposals for a new Patent Office to be erected on a block bounded by G and F and Seventh and Ninth streets, which L'Enfant had intended for a national pantheon. Besides being the first major federal commission in the District since Hoban's State and War departments, the Patent Office was regarded as an essential factor in achieving technical advances fundamental to the development of American agriculture and industry. The interest in technology had led to the founding in 1824 of the Franklin Institute at Philadelphia (where Thomas U. Walter gave lectures on architecture from 1825) and fueled the idea of the superior inventive genius of the free American. "The invention of the cotton gin, the steamboat, the spike machines-card machines, the telegraph, and nearly ten thousand other patented inventions," a contributor to the 22 January 1851 issue of *Scientific American* would declare, "are some evidences of the benefit confirmed upon our country by the genius and labors of inventors." Similar sentiments had motivated the House Committee on Patents on 2 April 1834 to seek estimates for a new "fireproof building" to replace the unsatisfactory accommodation in the former Blodgett's Hotel.

Mills handed two related designs to Commissioner of Public Buildings Major William Noland, the first on 9 April 1834 and the second a week later.[78]

Each faced stiff competition from the plans entered by Superintendent of Patents John D. Craig, and by Town and Davis in collaboration with William Parker Elliot, Jr., who like his father, William Sr., had been employed in the Patent Office.[79] Craig drew a rectangular structure measuring 120 feet by 50 feet, supported internally on cast-iron pillars and roofed with wrought-iron plates, inspired by recent British and European warehouse and factory design. Town, Davis, and Elliot delivered an altogether grander E-plan Greek Revival scheme, whereas Mills aimed his designs toward a lower budget, concentrating on the overriding requirements of fire prevention and capacity. The main block measured 150 feet by 60 feet, flanked by two wings linked across the front by a raised colonnade (although unspecified, it was probably to be of the Doric order). Standing on the basement, this colonnade both recalled his Southern Palladian architecture and anticipated the Neo-Greek stoa of his 1836 Treasury design. He could also have been influenced by a famous French building he much admired, Louis Le Vau's east front of the Louvre (1667). Mills's colonnade would have shaded the southern exposure of the two upper floors reached by the "roomy" staircases at each end of the central corridor branching from the entrance vestibule. Those stairs led to the administrative offices on the main floor, arranged about cross-axial corridors, and to the "grand Model Saloon," 146 feet by 52 feet, on the second floor, with potential for a third floor. Depending on the extent of fireproofing, he calculated the cut-freestone and brick structure at $60,000 or $70,000. Not surprisingly, Noland questioned Mills's figures and asked Richard J. Holdsworth, a clerk in his office, to check all the estimates. Holdsworth reckoned that Mills should have allowed $105,423.76, not least because he intended to use 116 tons of iron for window sashes, roof plates, and "columns and joists" in the Model Saloon. By comparison, he tallied Craig's plan at $67,346.50.

A disconcerted Mills disputed these estimates on 15 May, in part because he learned that Holdsworth had himself entered a design.[80] To keep the initiative, Mills sent in a revised scheme having the same H plan but in which the dimensions were reduced to 120 feet by 50 feet, fireproofing was confined to the brick vault, and iron was employed only for the window sash. He broke his second design into four alternatives: the first was limited to the erection of the center block in brick for little over $36,000; the second included the wings for an extra $5,000; the third called for the colonnade, also called the "Doric portico," raising the price to $47,316.30; while the fourth option envisaged the whole structure encased in cut stone for a total of $59,316.30. "The above estimates," he stated, "are predicated upon the plan of *arching* all the rooms with *brick,* the cheapest as well as the most secure from fire, compared with cast iron, as a substitute." Each version was also to have been roofed in copper or zinc. Not long thereafter he sent Noland a third design almost as large as his first, the main block of 150 feet by 54 feet, but again divided into four separate estimates.[81] Now he costed the variation between the brick and stone alternatives at $48,816 and $70,000, and, to quash Craig, reiterated that his brick vaulting would be "the cheapest as well the most secure from fire, compared with cast iron."

Despite the urgings of Craig, his successor Henry Ellsworth, and Senator John Ruggles, chairman of the Patent Committee, more than two years passed before Congress granted the necessary appropriations in July 1836 under the Patent Law for what would be described as the "National Gallery for the exhibition of specimens of American skill and ingenuity."[82] By then, the models were piling up in Blodgett's Hotel, but the hiatus benefited Mills, since his first unrealistic estimates escaped congressional scrutiny. He also had time to publish a profitable handbook for both tourists and lobbyists, following the lead of S. A. Elliot's *Washington Guide* (1830).[83]

The title was lengthy but explanatory: *Guide to the Capitol of the United States embracing every information useful to the visitor whether on business or pleasure* (1834). Amid the keyed plans, Mills allowed himself a scattering of criticisms of the building. The north and south fronts appeared "too flat and unmeaning," while Bulfinch's crypt was a "complete forest of massy doric columns." With the exception of the Supreme Court, flawed by "several radical defects," he lauded Latrobe's work, as well as the pictures in the rotunda of incidents from the Revolution painted by Colonel John Trumbull.[84] He also slipped in a couple of his own ideas for improving the Capitol. One was the addition of porticoes with curved steps on the south and north flanks; the other was for a staircase into the gallery of the rotunda (to be taken up by Walter when he extended the structure two decades later).[85] Without doubt, Mills's ulterior purpose was to lay claim to further federal architectural assignments, and with some success.

On 9 July 1834 Mills wrote to Noland, "With a view to devote my attention exclusively to my proffesional business I have resigned my situation as draftsman in the General Land Office and would request of you to give me what professional business you may have to do about the public buildings—the *Avenue* & c."[86] The resignation seems foolhardy; yet besides the resumption of work on the customhouses, he appears to have had reason for believing that he would continue to receive federal commissions. He even felt able to move his residence to a property on a north corner of E and Eighth and Ninth streets, quite close to the current Patent Office and Post Office, perhaps partly to afford Eliza additional space for her academy, which seems to have been attached to their household. One positive indication had been the invitation in 1834 to install a fountain at the center of the basement arcade on the west terrace of the Capitol to discharge water piped from Smith's Spring.[87] The ensemble, replacing an old iron pipe, originally served by a well, was fashioned after a Classical grave stele and praised in the 11 November 1834 issue of the *National Intelligencer*.[88] Placed on "a square pedestal of white marble, at each corner of which is a beautiful column of Philadelphia clouded marble," the fountain was "surmounted with a fanciful capital of Italian marble richly carved [by Hiram Powers, resident in the District 1834–1837]" and "discharged into a large white marble basin of beautiful workmanship, which is supported by a handsome column of Potomac marble." Although it was named for Powers rather than for Mills, the fountain, as the newspaper subsequently noted, provided a "constant stream of pure spring water, about 20 gallons per minute." Noland, in his 1834 annual report, accounted the "tasty work" at $1,021.77.[89] That might have included a fee for Mills's drawings, unless it formed part of the $100 payment he received on 6 February 1835, ostensibly for superintending the recoppering of the main dome of the Capitol.[90] The fountain remained in use until 1884, when removed to St. Elizabeth's Hospital prior to the reconstruction of the west front of the Capitol by Frederick Law Olmsted.

Mills's letter of resignation also shortly preceded an official directive from Treasury Secretary Levi Woodbury, ordering him on 28 July 1834 to visit each of the customhouses "with a view to suggesting certain improvements in the plans designed by you."[91] In all likelihood, he boarded a sailing packet at the Navy Yard in Washington bound for either New York or New Bedford, Massachusetts. To that whaling port on Buzzard's Bay, Eliza addressed a brief report of the family's doings on 8 August.[92] Eleven days later she mailed a letter to Middletown on the Connecticut River, suggesting that Mills had already journeyed north to Newburyport on the Merrimack River and thence to New London. Despite an arduous itinerary, he found time to reply from New London, for, on 19 August, Eliza hurried to acknowledge the receipt of his letter "with its enclosure of $5—tho' small the offering has proved very acceptable for indeed I have been much distressed for the want of it." The tentacles of earlier debts still threatened her peace of mind, especially in his absence; she had opened a letter about "your bath lands" and "a protest notice on the note [from] Mr. Nourse & others due at Bank." She had become practiced at handling his affairs, dealing with "several persons [who] have called in your absence wishing to get drawings made & engineering."

Undoubtedly, Mills's direct intervention in the building operations for the New England customhouses trimmed costs and ensured efficient construction. The official accounts published in the *Receipts and Expenditures of the United States* upheld his later claim that he had reduced the contractors' proposals "from 44, 42, & 33 thousand dollars to 10, 16, & 23."[93] Throughout his tour, he had "found not a single bricklayer that knew how to turn a groin," recalling in a letter of 21 February 1838 to the House Committee on Public Buildings that he "had to instruct the workmen, both in forming the centers and cutting the groins." He did not always succeed, the walls at Newburyport leaning outward and requiring the insertion of iron bars.[94] Much to his dismay, however, those visits were deemed by the Treasury to be ineligible for a refund of expenses, since the officials claimed that he was protecting his good name as much as the public exchequer.[95] He bewailed the assumption that the architect's responsibility ended with the supply of designs and specifications when writing on 23 July 1834 to apprise the Middletown collector, N. A. Phelps, of his impending visit.[96] Nonetheless, he convinced Woodbury to order fireproof vaulting in all the customhouses, as stated in the draft specification for the smaller of the two types with the word "Newburyport" penciled in on the title, "Description of Erecting and furnishing a certain building to be built in the City of Middletown—State of Connecticut for a Custom house... which is further explained by Drawings hereunto annexed."[97] Notwithstanding differences in dimensions, the specification was also used at New London and with the addition of a pedimented front and pitched roof, at Newburyport.

The contents follow the arrangement of his South Carolina specifications, detailing the outer dimensions, then the structure from foundation up, followed by instructions to the individual contractors. The external dimensions of the Middletown customhouse were to be 48 feet wide by 52 deep, while those of Newburyport were 40 feet by 50 feet and of New London, 45 feet square (63). The outer walls of brick faced with granite were to rise 39 feet and contain a 9-foot-high basement for storage. The internal walls and angular piers were to be of stone 1.5 feet thick, the spring or lower curve of the groin arches one-quarter of the span, and the intervening space "solidly filled, & grouted as well as all the walls." The instructions to the individual contractors were equally precise, for example detailing the mason's work on the dressed-stone single-story portico of two unfluted baseless columns in the refined modification of the Greek Doric he had developed in South Carolina; the bricklayer's method of fabricating thin brick and hydraulic-cement groin vaults, including the interweaving of the bricks along the ribs, much as in the Charleston Powder Magazine; the carpenter's provision of reusable scaffolding, or centering, for supporting the vault under construction, and of "a platform on the top [of the hip roof] for an observatory"; the iron founder and blacksmith's installation of cast-iron sashes and railings; or the painter's three coats of paint, lime based for the inside walls and ceilings, reduced to two in the privy, and oil based on all the metal. The contractors, of course, also had working drawings, although only those for New London survive. The plans show the central corridor bisecting the offices on the main floor and, to one side, a staircase to the other stories. The elevations depict the appropriately dignified facades in which federal authority was expressed not only by the portico but also by the broad corner

b

a

63.   Mills, customhouses at (a) New London, Connecticut, and (b) Newburyport, Massachusetts (1834–1835).

pilasters and deep entablature encircling the fabric; budgetary constraints caused the use of hammered stone for the fabric, only the ornamental features being smooth cut. The sense of order was further marked on the front by a horizontal molding between the floors and by the slight projection of the center bays. The Newburyport and New London customhouses still display their handsome utility, each restored as maritime museums. Sadly, the Middletown customhouse was first robbed of its pleasing proportions by the addition of a bulky French mansard roof in 1866–1867, and then demolished in 1918.

One omission from the Middletown specification was the description of the "apartment for the Post Office," a facility also included on the main floor at the east, William Street, side of the New Bedford customhouse. This was an aggrandised version of his smaller type, having longer outer walls of 50 feet by 52 feet, while retaining a similar plan as well as broad corner pilasters and continuous entablature (64). After 28 March 1835 when he apprised Mills of preparing the stone, the contractor Seth Ingalls added the pedimented portico of four modified Doric columns rising the height of the two main stories. Although Ingalls reversed the placement of cut and hammered stone in its entablature (much as the capitals of the New London portico were squared), the portico is effectively integrated with the existing monumental articulation, recalling Mills's earlier experimentation with the giant order and attic Classical adaptation of the Palladian mode he had perfected in South Carolina. The novelty of his architectural concept is highlighted to this day by comparing the New Bedford customhouse with the conventional temple-fronted Greek Revival Merchant's and Mechanic's Bank (1831–1835), erected nearby at the

64.   Mills, customhouse, New Bedford, Massachusetts (1834–1835).

foot of William Street by his erstwhile contractor Russell Warren. The convincing scale and use of granite, shared by Mills's three smaller customhouses, represent a distinctive American idiom, conceptually rational yet symbolically historical. What the Newburyport collector Samuel Phillips wrote to Mills on 20 November 1835 applies, indeed, to all four New England buildings: the "house was completed in a style, which, all acknowledge, reflects credit on the architect & contractor."[98] For Mills not only attained a greater measure of sophistication in forging symbolic form with economic planning but coincidentally advanced structural technique within the locality of each customhouse.

The contractors for the Appraisers' Stores in Baltimore were better able to comprehend and thus execute Mills's specifications for vaulting the four-story

a

b

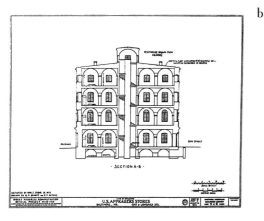

65. Mills, Appraisers' Stores, Baltimore (1835–1839): (a) facade in ca. 1930, and (b) section.

tructure, having the precedent of Latrobe's Baltimore Exchange (1817). The stores were built between 1835 and 1839 on the corner of East Gay and South Lombard streets across from Latrobe's Exchange and not far from the Baptist church, at a cost of nearly $242,000, including the site, under the supervision of Joseph White and James Howard (65a). That sum was a consequence of the size of the structure, measuring 85 feet wide by 99 feet deep, with a capacity of 340,000 cubic feet, and the complexity of the vaulting system.[99] To provide the maximum floor space, Mills adopted the cellular system favored by La-

trobe, comprising brick cross-vaults supported internally on granite piers
(65b). At the center was a light well, containing a stone cantilevered circular
staircase having a central newel of 4 feet diameter and probably a hoisting
gear.

In use almost up to demolition in 1938, the custodian of the Public Building
Service would in 1900 commend the stores as "one of the most substantial fireproof buildings in the United States."[100] The determinedly functional internal
arrangement was signified by the design of the exterior, which responded to
the design of Latrobe's Exchange. Alike most austere at street level, Mills
articulated this register of the stores by broadly spaced thick granite piers.
Between those piers, large, oak double doors were hung alternately with
smaller windows framed by squat antae. The piers, welded by a deep entablature, advanced massively around the building—seven bays on East Gay and fifteen on Lombard Street—part primitive peristyle, part modern structural
frame. Above this brilliant device for resolving function and aesthetic (on a par
with the progressive historicism of his great contemporary, the German Karl
Friedrich Schinkel), Mills turned to the more urbane Classicism of the Italian
Renaissance. The transition began with a continuous arcade akin to the
Roman-aqueduct motif used by Latrobe, pierced by narrower arched windows.
Above he ranged rectangular windows seated on horizontal moldings and diminishing in size upward toward the deep crowning cornice. Thereby he
adapted an essential theme of Classical and Renaissance architecture to contemporary requirement and achieved a new level of mastery in managing the
relationship between practical and ornamental features.

The satisfactory progress on the stores and New England customhouses
quickly brought Mills another Treasury commission. It was for a slightly enlarged version of his smaller standard customhouse design, to be built in Mobile, Alabama. The plans he mailed to the collector, since lost but described in
the specification, called for a brick building 66 feet square and 39 feet high,
fronted by a two-column portico of "plain Doric proportions" with a hip roof
covered by lead or slate.[101] The single divergence from the Middletown layout
was the insertion on the upper floor, above the custom hall, of a courtroom
"with a cove ceiling, extending up into the roof." Erected on the southwest
corner of St. Francis and Royal streets, but altered and repaired from 1843, it
was one of the new edifices built along the broad north–south avenues and
stood until 1851.[102]

The successful prosecution of those commissions aided Mills's pursuit of the
greater prize of designing a new, urgently needed, Treasury building. The solution that initially held greatest promise for Congress was a single new building to house all the executive departments: State, Treasury, Navy and War.
The idea appealed to those intent on controlling the growth in public expendi-

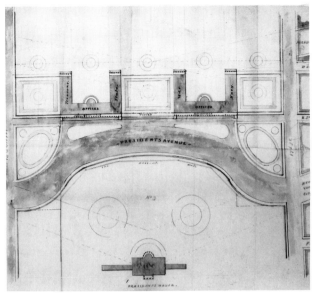

b

66. Mills, "New Executive Buildings," Washington, D.C.: (a) design (1834) and (b) sketch plan (ca. 1835).

a

ture and to those who saw an opportunity to construct a monumental building worthy of the federal capital. Such potentially opposite aims were adroitly handled in the report published on 5 February 1835 by the Maine Democrat Leonard Jarvis, whom President Jackson had endorsed as chairman of the House Committee on Public Buildings only six days earlier.[103] To compile his report on the "New Executive Buildings," Jarvis had consulted plans that Mills and William Parker Elliot, Jr., had evidently outlined for the committee in 1834. Mills had submitted at least three, apparently exhibited in Congress, of which drawings survive for only two. One shows two buildings having longer fronts and right-angle wings, linked by a colonnade and located on the north side of Lafayette Square facing the President's House (66a).[104] This may well be the scheme for unified public offices that Mills was to mention having completed before 1836 in a letter of 27 March 1838.[105] The second sketches an open quadrangle surrounded by a colonnade, with four external and two internal porticoes and occupying the site of the existing Treasury and State departments, west of the President's House (66b).[46] His third design, described in Jarvis's report, was for a building on the same location based on his Patent Office scheme. Although each design contained features of the plan he would be engaged to construct in 1836, none followed its entire form and should, therefore, be considered now.

The opening sentences of Jarvis's report must have gratified Mills. The "public edifices in the capital of our confederated republic ought not to be inferior to those erected for Federal or state purposes in our large commercial cities," surely, Mills concluded, a plaudit for his New England customhouses.

Better yet, Jarvis recommended proceeding with what on first glance seemed his third design. This envisaged an H-plan three-story building, placing two wings, each 160 feet by 60 feet, astride a central block 286 feet by 60 feet to furnish 160 rooms within, respectively fronted by the eight- and six-column porticoes. Then, in shocked disbelief, he read that Jarvis attributed this impressive congruence of form and function to Elliot. To compound the error, the report was reprinted on 13 February 1835 in the *National Intelligencer.* Within three days, Mills had mastered his chagrin and informed its editors that "Mr. E. has been only the draftsman, in this instance the original design being mine." That design has disappeared, perhaps destroyed with others of Mills's papers said to have been consumed by fire in a hotel at Long View Junction, Texas.[107] Nevertheless, the printed description certainly summons up a grandiloquent version of Mills's Patent Office proposals, temporarily consigned to limbo about the time the committee must have contacted him. Elliot, Mills contended, had simply switched the Greek orders used in this and another of the alternatives he had placed "before the appropriate Committee for more than a year past," continuing "various modifications of the plan suited to the present sites [on Lafayette Square, and along Fifteenth Street] were presented by me to the Committee; the most reduced is that selected." In corroboration, he reminded the public that Elliot was "no architect," having never "erected a building." The temperate complaint rings true when compared with the vindictiveness of Elliot's reply. Not content with stating, "There is not one idea in my design taken from his," Elliot satirized Mills's "colonnades, without use or meaning; his bare and naked and factory-like walls; his pidgeon boxes placed over the pediments . . . and his disproportions in the whole building" and scorned his "wild and visionary schemes," such as the *Substitute for Railroads* (1834). The next day, 21 February, the editors allowed Mills the last word. His response ignored Elliot's jibes in favor of clarifying his superior qualifications, trained by the "first Architect of this country, B.H. LATROBE, Esq" and "imbued with a *practical* knowledge of the art."

Confident in his public defense, Mills sought support in the Executive. That day he wrote to Treasury Secretary Woodbury, "respectfully" offering his professional services to "design etc., the public buildings which by act of Congress may have been placed under the Department to carry into effect."[108] But his tussle with Elliot and, indirectly, with the powerful New York firm of Town and Davis, which was responsible for major federal and state commissions such as the customhouse in New York and the North Carolina State Capitol, let alone the embarrassment caused to Jarvis, delayed the administration's decision.

Consequently, Mills persevered in casting about for other jobs, some time before 8 April presenting a plan for a national foundry to the Army Corps of

Engineers; he was to make notes for a fuller proposal when the subject of a Federal Arms Manufactory resurfaced in 1838 and the early 1840s.[109] About April 1835 he also sent Amos Kendall, the postmaster general, an unsolicited drawing for a "National Clock" to be built onto the existing post office in the former Blodgett's Hotel.[110] Perhaps along the lines of the sketch for an octagonal tower with a square superstructure drawn into his Washington notebook, his main purpose was to bring his skill and keenness to the attention of another member of Jackson's cabinet.[111]

There is also circumstantial evidence that Mills then enjoyed the patronage of President Jackson, who was intent on pushing through an ambitious building program in the District as capstone to the many federal commissions he had set in train across the states. However, although still determined to advance his policies, Jackson was contemplating retirement to the Hermitage, his plantation near Nashville, Tennessee. The Washington climate and tremendous stress of the presidency had exacerbated his debilitating chest condition, compounded by his inveterate use of tobacco, at times chewing or drawing on his favorite long-stem Powhaton pipe—rather than taking powdered snuff, as did Mills.[112] Fellow Southerner and Unionist, he could have met Jackson at the First Presbyterian Church in Washington, where the president occasionally worshipped. Mills's excellent artistic credentials make it quite likely that he was, in the words of the entry for 5 July 1836 in William P. Elliot's diary, "recently employed by General Jackson to make drawings for the Hermitage."[113] In 1819 Old Hickory had built a brick residence to which he had in 1831 added a four-column portico and a side wing, all damaged in a fire three years later. Jackson thereupon decided to restore it with a new balancing wing, transforming the portico into the in antis form. Contracts for this reconstruction, amounting to almost $4,000, were signed on 1 February 1835 with Joseph Rieff and William C. Hume.[114]

However, it is probable that Mills, who had already corresponded with Jackson, did conceive the "Design for the Hermitage the Mansion of Genl. Jackson President U. States" (67).[115] While not inscribed in his usual handwriting, this sheet illustrates the plan, section, and side elevation in a manner akin to other of his drawings. The combination of H plan and colonnade resembled his scheme for the Patent Office. The attribution to Mills of the design, if not the actual drawing, receives further support from the miniature sketch of a house for "Mr. Swan" on a scrap of paper in the pouch of his Washington notebook. The slight pen strokes outline a similar composition of a taller centerpiece shaded by six columns supporting a flat entablature and flanked by single-story wings. Moreover, Mills exhibited a proprietary interest in the Hermitage when he wrote to Jackson on 3 August 1836 hoping that the president "found your new mansion agreeable to your wishes."[116]

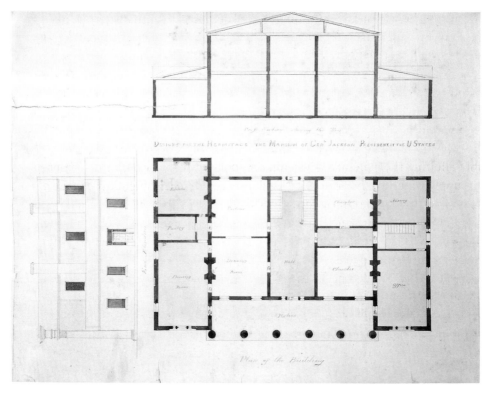

67.   Mills, design for the Hermitage, near Nashville, Tennessee (1836).

While the new Hermitage was rising Phoenix-like, Mills's third daughter, Mary Powell, married Alexander Dimitry in the spring of 1835 in Washington.[117] Born in New Orleans, Dimitry had graduated from Georgetown College in 1820, returning south to teach at Baton Rouge College before becoming the first English editor of the *New Orleans Bee* from 1830 to 1835. He regularly contributed short stories after moving to Washington in 1834, as a clerk in the Post Office Department. He soon shone in the Union Literary Society and surely met Mills through the small cultural network in the District. Apart from their shared interest in literature and education, Dimitry was a historian, nationalist, and devout Christian, although of the Roman Catholic faith. Mary and Alexander would enjoy a marriage as compatible as that of her parents, but one not troubled by economic uncertainty. The first of their five children was to be born at Washington, surely to the joy of Eliza and Robert; of their other daughters, only Sarah bore children.[118] Dimitry was to remain in the Post Office until 1842, and in 1847 he would become the first superintendent of education in Louisiana. Generous in his success, he boosted the shaky finances of his parents-in-law, and, in 1854, a matter of months before Mills's death, went back to Washington as a translator in the State Department.[119]

After the nuptials, Mills resumed his search for new commissions, finding time, nevertheless, to answer a query from the Scots immigrant architect David Paton (who took over from Town and Davis in 1835) about the best material for roofing the North Carolina Capitol at Raleigh.[120] On 17 March 1836 Mills solicited Poinsett's "interest to obtain for me professional employment," and on 29 March, General Gratiot, chief of the Army Corps of Engineers, ostensibly eliciting the general's advice on an enclosed plan for building a reservoir to supply water to Charleston.[121] Evidently rebuffed, he might have made a better impression had he sent Gratiot a description of the patent taken out before 21 September 1835 with Henry B. Fernald of Portland, Maine, for the "application of Hydrostatics" harnessing tidal movement in large chambers to compress air for motive power.[122] Then on 28 May 1836 Mills sent the Virginia Democrat Charles F. Mercer, of the House Committee on Public Buildings, a scheme for a "New Hall, House of Representatives on the site of the old Library of Congress."[123] This plan, which developed his 1835 idea of a western extension of the Capitol, provided a semicircular chamber with galleries and a ceiling height of only 20 feet, half that of the existing hall, in order to leave room for a "Library room" above. Although nothing specific resulted from this correspondence, it proved a timely promotion of his abilities. For on 2 July, Congress was forced by a fire in Blodgett's Hotel to vote appropriations for the construction of a new building for the patent office for $106,000; at the same time, it set aside $100,000 for a new Treasury.

Two days later, Mills petitioned President Jackson for appointment as "architect to the public buildings."[124] This time he enclosed "a few letters of recommendation," including one each from Governor Powers of South Carolina and Leonard Jarvis. Jarvis unreservedly reversed his earlier apparent support for Elliot, commending Mills as "the only person to whom the Committee on Public Buildings is indebted for any information" on the Executive Offices and his "competency & his practical ability. I shall be gratified in knowing that he has been selected." At long last, Mills's determination and ambition were rewarded. On 6 July, Jackson appointed him

> Architect to aid in forming plans, making proper changes therein, from time to time & seeing to the erection of said buildings [the Treasury and Patent Office] in substantial confirmity to the plans hereby adopted, which are in their outlines to be, as to The Treasury Building, that plan annexed by said Mills and as to the Patent Office, that annexed to Mr. Elliot—the former building to

be erected on the old site, and the latter one on the square north of the Post Office. [125]

Beyond its prestige and executive authority, the appointment as "Architect" would have appealed to Mills's sense of history. He was successor to the nation's most renowned architects, every one his own teachers: Hoban, Bulfinch, and Latrobe. He enjoyed the trust of a president intent on an extensive building program sustained by his January 1835 order to swell the federal reserves by the sale of public lands, who boosted Mills's modest salary of $1,800 (actually slightly less than that received by his predecessors) with a $500 payment for drawings. Mills also then had the advantage of being responsible to an acquaintance, Major Noland, the current commissioner of public buildings and grounds. [126] In those halcyon days of July 1836, confident in his ability to marry magnificence with practicality in an American idiom, he anticipated the chance to realize the sentiment he was to express in his essay on Virginia architecture: "We have entered on a new era in the history of the world; it is our destiny to lead, not to be led." [127]

Persuading Noland to lease for him an office near the site of the new Treasury on Fifteenth Street, [128] that "all my drawings & papers [specifications, estimates, and contracts] connected with this building, [would be] convenient of access for reference," [129] he determined to oversee personally the entire building process aided by a clerk, J. B. Rooker, and, as general superintendent, Robert Brown. He also soon began identifying books of potential utility to the architect and commissioner—for example, telling Noland on 9 August 1837 that he had "examined [Peter] Nicholson's Architectural Dictionary [published in two volumes (London, 1812–1819), and by then a standard technical reference book] and I found it a very useful work and think it would prove a valuable acquisition to the office as a book for general reference on all subjects connected with architectural and engineering subjects as well as mechanical." [130] A related concern was his attempt, once the commissions were under way, to augment the federal patronage of artists. Thus on 20 May 1837 he would confide to Gilmor, "We are going to give Mr. Pettrich [the sculptor Ferdinand Federick August Pettrich] something to do at the Capitol & The Treasury columns until something better offers." [131] The ledger of the Office of Public Buildings and Grounds records payments to him of $625 through 1838, the latest for three terracotta mantles in the Etruscan style. Unfortunately, Pettrich's progress was as slow as his prices were high, but with a characteristic but ingenuous generosity Mills placed his own reputation in jeopardy for Pettrich. To Benjamin Ogle Tayloe, a Virginia congressman, he wrote on 9 August 1838 stressing the "public benefit in securing the services of a man of real merit, who promises on this occasion to enrich our country in works of art, useful as well as ornamental."[132]

Interestingly, Mills's efforts to elevate the status of the architect coincided with the ill-fated attempt to organize a professional body for American architects spearheaded by Thomas U. Walter and Alexander Jackson Davis. At Isaiah Rogers's Astor House Hotel in New York City, on the evening of 7 December 1836, Walter won over the assembled "Architects from different parts of the United States" to establish the "American Institution of Architects."[133] In fact, a mere eleven architects were present, mainly from New York, including Rogers, William C. Kramp, Charles F. Reichardt (soon to head south to Charleston), F. Schmidt, Thomas Thomas, Sr., and Thomas Thomas, Jr., with Strickland and Haviland from Philadelphia and the Bostonian, Richard Bond. Their purpose was best summarized in the letter that Robert C. Long mailed from Baltimore on 6 November to Walter apologizing for his absence: "The Establishment of a general Architectural Association in our country, like the British Institute of Architects [founded in 1834, soon to number Town and Haviland as corresponding members] has been for some time . . . a cherished desire of mine, and the near prospect of seeing it accomplished is most gratifying, and ought to be to Every man who loves the Art." Those who attended resolved to hold an inaugural meeting of the Institution at the Pennsylvania Academy of Fine Arts "on the first Tuesday of May next, at 7 O'clock P.M." Again, Mills was not present, either loath to leave the federal commissions or resentful that despite his position as federal architect he was accorded the same treatment as the junior Elliot. Apparently he did not even send an encouraging letter, as did Rogers, Minard Lafever, and James Dakin, who wrote from New Orleans on 20 April: "I am much elated to hear that something is doing for Architecture besides drawing & executing, which until now has been the only public demonstration of its existance in our country."[134] That point was to be made much later in an article headed "Architecture" printed by The Crayon in May 1856, claiming that Americans judged architecture "not as Art, but as building . . . for its fitness of purpose and general impressiveness, and not for any thought or idea to be given by it." Nevertheless, Mills might have been among the twenty-three professionals, two associates, and twenty-five honorary members listed but not named in the minutes of the inaugural meeting of the institution on 2 May. Within a year, it had collapsed due to the panic of 1837, and, indicative of the failure to create a sense of professional unity, Walter was to be party to an essentially political attack on Mills's professional competence.

Unwittingly, Mills provided ammunition for his detractors almost from the day he took office in July 1836. He depended too greatly on presidential

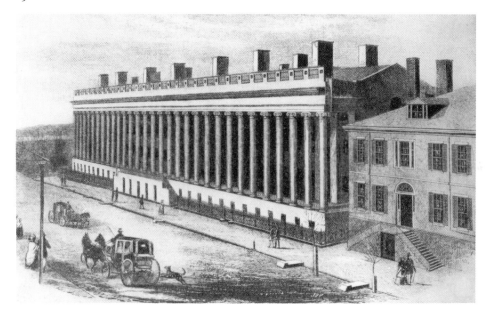

68. Mills, Treasury, Washington, D.C. (1836–1842), showing the old State Department.

decree—for example, having accepted unwillingly the use of Aquia Creek sandstone for the front and colonnade of the Treasury (68) and then petitioning Jackson directly on 3 August 1836 to increase the Patent Office appropriation.[135] He estimated that the Town and Elliot design required at least $150,000, or he would be forced to "reduce its proportions" and omit dressed stone for the rear. He further pointed out the uncertainty surrounding both plans by noting that the Patent Office appropriation of $106,000 had been calculated on a "brick" building with "floors of wooden joists, and consequently not fire proof," contrary to a congressional directive. While he hoped to circumvent bureaucratic delays, and to gain an immediate raise in salary to $2,000 since his predecessors had not faced such extensive duties of design and supervision, he inadvertently provoked the distrust of several congressmen conscious of a widespread antagonism toward federal authority in a society divided by economic and ideological disparities. Although by 10 July he could tell Gilmor, "We are progressing with our Public Buildings here rapidly—The basements of both are to be faced with granite [from the Patapsco quarry in Maryland]," the building policy for both commissions rested in part on verbal agreements essentially between Mills, the president, and the commissioner.

In the case of the Treasury, Jackson, according to an unsubstantiated report, had walked with Mills, still advocating the site on Lafayette Square,

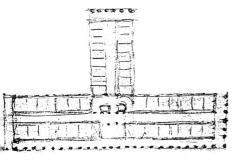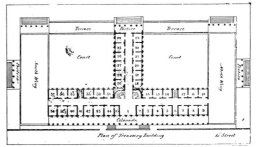

69.   Mills, Treasury, Washington, D.C., sketch of plan (1838), and engraved plan as built.

from the President's House eastward to Fifteenth Street and had paced out the facade line between the burned-out Treasury and State departments.[136] That resulted in obstruction of the view from the White House to the Capitol, and in Mills being held culpable by several irrate politicians. As harmful, in the retrenchment following the panic of 1837, Jackson had approved by word of mouth only the most comprehensive plan for the building before the contracts were advertised on 12 July 1836. This plan, Mills was to contend right up to his death, envisaged an E-shaped complex, having three wings projecting from the rear of the colonnaded main block along Fifteenth Street. Probably somewhat plainer than the version he was to reenter in about 1850–1851, when the Treasury stood in need of more accommodation, the three-wing scheme might well have begun as the alternative to his T-plan design, which was accepted by Congress in 1836. He had delivered the last version to Jackson on 6 July, together with a letter estimating the cost of adding south and north wings (respectively then intended for the General Post Office and State Department) at $265,000. The actual design is no longer in the official archive, but further information appears in his evidence to the House Committee on Expenditures in 1842, reiterating that his "original plan" comprised three wings 200 feet deep behind the 400-foot front, to be screened by forty-two columns. If Jackson had commended that magnificent blending of the Palladian domestic style of the first federal buildings with the templar architecture of the Classical era, Congress assumed Mills would build the T plan, and as cheaply as possible.

The T plan, which he incidentally sketched in the copy of his 1838 report to the commissioner still in the Office of the Architect of the Capitol, nonetheless enclosed extensive, fire-resistant accommodations within an appropriately monumental exterior (69). The main front on Fifteenth Street is aggrandized by the authoritative march of Greek Ionic columns (taken from Stuart and Revett's engravings of the destroyed Temple of Ilissus near Athens) raised on a basement to counteract the sloping grade as well as for monumental effect. The result was an imaginative combination of the ancient Greek stoa (adapted by Karl Frederich Schinkel for the Altes Museum, Berlin [1823]) with a modern version of the Renaissance and Palladian raised colonnade. When questioned about its design in February 1838, Mills would acknowledge the influence of "The Bourse in Paris" by Alexandre Theodore Brongniart (1808–1813), which had "extended and unbroken colonnades, [and] is regarded as the most magnificent of modern structures," and the east front of the Louvre, "admired and often celebrated for its extended and lofty colonnade, elevated upon a *high basement*."[137] He also cited the Temple of Diana at Ephesus in Greece as the specific source of the entrance, illustrated in Latrobe's 1730 English edition of J. B. Fisher Von Erlach's *Entwurfeiner historischen Architectur* (1721). Such uncharacteristically detailed historical sources reflected Mills's desire to match the grand European tradition, and with success—the Scottish visitor Robert Baird, for one, accustomed to the sophisticated Neoclassical architecture of London, Edinburgh, and Glasgow, declaring the Treasury to be "very striking as well as an exceedingly handsome erection."[138]

Whatever the tally of Mills's architectural sources, their adaptation is novel, even experimental, and hence distinctively American. The columns of the colonnade stand on neither a proper basement nor a true stylobate, are crowned by an ornamental balustrade, and are enclosed at either end. Similarly, the scale exceeded ancient practice—the Parthenon at Athens measured only 101.5 feet by 228 feet—intended to express the vast expanse of the New World, while retaining a visual association between American and Greek democracy. The *"effect,"* as Mills further argued in 1838, was both "grand and imposing," adding that "utility justifies" its "introduction" presumably as a sun break—venerable ancestor of Le Corbusier's Modernist brise-soleil—as well as the means of regularizing the facade along the incline of Fifteenth Street. Behind, Mills's American innovation is as evident, since the interior remains as he completed the original T-plan block in 1842; the north and south wings were added under the direction of Thomas U. Walter and Ammi B. Young between 1855 and 1865.

The unostentatious elevated entrance leads directly into the junction of the brick and stucco barrel-vaulted corridors that run straight ahead and to either side between the groin-vaulted cellular offices. The appearance of this lucid integration of structure, plan, and circulation evokes the "calm grandeur and noble simplicity" that the celebrated German antiquary J. J. Winckelmann discerned in ancient Greek art. At their intersection ascends the main staircase, Piranesian in scale but Aristotelian in its logical utility. Guarded by Greek Doric columns, the gracefully grand paired quarter-circular cantileveral flights of steps climb rhythmically through the three floors, even the curved bases of

70.   Mills, Treasury, Washington, D.C., staircase.

the risers reinforcing the sense of upward movement (70). Besides visually expressing effects that correspond to material characteristics of the building, this
staircase and those smaller on the lateral corridor symbolizes both the ideal of
bureaucratic efficiency and the idea of the authority vested in government.
That analogy continues through the unified structure, even with the varied dimensions of the individual offices, of which there were 114 when the building
first opened and 135 as enlarged, and most well lighted, ventilated, and
heated. The direct relationship between the major and minor spaces, further
united by the spare abstracted classical decoration, is truly modular and under-
scores Mills's continuing debt to Latrobe's teaching, but also his own individu-
ality. Where contemporaries were increasingly preoccupied with archaeology
and new technology, Mills sought to conform appropriate historical and American architectural themes with functional planning and economic structure.

    The selection of Town and Elliot's Neo-Greek scheme as the basis for the
Patent Office confirmed the current prestige of the revival in the United
States. They had conceived a quadrangular building, measuring 413 feet by
280 feet, with an internal court of 270 feet by 112 feet, rising two stories
above the basement and dominated on the main front, on F Street, by a massive Doric portico modeled on the Parthenon (71a). This was eight columns
wide and two deep, repeated with fewer columns on the north facade. The intervening walls and side pavilions were to have been ringed by thick pilasters

a

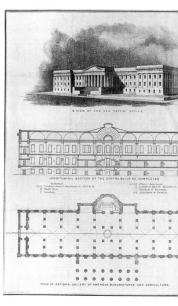

71. Ithiel Town and William Elliot, revised Mills, Patent Office, Washington, D.C. (1836–1842): (a) facade and (b) engraving of main building with floor plans.

b

72. Mills, Patent Office, Washington, D.C. (1836–1842): (a) Grand Exhibition Room and (b) vestibule.

a

inspired by the ancient anta, creating a severity that Mills considered to be excessive both formally and economically. Mills began his campaign to revise its external articulation in his 8 August 1836 letter to President Jackson, helped by the absence of detailed drawings (although Elliot was paid $174 for "drawings" for both the Patent Office and the Treasury on 3 March 1837, with an additional $300 on 15 December).[139] Again, the official record can to be supplemented by reference to later documents. The "idea" of the main block on F Street, Mills would write in the 1848 edition of his *Guide to the Capitol*, repeating evidence given to the House Committee on Public Buildings in 1838, was derived from a plan "presented by Messrs Town & Elliot," but the "interior arrangement" was "principally that of Mr. Mills."[140] He supplied a fuller account when replying on 23 August 1851 to articles published anonymously in *Scientific American* on 22 January and 1 February 1851 describing and illustrating Elliot's Patent Office design:[141] the Senate had voted "$110,000" for the main block as designed by Town and Elliot to be built of brick with "*wooden floors,* filled in with brick," the House adding "*cut stone*" walls but no money, while prior to digging the foundations (complicated by the "inconsistent nature of the ground"),[142] "no such plans were to be found, and, . . . I was compelled, *de novo,* to form plans of my own conception, following substantially the outline of that approved by the President." He dispensed with Town and Elliot's layout of central corridors, serving smaller rooms in the F and G street blocks and larger halls on the Seventh and Ninth street ranges, with double-flight staircases behind the north and south porticoes. Instead, he placed the vaulted offices in the eastern (Seventh Street) half, the "Model Rooms of vaulted ceilings being supported on columns" on the western side, and substituted more compact curved stairs linking the floors as well as stone for brick and wood flooring (71b). The upper floor "throughout" had been "thrown into one Grand Exhibition Room each section being 270 feet long, 64 feet wide, and 30 feet high, all vaulted with groin arches, supported on massive columns."

In fact, the congressional appropriation was sufficient to build only the main block (1836–1842); the original quadrangular edifice was completed largely following the Mills pattern, beginning in 1849 to 1851 with the east wing mainly under his own supervision, but the remainder and west wing from 1851 to 1855 by Walter and Edward Clark. This included the superb brick-vaulted Grand Exhibition Room, although in 1838 Mills was ordered to place additional columns in the two rows of columns supporting the vault (72a). Despite the intrusion of the columns, the room provided a capacious space to show models of American invention; it survived the 1877 fire that damaged much of the Patent Office, but was replaced by a more ornamental and cumbersome cross-vault designed by Adolph Cluss and Paul Shulze in 1879. Mills's original layout was preserved on the lower floors of the main block, which has housed the National Portrait Gallery since 1962. Entering through the F Street entrance, the visitor encounters one of the most striking interiors in the United States, even if in 1838 Mills was also told to insert barrel vaults at right angles to the groin vaults, necessitating the insertion of entablatures and extra columns (72b). Still apparent is Mills's original concept for a monumental yet picturesque spatial experience formed by the vestibule, curved cantilever double staircase, and contiguous old model room on the west side. Ennobled by the six stolid, modified Delos-type Doric columns and contrasted by the rhythmic arching of the groin vault, the graceful flights of stairs are etched against the light from the windows behind.

Mills's changes to the exterior were not less significant. He was responsible for selecting granite to face the basement and freestone for the upper stories, which would cause the anonymous author of the 1 February 1851 *Scientific American* article to regret that the contrast made "the subordinate parts superior in finish to the principal." That author also asserted that Mills had enlarged the basement windows but reduced the width and depth of the pilasters to the detriment of "a portion" of the building's "boldness and strength." Another change appears to have been the addition of sills to the windows. Those revisions had the effect of moderating the austere Greek Revival of Town and Elliot's design while injecting a modicum of the Palladianism he admired, and which had inspired the earlier Federal edifices.

Mills's underlying admiration for the American Palladian heritage was manifest in two series of unexecuted designs just postdating the original Patent Office and Treasury commissions. The least developed were two sketches of a three-story house for the distinguished Pittsburgh lawyer and Whig congressman Harmar Denny, who resigned in 1837.[143] Both show a raised portico, of four or six Greek Doric columns, flanked by curving stairs and three-sided projections at each side of the house (73a). Inside, Mills envisaged intersecting semicircular walls between the dining and drawing rooms along the front and, at the rear, three interconnected rooms shaded by a deep columned piazza reminiscent of his Ainsley Hall House. Dated "Jany. 27th 1837," but drawn on several pages near the end of his Washington notebook, are proposals for the library of the South Carolina College in Columbia.[144] He had time to sketch four variants when winter brought a halt to construction in Washington. The invitation probably came from George McDuffie, by then in the last weeks of his term as governor of South Carolina but still president of the college board of trustees. Ranging from 105 feet to 100 feet long and 65 feet to 54 feet deep, with the main front on Bull Street, each plan played upon the Palladian tripartite composition and a refined distillation of Classical and Renaissance features: a rusticated and arcaded basement, shouldering pedimented porticoes with four or six Greek Doric columns, transformed into pilasters on the rear,

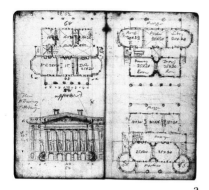

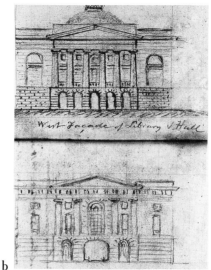

73.   Mills, sketch designs for
(a) Denny House, Pittsburgh, and
(b, c) South Carolina College
Library (1837).

a

b

c

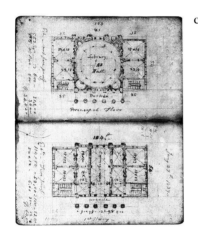

and a low dome (73b). He was redefining his Fireproof Building and Lunatic
Asylum from South Carolina, augmenting the Classical effect by the addition
of the dome and even by the central carriageway which was to become the formal entrance onto the campus. The plan of proportionally related vaulted
rooms on the ground floor and around the upper circular library simplified the
Palladian canon, like the Neoclassical square and arched windows (73c). He
sent a finished set of drawings (although only the two floor plans survive) to
the college, closely based on the first of the schemes in his notebook showing a
six-column portico and a 50-foot-diameter library estimated at $39,000. The
trustees were perturbed and abandoned Mills's beautiful design in favor of a
cheaper, less distinguished red-brick building, probably from a local contractor, which still stands at the northern corner of the campus on Bull Street.[145]

Progress on the federal buildings left Mills little time to brood over the failure of the Denny and South Carolina College projects. He was especially busy training the Washington contractors in the use of the brick and hydraulic-cement vaulting system. By blending Southern Palladian and Latrobean practice, Mills once again diverged from his chief rivals. The walls of Town and Davis's New York customhouse were 5 feet thick, partially strengthened with iron; Walter, at least for Girard College, combined cast iron with stone, while Strickland in the New Orleans Mint placed narrow brick arches within horizontal cast-iron frames. By the mid-1830s, as the Patent Office competition had intimated, cast iron was considered superior for fireproofing, strength, and utility; in New York, Stillman and Allen's Novelty Iron Works, at the foot of Twelfth Street, was producing structural ironwork as well as boilers, engines, ships' hulls, and machinery, including, incidently, the first steam locomotive built in the United States, named the Best Friend of Charleston. Although the inherent deficiencies of cast iron, with its tendency to fracture, especially when exposed to great heat, were not fully appreciated in 1836, Mills remained firm in his commitment to the economic, structural, and fire-protection advantages of the hydraulic-cement and brick vault. The statistics of the Treasury and Patent Office commissions would indeed prove Mills's case. Whereas the main block and single wing of the Treasury were to cost some $660,000, and the central block of the Patent Office, $418,000 (including the expensive main portico), Town and Davis's considerably smaller customhouse in New York reached almost $1.4 million (including $270,000 for the site); Girard College, $1,427,800; and the New Orleans Mint, $254,740 (three times its original estimate). And Strickland's Second Bank of the United States at Philadelphia, completed more than a decade earlier in 1824, when the scale of building charges and inflation were much lower, had cost nearly $500,000.

Mills's superficially more conservative approach proceeded from his essentially practical idea of design, explained in a retrospective letter of 21 April 1838 to Levi Lincoln, chairman of the House Committee on Public Buildings.[146] The fire resistance, structural integrity, and economy were achieved by the brick vault, strengthened by "massy granite braces crossing over the spandrels of the arches, binding the front and cross walls together," by the hydraulic cement that transformed the vault into "one mass of masonry, [further] relieving the lateral, and increasing the perpendicular press of the arches," and lastly by "bars of iron" let "into the blocks of stone forming the pilasters, reaching from the spring of the arches some 16 or 20 [inches] long through the cross wall." The proper structure decided, he had "determined the sizes of the rooms by the business that would be transacted in them," following the average dimensions in the neighboring State Department but ensuring that all, together with the corridors, were reasonably illumined. Only when those practical require-ments were satisfied had he turned to the aesthetic considerations, aimed at denoting the authority of government and enhancing the image of the republic.

Mills carried a similar practical method into the management of the Trea-sury and Patent Office commissions. The evidence can be found in the records of the Commissioner of Public Buildings and Grounds (between 1838 and 1841 having the additional minutes of the Committee on Public Buildings instituted by President Van Buren as part of his cabinet), embracing letter books, led-gers, voluminous packets of estimates, Mills's own printed annual reports to the commissioner, and many entries in his leather-bound notebook, which must have seldom been out of the pocket of his jacket from about 1835 to the late 1840s.[147] As early as 12 July 1836 he had compiled a long list of materials to be advertised for tender in the *Washington Globe, National Intelligencer,* and *United States Telegraph,* such as the purchase for the Treasury and the Patent Office of 300,000 and 281,000 burnt bricks, respectively (probably following the dimensions ordered by the city council on 6 October 1802: 3 inches to 4 in-ches long, 4.5 wide, and 2.25 thick), or for each building 3,000 2-inch planks 14 feet to 16 feet long. Later in October he called for 600 straight scaffold poles, 35 feet in length tapering from between 8 and 10 inches wide to 4 in-ches, for delivery by 10 November; on 31 October, Mills had accepted an offer of $2.62 per barrel for hydraulic cement to be on site by March 1837 at the be-ginning of the next building season.

The ledger and estimates also yield a fascinating roll call of the Washington building trade. Most were individual operatives, apart from the marble ma-sons, Masterton and Smith or Morrow and Prevost; some were family firms, such as William and Joel Downer Digges, one a carpenter and the other a sup-plier of bricks. The names of public officials occasionally appear as suppliers, notably C. J. Nourse, son of Eliza's godfather and still in the Treasury, who sold lumber to the commissioner in August 1836. The proposals also reveal the existence of an information network between the tradesmen, A. M. Jones of Philadelphia writing to Mills on 13 April 1837 that he had heard about the ad-vertisement for 6-inch pipes "thro' our mutual friend J. Graff." Interspersed through the agreements were exchanges about problems in delivery and quality control. Thus on 31 August 1836 Mills was reimbursed $7 for a visit to Balti-more to examine granite, but often he relied on his superintendent, Robert Brown.

All the records testify to Mills's conscientiousness. In his first annual re-port, for example, he regretted that insufficient masons had been hired to fin-ish the initial phase of stonework on both buildings. To compensate, he had ordered the preparation of stone on site under cover during the winter months. Besides requesting $257,617.18¾ for the Treasury and $273,794.10 for the

Patent Office in the 1837–1838 building season, he had also taken it on himself to enclose an estimate of $100,000 for the south wing of the Treasury, now to rehouse the State Department, and to forward his full E-plan scheme before the major expenditure began. Already, too, he was pressing for the continued upgrading of materials, although that campaign was really to be successful only once he began work in 1839 on the General Post Office, when the government accepted marble in place of granite.[148] In 1839, too, he would experiment with "Asphalte" for the Treasury and Patent Office pavements and to improve the system of contracting. From 1836 Mills had, as he was to write to Senator Robert Dale Owen in 1846, opposed contracting "for all the materials, . . . by the day to work them up," which "held out no pecuniary encouragement to the industrious and skillful workmen; the wages of all in their several callings, being much alike."[149] By spring 1839, as his correspondence with Noland proves, he introduced the method of compiling a "tariff of prices, and paying the same by measurement" and "each [trade] put under distinct contract, as far as practicable, and in accordance with the public interest." Every "Artisan" was therefore responsible for the "faithful performance of his department of the work" and "a watchful scrutiny induced on one contractor over another," with the result that the General Post Office was to exceed the Treasury and Patent Office in quality, speed of building, and economy.

Back in 1836 Mills had to proceed as best he might, meantime coping with a full schedule of other tasks for the government. Over the summer, he again supervised the recoppering of the Capitol dome and repairs to the roof over the main staircase.[150] While such tasks raised the standing of the architect, Mills unwittingly condoned the essentially informal status and poor remuneration of the post. But the monthly salary of $191.66 as architect fired Mills's innate desire to give his best. He became the willing workhorse of the Office of Public Buildings, ever keen to oblige his friend Noland. Early in 1837 he wrote a report on the ventilation and heating of the Capitol, which was implemented by the closure of a number of the lower entrances and installation of double doors and furnaces.[151] Coincidentally, he made fireproof the post office, document, and library rooms alongside the House of Representatives, having on 4 January 1837 handed Noland a long letter concerning the supply of water from basins on the east and west side of the Capitol through almost 2 miles of pipe with stopcocks for fire fighting, leading down to the Patent Office and on to the Treasury.[152] Between April and September 1837, he installed an air furnace and placed a screen behind the north entrance of the President's House, according to an outline drawing in his notebook, that cost a little over $6,000 to erect; and on 1 August 1837 he was paid $41.68 for installing ventilators in the building.[153] Such minor jobs were part of his legacy to the federal capital no less than his now altered or extended major public buildings. Poetic justice is fulfilled, for the majestic columnar theme he created for the front of the Treasury has been repeated in the raised colonnades that parade with a more insistent bureaucratic authoritarianism through the Federal Triangle and other executive offices completed during this century—testament to Mills's insufficiently acknowledged leadership in the creation of American architectural imagery.

Mills actively sought that goal, finding the time to answer the Washington National Monument Society's advertisement for a monument that would "harmoniously blend durability, simplicity and grandeur" and be erected for $1 million (74a).[154] He met the society's spring 1837 deadline, since on 6 June, George Watterston, secretary of the Board of Managers, would relay to him their "thanks." But the same message was sent to more than seven others, since no design seemed "coextensive with the Nation."[155] Still, he had the signal advantage of being federal architect, resident in Washington, and his monument to Washington in Baltimore was largely finished, the paving, inscriptions, and tripods being installed by 1838.[156] The indecision of the society would also allow him to revise his scheme, probably represented by the cursory sketch in his notebook, loosely Gothic in style, for a small, polygonal, buttressed structure with cusped pointed and circular windows, inscribed in the cornice "Washington" (74b).[157] The Gothic style was apparently favored by several board members, who as Freemasons, and like Washington, traced their legacy to the masons of the great medieval cathedrals.[158]

Mills explored Gothic symbolism in three other thumbnail drawings a couple of pages nearer to the beginning of the notebook, and apparently for a national cathedral, but quite possibly related to his entry in the Washington Monument competition.[159] The most detailed of the three sketches, an elevation identified as "Sketch of a Cathedral for W——," is comparable in articulation with the accompanying plan that, however, bears no indication of a site for the general's tomb (74c, 74d).[160] It traces out a Latin cross, approximately 190 feet long and 120 feet wide, with transepts each projecting 30 feet. That arrangement bears many similarities to the original Gothic project for the Baltimore Cathedral, which he had helped Latrobe prepare, even to the positioning of altars in the transepts as well as in the chancel. But Mills inserted semicircular apses framed by columns behind each altar and inserted a pulpit and lectern between the chancel and nave, which, if essentially practical and Protestant, anticipated the division between sacred and lay spaces advocated by the Ecclesiological movement.[161] Yet his advance toward medievalism, echoed in the rose windows and the towers and tracery in the crocketed gable above the main entrance, is tempered by Neoclassical symmetry.

Mills's intent of revising Gothic forms for modern American society was realized in his scheme for the New Orleans Marine Hospital. Its necessity had

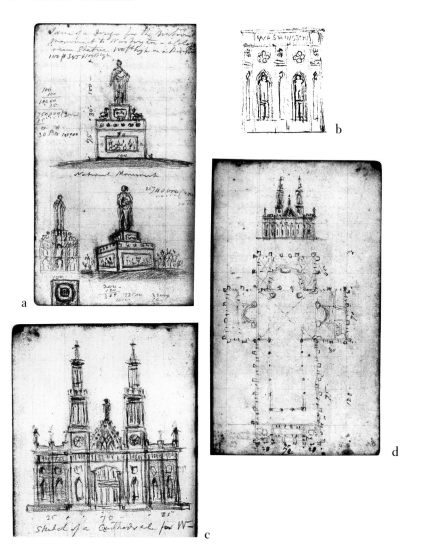

74.   Mills, sketch designs for (a) a Washington monument (1837) and a "Cathedral," Washington, D.C.: (b, c) elevation and (d) elevation with plan (1837).

been argued by Jefferson as early as 1802, and in 1837 the commission (the only one given under the March 1837 bill for hospitals along the "Western Waters") afforded a means of injecting funds into the local economy, ravaged by the diminished trade on the Mississippi.[162] On 1 September, Mills sent a set of plans and specifications to James W. Breedlove, the treasury collector at the Crescent City. He acted on his own initiative upon hearing that a site had been acquired for the hospital at McDonough on the south bank of the Mississippi, upriver from the city.[163] He might also have been spurred into action by seeing the designs forwarded to the Treasury from the Dakin brothers and

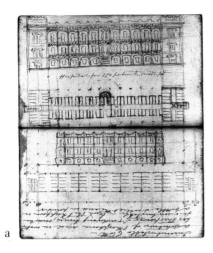

a

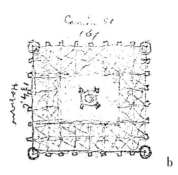

b

75.   Mills, (a) sketch design for a
150-bed Marine Hospital, and (b)
sketch plan for the New Orleans
Marine Hospital (1837).

Mondelle and Reynolds; indeed, he copied their grandiose Neo-Greek facades but less advanced plans into his notebook.[164] Breedlove received six sheets of drawings from Mills, five for a Gothic style hospital, but the sixth described as "geometrical Elevation of the Building (Grecian)."[165]

The Gothic scheme was based on the first of two sketches in his notebook, showing an H-plan building 150 feet long enclosed by two three-story battlemented pavilions with Tudor-style windows, inscribed "Hospital for 150 patients middle pt" (75a).[166] The plan, allowing for ample cross-ventilation, is rooted in his Burlington Jail and the publications on progressive hospital design. But he clearly liked the association with the medieval hospice, for a variant quadrangular plan marked "Harbour" and "Canal Street" is also Gothic in character (75b).[167] (The Gothic sketches are sixty-two pages apart, reflecting his random use of the notebook, a variation in pagination that applies to two bridge projects dateable to 5 July and 15 August 1837.)[168] In between the Gothic sketches are two initial outline schemes for his Classical-style hospital.[169] In both, he conceived a raised pedimented portico with curving side stairs and, to afford better ventilation than his competitors, piazzas front and rear, outside the wards that were served by central corridors. One scheme has an E plan and the other, also inscribed "Hospital," a T plan. By 1 September, he had, as he informed Breedlove, decided on the "plain Gothic or Anglo-Saxon" style as "being most suitable to the locality of this Building," an H plan 200 feet by 80 feet. Through its three stories the wards were concentrated in the central spine opening off a 15-foot-wide corridor leading to staircases at either end. Overlooking the "double Colonnaded Piazza elevated upon a lofty arched platform," the wards, "lofty and Airy," with "thin partitions so disposed that they should be as one great room." Equally practical, the attendant communal and service accommodations occupy the cross-axial battlemented pavilions. Behind their square-headed Tudor and pointed Gothic windows are the kitchen and refectory; rooms for the housekeeper, matron, and nurses; isolation wards; a bathroom; and a laboratory or pharmacy.

Mills's keenness was churlishly rewarded in Washington and doubtless deeply resented by rival architects in New Orleans. He was informed that his plans had been mislaid shortly after being returned to the treasury secretary on 27 October 1837. Fortunately for Mills, the Army Surgeon's Department, which had been invited to adjudicate, obtained a set of his drawings. They found for Mills, who entered into a tentative agreement with two of his Washington contractors, Joel Downer and William Digges, before 16 July, when he told Breedlove that no satisfactory alternative offer had been received from New Orleans.[170] Breedlove, however, had already signed with Mondelle and Reynolds on 15 May to build a three-story hospital measuring 176 feet by 78 feet for $63,000. An engraving in *Norman's New Orleans* of 1845 indicates that they stole several features from Mills's scheme, including the Tudor Gothic style, side pavilions, and ventilating roof lantern. Suspecting such plagiarism, Mills vainly sought compensation in the summer and again in January 1841 and October 1852.[171] His one consolation might have been the melancholy history of the commission, which was still incomplete in 1844 when Mondelle "failed" in the contract; the hospital did not finally open until June 1848. Within ten years, the first floor had become waterlogged, and the upper stories were used as a powder store until its destruction by an explosion in 1861.

Mills fared better in the overall federal marine hospital program. For Poinsett, recently called back from semiretirement by President Van Buren, invited Mills to compile standard designs based on information gathered by Dr. Benjamin King of the medical board. On 7 November 1837 King supplied Poinsett with an estimate of the accommodations required for the projected hospitals on all the inland waterways: 100 patients apiece at Natchez (Mississippi), St. Louis (Missouri), Louisville (Kentucky), and Cleveland (Ohio) and 50 at Napoleon (Arkansas), Paducah (Kentucky), and Wheeling (Ohio), plus an allowance for enlargement "without destroying their symmetry."[172] Mills conceived two designs based on his New Orleans plans, having two double-story piazzas front and rear with a central corridor. He had full sets of drawings ready by 1 December, enabling Poinsett to submit a report to the House of Representatives on 15 December. This was subsequently published with lithograph elevations and plans of both schemes, engraved by P. Haas of Washington.[173] "No. 1," the larger and in the Neoclassical style, has an H plan measuring 150 feet by 85 feet; "No. 2," in the Gothic, has a rectangular main block and projected corner towers measuring 75 feet by 63 feet. "No. 1" develops the Latrobean Neoclassicism of Mills's Baltimore phase, including modified Delos Doric columns upholding the piazzas (76a, 76b). "No. 2" substitutes medieval

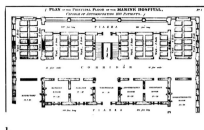

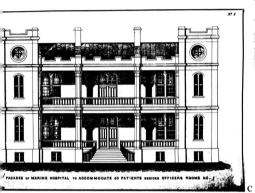

76.   Mills, (a, b) drawing and plan for a 100-bed Marine Hospital, and (c) drawing for a 50-bed Marine Hospital (1837).

detailing with multiple Gothic piers and tracery along the piazzas (76c). Behind those facades, clearly conceived to imply federal munificence, the respective plans revolve around the entrance axis and cross corridor, the first with a double-flight staircase at their intersection, and the second with dogleg stairs on either side. In both plans, the main-floor corridor divides the service accommodation from the cross-ventilated eight-bed wards. "No. 1" adds two wards with six beds in the rear projections, which in "No. 2" are earmarked for the staff. Only this set of plans indicated a "Future Extension" through the addition of side blocks, continuing the main layout.

Their qualities were recognized by the administration, the supervising surgeon of marine hospitals, as late as 1884 informing the House of Representatives that "the plans for marine hospitals drawn by Mr. Robert Mills have been followed . . . without material change, down to the hospital now being constructed at Chicago."[174] The program was under way from 1842, but not as swiftly as Mills implied in a letter of 21 March 1843 to Treasury Secretary John Spencer, claiming to have furnished the plans "for all the Custom houses, Marine hospitals (being eight in number) erected during the last twelve years."[175] For the computation actually refers to his five customhouses and the hospitals at Charleston, New Orleans, and most recently, in 1842, Mobile.[176] However, there is an entry in his notebook, estimating a hospital for Pensacola at $20,545.[177] The fact that he was not directly responsible for the individual hospitals does not diminish his achievement in providing excellent models for the eventual realization of this benevolent building program.

The marine hospital project, along with the panic of 1837, postponed Mills's ongoing campaign to win approval of his grandest plan for the Treasury Building. In October he proposed erecting a mirror image of his 1836 E-plan Treasury scheme on the west side of an aggrandized President's House. He sketched the skeleton idea on two facing pages of his notebook: a plan and south elevation headed "Improvement of the President's House," and a ground plan inscribed "Present arrangement of the Public offices on each side of the President's House—Octr. 1837—" (77).[178] He wanted to screen the north and south facades by extending the Ionic columns of the portico and south peristyle, which Hoban had added between 1824 and 1829 to Latrobe's designs. The columns were to continue along the east and west wings, now raised to the height of the main story above the existing low extension built by Latrobe in 1807.[179] The nobler scale was needed to support his redirecting of New York and Pennsylvania avenues to run diagonally between the public buildings up to the President's House. The complex to the east would accommodate not only the partially constructed treasury, but also the State Department and General Post Office. Opposite, a similarly composed fabric would house, from north to south, the Engineer's, War, and Navy departments. That arrangement anticipated the proposals he was to submit in 1841 and 1844–1845, while the overall layout prefigured another scheme of improvements to the President's House and public buildings drawn in about 1845.[180] However impracticable at that juncture, it was a superb vision not to be equaled over the ensuing decades, when the government could afford to provide the office space, space that executive departments already needed by 1837. Mills surely hoped that his proposal would provide employment in those troubled times and abort an anonymous plan for rebuilding the departments in two separate structures linked to the flanks of the President's House, copied into his notebooks as "Inappropriate & destroying the privacy &c. of the President's House."[181]

By then, the politics of restraint were starting to operate. On 21 September 1837 Mills had, via Noland, replied to complaints from Senator John Ruggles of Maine about the slow progress on the Patent Office.[182] Before the week was out, Noland asked Mills to field questions about the siting of the Treasury and the future of the adjacent State Department. Here was the tip of a veritable iceberg of retrenchment, the potency of which Mills at first misunderstood. By the new year, Mills was on the defensive and all too aware of the negative mood of Congress. The chairman of the Committee on Public Buildings, Levi Lincoln, was pressing for an investigation into the design, siting, and structure of both the Treasury and the Patent Office. After Lincoln had informed Mills of his intentions, nasty memories must again plagued the family in January

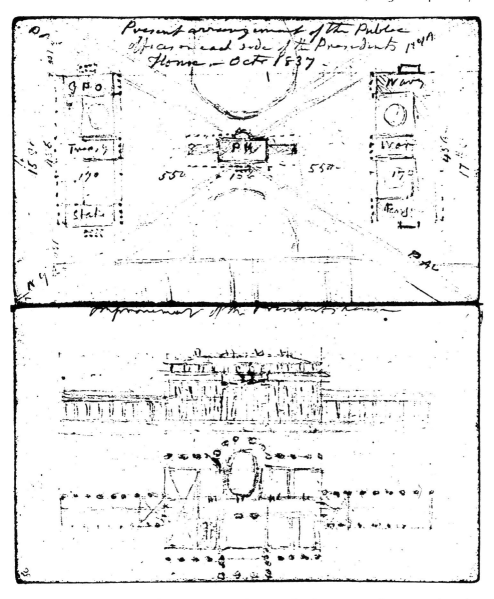

77.   Mills, sketch design for "improving" the President's House and environs (1837).

1838 and motivated his active participation in Eliza's work in establishing the Female Union Benevolent Society of Washington to provide employment for the indigent of the District.[183] News of the hardship suffered by so many of their fellow citizens in the recession surely assumed a particular relevance and likely became a constant refrain in their evening prayers. On 8 January, Mills steeled himself to draw up a long letter of justification to Lincoln.[184]

There is no official record of the receipt of this letter, probably because

Mills had not made a finished copy before Lincoln engaged Thomas U. Walter on 11 January 1838 with a fee of $500 to report on the construction of the Patent Office and Treasury.[185] The commissioners' letter books prove that Mills attempted to short-circuit the investigation, on 20 January suggesting to Lincoln that the main 400-foot block of his Treasury be finished, keeping the basement of the rear wing as a link to a parallel block 180 feet to the west with six column porticos at each intersection.[186] The two blocks would be further joined at their northern end by another, inscribed "State," alike graced externally by a colonnade continuing across the 230-foot southern expanse of the resulting "open court." Lincoln and the committee were not impressed, and no response is recorded. Whether or not antipathetic to Mills personally, whose professional enthusiasm might have been mistaken for conceit, they were daily confronted by the tottering national economy. In any event, Lincoln, a Whig and Northerner, Harvard educated, and former governor of Massachusetts, uncharitably allowed no quarter to Mills, a Democrat and Southerner despite his radical views.

Walter had accepted Lincoln's invitation with alacrity, despite purporting to find the task "delicate and unpleasant in the extreme," since he admired Mills as a "venerable and accomplished" architect.[187] That glib protestation, printed in the Lincoln committee report, belied Walter's matter-of-fact answers to the questions set by Lincoln. The site of the Treasury, Walter contended, ruined the view of the Capitol from the President's House and vice versa. The structure was weak; the external walls should have been at least 3.5 inches thicker. The internal plan was not functional, the passages being too narrow, the rooms too small, and the thirty-seven rooms in the basement too dark. Finally, the colonnade along Fifteenth Street was aesthetically monotonous. With regard to the Patent Office, he neatly concentrated on those features attributable to Mills alone, recommending that the antae be thickened, and the basement vault be reinforced with cross-walls plus iron bars, while noting that the upper exhibition room was unnecessarily large. His summation was alike double-edged. He recommended that the public buildings flanking the President's House should be demolished and replaced with a single complex on Lafayette Square based on the "design furnished by your architect in 1834, with such improvement as his mature judgment would no doubt suggest." Apart from failing to clarify whether he meant William P. Elliot, Jr., or Mills, the commission would once again be open for competition, with Mills at a distinct disadvantage.

Mills took nearly three weeks to respond, on 21 February composing a letter that would be included with Lincoln's report No. 737, published by the second session of the Twenty-fifth Congress on 29 March 1838. The site of the Treasury, Mills declared, had been chosen by Congress, sensibly bypassing reference to Jackson's legendary intervention to avoid any partisan backlash. The obstruction of the view between the Capitol and the President's House was only partial, and the slope on Fifteenth Street was to be reduced. The structural system adopted for both the Treasury and the Patent Office was conservative when compared with the thinner dimensions of earlier structures such as his New England customhouses, while as durable as Walter's costly massive stone and iron-reinforced vaults in Girard College. Despite Walter's strictures, neither the Treasury nor the Patent Office vaults had "the least fissure, settlement, or giving in any part of the work." As for the internal plan of the Treasury, the room sizes were determined by existing federal standards and provided 114 suitable offices. The attic rooms along the front would be for records, but they could be upgraded to offices by the installation of skylights; the passages were adequately lighted and wide. Finally, on the Treasury alone, the colonnade was appropriate and had precedents in French and Classical architecture. A neat thrust that, since most Americans admired the French as their allies in defeating British colonialism, and the ancients as an inspiration for their Constitution. He was equally astute in reverting to the program as a whole, reminding the budget-conscious Congress that the choice of lower quality stone for the Treasury and poor finish of the side walls of the Patent Office (to which wings were to be added) had been dictated by economy. Secure in his logic, he aimed a Parthian shot at Walter's pretensions to superior qualifications by regretting the "necessity which has here compelled me to enter into the defence of my professional practice, which for the first time, has been called in question."

Mills acquitted himself forcefully enough to concern Lincoln and his committee. On 28 February they called in Parris, ostensibly as an adjudicator, but charged with answering a slightly longer set of questions. Nowhere did Parris find for Mills, even if he acknowledged that the completed vaulting was sound. But he recommended that the system be replaced by the iron-hooped "spheroidal form" used in Britain and being employed in Ammi B. Young's Boston customhouse, and that the fireplaces be replaced by hot-air furnaces. While Mills was to follow up that idea, he sensibly ignored every issue except the vaulting system when he replied to Parris on 14 March. Thereby, he moved the argument toward his proven expertise and cited two independent authorities: the British scientist Charles Hutton, author of *The Principles of Bridges* (1801), and the French engineer and architect Jean Baptiste Rondelet, author of *L'Art de bâtir* (1802). He tabulated their rules for the relative thickness of pier to vaulting arch and compared the dimensions he had decided for the Treasury, Patent Office, State Lunatic Asylum, and customhouses, adding, for good measure, those the former architect of the Capitol, Latrobe, had ordered for the Bank of Philadelphia. The resulting figures were effective testimony.

In all Mills's buildings, the piers were thicker than either Rondelet or Hutton advocated, and those in the Treasury and Patent Office, respectively at 4 feet 3 inches and 4 feet 6 inches thick, were nearly twice those in Latrobe's bank.

Mills had again discomforted Lincoln and his committee, who now ferreted out adverse comment from Brown, the superintendent; Wood, the head carpenter; and William Archer, whom they generously rated as a master builder. In fact, Archer's Bridge Street Presbyterian Church, at M and Thirtieth streets, was constructed from 1820 to 1840 and was greatly over budget.[188] Prepared to countenance the grudges of men whose competence Mills had very likely questioned, Lincoln seems to have ignored his last attempt at a compromise, drafted on 26 March.[189] Mills, temporarily loosing his nerve, suggested that the new Treasury be roofed at the level of the second floor to create temporary accommodation and storage awaiting the completion of the new public office complex. He only asked that the committee decide on an appropriate site for the complex and secure "better materials" for its external fabric. If Lincoln actually received Mills's letter, he was unmoved and let his committee's highly critical report go to press unchanged.

House Report 737 found against Mills in every respect, despite the inclusion of his telling rebuttals, and the committee's ironic proposal that future federal buildings be faced with marble or granite. First, the members recommended the demolition of the partially built Treasury. Then they introduced a maliciously irrelevant issue by calling for the abandonment of Mills's unofficial 1837 scheme of a "Corresponding structure on the opposite side of the President's Square, on seventeenth street." Finally, they proposed a bill for the "removal" of the walls of the new Treasury in order to construct a "fireproof building for the Post Office Department" designed by "a skillful architect."

"The Committee have allowed themselves to listen to idle reports from idle men in this City," Mills moderately complained in a letter posted on 27 March to his fellow Charlestonian Hugh Swinton Legaré, founder of the *Southern Review* (1828) and at this time a Union Democratic congressman.[190] Possibly encouraged by the politically astute Legaré, Mills sent an address to the House on 2 April making just that point. Likely Legaré, a respected figure in Washington whom President Tyler was to appoint attorney general and interim secretary of state two years before his untimely death in 1843, steered the address into print on 4 April annexed to House Report 737. In it, Mills strengthened his case by reiterating that the Treasury and Patent Office vaults had no cracks. He also wakened Congress to the expensive "inexpediency, indeed fearful responsibility of removing a fire-proof building near completion, so absolutely needed for the safe keeping of the public records, until another equally safe building should be first erected."

Contrary to his desolate aside to Legaré—"I have no one here to defend me"—an articulate band of congressmen, mainly from the southern and western states, rose to demolish Lincoln's assertions. First up was Archibald Yell of Arkansas, who had served with Jackson at the Battle of New Orleans. Yell launched into the illogicality of Lincoln's bill, which in the name of economy would involve greater expenditure and destroy a building "good enough for all the purposes for which it was intended."[191] The next day, Ratliff Boon of Indiana came to Mills's defense. Endorsing the opposition to the bill voiced by Francis Pickens from Edgefield, South Carolina, Boon warned, "If we are to pull down the work of one architect, upon fault being found by another architect who may want a profitable job, there will be no end to putting up and pulling down the public work." What a sharp piece of homespun oratory, and what an incisive commentary on the ills of the American architectural profession and federal patronage! That wise witticism brought Levi Lincoln back to his feet to repeat the accusations against Mills in a speech occupying almost five pages of small print in the appendix to the *Congressional Globe* for 1838.[192] "This is no party affair," he averred, adding, "No unfavorable bias preoccupied the minds of the members" of his committee, "to the prejudice of Mr. Mills." But his argument was sullied by an assortment of unsubstantiated jibes—for example, when the designs for the public offices had been exhibited in 1835, the majority of congressmen preferred Elliot's submission as "simple, neat, convenient and economical," to that of Mills, which was "complex, ornate, incongruous, and extravagant."

Frustrated but tenacious, Lincoln petitioned President Van Buren for aid.[193] Van Buren, however, who was schooled in the realities of politics while holding office in New York and then in Washington, set about finding a compromise policy. On 23 April, he appointed three of his senior cabinet secretaries as commissioners of the public buildings. None could be accused of being prejudiced against Mills, and two were, if anything, sympathetic to his cause and to that of public architecture. They were Secretary of War Joel Poinsett and Treasury Secretary Levi Woodbury. Nor would the choice of the third commissioner have weakened Mills's growing sense of salvation in the last week of April. For John Forsyth, secretary of state, was Virginia-born and a Jacksonian Democratic senator, originally appointed to his present post by Old Hickory himself.

The commissioners were charged with assessing Levi Lincoln's report. Unlike Lincoln, they solicited information from Noland, who on 1 May praised Mills's expertise, especially in fireproof-brick construction.[194] Their judgment was further affected by the resumption of the debate in Congress on 8 June. Lincoln persisted in pushing his bill for demolishing the Treasury. Now, however, he fell back on Walter's opinion and moderated his attack on Mills, for whom he insincerely expressed a "long personal regard."[195] Few members came to his support. One, Zadok Pratt, a tanner from New York and a Democrat of the Van Buren circle, received a verbal drubbing from Pennsylvania Democrat George M. Keim, who was reminded of the conflict in the Homeric epics he had studied at Princeton, "We have now Mr. Mills and Mr. Walter, the very Ajax and Hector of this modern seize."[196] Keim had done his homework well, perhaps tutored by Mills, who could have been in the public gallery for the debate. He devastated Walter's credentials: not "one syllable" in Stephen Girard's will could be "found to justify the massive display of truncated pyramids, or those marble columns, the cost of whose entablature alone would have brought personal comfort and intellectual blessings to numerous suffering orphans." Vintage congressional debating this, even if it unfairly omitted the intervention of Biddle and the trustees in the Girard College commission, requiring Walter to continue the columns of the porticos along the flanks. Keim went on to declare roundly: "The veracity of Mr. Mills with his most exemplary character, are too well established in this community to be impunged. . . . The filthy slang of the Billingsgate School [a colorful allusion to the fish market in London] illy becomes any censors of public taste." Both Walter and Parris, as well as the Lincolnites, had failed to appreciate that Mills's "perfectly simple" and functional design for the Treasury represented an appropriate American style, which Keim efficiently summarized: "If science is progressive, so should the polite arts keep pace with them, and American architecture become a new school, in which might predominate, as a characteristic feature, the principles of economy, simplicity and convenience."

The mettlesome opposition to Lincoln's report indubitably swayed the commissioners more than Mills's appeal to Woodbury on 5 May for the resumption of work to end the distress of the workmen's families and to provide fireproof storage for public records.[197] On 12 June, they ordered Noland to resume work, since it was "sufficiently apparent that the new Treasury Building is not to be removed or altered by any Act of Congress."[198] On 14 June, Mills wrote ecstatically to Gilmor, "We have recommenced the work on the New Treasury building, Congress having decided against the Report of the Committee."[199] After the heat of the debate had cooled, he wrote again to Gilmor on 29 June relating the commissioners' comment that the "only error I committed in this business was in not getting the President [Jackson] to endorse the paper on which the Plan was drawn, on the one adopted [the E plan]. The members of the Cabinet (Gen. Woodbury, Mr. Kendall, Mr. Dickerson), all testified to the fact that a Southern Building was to be attached to the present one under erection & to the future changes in the State department building." However, he had to be content with continuing only the main block and central rear projection of the Treasury. The commissioners declined to approve the request he drafted on 27 June that the State Department be modified to "adapt it to the style and fireproof character of the new building" and the grade on Fifteenth Street be leveled between New York and Pennsylvania avenues.[200] Although required to alter the vaulting of the main-floor vestibule and of the Grand Exhibition Room in the Patent Office, Mills had the satisfaction of publicly celebrating his victory in the annual report he submitted to Noland on 1 December 1838.[201] The treasury secretary had taken up his quarters in the central projection of the new building, most of which was finished, while at the Patent Office the centers of the vaults were struck in the upper story and the basement of the grand portico completed.

By then, however, Lincoln had gained a partial revenge. For in July he successfully moved that during the summer recess "the arrangement of the [speaker's] chair and seats of members" be restored "to the state in which they existed previous to the alteration" completed by Mills two years earlier.[202] Congress found for Mills on structure but not on acoustics, even if Lincoln's shuffle failed to render the members' debates any more audible. And the commissioners had entrenched Mills's position by unofficially awarding him the commission for a new courthouse at Alexandria on 7 July. Coming on top of the resumption of work on the public buildings, it put an end to any idea Mills harbored of responding to the advertisements announcing competitions for the state house and masonic hall at Lancaster, Ohio, which he had clipped and stuffed into the pouch of his notebook.[203]

By 17 July, he could show the commissioners plans for converting the former Bank of Alexandria to keep within the $15,000 appropriation, although, as he wrote two days later, the conversion would be "neither tasteful nor convenient."[204] That may have been true, yet it seems more than fortuitous that Mills also signed two drawings for a new courthouse on that same day.[205] The crisply rendered drawing of the facade illustrates how Mills attuned his main South Carolina courthouse type to the more rigorous classicism of his own federal architecture (78a). The portico of four Doric columns, unfluted for economy but spaced more widely at the center in emulation of the Propylaea gateway onto the Athenian Acropolis, sets the pattern of severe openings and compressed ornament. Their verticality, reinforced by the rectangular arcade beneath and the steeply curved steps, continues up to the side chimneys and central ventilator lantern, itself loosely imitated from the elegant Lysicrates Monument at Athens. The upward movement is nicely countered across the balanced 60-foot-square front by a finish of horizontal scored stucco, ornamental recessed panels, and continuous entablature. The interplay of vertical and horizontal lineaments is finally resolved by the low-pitched pediment and roof. Inside, the model of the ancient world reappears in the ampitheatral courtroom on the upper floor (78b). About it, Mills packed rooms for the judge, court officers, and jury, as well as the internal staircase. This descended to

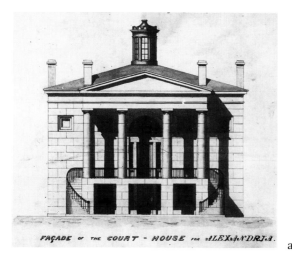

FAÇADE OF THE COURT - HOUSE FOR ALEXANDRIA.

a

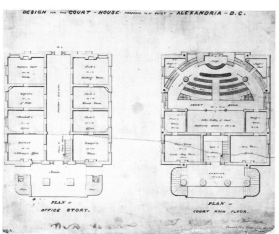

b

DESIGN FOR THE COURT - HOUSE PROPOSED TO BE BUILT IN ALEXANDRIA - D.C.

PLAN OF OFFICE STORY.

PLAN OF COURT ROOM FLOOR.

78. Mills, drawing for the courthouse, Alexandria (1838–1840): (a) front elevation and (b) plan (1838).

the central corridor running through the lower floor, its 14-foot width probably a consequence of the criticism aimed at those in the Treasury. On either hand were four interconnected offices for daily use, each with a separate window and fireplace. One innovation was the installation of water closets under the external staircases.

Perhaps wary after the Treasury episode, Noland delayed recommending Mills's design until late October.[206] Tenders were advertised on 17 November, and a contract for the zinc-roofed brick structure was signed with J. Dixon of Washington on 26 December for $11,699.58 with a deadline of 1 November 1839.[207] Progress was slowed, however, by the decision on 22 April 1839 to insert a 3-foot-high granite base and, no doubt chivvied by Mills, to introduce fireproof vaulting on the first floor. Subsequently, on 5 June, Dixon was ordered to further heighten the base and to vault the court floor. To check their proper execution, Mills traveled to Alexandria sometime before 26 November, when he was reimbursed $10 for expenses; not until 20 February 1840 did he receive a fee of $300 for his original drawings. Because of the alterations, completion was postponed until 1842, and costs increased to nearly $18,000. Unfortunately, Noland was much too sanguine about Dixon's progress in his own 1839 annual report, wherein he nonetheless fairly described the "whole arrangement of the building" as "convenient and comfortable for the transaction of court business, and the office rooms safe depositories for the public records."[208]

The best form for "court business" motivated Mills to write at about this time to his friend Judge William Cranch suggesting alterations to the two-story rectangular court in the east wing of the Washington City Hall.[209] Mills's specific proposals correspond with the sketch elevation and amphitheatral plan for a "Court May 22nd" in his notebook. The semicircular rows of seats face desks for the attorneys and clerk, and against the straight rear wall the judge's dais. On either side are benches for the jury, rooms for the court officers, and a staircase to a public gallery above the lobby, apparently supported on cast-iron columns. This more compact arrangement, which he estimated at a little over $3,000, was intended to permit the introduction of a second courtroom over the existing space. Cranch could have agreed with Mills's argument for more space, since the caseload of his court was growing. But the city had no funds to spare, and it was not until 1849 that Congress voted sufficient money to build a reduced version of Hadfield's original design for the center section of the city hall.

The administration preferred that available federal funds be expended on a new General Post Office, long overdue since the old post office in the former Blodgett's Hotel had burned on 15 December 1836. On 24 December 1838 Noland ordered Mills to prepare estimates for an entirely new building, rather than as a wing to the Treasury. Over Christmas, Mills worked hard on tracing out a design upon which to calculate the cost of using various materials for the facing, ranging from freestone to marble. The only interruption was the compilation of a specification requested by his friend Asbury Dickins, now in his third year as secretary of the senate, to rectify the inadequate heating in that wing of the Capitol.[210] By 9 January 1839 the tireless Mills had submitted a "book of drawings" and a list of estimates for the new General Post Office. These began at $280,000 for a split-granite fireproof structure, rising to $328,000 for one clad in marble "according to ancient practice."[211] From the outset he anticipated the future needs of the government by proposing that it buy the whole square between E and F and Seventh and Eighth streets to permit future enlargement of the Post Office, and he continued to polish his initial design between 9 and 30 January.[212] The month's effort established the essentials: a half-quadrangular plan that would permit easy extension by repetition on the northern section of the block, a fireproof brick- and granite-faced structure of three stories above a basement, and a six-column engaged and pedimented Ionic portico (later changed to the Corinthian order) to grace the entrance at the center of the 200-foot main front on E Street. The portico was to be lifted up, in the Palladian manner, to the first-floor level and its columns to reach 50 feet to the entablature. Above the portico would rise "a tower," 140 feet high, modeled after the Egyptian obelisk and containing "an illuminated clock with its great bell, contemplated to be of a size to be heard in every part of the city."[213] The corners were to be decorated with pilasters and the windows on the second floor divided into three vertical sections, distantly reminiscent of the Palladian or Venetian type, if essentially functional "so as to give large central light to the office rooms, and afford in the exterior a greater mass of unbroken masonry—giving the appearance of superior strength."

Grace more than strength was to become Mills's paramount aim as he further refined the design up to his official commissioning on 3 March 1839. This development was spurred by the commissioners' rejection of the tower as too expensive. Here government economy served Mills well, for it would have disrupted the stylistic integrity of his General Post Office. Fortunately, however, the commissioners did allow him to upgrade the quality of the ornament and materials. The basement and first floor were beautified with channeled rustication, the facade ennobled with pilasters, the second-floor windows capped with triangular and elliptical pediments, the entablature crowned with a decorated cornice and balustrade, and the side wings each aggrandised by two-column pedimented porticos. Most important, on 4 May the commissioners ordered the facade to be faced with marble above the first floor, granite being used for the basement and on the rear.[214] That upgrading accorded Mills the distinction of truly enhancing the standard of federal architecture and might have prompted him to substitute the more complex Corinthian order of the Temple of Jupiter Stator, which, in addition to being the first marble building in ancient Rome, had been used by Latrobe as a model for the House of Representatives (79). Mills also echoed the ornamental pattern of the Capitol facade as refurbished by Bulfinch in the projected channeled rusticated piers of the basement and first floor, triangular and elliptical headed windows, and surmounting ballustraded cornice. Perhaps the resemblance struck President Van Buren as he looked over Mills's design on the occasion of laying the foundation stone on 25 May. But not until the fabric neared completion in 1840 could the knowledgeable appreciate the extent to which Mills had drawn on the Renaissance and Palladian sources of American architecture. For the General Post Office heralded the demise, in the northeastern states at least, of the Greek and the rise of the Renaissance Revival; its opening in 1841 coincided

79.   Mills, General Post Office, Washington, D.C. (1839–1842), in ca. 1865.

with the publication of Andrew Jackson Downing's *Landscape Gardening*, promoting the architectural style of the Italian villa. No wonder the architecturally well-informed and astute Robert Dale Owen could hail the General Post Office as a "graceful example" of the "Italian," adding, "It may be considered Palladian in its general character, but is simpler than most of the Vicentine's designs."[215] Mills would also acknowledge that influence in 1848 when, on a card listing the major statistics of the public buildings, he denominated the General Post Office "Grecian (Italian)."[216]

The facade, impressive and homogeneous even after the street was lowered in 1871, expressed the intelligently designed and capacious brick-vaulted interior (80).[217] The main entrance portico formed by two Doric columns cleverly reduced the scale of the external Corinthian order to the height of the office floors. Behind that he introduced a broad hall, 31 feet by 34.5 feet, screened by two more Doric columns from a broad cross corridor. This passed two semicircular staircases to intersect with the narrower corridors giving access to the offices in the wings. All the passageways were decorated with a frieze having the Greek anthemion pattern from the Erechtheion on the Acropolis. Every office had individual windows and separate entrances, as well as interconnecting

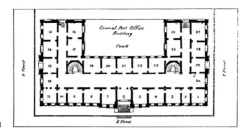

a

b

80.   Mills, General Post Office, Washington, D.C.: (a) plan and (b) engraving.

doors. They varied in size from 19 feet by 19.5 feet to 19 feet by 50 feet; one, 50 feet by 39 feet, which was earmarked for the city post office on Seventh Street, was deleted.

With the Whigs at bay and the commissioners supportive, the structure was executed according to Mills's reformed building practice. In conjunction with Noland, he compiled lists of proposals from each contractor, signed separate agreements with each tradesman and supplier, and ensured their strict adherence. Consequently, the relevant documents are remarkably complete, from the contract signed with J. Dove on 5 April 1839 to clear the site at 18¾ cents per perch of earth removed, to that signed on 29 June with Masterton and Smith for the marble work, using stone from the Kain and Morgan Quarries in East Chester, New York, but prepared with their own machinery, for a total of $101,107.99. Emery and Gault were the granite masons, working stone from quarries near Ellicott Mills in Maryland, while J. Dixon cut the sandstone from Towson's or Been's quarry in the same state. Through 1839, 1840, and 1841 came myriad minor agreements, as that on 24 May 1839 with G. Reynolds to supply 3,000 bushels of hydraulic cement at 37½ cents a bushel or, on 15 October 1840, with T. Corcoran to supply 300,000 bricks at $7.25

per thousand. Earlier, on 26 June, the commissioner signed with the Philadelphian John Skirving to install three large furnaces and apparatus "for conducting and diffusing of the warm air throughout the corridors and passages" before November for the price of $2,790, including the gas pipes. Here was proof that Mills did not allow rivalry to cloud his selection of first-rate contractors, since Skirving had been recommended to him by Strickland.[218]

The commissioners' ledger also discloses the greater care for detail that Mills had helped to introduce. Thus it records his monthly salary payments (now averaging between $208 and $250) and such fascinating details as W. P. Elliot "laying down lines" for the building on 19 July 1839, or on 20 May 1841 the stonecutters and laborers receiving $94.31 compensation for time lost during the "funeral of the late President" William Henry Harrison, who died of pneumonia contracted at the time of his inauguration. The building was finished remarkably quickly for a total of $475,437.41, which, allowing for the substitution of marble and inflation, was only $100,300 above the appropriation; Mills's actual commission of March 1839 had set the figure at $280,000. This compared well with the more than $650,000 that would be expended on its extension by the erection of its mirror image at the rear, as he had proposed in 1838 and would again in February 1851. That commission, though, went to Walter who squeezed in more ornament and substituted a cast-iron and brick vaulting system; from 1858 Walter was demoted and the work carried on under the direction of Captains Montgomery C. Meigs, W. B. Franklin, and Edward Clark.

Once Mills's General Post Office was opened (the water closets were fitted up in 1842, and the railing and tripods erected two years later), the usually prosaic Noland was moved to describe it in his report to Congress as "this Beautiful building."[219] Most agreed with his opinion, even the critical Charles Dickens, who, in 1842, declared it to be "very compact and very beautiful."[220] His sentiments were to be amplified, and politicized, by Anthony Reintzel in the *Washington Directory and Government Register* (1843); he compared its "lively, brilliant, and spangled whiteness" begetting the idea of "youthful, healthy and elastic beauty" with the "sandstone structures" suggestive of the Union crumbling to pieces by its own weight. Four years later, the Irish-born architect Charles B. Cluskey, who had produced some fine Neo-Greek edifices at Augusta and Millidgeville in Georgia, singled out the General Post Office in his *Report on the Public Buildings to the House of Representatives* as "the most chaste and best proportioned of the public buildings in the metropolis, and the only one that is built of materials that will stand the test of time—marble and granite."[221] That same year, the pioneering woman architectural historian Louisa Tuthill, in her *History of Architecture,* welcomed it as "a magnificent building" that, if extended according to Mills's wishes, would become "one of the most splendid buildings in the United States."[222] Still more gratifying for Mills, keen to place American architecture on an international footing, the influential London architectural magazine *The Builder* published an unsigned letter accounting the General Post Office "finely proportioned... and an elegant piece of architecture."[223] Those words hold true to this day, as the enlarged building continues to serve the republic, housing the Federal Trade Commission and, with the nearly contiguous Patent Office, now the National Portrait Gallery, part of a pleasant pedestrian mall.

When Dove was clearing the site for the foundation of the General Post Office, Mills on 18 March 1839 had heard more good news from Noland. In response to a recent appropriation of $39,000, the Commission of Public Buildings had accepted his "Design for the New Gaol. Proposed To Be Erected In The City Of Washington By Robert Mills Architect of the Public Buildings" (81).[224] This combined a plan of the main floor and an elevation of an utilitarian Neo-Gothic front. The Gothic dressing was pared down as much as the internal layout was compressed. The buttresses, closer spaced across the middle five bays, reinforced the plain walls and with the battlementing summoned up the medieval fortification, imprecisely defined in his 1841 annual report as "Anglo-Saxon."[225] The squat spired tower at the center ventilated the staircase and corridors, while the simplified iron-sashed Tudor windows would provide ample light and air and divest the public front on Judiciary Square, adjacent to the city hall, "of the painful appearance of a prison house."

The quantity of accommodation clinched the approval of the commissioners. Behind the raised entrance, a 10-foot-wide hall intersected the staircase and corridor that communicated with the cross-vaulted front rooms, measuring 21.5 feet by 15 feet, assigned to the warden and his assistant, and wards of 19 feet by 15 feet for debtors. In addition, the corridor let air through slits into the chain of eight cells, each measuring 8.5 feet by 10 feet, for criminals at the rear. Their iron-latticed doors could be reached only from a narrow passage across the rear, accessed from the staircase and terminating in privies. The secure division of criminal, debtor, and service accommodations was repeated on the upper and lower floors without loss of reasonable illumination and ventilation. The risk of fire was minimized through an entire brick-vaulted structure, stone stairs, and paving. The commissioners could feel assured that it would represent a considerable improvement on the inadequate and unsanitary ten-year-old jail that Bulfinch had built for a mere $1,609.32.

They rewarded Mills by engaging him to supervise the construction of the jail, assisted by a clerk, and agreeing that "the Architect shall have full power at any time during the progress of the work to make such changes in the plan... as he may deem best for the public interest."[226] Moreover, they raised his annual salary to $2,500, a decent remuneration, from 1 April 1839. On the

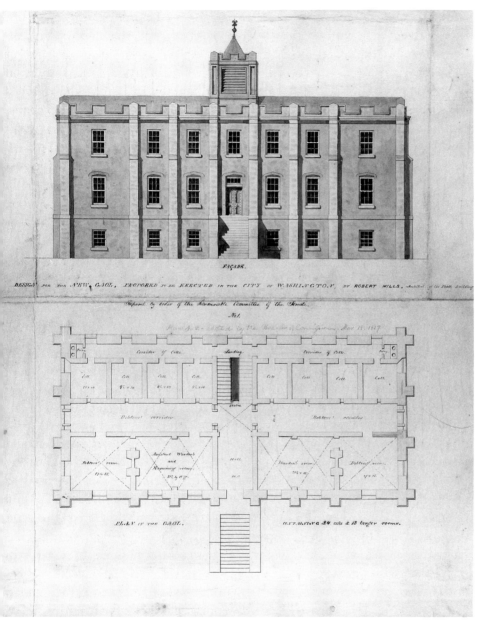

FAÇADE.

DESIGN FOR THE NEW GAOL, PROPOSED TO BE ERECTED IN THE CITY OF WASHINGTON, BY ROBERT MILLS, Architect of the Public Buildings

Prepared by Order of the Honourable Committee of the Senate.

No 1.

PLAN OF THE GAOL.   CONTAINING 24 cells & 13 larger rooms.

81.   Mills, drawing for the "New Gaol," Washington D.C. (1839–1841), elevation and plan (1839).

strength of his new salary, he moved to a house on P Street on the north side between 4½ Street and Delaware Avenue in the pleasant residential area being developed at Buzzard Point near the Arsenal (close to the modern Fort McNair) and purchased goods and real estate, to judge from the series of transactions witnessed before the Washington Recorder of Deeds.[227] At this time, Eliza may have closed her Washington Female Academy, since two of her daughters were married. The location of their new home may have been less convenient for conducting business but was more salubrious. Mills's confidence spread into the contracts that he and Noland wrote with the major tradesmen R. Staunton and R. Brockett, who were responsible for the masonry and brickwork. Although another spate of congressional parsimony delayed construction of the enclosing wall until 1841, the jail was finished under budget, $37,851, and in operation from 1842 to 1864, being demolished in 1874. By then, James Renwick's Neo-Norman Smithsonian Institution on the Mall had wrought a more indelible change in the aesthetics of federal design.

Mills's interest in the Gothic style was further rekindled by an invitation to advise on the design of a new building for the U.S. Military Academy in West Point, New York, overlooking the Hudson River, a setting that many at the time believe was appropriate for irregular composition, diverse surface, and naturalistically inspired decoration of that style of architecture. In February 1838 the old academy building, formerly the chapel and then housing the library and observatory, had burned.[228] As a result, the superintendent, Major Richard Delafield, approached at least one architect, Isaiah Rogers, for a design of an observatory,[229] which was needed to provide instruction in the rudiments of astronomy, vital for the officer cadets' training, notably toward their duty of patrolling and surveying the frontier. War Secretary Joel Poinsett was keen to improve the academy's facilities as part of his program for universal military training and engaged Mills to refine two elevations "of the building for the Library and Philosophical Apparatus of the U.S. Military Academy as originally designed by Major Delafield" (82).[230] Mills retained the major features on the two elevations he returned and signed on 4 June 1839.[231] They consist of a central observatory and two-story ranges and corner towers, clad in a Neo-Gothic uniform of battlements and turrets. But if he followed Delafield's overall composition, Mills mustered a more accomplished Tudor mode evidently by reference to engravings in Britton's *Architectural Antiquities of Great Britain*. The domed polygonal turret, for instance, recalls the ogee-arched canopies capping the market crosses in Malmesbury, Wiltshire, and Chichester, Sussex, engraved by Britton, each of which had buttresses topped by finials comparable with those of both Mills's elevations.

Poinsett was not much impressed with Mills's drawings, perhaps disliking their lack of archaeological conviction. He rejected his bill for $100 dated

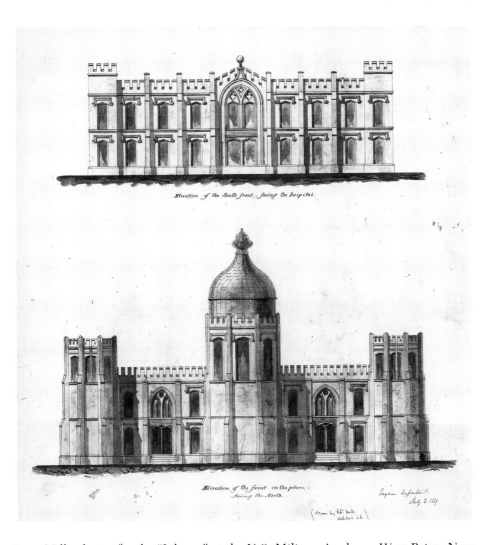

Elevation of the South front,—facing the hospital.

Elevation of the front on the plane,—facing the North.

Engineer Department
July 2, 1839

[Drawn by R.A. Mills,
Architect &c.]

82.   Mills, design for the "Library" at the U.S. Military Academy, West Point, New York, front and rear (1839).

1 August 1839 and ordered Captain F. A. Smith of the Corps of Engineers to send Mills a fee of $50 for a "very imperfect design."[232] However, a version of the Mills and Delafield scheme was erected in 1839–1840 for $50,216.[233] Faced with red sandstone and measuring 160 feet long by 78 feet wide, it housed offices for several of the senior staff of the academy together with an equitorial telescope in a central dome of 27 feet diameter. About the time building commenced, Mills, pleased that his efforts had been partially recognized, on 30 January 1840 presented the War Department with a prized possession from the hand of Colonel John Senf, one of his earliest heroes: the

"Plan of an enclosed Battery for 8 guns, prepared to be built On the Publick [Land]—and on James Island, near the Place of the old Fort-Johnson 1787— Ch. Senf Col. Engineer."[234]

Poinsett, nonetheless, almost two years later used Mills's comparable Neo-Gothic scheme when endeavoring to acquire for the National Institution for the Promotion of Science, of which he was president and Mills a founding member, the munificent bequest willed to the American people by the wealthy English dilettante James Smithson. A bachelor, Smithson had died in 1829, but his estate was not finally settled until May 1838, when 105 bags of gold sovereigns, then the equivalent of $508,318.46, had been dispatched by ship to New York.[235] Poinsett wanted to seize the initiative before both he and President Van Buren left office in March 1841, Van Buren having lost the Democratic nomination in 1840 to Harrison. On 4 January 1841, Poinsett had read "Discourse on the Objects and Importance of the National Institution for the Promotion of Science" to collect the "national productions" of America and encourage "a taste for literary and scientific pursuits," especially necessary "owing to the condition of our country, which requires all her sons to labor, and does not admit of a class of learned men of leisure." Then he persuaded Lewis F. Linn to present a bill in the Senate proposing that the chief cabinet secretaries be appointed trustees of the Smithson Bequest and that the National Institution organize the establishment of a suitable building on the Mall.[236] The bill was entered for debate on 10 and 17 February but did not pass. Meantime, however, on 16 February, Mills gave Poinsett a deftly drawn pen-and-wash rendering (83):

> Plan of the Mall with the adjoining streets and Avenues: the relative position of the Capitol, President's House and other Public Buildings: and particularly the improvement of that part of the Mall situated between 7th and 12th Strts: with a view to a Botannic Garden, connected with the establishment of the Smithsonian Institution, proposed to be in charge of the National Institution for the promotion of science.[237]

Mills's plan visualizes a remarkable transformation, particularly of the barely developed Mall area, which had been allocated by President Washington in 1796 for a botanical garden and granted to the Columbian Institute for that purpose in 1820 by Congress. The Washington Canal would be refurbished and given two new bridges in order to incorporate it into an overall landscape scheme. The Capitol grounds were to be laid out formally, only the lower section between Pennsylvania and Maryland avenues having an irregular planting of trees. The Capitol itself would be extended eastward, in line with

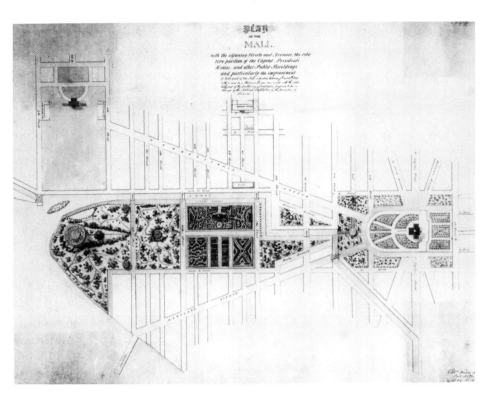

83.   Mills, plan for the Mall, Washington, D.C. (1841).

Mills's 1835 proposal for a new House of Representatives. On its axis, he projected a rectangular Neo-Gothic National/Smithsonian Institution building surrounded by a botanical garden, with to the west a large circular monument overlooking the Potomac and aligned with the President's House, anticipating the glorious present-day vista from the Capitol: down the Mall to the Washington Monument and Lincoln Memorial, symbolizing the most momentous phases in the creation of the nation. Yet Mills, unlike the 1902 McMillan Commission, which established the basis of the modern layout, did not forge a direct link with the ground south of the President's House. Apart from extending the existing streets, he wanted to introduce a semicircular driveway to its main entrance and drew the flanking public buildings as matching three-sided blocks. Thus besides answering the needs of the institution, Mills coincidentally sought to alter congressional opinion in favor of his proposed Treasury extension and to reactivate the Washington National Monument Society's request for a site on the Mall, rejected by the Senate in 1838.

 Mills, aided by the draftsman John E. Scheel, also worked up more detailed drawings of the elevation and plan for the institution together with alternative arrangements for its grounds. One larger ink drawing depicting the main,

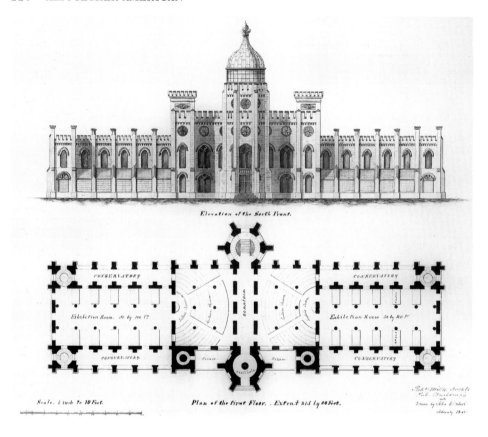

Elevation of the South Front.

Scale. 1 Inch to 10 Feet.   Plan of the First Floor. . Extent 315 by 80 Feet.

84.   Mills, design for the National/Smithsonian Institution, Washington, D.C. (1841), drawn by John Scheel.

south, front, and floor plan, was signed in a shaky hand by Mills but inscribed "Drawn by John E. Scheel February 1841" (84).[238] The signature perhaps indicates the beginning of a disorder of the motor nerves controlling Mills's hand, which was to cause him to depend on the services of draftsmen and on members of his family to write his correspondence and articles. He was able to execute two smaller designs for the grounds with color washes, one being inscribed "Picturesque View of the Building and Grounds in front," although depicting jets d'eau typical of the more formal French seventeenth-century landscape garden, much as the front of his institution has Gothic features attached to a basically Palladian tripartite framework.[239] The design of the facade develops his West Point Library proposal. Its 315-foot length is dominated by an ogee-capped octagonal tower climbing 130 feet in front of a three-story battlemented block framed by square turrets and containing one of the main staircases; the other occupied a tower at the rear. The disparate forms of the exterior are bonded together at the upper level by circular openings containing quatrefoil tracery, and below by Tudor windows with hood molds. In turn, the battlementing and buttressing continue along the lower side ranges, which nevertheless lack definition because of the omission of the flank turrets included on his plans for the grounds. The outer buttresses imitate the Gothic flying buttress, except on the end bays, where they rise straight up to enclose further circular staircases. At the first-floor level, the buttresses support 15-foot-deep glazed conservatories sandwiching the 50-foot-wide exhibition rooms, at their upper stage strengthening the walls of the second-floor exhibition gallery. Another sheet, drawn for Mills by Scheel in March and inscribed "Plan No. 5," delineating the two upper floors, shows that this gallery was to be vaulted and to extend across the full width of the building.[240] In the tremendous space, measuring 310 feet by 50 feet, exhibition cases placed at right angles to the buttressed walls would contain specimens culled from the present and future states of the Union. Off the exhibition gallery, within the central block, were to be smaller cabinets. Above them are two more amphitheatral lecture rooms, like those below supported on two ranks of six columns and reached either from the subsidiary staircases in the front turrets or by the main staircases in the octagonal towers.

Mills buttressed his drawings with an explanatory letter addressed to Poinsett on 29 February (presumably when he employed Scheel to draw "Plan No. 5").[241] Describing its style as "Anglo-Saxon," he went on to define the function of each element, giving the size of the lower exhibition rooms as 95 feet by 50 feet by 20 feet and noting that the octagonal towers might be used as observatories. He particularly pointed out the value of the lecture rooms, stating that "*verbal* instruction" represented the most effectual means of "*increasing knowledge.*" Perhaps because he was in frequent contact with Poinsett, Mills did not then bother to explain the appropriateness of either the style or his adaptation of it to the purposes of the institution. Only when he resubmitted, largely unchanged, the designs in the 1846 competition for the actual Smithsonian Institution via Senator Owen did Mills write how the medieval style yielded excellent internal lighting, spacious fireproof vaulting, and separation of service facilities into the various towers and turrets. This November 1846 letter proves that he had in February 1841 pored over several books by the early British Gothic Revivalists before making a design for the National Institution.[242] Of course, there was his own copy of Britton's *Architectural Antiquities*. But he had also consulted John Carter's *Ancient Architecture of England* (two volumes, 1795–1807) and issues of the journal of the Society of Antiquaries of London, each outdated and superseded by Britton's own *A Dictionary of Architecture and Archaeology of the Middle Ages* (1832–1838), and the archaeologically meticulous *Specimens of Gothic Architecture* (1823–1825), compiled with A. C. Pugin. Consequently, when defining the style of the facade to

Owen, Mills was to follow the old imprecise terminology, citing the "ancient English style" in one sentence and "pointed arch style or the Anglo-Saxon" in another. He would even rehash the discredited theory peddled by the late-eighteenth-century British antiquaries that the pointed Gothic (Norman-style) arch originated from the intersection of round-arch arcades as "practiced by their Saxon predecessors." Still, his letter to Poinsett reflects the genuine enthusiasm for the aesthetic and practical attributes of the Gothic, which had inspired the 1841 design for the National Institution, and his earlier Neo-Gothic work: "The ceilings of their churches were formed by groined vaulting, their points of springing being against the buttresses along the walls, by which means those parts intervening were not required to be massy, and allowing the introduction of the immense openings found here."

The project was put on hold, so that Mills could concentrate on finishing the federal commissions. While being ultimately responsible for every aspect of the federal buildings, through 1839 costing the then tremendous sum of $326,111 according to Noland's annual report, Mills also organized such lesser jobs as the erection at the Capitol of "three handsome cupolas, in place of the old decayed skylights over the library room [the Library of Congress then in the west projection]."[243] Noland expressed satisfaction with Mills by assuring Congress, "The beneficial effects of using the hydraulic cement in the construction of the arches has been fully realized, by affording the means of occupying the building [Treasury] at an earlier period than if they had been constructed with common mortar." Mills petitioned Levi Lincoln on 22 January 1840 to erect a new city post office,[244] a foolhardy action because deficiencies had been discovered in the marble and workmanship supplied by Masterton and Smith, causing the commissioners, now swelled to five by the addition of the navy secretary and postmaster general, to chide Mills on 11 March about the consequent cost increases.[245] He was, therefore, required to produce a detailed statement of the additional sums, highlighting those caused by the use of marble, and revised estimates for the total cost. The atmosphere was more antagonistic again, goading him into arguing forcefully for the completion of the Treasury colonnade and marble steps up to the equally magnificent portico of the Patent Office. During the debate on the 1840 appropriations, Pennsylvania congressman Charles Ogle unsuccessfully moved the denial of $3,665 for repairs to the President's House, accusing Van Buren of "wasting public funds" to transform it into a "Palace as splendid as that of the Caesars, and as richly adorned as the provident Asiatic Mansion."[246]

However, the sight from the Capitol of the three nearly completed public buildings convinced most congressmen of the value of the federal architectural program and ability of their architect. At the behest of Senator William C. Preston of South Carolina, they engaged Mills in March to design "suitable foundations" to support Horatio Greenough's "colossal statute of Washington in the centre of the Rotundo," which weighed all of 10 tons and cost $2,000.[247] Had the congressmen seen the statue (it did not arrive at the Washington Navy Yard until 16 August 1841), they might have endorsed two other proposals Mills submitted.[248] For against their orders of 1832, Greenough had represented Washington not standing but sitting in the idealized guise of a seated Classical philosopher or judge, naked to the waist and with his right hand pointing upward in a gesture as ineloquent as the figure was inelegant. Realizing that it might be overwhelmed by the great space, Mills drew a sketch "showing the manner in which lights [windows beneath the drum] may be introduced for properly shadowing the Statue of Washington."[249] He also revived two features from his own 1832 proposals for a vault in the crypt and "a grand flight of steps . . . winding around the pedestal" of the statue into the rotunda, by which "the beauty and grandeur of the second rotundo [would] be brought into view." Wary of the mounting costs, the congressmen even refused Greenough's request via the current president, John Tyler, that the statue be elevated and were relieved when Greenough suggested that it be placed outside.[250] However, they rejected Mills's hopeful preparation of two sensible designs, one in the Renaissance Classical mode and the other, more remarkable for him, a delicate octagonal cast-iron and glass shelter (85).[251] Unprotected, the statue suffered weathering and much public derision, until removed first to the original Smithsonian and then to the National Museum of American History, where it exhibits the faults that Mills later castigated in a draft for his 1853 article on architecture in Virginia.[252]

Understandably, during the spring of 1840 Mills's major concern was to answer the commissioners' queries about the cost overruns on the General Post Office. In a letter of 23 March, he attributed them to the substitution of marble for granite and the consequently inflated cost of the ornamental features, together amounting to about $90,000 and raising the total to $450,000.[253] Furthermore, he had been permitted on 25 February 1839 to increase the thickness of the marble blocks in the walls from 6 to 9 inches, so that he predicted a final expenditure of $450,000. But he confused the situation by declaring that the original granite scheme would in fact have cost about $410,000. The commissioners passed on his letter without comment to President Tyler.

Other incidents could have lulled Mills into imagining that his critics were quiescent. On 5 April the Senate Committee on the District of Columbia invited him to report on the possibility of lighting the Capitol, President's Square, and Pennsylvania Avenue with gas lamps. As usual, he was enthusiastic about the new technology: "The gas-light can be transmitted, or conducted, any where, and disposed in the most beautiful and picturesque forms for ornament or use."[254] The whale-oil lobby in the eastern states extinguished that pro-

DESIGN FOR CANOPY FOR THE STATUE OF WASHINGTON. CAPITOL GROUNDS.

85.   Mills, designs of a canopy for H.
Greenough's statue of Washington
(1841).

gressive idea—gas not being installed in any public building until 1848—but
voted in 1842 for Pennsylvania Avenue to be supplied with oil lamps, making it
for several years the only properly lighted street in the capital. Although the
result was to be equally in vain, Poinsett asked Mills in September to design
for him a modest brick house, 44 feet by 38 feet, before he resigned in the
summer from the War Department.[255] In October, Commissioner Woodbury
sought his advice. Ammi B. Young had applied for a grant to study heating
methods and marble quarries in Europe. Perhaps still resentful about the customhouse episode, Mills warned that the grant would establish a "bad precedent, as every Architect or undertaker of a public building would consider
himself entitled to improve his knowledge in his art at the public expense," besides undermining American technology and artistic development.[256] His commitment to the development of American ingenuity had already inspired him to
join the National Institution; on 8 June 1840 he sent the membership fee and
soon thereafter secured the display of its collection in the Grand Saloon of the

Patent Office.[257] Those sentiments would also lead him to endorse a fellow member, Francis Benne, who advertised an "Evening School for Architectural Drawing" in November 1841, including Mills's name among those supporting the school.[258]

Meantime, as fall colored the still dense deciduous woods around the capital, Mills's sister Sarah Lusher was sending amusing reports along her eventful journey to the Deep South and "knitting" him a "couple of pairs of socks."[259] As Martha headed toward Memphis, Tennessee, in December, Mills compiled his 1840 annual report, which included an indirect plea for further federal work.[260] He was motivated by the approaching end of the government commissions and aware of stirrings against fresh expenditure due to another recession caused by uncontrolled expansion of credit following the closure of the Second Bank of the United States. He began by celebrating the functional and aesthetic qualities of the completed federal edifices before outlining "The South Wing of the Treasury," budgeted at $150,000, and "addition of the wings embraced in the original design" of the Patent Office. Neither the commissioners nor Congress rose to the bait. Undeterred, Mills took his case to the public by including those prospective wings on the plans of both the Treasury and the Patent Office in his *Guide to the National Executive Offices and the Capitol of the United States* (1841). By the time of its distribution between March and September when he secured the services of John Skirving to install heating systems in the General Post Office and House of Representatives, the economy and thus his own position deteriorated sharply.[261] In May, this new financial recession shocked Congress into appointing the Committee on Public Expenditure, which focused on the performance of the commissioners and the architect. Again, Mills tried to deflect the politicians from scapegoat hunting by presenting proposals for constructing the Patent Office wings, baiting one scheme with a $150,000 estimate for also building a compacted south front to accommodate the National Institution for the Promotion of Science.[262] But his only executed commission that spring seems to have been the completion in Alexandria of a simpler version of the Maxcy Monument at the College of South Carolina to commemorate one of its beneficent citizens, Charles Bennett.[263]

Mills must have been increasingly anxious in May and June, when he was required to submit written answers on his conduct of the federal commissions to the House Committee on Public Expenditures convened by Secretary of State Daniel Webster. Not that he stopped trying to line up a major new project. The day before he submitted his annual report to Noland on 21 December 1841, he sent War Secretary J. C. Spencer plans for a three-story range to be erected between the central bays of the existing War and Navy departments (86a).[264] Providing fourteen vaulted offices astride a central linking corridor on the first two floors and larger rooms above for the Topographical Bureau, it

a

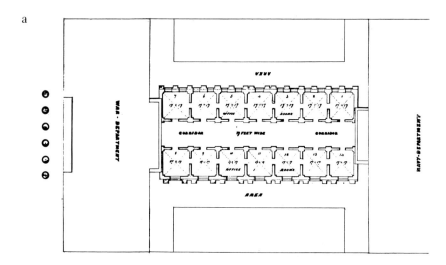

b

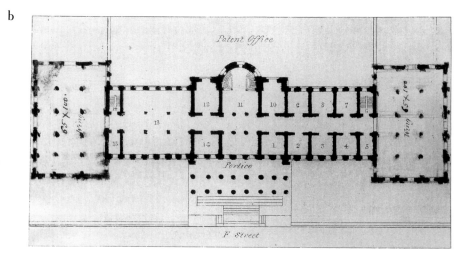

86.   Mills, designs for (a) linking the War and Navy departments and (b) Patent Office wings (1842).

would cost a maximum of $165,000, including marble facing. Spencer and his officials might have favored Mills's solution to their want of space, but could not proceed in the climate of restraint. Finally, on 29 March 1842, the Committee on Public Expenditures distributed its report, to be followed shortly on 1 April by a separate, shorter review of the Treasury Building undertaken by the Whig congressman from Massachusetts, Charles Hudson.[265] The report of the Expenditures Committee had been compiled by the three-man Commission on Public Works, made up of the clerk of the House, Hugh Garland; his successor from May 1841, Matthew St. Clair Clarke; and the obscure W. S. Murphy (not to be confused with Henry C. Murphy, the New York Democrat and mayor of Brooklyn, who would be elected to the House in 1843). They had finished their investigation by 15 July 1841, although their findings were not officially released until eight months later.

The conclusions of Garland, Clarke, and Murphy were devastating, especially for the politically weak Noland and Mills. From the opening statement, Mills was castigated as the perpetrator of "extravagances," as in his recent request for $47,000 to finish the Patent Office portico when expenditure had already exceeded the appropriation at least fivefold. Then came the horrifying summary: there "has been a great want of system and order," and "for years they [the public buildings] have been carried on amid scenes of confusion and disorder, arising in a great measure from private bickerings, mutual resentments, and personal quarrels among the superintendents and workmen." That set the unsympathetic tone of the succeeding analysis of the federal commissions in Washington and Alexandria, barely mitigated by their brief admission of larger overruns on the Boston and New York customhouses. The commissioners were not prepared to acknowledge the difficulty of precise quantity surveying (then in its infancy) or the effect of inflation, let alone admit that Mills was motivated by a desire to raise the architectural quality and capacity of the federal buildings. So while moderating their criticisms of the high cost of the Patent Office with praise for its "faultless" workmanship and "majestic" style, they decried the construction of the Alexandria Courthouse and facilities of the Washington jail. Unfortunately, Noland and Mills had left themselves wide open to censure by their optimistic statements to Congress, which were aimed at keeping up the appropriations. According to their 1840 annual report, the jail was well built and entirely finished when, as the triumvirate could see for themselves, it was discovered that the walls were defective and some $3,000 worth of work remained to be done. Similarly, they dredged up Mills's initial claim that the substitution of marble for cut stone in the General Post Office would be cheaper. They discounted both his revised estimates and his subsequent increased use of marble in order to infer that he had adjusted the bids to the advantage of Masterton and Smith. Hudson, an ordained Universalist minister who later edited the *Boston Daily News,* also accused Mills of having engaged in a "sort of covert design" to erect his grander E-plan scheme for the Treasury and subsequently for its south wing, entirely ignoring the future expansion of government business. Thus it came as no surprise that Hudson voiced New England prejudice against expensive architecture and art by selectively quoting from Mills's reports:

If the wants of Government require an edifice which costs one million and a half of dollars, Congress ought to make the appropriation; but if the appropriation be asked for to furnish the "richest decorations of the Grecian Ionic order" or to furnish "terraces, corridors, and colonnades, as agreeable promenades for the officers of the Department during their leisure moments," or if the money be wanted to provide a "fountain and *jets d'eau,* enriched by grass and shrubbery," we have no hesitancy in saying that the appropriation ought to be withheld.

Mills surely recognized that he was, for the second time, the victim of political exigency. By now better experienced, he moved quickly to his own defense in less than two weeks, on 16 April 1842 preparing a "statement of all the facts in this case," which he directed to his friend Isaac Holmes, a native of Charleston who had served in the state legislature before being elected as a Democrat to Congress in 1839. Then on 3 May he wrote to William Boardman, a Whig from Connecticut who was chair of the House Committee on Public Buildings, to ensure the publication of his replies to the committee together with a covering statement.[266] Perhaps with pressure from Calhoun, again in the cabinet as secretary of state, the House printed the "Memorial of Robert Mills" on 10 May as an appendix to the findings of the committee.[267]

Mills gave a good account of himself, first retaliating against Hudson. He had been forced to accept estimates for the Treasury on the basis of day work and to teach the bricklayers how to construct his system of hydraulic-brick vaulting. Difficulties had arisen between superintendents and some of the tradesmen, but the major cause of the relatively slow progress of building—and the reason for an increase in the costs—was the suspension of work in 1838. Regarding the original scheme, he had in 1836 shown the "full drawings" to Congress and the president, who instructed him to "spare no expense in having the work done well, and with all due dispatch." Then Mills turned to the triumvirate, typifying their misinterpretation of events by recalling that the initial appropriation for the Patent Office allowed only for a conventional brick structure and that in 1838 the "offspring of ignorance" about the integrity of his vaulting system had led to the unnecessary expenditure of some $60,000 to thicken the upper part of the structure. Regarding the General Post Office, he was prepared to admit that the statement of bills for the marble had been done "hurriedly," even though they had not involved much money, although he would argue somewhat differently when the question resurfaced in 1851. Having, he believed, dealt effectively with their charges, Mills made public the correspondence with the committee in order to counter specific criticisms. Thus the letter he wrote to Clarke on 17 June 1841 stated that he had not superintended the Alexandria Courthouse and that completion had been postponed due to unexpectedly cold weather, which in turn caused the damage requiring repair. He also included information on his practice, noting with regard to the selection of the bid by Masterton and Smith for the marble work on the General Post Office that he had checked the figures against the *Builder's Price Book* (1836) by James Gallier, Sr.; in his 21 May letter to Clarke, he recalled insisting that only "first-rate mechnics" be hired. Yet the more thorough his explanations, the less plausible they might seem, as with the issue of the marble contracts for the General Post Office. At the other extreme, his responses to questions of detail could appear to be too facile. Open-lattice iron doors had been adopted in the Washington jail, he told Clarke on 30 June, because the "safe-keeping of the prisoner" demanded that "he be as much exposed to the eye of the keeper as possible." The unkindly could attack him for concentrating on security to the detriment of humanitarianism, ignoring the fact that the cells faced onto an enclosed passage and hence enjoyed comparative privacy. And who was he, merely an architect, to brag "that there has been no building of the same magnitude, character, and beauty of decoration" as this constructed with "greater diligence, fidelity, and discriminative economy"?

Perhaps overconfident that the publication of his memorial in May 1842 boded well, Mills drafted at least two letters to Boardman, proposing that the foundations of the south wing of the Treasury be laid and that the Post Office and jail be finished.[268] In May he also tackled the task of converting Bulfinch's decrepit jail into a lunatic asylum, long needed in Washington. Two sketch plans, one inscribed on the back "Penitentiary Washington," possibly illustrate his initial idea for adding cell blocks on either side of, and two large workshops together with a "Chapel Hospital" behind, the Bulfinch facility.[269] On 17 May he presented Noland with a detailed proposal exchanging the "idea of a prison house" for an "air of cheerfulness."[270] The old perimeter walls were to be replaced by a fence screened with shrubbery, the cells enlarged and iron gratings removed from the windows, and refectories introduced to promote the "good effect of social intercourse" among the twenty-four inmates. Notwithstanding the modest estimate of $4,050, Noland stalled, awaiting the passage in July of an enabling bill, only to award the commission to Skirving in November, despite his higher estimate of $6,750.[271]

Mills refused to be swamped by melancholic lethargy as he awaited his fate at the beginning of June 1842. He drew up an economical proposal for increasing the seating within Latrobe's pretty Neoclassical St. John's Church on Lafayette Square (1816–1817), adjacent to the President's House. Because of its presidential pew, this neat house of worship, with its Greek-cross plan and dome, had, in Latrobe's words, made "many Washingtonians religious who had not been religious before."[272] It had been remodeled somewhat unsympathetically between 1821 and 1822 by the addition of an entrance portico and a steeple. Whether on his own initiative or at the request of its rector, his friend

Dr. William Hawley, Mills outlined two plans, accompanied by a letter penned on 8 June.[273] For a total of $1,276, he undertook to provide ten additional pews and to rearrange the interior somewhat along the lines of his sketch plans for the Washington Court delivered to Judge Cranch, by enlarging the east projection to accommodate a vestry and session room below and the organ and choir above. The original space would be "thrown into the body of the church and then afford four more pews" disposed, like those in the chancel, so "that the communion service may extend all round it." That was a liturgically radical idea that anticipated the twentieth-century practice of locating the altar centrally.[274] Whether this idea was too controversial or the estimate too expensive, the vestry decided not to proceed.

Soon after submitting the designs for St. John's, Mills sought other means to assert his competence and position as federal architect. On 22 June he sent Poinsett a plan for the wings of the Patent Office, inked in on either side of the engraving of the main block from the 1841 edition of his *Guide* (86b).[275] They were to measure 65 feet wide and 100 feet deep and be fronted by coupled pilasters, with single ones along the flanks. Internally, the groin-vaulted ceilings would be supported on two rows of four columns, in order to allow the maximum floor area for exhibiting the patent models. In sending this imprecise draft scheme, Mills made the error of assuming that those who received the sketch would comprehend his ideas with the completeness and lucidity that they assumed in his mind. In any case, he entirely misjudged the tenor of Congress, in which arena his scheme was, predictably, rejected.

Just two days before the celebration of the nation's independence, which he cherished, Mills received a brief letter. It came from President Harrison's acting secretary of the treasury, Thomas Ewing, who summarily ordered Mills to vacate the room he had been using as an office in the Treasury within three days.[276] There Mills had drafted the working drawings and specifications for the series of buildings that had so enhanced the District. What a reward for creating an architectural heritage worthy of comparison with the contemporary developments in the capitals of Europe and Britain, one that would not be equaled in Washington until the twentieth century. As Noland was to regret in his 1842 annual report, Mills's position was terminated only after the government had "had the full benefit of his services in the execution of his several designs."[277] In other words, Congress still did not consider that the government had a responsibility for the day-to-day upkeep of the buildings under its control or indeed for the support of American culture. The post of architect of the public buildings was officially expunged from the federal rolls on 6 February 1843.[278]

Mills must have been profoundly despondent, even though he bravely launched a major, if ultimately abortive, literary project described in a printed questionnaire as "a statistical history of the State of Virginia."[279] He faced poverty anew, and his genuine patriotic idealism had been abused. Not surprisingly, he removed most of his drawings, a regrettable loss to the nation's archives. Yet he had one more official task to fulfill, the writing of his report to Noland. Composed in his own home, it affords remarkable proof of his fortitude and good will. "In closing this my Report," Mills wrote on 19 August, "and my official connection with you Sir, it is a source of gratification to me to recollect the harmony of action which has existed between us in executing the several duties devolving on us, during the course of six years, permit me here to render you my sincere thanks for your kindness, and confidence at all times, and to salute you with esteem and respect."[280]

6

Washington, 1842–1855
"original and peculiarly American"

After his dismissal, Mills's attention increasingly turned to the western expansion of the United States, its Manifest Destiny to dominate the continent and eventually the Pacific. The policy, which he would indirectly endorse through a series of pamphlets on transcontinental railroads and telegraphs, received a boost with the signing in August 1842 of the Webster-Arbuthnot Treaty, establishing the boundaries between Maine and the British colonies of New Brunswick and Lower Canada (Quebec), and four years later the negotiation of the forty-ninth parallel as the transcontinental demarcation line. Upon his inauguration in 1845, President James K. Polk would admit Texas into the Union, seize San Francisco in June, and seven months later command the invasion of Mexico. Within two years, the Treaty of Guadelupe Hidalgo ceded New Mexico, Texas, the Rio Grande, and Upper California to the American republic.

The inexorable tramp westward of horse and settler intensified the zeal to bind the vast frontier lands into the Union by railroad and telegraph; in February 1843 Congress would grant Samuel F. B. Morse $30,000 to develop his telegraphic system. Beginning in 1845, a series of railroad schemes was to be proposed, converging on a northern route tracing the Lewis and Clark Trail to the Columbia River; a central one from St. Louis to San Francisco; and two southern routes, either from Memphis linking with the Santa Fe Trail to Los Angeles, or from New Orleans across Texas (and present-day Arizona) to San Diego. Yet their promoters, who like Mills looked to the American development of the Pacific and Orient trade, failed to appreciate that expansion would exacerbate the slave issue. The uneasy accommodation on that and other divisive questions would begin to disintegrate rapidly after the Compromise of 1850 under President Franklin Pierce.

The "defense of the western frontier," established by President Jackson along the Missouri and Mississippi rivers mainly to control the dispossessed Indian bands, had prompted another of Mills's attempts to remain in the federal service. On 31 October 1842 he wrote to War Secretary Spencer purporting that General Macomb "a short time previous to his decease requested me to furnish the War Department with a copy from the original drawing in my office of the Design I made for the fortified Barracks, adopted by the Department . . . a larger drawing made for the Department, having he said, got lost or mislaid in its transmission to the West."[2] Later, when writing to Treasury Secretary Thomas Corwin on 18 October 1850, he would recall giving the drawing to Poinsett during his tenure as secretary of war (1837–1841), together with a "report on the fortifications proposed on our Indian border to be constructed of Piza [from the French *pisé de terre,* or "packed-earth construction"]."[3]

Mills's letter to Spencer is now bound in with a large sheet inscribed "Diagram of Fortified Barracks to Accommodate 10 Companies of Infantry and 4 Companies of Dragoons with the requisite Quarters for the Officers & Attachés scale of the Drawing 50 ft to the Inch" (87). The plan and explanatory inscriptions occupy most of the sheet, fringed by elevations of the officers' quarters, headquarters, and barrack blocks. The two former facilities line the southeastern range of the 256-foot-square "Parade Court," the larger officers' quarters having three raised porticoes deployed with three detached pilasters, while the headquarters block has a full temple front of four pilasters, alike served by curved steps. On the three other sides are two-story barracks abutting the defensive wall, and a deep triangular section accommodating four stables for a company of seventy-one dragoons. The barracks are accoutred with tall arches at the center and ends of the shading colonnades, affording speedy access and symbolically echoing Roman military architecture. At each corner, polygonal pointed projecting bastions were to have housed the hospital, magazine, quartermaster, and sutler, as well as defensive artillery. Reminiscent of the fortifications of the great seventeenth-century French military engineer Vauban, Mills's papers include a translation of "The memoirs about military barracks" by Colonel J. V. Belmas, author of "Mémoire sur les fourneaux de casernes par M. Belmas," section 9 (1833) of *Mémorial de l'officier du génie . . .* (1803–1892).[4] Belmas stressed the need for large, well-ventilated internal spaces and external galleries for ease of inspection and quick muster, specifications obviously within Mills's powers of analysis and manifest in his plan. Nonetheless, its sophisticated structure, albeit monumentalizing the expanding federal presence, seems better suited to European conditions, despite the

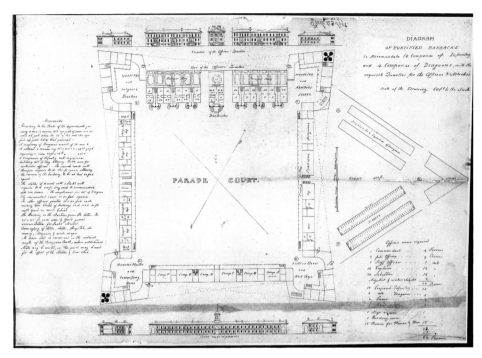

87.   Mills, design for fortified (frontier) barracks (ca. 1842).

implication that he had followed the "Rule of the [War] department" inscribed "Memoranda" on the left side of his drawing. This required 225 square feet for every six men at posts above the thirty-third degree of latitude, or 256 square feet below it. Although one official noted that Mills's plan appeared useful, the War Department really wanted much cheaper forts, predominantly for the cavalry detachments that policed the borders, Indian reservations, and advancing settlements.

In resubmitting the design of the fort, Mills was scouting for the larger architectural objective of "Additional Building for [the] War and Navy Departments."[5] He took to the field with two schemes reinforced by explanatory estimates, actually delivered to the secretaries of War and the Navy on 17 January 1843 but under preparation for several weeks. Colonel Abert of the Engineers tacked them onto his "Letter" of 25 January 1843 reviewing the proposals he had requested from William Strickland, alike based on a specification that Colonel J. G. Totten had compiled in February 1842, proposing to build two new structures on Pennsylvania Avenue, one 75 feet north of the present War Department and the other a similar distance south of the extant Navy Department. Each would stand three stories high; contain sixty-four rooms; be built of granite and brick, with iron and brick arched fireproof ceilings and Roman Ionic porticos; and cost $113,490. Conscious of his disadvantage but clearly

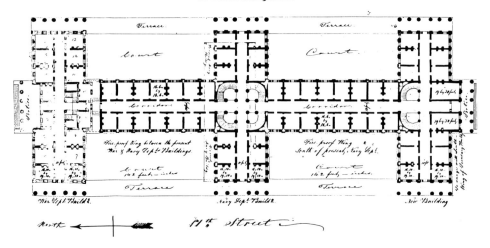

88.   Mills, design for enlarging the War and Navy departments, Washington, D.C. (1843).

possessing intelligence of Strickland's dispositions, Mills determinedly advanced a different configuration.

Mills's first scheme was supported by three plans, loading 108 rooms into a three-story T-plan fireproof, brick-vaulted building anticipated in a scheme reworked the next year (88). It was to be positioned south of the Navy Department, but linked by the 140-foot-deep rear wing. The main front, 198 feet long, would be commanded by a raised six-column Greek Ionic portico, repeated on either 63-foot-wide flank. For the sake of parading fine architecture in the vicinity of the commander-in-chief's residence, he included estimates for cut stone and marble facings in addition to brick: from $229,332 up to $417,337. More economical was his second scheme, now of four floors, entirely of brick, and stripped of the terraces atop storage vaults on either side of the central wing, totaling $253,843. Ten days later, on 27 January 1843, Mills delivered a supporting thrust, advancing his cheaper scheme but again infiltrating the estimated costs of using higher quality facing:

> As the character of a nation is judged of by the character of its public buildings, I considered it my duty, as an American, having the honor of his country at heart, to recommend nothing that would compromit [compromise] its honor. Where imperious necessity compels us to economize the public expenditures in its necessary works, we should not lose sight of giving that final finish to it which will prove creditable to the country.

Congress neither obeyed Abert's recommendation nor responded to Mills's exhortation. In military terminology, Mills's position was fast becoming untenable. "I have presumed in my extremity," he wrote to Poinsett on 8 March 1843, still without work, "to anticipate your acquiesence in my request of the 5th instant to be allowed to draw upon you for the amount of your inscription to my Atlas in advance."[6] He hoped that another old Charleston friend, Thomas Bennett, Jr., would lend him $300 to pay the Philadelphia engraver Tanner prior to reissuing the *Atlas of South Carolina*. Impoverishment had already forced him to stop paying fees to the National Institution as well as to the Apollo Association of New York, founded in 1840 to exhibit contemporary American art and hence an organization that Mills would have been keen to support.[7] The welfare of Eliza and his unmarried daughter Anna, who probably acted as his scribe, impelled him to petition Navy Secretary Abel P. Upshur on 10 March 1843 to superintend the construction of a fireproof building "for the department of charts & c.," pleading that he would be "satisfied with a small compensation for any services rendered, as I am at present out of employment, and destitute of means to support my family."[8]

However humiliating to him, he repeated that plea when on 21 March he asked Spencer, now treasury secretary, "to arrange the plans, estimates and specifications for the Custom house proposed to be erected at Wilmington, N.C."[9] Spencer coldly replied two days later that there was "no occasion for your services." Ironically, the building erected there to the designs of John S. Norris of Savannah between 1844 and 1846 on North Water Street emulated Mills's refined American Classicism, being fronted by a pedimented and engaged Corinthian portico raised on a rusticated basement. Mills was to be no more successful when offering Spencer on 25 April that he would furnish plans for the delayed marine hospitals "at half what was formerly paid me by the Dept.—I am suffering for want of employment in my profession, and you would confer a great favor on me by meeting my wishes at this juncture."[10] Only in 1844 were his 1837 proposals for the marine hospitals to be resubmitted to Congress and eventually passed in 1845, but not to his personal advantage.[11]

Something of a pariah, Mills bravely advertised his professional services as "Architect" in Reintzel's *Washington Directory* for 1843. Meanwhile, most of his former responsibilities were assumed by Skirving, and his improvements within the Capitol under censure. On 15 October, Engineer Lieutenant A. Humphreys criticized the poor acoustics in the House and suggested the construction of a new chamber. He favored a design by the "eminent architect" Strickland for new accommodation in an extension to the south wing, measuring approximately 153 feet by 104 feet and estimated at $282,789. This report was published by the House on 8 January 1844 and again on 24 May.[12] By that time, Zadok Pratt, Democratic chairman of the House Committee on Public Buildings, had rejected Mills's memorial "Proposed alterations in [the] Hall of Representatives, and comparison with other Legislative Halls."[13] In it, Mills reminded the congressmen that his 1829–1830 proposals had never been implemented fully—no mention of the restoration of the original seating arrangement in 1839—and recommended that the ceiling be lowered to a height of 46 feet. Noting that the Chamber of Deputies in Paris was not much bigger, he proposed that the resulting space above the new ceiling be transformed into a library room (89). His opportunistic but abortive counterattack against Humphreys is illustrated by two drawings, the second of which may have offended Pratt's committee because it referred to the new House of Commons in Barry and Pugin's Neo-Gothic British Parliament (a chamber 50 feet high, like the French chamber, which was still under construction).[14]

Everywhere Mills turned, Strickland appeared to be in an advantagous position. On 5 December he wrote to Secretary of the Navy D. Henshaw regarding congressional bill 199 "for the construction of a fire proof building South of the Navy office for the joint use of both [the Navy and War Departments]"[15] and because no action had been taken regarding Colonel Abert's 1843 "Letter."[16] Strickland's two blocks would destroy the "harmony of the President's Square," and their cast-iron and brick vault would be subject to dimensional variation and fire damage, besides being more costly than his own hydraulic-cement brick vault. That system achieved "great lightness, beauty and permanence," the "bug-bear that Arches require great thickness of walls, is now done away, as shewn in the many fire proof buildings erected by me, where the common thickness of walls was used." As reinforcement, four plans rendered by Francis Benne and corresponding with descriptions in his letter remain in the National Archives.[17] Essentially, it would have synthesized his 1837 scheme for transforming the War and Navy department buildings into a mirror image of the original E-plan Treasury with his 1841 proposal for linking fireproof wings, thereby providing dignified and serviceable accommodation in harmony with the existing architecture. A block containing ninety rooms on three floors was to be erected south of the Navy Department and connected with it and the War Department by wings placed either centrally or closer to Seventeenth Street. The central-wing version depicted six-column porticoes on the north and south fronts, while the side-range variant added six-column porticoes on the east and west facades of all three buildings, that on the west front of the old Navy Building having eight columns (90). Mills had estimated the basic costs in a separate submission to Congress as $67,000 for the linking ranges and $112,000 for the new south block, in all about $236,000, as against Strickland's less capacious blocks, estimated at almost $227,000.[18]

Henshaw was noncommittal, still suffering shock from the explosion of a

89.   Mills, design for improving the Hall of Representatives (1844).

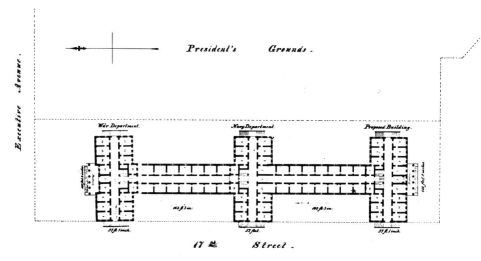

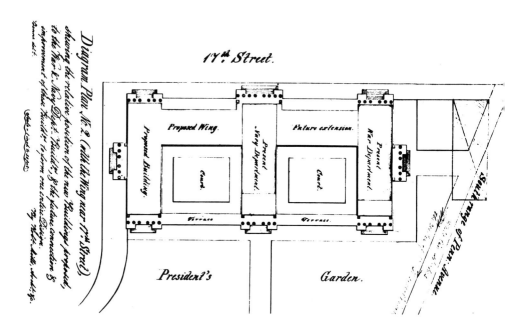

90. Mills, designs for enlarging the War and Navy departments, Washington, D.C. (1844) [positioning both plans to correspond in orientation].

large experimental gun aboard U.S.S. *Princeton* in the Potomac on 29 February 1844, which had killed a number of dignitaries, including Secretary of State Upshur and Navy Secretary Thomas Gilmer. Hence Mills, versed in the necessity of lobbying, pressed the superior merits of his plan in letters to congressmen across the political spectrum: the Virginia Republican Edward Dromgoole, president of the Washington Teetotal Abstinence Society, and the Michigan Democrat Lucius Lyon.[19] To Lyon he indicated that he had offered the government a yet cheaper alternative, proposing "*now* to connect the two buildings [the War and Navy departments] together by a wing, & elevate another story upon the present buildings to perfect the block (the raising of buildings is proposed in the bill)." To both he claimed endorsements from Isaac Holmes, the Charleston-born Democrat; Senator Robert Dale Owen, the literate Radical from Indiana; and Robert C. Winthrop, scion of the founding dynasty of Massachusetts. Dromgoole, Holmes, and Owen, together with thirteen congressmen, signed a petition commending Mills's architectural abilities to President Tyler at this time; Owen added his name to a second petition, dated 17 June 1844, with another eleven members.[20] Mills drew Lyon's attention to two other matters. He wanted Lyon to help quash Pratt's bill for erecting the Patent Office wings upon a plan contrary to his own concept as recently passed by the Senate.[21] In this, Pratt might well have been backing a design by Strickland, for on 12 April 1844 he was to publish a report entitled "National Monument" aimed at preempting the Washington National Monument Society.[22] It illustrated the plan and elevation for a marble circular domed temple rising 120 feet above a 100-foot-high square pedestal, drawn by Strickland but captioned "designed by the Hon. Zadok Pratt of N.Y." Adding insult to injury, Pratt published a further report on 25 May headed "Monument Square," proposing that it be constructed not north of the Capitol, but on the Mall between Seventh and Eighth streets, the very location the National Institution had wanted for Mills's building and botanical gardens.[23]

Yet by the summer of 1844 Mills had gained some influential support for his appointment as architect of the War and Navy Departments Extension. John Tyler, distinguished in Virginia and federal politics before assuming the presidency on the death of Harrison in April 1841, had brought Calhoun back into the cabinet as secretary of war. When, on 18 June 1844, Mills petitioned him "to carry into effect" the extension of the War and Navy departments and to [extend the Patent Office]," President Tyler added his endorsement to the accompanying testimonials: "Mr. Mills is well known by his public works—The Secretary could not select, according to my understanding a better person— J.T."[24] Mills must have been delighted, perhaps believing himself set fair to regain his authority as federal architect. By the end of September, Pratt had to acknowledge the defeat of his bill 199 and to report the "substitute" scheme for erecting a fireproof block according to Mills's proposal "upon the enclosed lot south of the present Navy office" for less than a $100,000 appropriation. And in his annual report, dated 31 December 1844, Pratt even echoed some of Mills's ambitions for federal architecture and postulated that democracy in the United States showed a tendency "to combine elevated considerations of the arts and sciences with whatever is useful."[25]

Pratt, though, was insincere and aware that Tyler and Calhoun would soon lose political power. On 28 January 1845 he published another report on the public buildings, accompanied by an engraving of only one of the three schemes under consideration for the War and Navy Departments Extension.[26] Conspiring with Colonel Abert, he had plumped for "Plan C"—by Strickland. In fact, it corresponded precisely with a description that Strickland had rushed to finish the very day before, under instructions received from Pratt on 21 January, themselves influenced by a letter of 20 January from Mills.[27] Strickland proposed a building 550 feet long with two wings at either end, to be of four stories, and to contain 160 rooms for a cost of $480,000 in marble or, in cheaper materials, $375,000. Mills would not have been at all gratified to learn that Strickland derived the main elevation, aside from the raked attics in place of pediments over the central and side porticoes, from his own General Post Office. Pratt was doing Mills no kindness by printing his letter in the report, since the arguments were angled toward Strickland's previous two building plans, which were no longer under serious consideration. Conversely, it commended his own Neo-Greek-style design, obviously to match his Treasury but which was outmoded by the Italianate fashion he had pioneered in the General Post Office. Mills's plan was estimated at $1 million. Therefore, Pratt and the committee could justifiably promote a scheme, conforming in most respects with that of Strickland, having four stories, cast-iron structure, and a central building 600 feet long and 200 feet deep (to be constructed first), flanked by two wings to the north and south of the existing departments, which they would replace. In fact, it was comparable with the full E plan that Mills had projected for the Treasury Building and, in external style, with his General Post Office.

Nor had Pratt yet finished with squeezing out Mills. On 8 February he asked Strickland to prepare a design for the "Proposed Residences for Heads of Departments." A week later, Strickland handed him a plan for five contiguous four-story houses, each 50 feet square, fronted by a portico and having four rooms per floor, together estimated at $154,500. It was published on 25 February, with a list of accommodations required by all the government offices and a letter from Isaiah Rogers outlining a plan for the War and Navy departments, priced at $792,400, in a report headed "National Edifices at Washington."[28] Mills was cast further into the wilderness when Congress, exasperated that

$5,250 was being spent annually on temporary office rental, appointed the unsympathetic Colonel Abert to organize a competition for a new building. Unwisely, Mills merely resubmitted the $1 million proposal the committee had sidelined, conceding only to Abert's known dislike of central heating by specifying fireplaces in the new offices as well as a hot-air system. But he ignored the attraction that new solutions generally held for politicians and Abert's inevitable concern with budget. While his plan came in below those entered by Young and Rogers, respectively of $1,500,000 and $1,061,389.50, it was beaten by William Archer at $850,000, Strickland at $750,000, and John Notman at $678,590. Abert, not surprisingly, concentrated on the cost factor and singled out the designs by Strickland and Notman when he reported to Congress on 14 April 1846. He was not swayed by the intervention of Robert Dale Owen, who had written Treasury Secretary G. M. Bibb on 9 March to state that he and "as I believe our House generally" preferred Mills's scheme, with his tried system of brick fireproof vaulting.[29] Owen appears to have been right, for Congress hesitated, awaiting the formulation of policy by the newly elected Polk administration. By August, Mills thought it worthwhile to contact the secretary of war, who referred him to Navy Secretary George Bancroft, the celebrated Harvard historian who shared his antislavery sentiments and was in the middle of writing his pioneering *History of the United States*.[30] On 28 August he asked for an interview, "desirous of presenting other designs." As a result, he compiled a synopsis of all the proposals sent to Bancroft on 20 November, advocating a 557-foot "hollow square" along Seventeenth Street with 200-foot-deep wings of four stories containing 300 offices. It was to be erected in stages, beginning with the south wing, with 110 rooms, and then the north wing beyond the present War Department, having 60 offices, together estimated between $466,000 and $567,000. The final range, with 130 offices, would bring the total to $1 million.[31] Whatever Bancroft's reaction, Mills's latest overture went into limbo.

Polk's declaration of war against Mexico in May 1846 would end the skirmishing about the commission. Yet Mills won a Pyrrhic victory. In 1847 General William H. Winder of Baltimore engaged him to design an office building for lease to the War Department.[32] It was one of two completed by private speculators under the dispensation of Secretary of War William L. Marcy; the other was the more flamboyant Italianate and Second Empire Corcoran Building on Fifteenth and F streets, financed by the banking house of Corcoran and Riggs, the firm that floated the bonds for the war in Texas. Marcy, who had entered the Senate in 1831 as a Jacksonian Democrat, perhaps had sympathy for the plight of Old Hickory's architect. It is probable that he recommended Mills to Winder when arranging for a site on the northwest corner of Seventeenth and F streets, just opposite the proposed War and Navy Departments

91.   Mills, Winder Building, Washington, D.C. (1847), in ca. 1900.

Extension Building, which he was to postpone during his four-year secretary-
ship. Winder anyway could have recognized Mills's talent for comely and economical architecture, since he lived not far from the Baptist Church and
Appraisers' Stores in Baltimore.

In designing the two exposed facades of the Winder Building, Mills did echo
the unassuming nobility of the stores (91). Its four and a half stories are divided vertically into three registers, akin to the Italian palazzo: the channeled
rusticated first floor, or basement; the *piano nobile* section, which actually em-
braces three floors; and the mezzanine, which is integrated into the projected
cornice. Within its L plan, 209 feet on F Street and 101 feet on Seventeenth
Street, were originally 130 offices served by central corridors, entered through
two doorways at either side of the F Street facade, and one in the middle of the
Seventeenth Street front. Behind the Seventeenth Street facade is one of the
three staircases, the others being placed beyond the western vestibule off F
Street and on the northern end of the corridor in the Seventeenth Street range
(aligned with the eastern F Street entrance). The basement is constructed of
stone, and the upper walls are of brick finished with stucco. Also of brick are
the internal vaulting of the vestibule, corridors, and offices, wherein the brick
arches spring from iron beams set about 8 feet apart. The brick arches may be
a concession to Winder, who might have had an arrangement with one of the
Baltimore iron founders. The Jayne Building in Philadelphia (1848–1850),

climbing up six floors and among the earliest "high-rise" buildings in the United States, was shortly to be begun with iron beams, piers, and external cladding to the designs of William L. Johnston.[33] The original records of the Winder Building are sadly lost, but some indication of cost can be gleaned from the lease that the general signed with Marcy. The War Department paid an annual rent of $175, including fuel, until 1854, when the federal government purchased the building for $200,000.

Mills had certainly equipped the department well and would have been entirely gratified that as late as 1929 an official of the State Department declared that the "building was thoroughly well constructed." During his lifetime, it helped outflank Walter's 1852 proposals for a large quadrangular building with a central range for the War and Navy departments. Only in 1871 was the British-born Alfred B. Mullett commissioned to execute his grandiose and disharmonious Second Empire–style Executive Office Building on the other side of Seventeenth Street to house the War, Navy, and State departments. Eighteen years in the building, it cost the colossal sum of almost $10.5 million. Mills's compact and unostentatious Winder Building even now faces Mullett's strutting braggart like a seasoned soldier, disciplined and capable.

During the protracted struggle for the commission for the War and Navy Departments Extension Building, Mills retained the solicitude of some highly placed friends, among them the Whig Democratic senator from Michigan, William Woodbridge, chairman of the Senate Committee on Public Lands. On 31 May 1844, the senator had agreed to print his memorial on trigonometrical surveys for possible use in the mapping of routes to the far west, although the commissioner of the General Land Office questionned its relevance to the "admeasurement and subdivision of small public lands."[34] More successful was Mills's petition to Calhoun and Treasury Secretary George Bibb at the beginning of July for the Marine Hospital in Key West, Florida, toward which Congress had recently appropriated $25,000.[35] He enclosed a revised version of his larger standard 1837 design, separating the central block of the three-story structure from the side wings by passages and staircases (92).[36] Shaded by broad piazzas, this block would contain the warden's quarters on the first story and two floors of wards above, the service accommodations being in the wings together with further small wards on the upper story. Even in 1886 the surgeon general could aver that, "excepting the modern pavilion hospital," no other plan was "better adapted to [the] climate for the purpose intended." Mills had also taken great care in writing the specifications, delivered on 6 August, and in discussing the construction with the contractor, J. W. Simontown, who on 16 August undertook to build the hospital for $24,950 between December 1844 and May 1845. The brick and hydraulic-cement walls were covered with white painted stucco, and the wood-floored interior was given

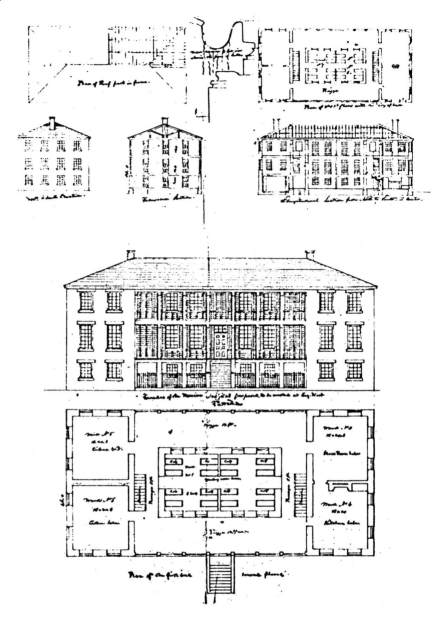

92.   Mills, drawing (1844) for Marine Hospital, Key West, Florida (1844–1845).

added shade by green blinds. The structure remained virtually unchanged until its demolition in 1942, apart from the reconstruction of the piazzas in 1907.

Mills had plenty of time on his hands, except for the small jobs that Asbury
Dickins, especially, was able to direct his way. One such, of great historical
moment but little professional significance, was the addition of six desks for
the senators from Iowa, Utah, and Texas, states officially admitted into the

Union in 1845. One desk became the throne of the "King of Texas," Sam Houston, who was such a showman that he often sat wrapped in an Indian blanket and shod in moccasins, whittling wooden hearts during the debates that became evermore preoccupied with the slavery question. Mills's fee was a paltry $5, paid on 3 May, but it was sweetened by an invitation from the Texas senators to design the state coat of arms in 1852.[37] In the oppressive days of August 1844, his old friend Noland, who served on the Commission of Public Buildings until his voluntary retirement in November 1846, also found work for him. He asked Mills to check Skirving's installation of four furnaces in the President's House, for which he received a few more welcome dollars on 4 September.[38] However, the callous treatment generally meted out by the Polk administration explains a cryptic note dated 28 February 1845: "Robert Mills withdraws his papers."[39] That would seem to record his final removal of drawings and documents for federal commissions, perhaps intended for a book on his architecture.

Through the fall he sublimated frustration and financial anxiety in new endeavors. By the beginning of 1845, he had finished the second edition of his *American Pharos,* published by W. M. Morrison as the *American Light-House Guide* (1845). He was also mulling over a new design for the Washington National Monument, reverting to the form that, coincidentally to be capped by a navigation beacon, he had favored to commemorate the Battle of Bunker Hill. He deposited it with the Washington National Monument Board's selection committee, including old acquaintances such as Watterston, Force, and Seaton, who awarded Mills the victor's laurels on 26 April.[40] This marvelous reversal of fortune, however, would be stalled for almost three years but restored his confidence and creative energy, resulting in a further project for the Patent Office wings and subsequent agreement of the House of Representatives to print his "new plan of roadway" on 18 February 1846.[41]

Mills's "roadway" envisaged "a system of inter-communication with Oregon, and a commercial highway to the Pacific ocean" but utilizing the steam carriage, already rejected as inferior to the railway in Britain. Conjecturing that the requisite roadway could be built for a mere $5,000 per mile, as against $22,000 for a railroad, he calculated a figure of $9 million for the construction of a northern roadway stretching approximately 1,800 miles from the East Coast to the Platte River in Nebraska, over the mountains to the Columbia River, and on to the Pacific. Realizing the multifarious difficulties of building roadways, particularly across the barely surveyed northwestern territories, he also proposed a southern route from Charleston via Vicksburg on the Mississippi River, with a branch to New Orleans, to the Rio Grande and Huagui Yaqui River onward to Guaymas on the Gulf of California with a sea link to San Diego, Monterey, and San Francisco. Apart from promising some relief to his

economically hard-pressed native state, which was daily losing its white population to the New South, this offered "the shortest and best route across the
continent." But it was predicated on two unreliable propositions: highly optimistic reports that General T. J. Greene had recently published on the potential of the banks of Rio Grande for transportation through the Sierra Madre,
and the assumption that the United States would gain permanent control of
the territory south of the Tropic of Cancer. While the United States never assumed that control, Mills anticipated the economic and political development
consequent on the 1849 California gold rush and eventual American acquisition of the then British-administered Sandwich Islands (annexed by the
United States as Hawaii in 1898). The islands, Mills realized, could be the
staging post to Imperial China, with which the United States had signed a
trade treaty at Nanking in 1844.

   Those prospects for American expansion, together with General Zachary
Taylor's victories in the Mexican War, encouraged Mills to present further
schemes to Congress in 1847 and 1848. The first was headed "Memorial of
Robert Mills respecting A new route to the Pacific ocean, with a plan for the
transportation of dispatches to Astoria in fifteen days." Without declaring a
preference for the steam carriage or railroad, his purpose was to offer routes
that would secure the Oregon Territory against possible harrying from the
British Hudson's Bay Company in New Caledonia (later British Columbia).
Printed by the Senate on 18 February 1848, before the Treaty of Guadelupe
Hidalgo limited the territory to be ceded to Upper California (within the
boundaries of the modern state), the memorial laid out four routes to the Pacific.[42] Three began at New York, one following a northerly course, based on
Whitney's 1845 survey of Nebraska, to Astoria.[43] The other two would run
south via Charleston, either to Memphis (the Memphis–Albuquerque route)
and San Diego, or to Vicksburg and on to Guaymas (the Vicksburg and New
Orleans route, served by a branch line to the Crescent City). The fourth,
more southerly "Mills route" joined Charleston to the Gulf of California via
Laredo and was to include a telegraphic line. In his second scheme, he accepted the conventional preference for the railroad and took account of the
Mexican treaty by concentrating on the route through the American Midwest
to San Diego. Published by the House as "Railroad from the Mississippi Valley, to the Ports of San Diego, Monterey, and San Francisco, also the con-
nexion of this road with those of the Atlantic States leading west as far as the
valley of the Mississippi," it was 167 pages long.[44] The substance comprised reports from Colonel P. St. George Cooke, who in 1845 had discovered the passage through the southern Rocky Mountains, and Lieutenant Burford, also of
the U.S. Dragoons. Mills far-sightedly predicted that such a transcontinental
railroad could help to channel trade between Europe and Asia across the

United States (later realized by Commodore Perry's 1853–1854 negotiations with Japan).

Although the schemes faded into obscurity, he had kept his name before the legislators. On 25 March 1846 the Senate circulated a report from Illinois Democrat Sidney Breese, seconded by George M. Dallas of Pennsylvania, about the deficient space within their chamber. Inured to discomfort from service in the Black Hawk War and home-spun circuit courts of Illinois, Breese was chiefly concerned with improving press and public access, rather than with the woeful ventilation and heating; during the winter, the senators endured the smoky and dank atmosphere caused by the ineffectual hickory-wood stoves, while they were periodically fortified by extra clothing, blankets, or spirits imbibed in the notorious Hole-in-the-Wall bar.[45] "With a view to avoid incautious alterations," Breese advised, "I would suggest the expediency of consulting Mr. Mills or any other skilful architect, now in the city."[46] Thereafter, Breese and Dallas commended the proposals that Mills had delivered to them on 18 March. The press reporters were to be penned in boxes fitted into two quadrants and contiguous eastern section of a new "Gentleman's Gallery" around the arc of the chamber. The south side of the gallery, entered from the staircase in the elliptical vestibule, would be screened off for unspecified "special purposes," perhaps for political horsetrading. The seating in the extant ladies' gallery behind the speaker would also be enlarged, and the ventilation and illumination augmented by an enlarged skylight. This tinkering Mills estimated at $3,320, knowing that the only viable solution was a new chamber, preferably in part of the space on the west side of the Capitol then occupied by the Library of Congress. Most senators also wanted new quarters but occupied themselves with other matters, leaving Dickins, still their secretary, to pay Mills $50.[47] He certainly needed the cash, although his son-in-law Dimitry had on 15 January agreed to purchase the Bath Lands, simultaneously conveying them in trust to Eliza.[48] This generous maneuver enabled Mills to retain the family house at Buzzard Point and his office on Louisiana Avenue. Noland, too, paid him $190 in fees before he retired in November, for checking on several repairs undertaken by Skirving in the north wing of the Capitol.[49]

Mills could not rely on the charity of friends and was constantly on the watch for commissions. "May I submit to you some Plans for the Memphis *Depot*," he had asked Navy Secretary Bancroft in a letter dated 12 March 1846. "I have paid much attention to the subject and collected many facts connected with the arrangement of the best foreign Navy Yards, and adapted them to the peculiar circumstances of the Memphis locality—and objects."[50] These were not required, and only occasionally was the debilitating pattern of rejection broken. On 12 October he was writing to Benjamin Ogle Tayloe, replying to the redoubtable Virginian's inquiry about the cost of the addition of a fifth story and improvements to his City Hotel.[51] The plain Federal-style building had become run-down despite its prime location on Fourteenth Street and Pennsylvania Avenue, but Tayloe flinched at Mills's estimates. A similar fate apparently awaited his "Specifications of the work of Mr. McDermott's building," which probably dates from this period. An incomplete draft of the specifications states that one of the shorter sides of a four-story, stone and brick building would stand on Louisiana Avenue, possibly near his office. The first floor was to be supported on a series of 11-foot-high stone piers complete with a 2-foot-deep frieze, not unlike the lower part of the Appraisers' Stores at Baltimore.[52] Mills's patron was possibly M. McDermott, who operated a coach factory on the south side of Pennsylvania Avenue between Third and 4½ streets W., close to his office.

A proud man, Mills might have preferred to sustain his faltering career by such irregular speculative commissions. But in February 1847 the welfare of his family, especially Eliza, whom he knew was becoming too old to supplement their income through teaching, demanded that he accept the post of supervising James Renwick's winning design for the Smithsonian Institution. Mills's employment as "Assistant Architect & Supt." from February 1847 to March 1848 with a monthly salary of $83.33½ was by way of a consolation for the rejection of the revised version of his National Institution design, which he had entered in the 1846 Smithsonian Institution competition, and was probably arranged for him by Senator Robert Dale Owen.[53] By 10 August 1846 the Smithsonian Institution had been established by Congress and approved by President James Polk to be under the direction of a board of regents chaired by Owen, who had passed on Mills's design to his brother David, and at the second meeting of the regents on 9 September 1846 had submitted their collaborative scheme for a building to be located on the Mall.[54] This essentially represented Mills's conception, being described in his already quoted letter to Owen.[55] The wings measured 470 feet by 50 feet to house the "grand exhibition room" on the second floor, which was divided under its 20-foot-high ceiling into three aisles. The library, 240 feet by 50 feet, occupied the center of the first story with four lecture rooms and accommodations for offices on either side. On the third floor, the main space was reserved for the exhibition of "works of art, lecture rooms, studios and cabinets of Art." The octagonal tower at the middle of the north front was now to rise 150 feet, display a statue of Smithson, and be used for an observatory. The interior was still to be constructed with fireproof-brick groin vaults, while the exterior would be faced with Potomac and Susquehanna stone, ornamented in the Norman style. Wary of seeming to be Owen's cynosure and to prove its impartiality, the building committee studied the latest material on international museum architecture, interviewing the other leading architects from throughout the nation—Renwick, Rogers, Walter, and Young—and two immigrants from Britain proficient in the Gothic mode—Notman and Richard Upjohn—who could have commented on the archaeological imperfections of Mills's design.[56] Each member of that formidable group, together with Mills, was invited to present plans in the competition. Equally discouraging for him, it became apparent even before the 25 December deadline that Renwick was in the ascendant, despite Rogers's diary entry for 26 December: "talked over [with William Parker Elliot] about the best mode of setting about to counteract the clique in this city [Washington] in favor of Mills and Mr. Renwick."[57] Renwick's father was a well-known scientist, a close friend of Alexander Bache, the superintendent of the U.S. Coast Survey, and a member of the board of regents. Moreover, Renwick, Jr., was the "new man," architect of two New York churches: the Neo-Gothic Grace Church (1843–1846) and the more novel Neo-Romanesque Church of the Puritans (1846), which had attracted much attention. Even Owen joined the majority of regents by singling out two projects for the Smithsonian by Renwick in the Lombard (North Italian) and French Romanesque styles, lauding the former in *Hints on Public Architecture* (1844), published under the authority of the regents. Once Renwick had agreed to adjust his internal plan to the one David Owen had designed in collaboration with Mills, and to add battlements, the regents declared him the victor in February 1847. Less in harmony with the architecture of the District than Mills's design would have been, Renwick's strident red brick Smithsonian still stands out discordantly on the formal magnificence of the Mall.

How galling for Mills to watch President Polk lay the foundation stone on 1 May 1847, wielding the mallet that had been used on the Capitol and his own Baltimore, Washington, and De Kalb monuments. Among his numerous duties, he assisted Renwick with the working drawings—for example, on 27 December sending to him in New York "a tracing of the two sheets of details signed by [James] Dixon [the main contractor]."[58] He checked the work of the other tradesmen, some of whom, such as C. Buckingham and T. Berry, had also been employed on his federal commissions, and wrote out the detailed contracts, including one with E. Walters of Sandy Spring, Maryland, for a medal of Smithson on 26 February 1847.[59] Mills's need of the monthly salary is hinted at in a short letter from Messrs. Halliday and Muller of New York postmarked on 30 July 1847, informing him of their inability to procure a loan on his behalf.[60] Hence it is not surprising that Mills held his peace about weaknesses in Renwick's design, at least until 14 February 1849, when he corresponded with Poinsett about the absence of fireproofing.[61] Within two weeks, he was to be replaced by Robert Brown, following complaints about the pace and cost of construction (and Renwick's layout) by the institution's first secretary, Joseph Henry, who had taught short courses on architecture at Princeton University.

Mills was sacrificed because his dismissal would cause the least political controversy.

Not that his reputation had been entirely eclipsed. On 11 April 1847 the *Baltimore Sun* reported that he had been approached "to submit designs in conjunction" with the American sculptor Hiram Powers, then resident in Rome, for a monument in Washington to President Andrew Jackson, who had died in June 1845.[62] Mills's idea is recorded in three pencil sketches in his notebook (93a/b), the third and largest clearly inscribed "To Jackson."[63] He imagined a massive triumphal arch approximately 130 feet high and 50 feet wide, supporting a heavy attic, a two-tier pedestal, and a standing figure. A taller and more geometrical interpretation of the base from his original Baltimore Washington Monument design, Mills's sketches formed the basis of the drawing made for him in January 1852 by the draftsman Emil S. Friedrich for $2.65, when the commission was finally put in motion.[64] However, it was awarded to a fellow South Carolinian, the self-taught sculptor Clark Mills, whose hobbyhorse-like bronze equestrian statue was placed at the center of Lafayette Square.[65] Mills must have regretted not honoring the man who gave his talents greatest rein, and he must have been envious that Congress voted Clark Mills substantial additional funding.

How different than the small sums paid him by Congress over the intervening years, mostly thanks to Asbury Dickins. On 23 July 1847 Mills had received $55 for a report on the stability of the gas beacon that James Crutchett had fixed atop Bulfinch's dome in the spring of 1847. Mills concluded "that Mr. Crutchett has left nothing undone to ensure complete success," happy that all the "braces, bands and bolts" sustaining the 96-foot-high mast and its polygonal lantern, measuring 20 feet high and 6 feet in diameter, altogether weighing some 3 tons, were "made of the best wrought American iron."[66] The beacon appears on the engraving of the Capitol in the frontispiece to his 1847–1848 edition of the *Guide to the Capitol,* of which 100 copies were acquired by the Senate in 1848 for $50.[67] Neither Charles Douglas, the new commissioner of public buildings and grounds, nor Congress shared his enthusiasm for the beacon and in the summer of 1848 ordered its removal.[68] Earlier that year, Dickins had paid Mills another $75 for replacing the Senate skylight and for four plans of the Capitol showing the gas system "for lighting the halls of Congress, rotundo, stairways, and other points" as installed during 1848 in response to his enthusiastic report.[69] Commissioner Douglas alike tried to help, paying Mills $20 for "drawings, specifications & c." necessary to repair the Potomac Bridge, completed between May and November 1847 for $23,205.[70] Glad though he was to be employed, such work was paltry and routine. Witness the $17,377 schedule of repairs to the President's House, including the introduction of gas lighting, that he would compile by 28 June

93.   Mills, sketch designs for a
monument to President Andrew
Jackson (1845).

1848 for Robert M. T. Hunter, chairman of the Senate Committee on Public
Buildings.[71] Among a litany of furbishments was renewing the fence and new
"bulkhead or ante Hall with suitable folding & other doors at the entrance of
the Principal Hall" in the President's House to replace the existing glass
screen.[72] He also graded and landscaped the mosquito-infested grounds to the
south.

   Having little to occupy his still abundant energy, Mills again tried his hand
at autobiography. His draft title was "The Architectural Works of Robt. Mills
consisting principally of buildings of a Public character executed in various
parts of the United States."[73] Loaded with deletions, the brief text is written in
the end pages of his abandoned "Manual of Rail Roads" and includes a "List of
Designs," sadly bereft of entries aside from a plan of Monticello but possibly to
include drawings of the federal buildings, since in 1848 he would distribute a
card listing the architect, cost, and style "of Public Buildings in Washington
City."[74] What remains of his autobiography outlines a cogent defense both of
the architect's professional status and of his principles of design. "The science
of architecture is perhaps the most difficult, important, and interesting of all
branches of study—when it is intended to form the ground work of practice,"

he asseverated in emulation of the argument in the third edition of Sir William Chamber's celebrated *Treatise on the Decorative Part of Civil Architecture* (1791). "Altogether American" in his "professional views," since his "studies" had "never been out of the United States," he acknowledged the "economy," "correct taste," and suitability to the "character of our political institutions and pecuniary means" of Greek architecture. But it should be adapted according to the Vitruvian principle "that beauty is founded on order, and that convenience and utility were constituent parts." This rationale was not developed further but demonstrates his opposition to the more thoroughgoing archaeological imitation espoused by contemporary revivalist architects—amusingly derided by an entry in Isaiah Rogers's diary: "At office nothing new occurs—swapped Arabian Antiquities for a Parallel of Architecture with Mr. Town. Received also three volumes."[75] Clearly Mills planned to illustrate his theoretical views by reference to his own work, listing the locations of his major buildings, and to record his contribution to the development of architecture in the United States. He had "acted as a pioneer" despite "many and great difficulties" and "little encouragement," the "value of his labor little appreciated"—phrases that resound with disappointment over the limited recognition of his synthesis of Southern Palladian and Rational Classical architecture to create an American architectural style, yet convey an underlying tenacity of purpose and idealism. Ever optimistic, he could opine that the "wealth and good taste of our citizens are every day aiding the cause of the Fine arts, and we may anticipate the time when the United States will rival the most enlightened countries of the old world if not in the splendor, yet in the magnitude, utility and good taste of its public works." That would eventuate after the Civil War and the 1876 Centennial Exposition at Philadelphia, but as late as 1857 Calvert Vaux, for one, in his *Villas and Cottages*, would regret the lack of an American style of architecture in the absence of educated patrons.[76] But then the final sentences read: "If it [architecture] constituted a part of a liberal education we should see a better taste and a more substantial character of building adopted in our country. Until our citizens can distinguish between the crude drawings of the illiterate artist and the design of the regular bred architect, it is not to be expected that a judicious selection of plans would always be made."[77]

Happily for Mills, one group of Americans was capable of the "judicious selection of plans." Back on 26 April 1845 the Washington National Monument Society had selected Mills's admirably rendered elevation with inset plan modestly inscribed "Sketch of Washington Nat.l Monum.t" (94a).[78] Added to its artistic attraction and optimistic estimate of $250,000, his monument promised to be stupendous. He had mounted a superbly tall obelisk on a massive circular Greek Doric Pantheon-like rotunda, itself atop a deep base and entered through a portico four columns wide and two deep. Besides developing aspects

SKETCH OF

WASHINGTON   NATL: MONUMT:

BY

ROBT: MILLS,

ARCT.

a

b

94.   Mills, (a) design for the Washington National Monument (1846), and (b) Washington National Monument Society certificate.

of his Bunker Hill and National Mausoleum projects, it represented an inspired rethinking of the two-stage composition of his original design for the Baltimore Washington Monument, adapting its quadriga and tripods to facilitate the visual transition from the hugely powerful rotunda base to the obelisk. Thus he had imaginatively welded, but also transformed with a truly American innovation, three enduring ancient themes: the Egyptian obelisk, the Greek Doric order, and the Roman circular temple. Each enshrined sublime associations of immortality that through their juxtaposition assumed more forceful architectural form, more impressive and direct than the kind of sophisticated French design he had seen in Jefferson's books, such as J. Molinos and J. LeGrand's less powerful combination of peristyle and obelisk for a Bastille monument illustrated in Kersaint's *Discours sur les monumens publics*.[79] The thirty 100-foot-high columns Mills deployed around the 250-foot-diameter Pantheon appear sufficiently widely spaced to impart thrust to the 500-foot obelisk, while broad enough to suggest adequate support for its soaring mass.[80] The tremendous total height of 600 feet was enhanced by another brilliant counterpoint, between the large relief inscription at the bottom of the shaft and the American star near its apex. This had a low pitch in order to correspond better with the flat balustrade of the Pantheon and to resolve the elevation of the obelisk.

The subtlety of his reinterpretation of standard monumental precedents must have been obvious to the board.[81] The members could appreciate that the massive scale of the monument would appeal to the popular mind and that its didactic purpose was carried through into the ornamentation. Those details Mills probably outlined in an accompanying description, which seems to have been quoted extensively in Force's *Picture of Washington and its Vicinity* (1848), published soon after 25 January, when the managers finally initiated operations.[82] The first physical contact that visitors would have with Mill's spectacular structure was the "National Pantheon." Inside, its tremendous curving volume, 60 feet high and 50 feet wide with a circumference of 500 feet, would be divided by "radiating archivolts" displaying "national paintings," statues, and sculptural reliefs of leaders and battles of the Revolution, dramatically illuminated by four lanterns articulated as "small temple-formed structures" around the terrace above.[83] The terrace, having a breadth of 180 feet and a 15-foot-high balustrade, could be reached by a railway "curving up 75 feet around the inner wall of the "colossal central pillar." Another "easy graded gallery, which may be traversed by a railway," would ascend to a "circular observatory, 20 feet in diameter, around which at the top is a look-out gallery." From there, the visitors could also look down on the "colossal symbolic tripods of 20 feet high, surmounted by fascial columns," returning their attention to the inspiration of the monument. The tomb of Washington was to be installed at the center of the basement of the Pantheon, "the descent to which is by a broad flight of steps lighted by the same light [from openings sunk into the floor of the outer base] which illuminates his statue." The effect could well have matched that of the cult figure in the temples of the Classical world. But function was not sacrificed to effect. Thus the basement would also accommodate the "keepers of the monument" and "catacombs for the remains of which distinguished men as the nation may honor," while behind the deep, wreath-decorated entablature of the Pantheon should be 20-foot-wide rooms that were to be top-lit and used primarily for exhibiting works of art "or studios for artists engaged in the service of the Monument."

Conscious of the complexity of his design and its likely cost, Mills on 14 June 1845 had mailed the board of managers options for tailoring the magnitude of his design to meet budgets ranging from $100,000 to $1 million.[84] This had the effect of reviving the fund drive, placed in 1846 under the direction of a general agent, the Ohio congressman Elisha Whittlesley, a founder of the Whig party. Lithographs of Washington priced at $5, as well as $1 prints of Mills's design, were sold in each state and special appeals made to Freemasons and to the Navy. The society's coffers swelled to $87,000 by mid-1847, when the managers repetitioned Congress for a site on the Mall with enough certainty of success to determine on 25 January 1848 to proceed with the sublime obelisk and to organize the cornerstone ceremony for 4 July.[85] The legislation granting the society approximately 30 acres adjacent to the Potomac (facilitating the transportation of stone) was passed by Congress on 31 January, and the deed was signed on 12 April. Revived as always by practicing his vocation, and especially for this purpose, Mills had by 22 February delivered a "Plan of Operations" for the cornerstone ceremony. A month later, he had completed a report with Renwick on possible design modifications, including a contraction of the obelisk to between 300 feet and 500 feet and the substitution of a simpler, "American" order for the Pantheon, likely derived from his modified Greek Doric. Gratified by a payment of $100 on 10 May and annual supervisory fee of $500, Mills busied himself with choosing the contractors for digging out the foundations, which were nearly 90 feet square and 25 feet deep.

The members of the board of managers were also encouraged by the support of a wide cross section of political opinion in that era of growing dissension, and by the personal interest of President Zachery Taylor, who signed the society's membership certificates engraved with the proposed 500-foot-tall obelisk and "Mont. Complete With The Pantheon" printed on either side of a profile of General Washington (94b).[86] A good proportion of the 4-foot by 2-foot marble blocks required to line the internal wall were to be donated by the individual states, and Thomas Symington, who owned a quarry near Baltimore, had promised to donate the massive 24,500-pound cornerstone and to supply the external marble at reasonable rates. Better yet, the mounting publicity had brought an undertaking from the Susquehanna and the Baltimore and Ohio railroads to convey the cornerstone free of charge to the Washington Navy Yard. Many had already volunteered to haul it (via Fourteenth Street) to the site, where the senior mason, Matthew G. Emery (later to be mayor of Washington), would dress its surfaces while Doherty, superintendent of work, and Berry would cut a recess for a zinc case to contain a copy of the society's constitution.

The cornerstone was manhandled aboard a wagon on 7 June, heralding nearly four weeks of intense and joyful activity for Mills and increasing public excitement. Along Fourteenth Street, the volunteers strained to haul the weighty stone, urged on by spirited renderings of "Hail Columbia" and "Yankee Doodle" played by the U.S. Marine Band. At the site, laborers, predominantly Irish "navigators" whose number would peak at 300 men, were digging the foundations and, as Independence Day approached, leveling off the excavations to construct shaded seating on two sides for the distinguished guests. In their honor, Mills directed the carpenters to fabricate an arch covered with colored cotton "suitably embellished," upon which would perch a tethered live American eagle. All was ready by Tuesday, the Fourth of July, the excavations having been inspected by a somewhat unholy trinity composed of Renwick, Cameron, and Colonel Abert. Auspiciously, the weather brightened before midday when Mills climbed Capitol Hill in order to take his seat in one of the carriages reserved for the important personages under the direction of the marshall of the day, Joseph H. Bradley, mounted on a fine charger. The ceremony was indeed impressive and for Mills, so long involved in projects to honor General Washington, particularly moving.[87] The presidential entourage led the parade, escorted by detachments of the U.S. Dragoons and Horse Artillery. Behind marched a large body of regular infantry commanded by a hero of the Mexican War, General Cadwalader; militia contingents; city fire companies; and representatives from the Freemasons of 1,000 lodges (their leaders carrying Washington's masonic gavel and apron), the Independent Order of Odd Fellows, the Order of Red Men, the Washington and German benevolent societies, and temperance societies (one drawing a car with a "large cask of cold water inscribed 'Fountain of Health.' ") Next followed the carriages of the distinguished guests, Mills occupying one alone, "having in charge the books and other articles to be deposited in the cornerstone." How he must have relished the cheering "masses of people, of all classes, and sexes, and ages, and colors, gazing from the windows or thronging the sidewalks or grouped in countless thousands upon the Monument grounds." They stilled as House Speaker Robert C. Winthrop delivered a noble oration in praise of Washington, articulating the political ideal that Mills and many others standing nearby yearned that the monument should represent: "Let the column which we are about to construct be at once a pledge and an emblem of perpetual union!" No less would Mills have responded to the religious gloss that the Reverend McTilton added in the succeeding prayer: "We plant in earth the shaft that points to heaven. . . . It tells of Christian virtue and patriotic devotion." The sentiment was reinforced by Benjamin French, grand master of the District Freemasons, who likened the star intended to decorate the upper part of the obelisk with the Star of Bethlehem. Then French turned and presented his "brother" Mills with the "square, level, and plumb, which are the working tools you are to use in the erection of this Monument," enjoining him to build it to "stand until the end of time." That exalted command undoubtedly reverberated in Mills's mind when he attended the reception in the East Room of the President's House and, with the "immense multitude," watched the fireworks display that ended the celebrations in the evening. He had reached the zenith of his career and was embarked on the commission that would most assuredly reward his ambition to win fame through the exercise of his talents in the service of his country.

Experience, however, had taught Mills the vulnerability of the architect's calling. Hence, in his own and the Monument Society's interests, he composed a progress report on "the people's work," seeking to excite public generosity. Written while he was delineating the working drawings and the foundations were nearing completion, the article, signed "M," was published in the *National Intelligencer* on 15 September.[88] Perhaps advised by the editor, his friend William Seaton, then mayor of Washington, Mills appealed to the popular fascination with detail. The readers learned that the foundations were almost up to ground level, formed of blocks of blue rock hewn from the Potomac Valley, and weighing between 6 and 8 tons. These had been laid, under the superintendence of David Hepburn, in various shapes to effect a better bond, using "hydraulic cement and strong stone lime, with a proper proportion of coarse sharp sand, which will become as hard as the stone it binds in a very few weeks." The nearly 2,010 perches of masonry extended 80 feet square and ascended in steps 25 feet above a solid bed of gravel, 20 feet deep, drained by a force pump.

The conduct of those operations and the subsequent construction of the hollow obelisk earned Mills a monthly salary of $41.66 from 3 June until 1 August 1849, when it was reduced to $25 as a consequence of the diminishing resources of the society.[89] Their fund-raising was undermined by criticisms of the load-bearing qualities of the coarse-grained crystalline limestone marble supplied by Symington. Professor Walter R. Johnson, for one, registered his concern before the National Institution, first in a letter read at a meeting on 4 May 1849 and then in person on the 15 June, when Mills was present.[90] Mills did not choose to respond until 19 November when he assured the institution that Johnson's criticisms were "groundless," citing a report by Professor Charles Page sent to Interior Secretary Thomas Ewing. Yet he was not able to deny Johnson's riposte that Page had tested only samples personally selected by Symington for their lower quantity of unstable iron pyrites. Nevertheless, the masons continued to lay the squared marble blocks in 2-foot courses backed by rubble masonry without incident. No settling would be discovered in the investigation undertaken in 1859 by Colonel J. C. Ives.[91] However, when Congress finally decided to complete the obelisk as a symbol of the reunited Union, the aptly named colonel of engineers, Thomas Lincoln, was to buttress Mills's foundations with concrete between 1878 and 1880.

During the first building campaign, the inevitably slow progress had further diminished public interest. Therefore, the society instituted annual rededication ceremonies at the site from Independence Day, 1849. Unfortunately, these events fared no better than the special appeals directed to the Freemasons, the Oddfellows, and the military over the next four years; the 1850 ceremony, indeed, had a melancholy outcome. Already incubating cholera and forced to sit through an unusually long speech by Senator Foote, President Taylor succumbed to the disease within five days.[92] The next year, even the fixing by his successor, Millard Fillmore, of the block of marble donated on behalf of the District by General Jones (and laid with cement containing earth from the tumulus raised at Cracow, Poland, in memory of the revolutionary hero Kosciuszko supplied by Professor Lieber of South Carolina) failed to reawaken the popular imagination. The desultory pace forced the board to reduce Mills's remuneration again, from 1850 to 1853 paying him a fee of only $25 in the months of February, May, August, and November.

He tried to reverse the unfortunate trend, in the spring of 1852 collaborating with the artist Benjamin F. Smith on a "bird's eye view" of the design that incorporated the American order on the Pantheon (95).[93] To clarify its details and to suggest the overall magnitude, Smith positioned the portico facing toward the Potomac and set the monument within the left foreground of an exciting vista of Washington, stretching from the President's House, past Mills's Treasury, Patent Office, and General Post Office to the Capitol. Beyond, Smith depicted the westward spreading country, which, with billowing clouds streaming over the Capitol, cast the monument as the beacon of the republic. On 30 April, Smith sent Mills a bill for $36, suggesting that payment was Mills's contribution to the board's current campaign to rekindle popular enthusiasm. Later, on 20 July, Mills recommended that the board install a calcium gaslight at the top of the staircase to provide sufficient illumination and ventilation within the shaft to attract visitors. The use of such modern technology in the construction of the monument was recounted in the board's contempo-

95.   Benjamin F. Smith, panoramic view of Washington, D.C., showing the Washington National Monument (1852).

rary publicity. They prepared an article entitled "The Great Work," very likely at Mills's instigation.[94] It described the system of lifting the building materials by derricks at each corner of the rising obelisk, served by a 40-horse-power steam engine, and pointed out that a donation of just 10 cents from every citizen would provide "ample means" for its early completion. The rhetoric failed to swell the donations, although the structure would win international recognition, since the English topographical artist W. H. Bartlett included an engraving of it by H. Warren and J. C. Armytage in his *History of the United States* (1856), published on both sides of the Atlantic.

In the United States, however, the society's fund-raising was further harmed when, in January 1853, Congress appropriated $50,000 for an equestrian statue of Washington to be executed by Clark Mills.[95] Worse was to follow the next year, when the shaft had reached 153 feet and the expenditure some $230,000. The board of managers, glad of any aid, accepted a gift of stone from Pope Pius IX taken from the ruined Temple of Concord on the Roman Forum.[96] This act exasperated the stridently nationalistic and anti-Catholic American, or Know-Nothing, party. Some of the party's adherents hijacked the block, for which the board offered a $100 reward, and tossed it unceremoniously into the Potomac. In the disturbed state of contemporary American politics, irritated by opposition to the flood of immigrants from Roman Catholic Europe and Ireland, the board was unable to reassert its authority. Its petition to Congress for funds in 1855 was rejected, in part because

Know-Nothing sympathizers seized the board's papers and established a rival executive. To Mills, these events must have been horrifying, tainting the National Monument with the narrow sectionalism everywhere apparent in the political scene. Under the Know-Nothings' direction until 1858, the obelisk rose only another couple of feet, the poor-quality stone that was used had to be removed later, and the funds dried up. The forlorn stump, with its motionless sheer-legs and lifting tackle, stood all too visibly as a reproach to national dissension long after the president and Congress had incorporated a new Washington National Monument Society in February 1859.

This disastrous episode and ensuing fundamental changes in taste threatened the very survival of Mills's monument. Twenty-one years after his death, with no further progress in its erection, the American Institute of Architects would concur that Mills's conception was "unworthy of the spirit of the architecture of enlightened and civilized people" and insist on the "selection of some different and suitable design."[97] Fortunately, Congress thought differently and, in the renewal of Unionist spirit during Reconstruction, resumed Mills's "Great Work." By 1880, the blocks of New England granite and marble were being added above the still distinct top course laid under Mills's direction. Four years later, the obelisk was topped off with a capstone weighing 3,300 pounds and sealed by a cast-aluminum block measuring 8 feet, 9 inches high surrounded by 144 platinum-tipped lightning rods. The $1,187,710.31 bill was but a small price for achieving Mills's stupendous vision, one more expressive for the lack of the Pantheon. As the now aged Winthrop would declare at the dedication of the monument in 1885, no "more effective and appropriate" design could be imagined for Washington and the United States:

> Overtopping and dominating all its surroundings, beaming and glistening out at every vista as far as human sight can reach, arresting and riveting the eye at every turn, while it shoots triumphantly to the skies—Does not, I repeat, that Colossal Unit remind all who gaze at it, more forcibly than any arch or statue could do, that there is one name in American history above all other characters, one example to be studied and reverenced beyond all other examples?

So it continues to remind countless thousands of Americans and visitors, proof of Mills's conceptual accomplishment. The monument stands sentinel over the flags of the states of the Union that encircle its base, at night their floodlit shadows moving ethereally across the faces of the obelisk. Then the monument can assume the rocket imagery that Winthrop sensed, the red aircraft-warning lights at its apex signifying the power of the nation that General and President Washington had battled to create.

The commencement of the National Monument had in 1848 restored Mills's professional standing. His reputation was boosted further when, on 13 February 1849, the House Committee on Public Buildings published Cluskey's report, which, while not without criticisms, praised his work in general and the General Post Office in particular.[98] Cluskey's comments on the woeful acoustics in the House of Representatives encouraged Mills to contact Poinsett, again secretary of war, advocating the enlargement of the Capitol. On 14 February, Poinsett commended his "plan," but hoped he would "bear in mind that the New Chambers of the Senate & especially the House of Representatives should be free from colonnades, recesses or curves, depend upon it a simple plain parallelogram is best suited for speaking & hearing."[99] Poinsett's comments could identify Mills's proposal as a sheet combining partly revised engravings of the main floor of the Capitol with pencil-and-ink outlines headed "Sketch of Duplicate Building with outer Wing Buildings of Communication, forming a square court within with Galleries all around."[100] The wings correspond in length with the present east front, from the portico of which extends a continuous colonnade, whereas the internal arrangement of the Capitol and "Duplicate" is virtually unchanged. Not surprisingly, because, as Mills should have realized, the scheme perpetuated existing acoustical and functional deficiencies, Poinsett did not offer to promote the plan.

Mills's rehabilitation did eventuate with the appointment "Superintendent of the erection of the wings of the Patent Office building pursuant to the Act of the 3rd March 1849."[101] Those welcome words were dictated on 3 May by Interior Secretary Thomas Ewing. In fact, the ledger kept by the commissioner of public buildings records the payment of Mills's monthly salary of $125 from April, to prepare the specifications and working drawings, the drawing for the east-wing facade (now appropriately owned by the American Institute of Architects) showing dimensional variations in the basement windows and pilaster widths to allow for the northward-falling grade level and steps for the eventual rear portico. (The incumbent commissioner, Ignatius Mudd, formerly a lumber merchant, asked him to fabricate "several spacious apartments" beneath the Senate, "one as a holding room and the others for the storage of books and stationary," to advise on the Washington water supply, and to relocate the government greenhouses on the Mall.)[102] Congress, recognizing that applied science could be profitable as well as nationally prestigious, insisted on effecting Mills's 1836 plan, rather than one of his subsequent smaller proposals, including that presented in 1844 for wings measuring 100 feet square, having "iron pillars and girders" estimated at $75,000.[103] Aware of the limited government resources consequent on the Mexican War, Mills immediately set about obtaining bids on the various types of work, scrupulously listing each in a letter to the commissioner dated 16 June, which he transcribed into his annual report.[104] The variations in estimates were considerable; James Dixon, for example, bid $282,240.40 for the marble work, while Winter and Prevost (or Prevest) offered to do the work for $181,962.[105] Among the unsuccessful bidders for the stone, lime, and cement was Captain William Easby, like Mills a member of the National Institution, whose bids of 85 cents per barrel of 3 bushels and $1.62½ per single 300-pound barrel were roundly beaten out by Andrew Hoover (64 cents per 300-pound barrel) and John Coburn ($1.39). Already discomfited by the rejection of stone he had supplied in 1848 for the foundation of the Washington Monument, Easby nursed a grudge that would lead to Mills's dismissal from the commission two years later.

Yet Mills was too busy in March 1849 to worry about ruffling feathers, and too honest to consider favoring acquaintances over the public interest. The pace of construction was brisk incurring an arrear of $15,000 before the close of the building season. When writing his 1849 report, Mudd recorded that the east wing was nearly complete up to the basement ceiling and that Symington had already delivered marble for facing the outer walls.[106] Mudd thus confidently asked for appropriations of $200,000 for the east wing, and $150,000 to start the west wing. What is more, he put a roundabout case for reinstituting an ad hoc version of the "office of architect," if only on a commission basis. Congress disagreed and only after an acrimonious debate in the Senate between 12 and 19 April voted $90,000 for the east wing. Mudd thereafter tended to let Mills fight for the two-wing scheme, as when he wrote to D. C. Goddard, acting secretary of the interior, on 7 August and 5 September 1850 warning of the "perilous condition" of the temporary west wall and seeking an order to proceed with the foundations for that wing.[107] Goddard demurred, ordering Mills, on 6 September, to construct temporary abutments. Mills's urgency and Goddard's stonewalling proceeded from the extraordinary report submitted by the new commissioner of patents denying the need for additional accommodation. The chairman of the House Committee on Finance, in part due to the mounting pressure for new legislative chambers in Congress, even tried unsuccessfully to stop the latest appropriation for the east wing.

Midway through those frustrations, Mills published proposals for a sophisticated water system for Washington in the National Intelligencer and was approached by the Fort Necessity Washington Monument Association about an appropriate design to mark the site of the general's earliest combat.[108] His novel suggestion, a 50-foot hollow iron column, could reflect the problems he was having with the National Monument as much as it did the increasing use of

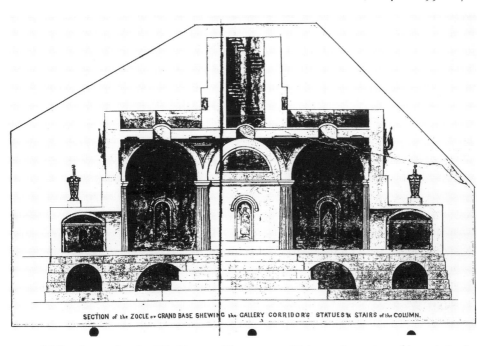

SECTION of the ZOCLE or GRAND BASE SHEWING the GALLERY CORRIDOR'S STATUES & STAIRS of the COLUMN.

96.   Mills, design for the Washington Monument, Richmond, section of base (1850).

structural iron. It was not taken up, although he would develop the columnar theme in response to a competition advertised in the *Richmond Enquirer* beginning in October 1849. The Monument Committee offered a premium of $500 for the design of a monument to Washington that would be erected near the Virginia State Capitol.[109] On 8 January 1850, the closing day of the competition, Mills "personally" presented to the chairman of the Monument Committee, Governor John Floyd, his scheme: "perspective views of the entire design, shewing the location of the Monument, contiguous to the Capitol at Richmond," a "model" that has since been lost, and an elevation, a section, and two plans of the "Grand Base," all probably rendered for him by an assistant.[110] These depicted a massive base, stepped in from an 86-foot-square and 10-foot-high terrace to a 60-foot-square and 30-foot-high "grand zocle [socle]" supporting a 120-foot-high column surmounted by a "Colossean statue of the *Pater Patriae*" (96). From his unused Baltimore designs, he also borrowed the four 7-foot-high tripods, military trophies, and statues, as well as the thirteen bronze shields and spears along the lower shaft of the column. From his National Monument scheme derive the large sculptural reliefs around the socle and the top-lit gallery within the base, ornamented with fresco paintings, illustrating the deeds of Virginia heroes of the Revolution, statues of whom would occupy the eight niches between the engaged Greek Doric columns ringing the gallery. The gallery would also contain "a secret door" into the 180-foot-high staircase boring up the shaft to a viewing platform atop the capital. This was to be "original and peculiarly American," being decorated with "the '*star-spangled banner*' festooned around and under its abacus, held up on each side front by an American spread eagle." Mills determined that the statue of Washington should display "his military character," all too conscious of the dangerous friction in current American politics. For, as he had written Floyd on 4 January, the monument was to be the symbol of "a grateful country" that would "thus join together what ought never to be separated." (The message amplified ideas in the "Description of the Monument proposed to be Erected in Charleston S. Carolina to the honor of Genl. G. Washington," which he probably prepared after April 1846, when the Senate had rejected a resolution that Hiram Powers execute an equestrian statue in the capital. That statute would have been a 10-foot-tall bronze mounted figure attired in "the Roman military costume" elevated above a 22-foot-high circular pedestal ornamented by shields of the various States, "the common standard of [the] Union between each.")[111]

Floyd and the committee chose as finalists Mills, E. B. White, James Renwick, and sculptor Thomas Crawford. However, some may have bridled at the Unionist or military allegory, and most would have been appalled by the $99,140 estimate for Mills's granite and marble, bronze-decorated structure. Therefore, on 2 February the committee opted for Crawford's cheaper sculptural scheme—a simplified version of a plan he had prepared in 1840—setting an equestrian statue on a pedestal surrounded by six statues and four symbolic trophies.[112] By way of compensation and because Crawford was about to return to Italy, the committee appointed Mills "Architect of the Monument" with a quarterly salary of $250.[113]

The work was not arduous, since the actual superintendence was conducted by O. H. Rand, allowing Mills in March to design a fireproof "granite or marble faced" customhouse for Charleston estimated at $370,000 that, however, failed to satisfy the Treasury.[114] Unfortunately, trouble arose when Rand insisted that the stonecutters work a daily shift of eleven rather than the usual ten hours and supply their own tools. Preoccupied in Washington, Mills failed to resolve the dispute, eventually precipitating an investigation by a select committee of the Virginia legislature that convicted Rand of incompetence and dishonesty.[115] Nor did Mills endear himself in Richmond by foolishly attempting early in 1852 to effect a major change in Crawford's design under the guise of a "slight modification." On 22 February he had written to the new governor, Joseph Johnson, suggesting that Crawford's equestrian statue be incorporated into the base of a 76-foot-high granite column surmounted by a statue of Liberty.[116] With a total elevation of 120 feet, compared with Crawford's 55-foot ensemble, his "*Column of the Revolution*" would supply that "*loftiness*" that was "an essential quality in a monument of this dignity." Besides opining that the statue would be better sited at the south front of the capitol, he asked rhetorically, "Shall Virginia disappoint the admiring stranger's expectations, by leading him to the *dwarf* monument, falsely so called, *behind the Capitol* [80 feet high], as if ashamed of its diminutiveness, and want of dignity?" The biting sarcasm spilled over into his description of Crawford's six figures of Virginia heroes of the Revolution as "*Menial.*"

This unusually acerbic missive, reflecting frustrations and reverses in Washington, was printed by the legislature on 9 March and dispatched to Crawford in Rome, although Mills claimed to have sent him the proposal in February. It offended at least one committee member, the Richmond lawyer Conway Robinson, and goaded Crawford to respond angrily on 12 August, dismissing his proposal as a "bastard column."[117] The taint of meddling also aborted another proposal he had made to the chairman of the committee of the Virginia Senate on 4 March 1852.[118] This was for a fireproof structure, 25 feet by 20 feet and 17 high, in which to display Houdon's "*priceless*" statue of Washington, then in the rotunda of the capitol. The enclosure was designed to stand in the middle of the terrace below the main portico; its facade would have four pilasters, framing side niches, and a central entrance and would support a deep entablature masking the roof. The estimate was a mere $2,000, since the stuccoed fabric would use rubble-stone surplus from the Crawford monument. Only concern about the mounting costs of the monument, up to $81,867.95 by March 1852, redirected antipathy toward Crawford and away from Mills, who retained his position until the end of October.[119]

The initial phase of the commission had, by contrast, been a time of optimism for Mills. In 1850, with the fees from Richmond and his other Washington commissions, he had purchased a house in Eliza's name to prevent her being subject to his indebtedness. Located on a quite spacious lot on New Jersey Avenue at B and South Capitol streets S.E., facing the Capitol across the Columbia Fire Engine House, the site is now occupied by part of the Longworth House Office Building. He also had an office on the south side of C Street between Third and 4½ streets, southwest of the Capitol, now covered by the modern urban freeway. The Millses' improved finances forwarded Anna's marriage to Fortunatus Cosby, a clerk in the Treasury Department, although she continued to spend much of her time with her parents. Then on 11 May 1850 he sent a letter of congratulation to his daughter Mary Dimitry on the birth of a son.[120] He thought she would be "acquainted with our whereabouts in this City, namely on the Capitol Hill, the 1st house on New Jersey Avenue south of the Capitol—from which we have a commanding view of the whole city West, South & North & East also from the sky light cupola." Mentioning the visit of Anna's friend, the daughter of the Arkansas senator and fellow railroad enthusiast Solan Borland, Mills continued, incidentally revealing how he tended to spend rather than save, "I have a suite of rooms comprising three apartments, a Parlor, splendidly furnished from New York this spring."

Mills had other influential acquaintances on the Hill. The most energetic was the Mississippi senator Jefferson Davis. Entrenched on the Senate Committee on Public Buildings, he reactivated the forces in favor of the Capitol extension, knowing that the 1850 census indicated the need for more senators and congressmen. He recognized a well-briefed potential ally in Mills, since on 25 February Congressman James Pearce of Maryland had submitted to the speaker of the House the "Memorial of Robert Mills, civil engineer and architect, asking an investigation of certain plans, models, and estimates made by him of improvements and additions to the Capitol."[121] Davis officially contacted Mills on 3 April 1850, just two days after he had listened to Daniel Webster deliver the eulogy to John Calhoun, whose death heralded the decline of the southern cause in federal politics, which was to affect Mills's position adversely;[122] like as not he was among the melancholy throng that watched Calhoun's coffin lifted aboard the deck of the steamer *Baltimore* in the Washington Navy Yard on 22 April bound for burial in the cemetery of St. Philip's in Charleston.

At first, Mills advised Davis that the best plan for the extension would be to carry "out the East front, to the same dimensions as the West projection."[123] The western projection had been designed by Latrobe in 1807 to house the Library of Congress and offices (1817–1820), which were built by Bulfinch.[124] Mills outlined the east extension on a sheet now among the Senate records inscribed "Plan of the Capitol as proposed to be improved" (97a) and in the draft for an undated letter to "the Honorable Jefferson Davis Comm. Pub. Buildings," wherein he called it his "original plan," a version having already been published on pages 51 and 52 of Owen's *Hints on Public Architecture* (97b).[125] Mills proposed that the new House be rectangular in plan with horseshoe seating, occupy the whole of the deeper eastern extension, and be fronted by the existing portico shorn of the innermost rank of four columns. The Senate should be relocated in a space approximately half the length in the west wing, leaving the existing chambers to be refitted, respectively, for the Library of Congress and the Supreme Court. Thereby he would maintain the *"relative position"* of House and Senate while providing separate entrances into each, and remove the *"awkwardness"* of the "appearance of the Capitol in from the *East* (the Baltimore Road)" by placing the dome "in proper position in the building, and bringing the whole into harmony of which it is now deficient." Construction of his proposal need not disrupt congressional and Court business, or require such expensive foundations as would north and south wings, and the project was estimated at less than $500,000.

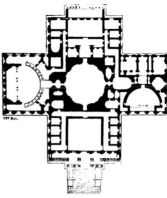

Capitol, with proposed Addition.

b

97. Mills, (a) sketch plan for
extending the Capitol (1850),
and (b) plan for extending the
Capitol, from R. D. Owen,
Hints on Public Buildings
(1849).

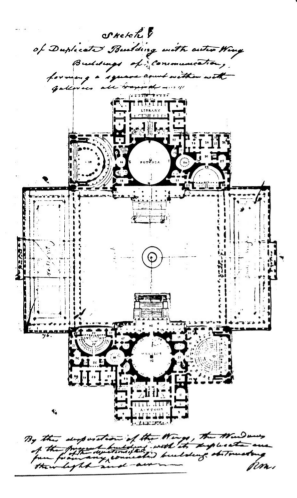

a

Later that spring of 1850, however, Davis persuaded Mills to adopt his own
idea for north and south wings. Accepting that discretion was the better part
of valor, Mills on 1 May submitted a report accompanied by at least eight
drawings on this basis rendered for him by W. S. Powell.[126] Davis passed the
drawings on to his close ally Robert M. T. Hunter, the Virginia lawyer who
had practiced in Winchester before entering federal politics in 1837 as a
states'-rights Democrat associated with Calhoun (whose biography he wrote in
1843). On 28 May, Hunter presented Mills's report, best termed the Davis–
Mills proposal, to the Senate, which thereupon ordered its publication.[127]
Hunter, on behalf of Davis and John H. Clarke, the other leading member of
the Senate Committee on Public Buildings, described the proposal as having
been "originally suggested by the topographical bureau [in 1844, drawn by
Lieutenant Humphreys and Colonel Abert, using Strickland's design], but altered by Mr. Robert Mills." It envisaged wings extending 100 feet from the
existing north and south sides of the Capitol and 200 feet from the east and

west facades, lengthening of the existing east and west colonnades to the wings, expansion of the Library of Congress in the west projection, and sundry improvements not embracing the alteration of the Senate or the Supreme Court for an estimated sum of $1,024,000. The estimate separated off the costs of contingencies, scaffolding, and Mills's superintendence fee, together totaling $80,000, and also a figure of $300,000 for crowning the rotunda with a two-tier circular drummed dome and lantern. This graceful replacement for Bulfinch's squat structure appeared in a larger alternative that Mills had offered, his drawing No. 1. It showed wings that were to be 240 feet long, raising the basic estimate to $1,109,500 minus the contingencies and new dome. The dome is further illustrated in the two surviving drawings from the series: "No. 4. Rotunda. Longitudinal Section through the Centre of the U.S. Capitol, shewing all the Legislative Halls; Rotunda and Supreme Court with the proposed improvement of the Centre and other Domes according to the Plan and Facade No. 3 By Robert Mills Architect," and "No. 6. Proposed Elevation of Facade No. 3—of the U.S. Capitol By Robert Mills Architect" (98).

The "lofty dome" manifested Mills's aesthetic and symbolic concept for the reconstituted Capitol. Besides monumentalizing the center and amplifying the effect of the entrance portico and rotunda, his proposal embodied themes in earlier designs for the building. The double-circular drum respectfully transmuted the great domed peristyle conceived by William Thornton in about 1793 to rise over his colonnaded Great Conference Room abutting the west side of the rotunda; it also echoed Stephen Hallet's 1792–1793 drawings for a drummed dome over the rotunda. Yet Mills had a much surer sense of proportion. By drawing the lower tier of his drum approximately three-quarters of the diameter and height of the rotunda, and then telescoping the upper tier while stretching the dome and lantern to virtually their combined elevation, he promised to achieve the magnificent and unifying feature so lacking in the Capitol as it stood in 1850: where the Bulfinch dome rose 70 feet, that of Mills would have ascended 210 feet. He appealed to the sophistication of mid-century Americans, their sense of taking over the mantle of Western civilization, as the British Prime Minister William Gladstone was to recognize in the 1880s.[128] The dome, Mills wrote with reference to drawing No. 3, an elevation of the whole extension, "assumes the architectural character of that crowning St. Peter's Church at Rome, St. Paul's, London, the Church of Invalids, Paris, and other like buildings." While these models may seem curious for a republican legislature, functionally they were germane to his aim of counteracting the low profile of the Capitol that would be exaggerated by the extension. Such an approach would "produce a grand effect," and "a total change in the architectural effect of the Capitol." Fair comment, to judge by his drawing No. 6 for the new side elevation, showing how he cleverly welded the Renais-

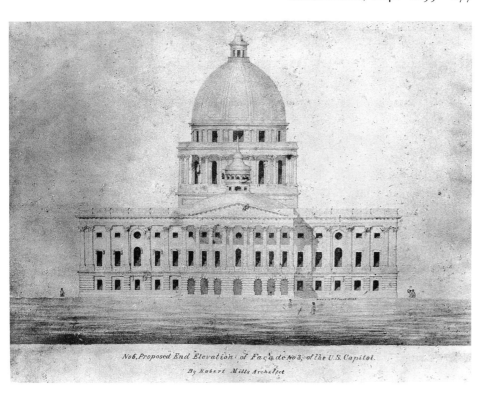

No 6, Proposed End Elevation of Façade No 3, of the U.S. Capitol.
By Robert Mills Architect

98.   Mills, design for extending the Capitol, showing the proposed new dome (1850).

sance and Baroque antecedents of the dome with the wing facades imitated from Thornton. The union was to be forged by the centralized upward movement, bonded by the motif of coupled columns and pilasters in the facade and drum. An architectural metaphor of the political union he yearned for the nation, Mills's composition prefigured that less subtle, if more stupendous, dome that Thomas U. Walter completed after the Civil War.

In designing the interior, Mills alike interwove European precedent with variations of the existing debating chambers. The new House was to measure 100 feet by 70 feet, and the new Senate 90 feet in diameter, both having a height of 45 feet, and respectively accommodating 300 and 100 delegates. Each was to be of the *"horseshoe* or semicircular form, surmounted by a *very flat dome*," proved "favorable to the voice and the ear" in the Chamber of Deputies at Paris and his own auditorium churches. The form had also been selected by Latrobe when rebuilding the House in 1816. Diplomatically silent on its faults, Mills reminded Davis's Committee on Public Buildings that he had been trained by that "gentleman of transcendant talents, of high scientific attainments, and perfectly master of his profession" to whom "the *whole Union*" was indebted "for introducing a *correct* taste in architecture into our country."

Nevertheless, to point up his respect for the history of Congress, he included an alternative plan for the House based on Hoban's elliptical plan "adopted for the hall erected for the *first Congress, which sat in Washington in 1800."*

Only drawings for the Senate remain: a "Section of the Senate Chamber looking north shewing a double tier of [cast-iron?] Galleries" and a "Plan of the New Chamber of the Senate" (99).[129] The desks were to radiate around the vice president's chair, placed at the center of a colonnade backing onto the ten-column portico on the new north front, the remainder arced by an 8-foot-wide lobby communicating with flanking offices and the old structure via an ante-room at the southern end. As for the existing chambers, the square recess of the House would be turned over to the representatives' library, while the "*circular* part" could be used to display the paintings and sculpture then in the Library of Congress. The library would occupy the whole western projection, a space 155 feet long by 60 feet wide and 45 feet high, capable of holding more than 250,000 volumes arranged in four tiers of alcoves (surprisingly not follow-ing the use of separate fireproof iron stacks in Henri Labrouste's Bibliothèque Sainte-Geneviève in Paris [begun in 1845]). Finally, the Supreme Court would be moved from its unhealthy chamber in the lower north wing into the old Senate, Latrobe's court being used as a law library.

The report was a persuasive document. Therefore, Davis through his associ-ate Hunter was happy to endorse its chief constituents. Accustomed from his military as well as his political experience to pick objectives that were capable of achievement, Davis decided to concentrate on those additions and alter-ations immediately required by Congress. He left the question of the dome, ev-idently of great moment for Mills, open for debate. That diffused accusations of extravagance and, taken with the flexibility inherent in Mills's other pro-posals, eased passage of the report through the Senate. The Senate ordered it printed and empowered the Committee on Public Buildings to act in concert with its counterpart in the House. This resolution became operative on 24 July after a brief debate in the House when, however, the extension fell foul of North–South tensions, being most strongly supported by Benjamin Woodward of South Carolina and R. H. Stanton of Tennessee. There was also a powerful undercurrent of opposition to further large-scale public expenditure. Thus when Mills rejoiced in the apparently good prognostications for his plans, the likelihood of their implementation was actually diminishing, and the publicity had attracted the interest of other architects, William Parker Elliot writing to Alexander Jackson Davis on 10 June, "Should you decide on submitting plans you will be in time."[130]

Untroubled it would seem by his identification with southern power brokers and yet again underestimating the strength of the cost-cutting faction in Con-gress, Mills returned to a long-standing preoccupation. While he waited upon

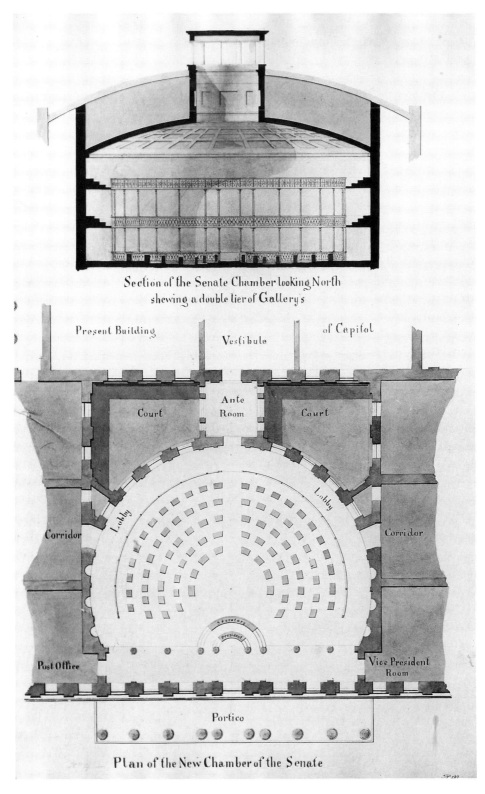

Section of the Senate Chamber looking North
shewing a double tier of Gallery s

Present Building

Vestibule

of Capitol

Court

Ante
Room

Court

Lobby

Lobby

Corridor

Corridor

Secretary

President

Post Office

Vice President
Room

Portico

Plan of the New Chamber of the Senate

99.   Mills, design for the Senate chamber (1850).

the deliberations of Congress—and attended to the east wing of the Patent Office and less closely to the Richmond Washington Monument—he wrote seven articles under the heading "Waterworks for the City of Charleston." They were printed in the *Charleston Mercury* between 7 August and 12 September 1850 and revived his 1825 proposal, but prefaced by a review of systems in the ancient world and contemporary America.[131] The articles fell on empty pocketbooks, but were a factor in the incorporation of the Charleston Water Company in 1854.[132]

As article succeeded article, so Mills's advantage in the potential Capitol commission was eroded, to no small degree by Jefferson Davis's dealing for a politically viable program for the extension. When he rose in the Senate on 19 September representing the joint committee, he stated that the members had inspected "various plans of different architects."[133] Evidently, the majority insisted on economizing, since Davis announced that Congress would be asked to vote "$100,000 for each wing." With regard to the precise plan, he would go no further than commend the solution he had asked Mills to devise, thereby detaching the extension from attacks on the architect or expenditure in general. The policy succeeded in the Senate debates that took place on 23 and 25 September 1850, but at the cost of Mills's special position.[134] On 25 September, it was agreed that the "Committee on Public Buildings be authorized to invite plans, accompanied by estimates for the extension of the Capitol, and to allow a premium of $500 for the plan which may be adopted." Two days later, the House concurred in voting the extension, but amended the procedure so that the plan and architect were to be "approved by the President" with an appropriation of $100,000.

Mills now knew that he was expendable. With Eliza or Anna as his scribe, he solicited support, sending one letter to his friend Walter Lenox, newly elected mayor of Washington.[135] Accompanying a copy of his report, the letter amplified his qualifications in acoustical design and enjoined Lenox to support his plea that the president "appoint a scientific and *practical* commission to visit the large rooms erected in some of our Cities for public speaking"—neither Baltimore nor Philadelphia with his churches and Washington Hall were far away—"by which means they would be able to test the merit of certain forms of rooms for Legislative purposes." No commission was constituted; instead, between 2 and 21 October 1850 the *National Intelligencer* and other Washington newspapers carried advertisements for plans and estimates for the Capitol extension, with a prize of $500. Apparently Mills entered the designs he had drawn for Davis that spring and also vainly tried to refloat his "original plan" for the east extension.

Less distressing for Mills were the consequences of the appointment in September of A. H. Stuart as interior secretary, when work on the upper floor of

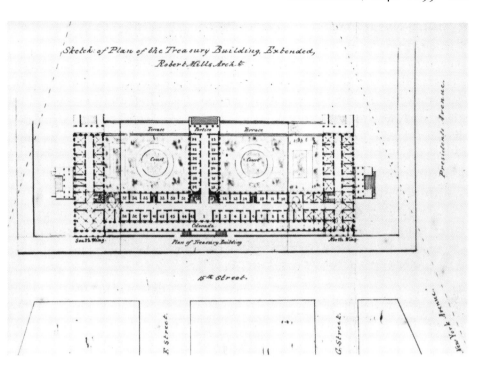

100.   Mills, design for extending the Treasury (1850).

the east wing of the Patent Office was about to begin. Elliot wrote to Stuart accusing Mills of altering what he called the original plan to accommodate offices at that level. Stuart agreed, forgetting that Congress had dictated the change, thereby enabling Mills to execute a spacious groin-vaulted hall supported on a double row of trim, widely spaced piers akin to his initial concept for the Grand Exhibition Hall. Still discomfited, Elliot wrote two critical articles on the commission that were to be published anonymously by *Scientific American* in the spring of 1851 but convincingly rebutted by Mills.[136] Optimistically, Mills had in the early fall of 1850 asked Treasury Secretary Corwin for commissions to complete the north and south wings of his Treasury and design a customhouse at San Francisco.[137] Corwin was sufficiently interested to read Mills's "Report on the subject of the *Extension* of the Treasury building, according to the original Design, as approved by the President of the United States" and study his handsome "Sketch of Plan of the Treasury Building, Extended" (100). On the latter, Mills traced the new wings alongside an engraving of the existing Treasury from his *Guide to the Public Offices*. The lower ground on the south side allowed that wing to have four floors containing some fifty offices, as against the three stories and approximately thirty-eight rooms of the north wing, to be built beyond the State Department to prevent interruption of its operation. Each wing was to project forward of the east colon-nade and have six-column porticoes, repeated on the north and south facades and on the westward side of all three wings. Between them, he drew raised terraces with fountains, increasing the estimate to a daunting $630,000. Considerably cheaper was his customhouse scheme because it would be con-structed, as he informed Corwin on 18 October, in "Pisé."[138] Also to compen-sate for the lack of skilled labor in San Francisco, he proposed that the interior be supported on iron joists. Bureaucratic indecision as much as its structural novelty doomed his proposal, since the commission was shelved until 1854.[139]

A week or so before Christmas 1850 Mills received a most gratifying letter from Andrew Stevenson, who sat with Hunter on the board of visitors of the University of Virginia. "I wrote to two eminent architects (Mills & Renwick)," Stevenson reported from Georgetown on 28 December to the rector, Professor Joseph Cabell, "to ascertain what they would charge to come up & visit me & draw plans, &c. for the Building."[140] The invitation to Charlottesville was to as-certain where new teaching and communal facilities could be erected without intruding on Jefferson's campus. In October 1849, the rector and visitors had considered that a solution to the lack of teaching facilities was "urgent," since the number of undergraduates continued to increase.[141] Perforce they heard lec-tures in all disciplines, except natural philosophy and chemistry, in the same two lecture rooms and crowded out the library room in the rotunda during "public exhibitions." Stevenson, therefore, had been appointed to form with Jefferson's kinsman, Colonel Thomas J. Randolph, "A Building Committee, with full power to select a suitable Artitect" with a budget of around $25,000. Their choice was Mills, "he being the most reasonable—He staid not two days, & we agreed on the plan." Belatedly he fulfilled Jefferson's invitation to visit his American temple of learning.[142] "I think," Stevenson assured Cabell on 28 December, "you will approve the plans of the Building & its location—as far better than those supplied by Mr. Hooper—It will add to the appearance of the Rotunda, & the whole of the Buildings." Stevenson was a man of sensibil-ity and wit, ending his December report to Cabell by likening the commission to the volatile political temper of the times: "There is no receding or seceding now!"

Stevenson's enthusiasm was warranted. By 3 January 1851 Mills had pre-sented him with full specifications and six "Sketch Plans"—since lost, but listed in the University Minutes—illustrating a four-story block, 105 feet long by 54 feet wide, linked to the rear, north side of Jefferson's rotunda.[143] "Cou-pled" might be a truer word, for two columns of its Corinthian order, replete with a spur from its continuous entablature, formed a respectful junction of old with new. The columns reappeared, three deep, on the opposite ends of the flanks, turning into the pedimented six-column portico spanning the rear as a tribute to Jefferson's other masterpiece, the Virginia State Capitol. Thereby Mills concentrated the new facilities, supercharged rather than diminished the significance of the rotunda, and exploited the least conspicuous available site. He even made a virtue of the adverse fall of ground behind the rotunda by inserting two basement stories, each having two lecture rooms, 50 feet by 45 feet and 14 high, separated by a 9-foot-wide corridor, and capable of accommodating up to 500 students. The tall Corinthian columns of the rotunda's portico were quite sufficient to encompass the two main floors of Mills's extension, containing a museum below and galleried hall-cum-exhibition room above. In all justice, Mills could claim what Stevenson wrote to Cabell on 3 January: the extension was "made subservient to that of the Rotunda & calculated to aid its appearance & add to its beauty" while providing a "vast deal of useful room . . . within a small extent of wall."

Economy dictated the brick-fabric cast-iron column capitals and pillars supporting the galleries in the hall, itself covered by a "coved ceiling" version of the de l'Orme system "formed of inch boards, doubled and cross-jointed."[144] Mills also persuaded Stevenson that the "work" should be "bid for *separately*" and to hire George Spooner to superintend the work of the principal contractors, Hudson and Lushbaugh. His own charges were quite modest: no fee for the plans and specifications, but a monthly salary of $83.33 from December 1851 to October 1852.[145] Three of the lecture rooms were in use by June 1852, although with wooden rather than fire-resistant iron benches. Expenditure had reached $40,907.71 ($10,000 above Spooner's estimate and $6,000 over their resources) by 29 June 1853, when the committee of inspection reported on the virtually completed extension. The members found the "whole building capacity of lecture rooms, Laboratory &c. is not surpassed by any institution of the kind. . . . Indeed there is nothing in the opinion of the Committee to prevent its development for the most perfect instruction in agriculture, manufactural & pharmocopeial Chemistry." The Charlottesville newspapers took up the refrain, describing the extension as "splendid," and so it appeared in the most famous illustration of the university, Bohn's bird's-eye view of 1853 (101).[146]

Mills, too, said that he was satisfied. In his article "Architecture in Virginia," published by the *Virginia Historical Register and Literary Companion* in 1853, he would stress the utility of the extension.[147] It was still his hope that a statue of Jefferson would be exhibited in the northern portico looking toward the Blue Ridge, incorporating a miniature version of the Choragic Monument of Lysicrates, which Jefferson had commended to him in 1825, atop a four-column temple and tall square pedestal.[148] The university could not fund this project any more than it could afford the fireproof brick vault and water supply that Mills had wanted. Luck alone delayed until 27 October 1895, the outbreak of fire that Mills and Randolph had feared. The blaze raged through his

101. Mills, extension to Jefferson's University of Virginia, Charlottesville (1851–1852), lithograph by Bohn (1853).

extension and spread to the rotunda.[149] All that remains of Mills's practical and harmonious structure are the grassed-over foundations and, adorning them, one of the cast-iron capitals from its main portico.

The satisfactory progress on the University of Virginia commission must have heartened Mills in the new year of 1851 while the Joint Committee on the Capitol Extension deliberated. The full tally of other competing architects cannot be ascertained, for when Davis reported the result of the committee's deliberations to the Senate on 8 February 1851, he merely referred to having considered plans by "many distinguished architects."[150] Walter definitely had entered two designs on 12 December, one placing the new House and Senate in an eastern extension possibly stimulated by Mills's proposal, and the second adding north and south wings, the option chosen by Cluskey, who also projected a cast-iron columned central rotunda.[151] None of the entries entirely satisfied the committee's criteria of efficient legislative chambers and adherence "to the architectural character and site of the original building." Therefore, perhaps feeling indebted to Mills, Davis had persuaded the committee to support a scheme "combined from various sources, especially from the drawings submitted . . . by Robert Mills, the architect in the employment of the government." Its main features were an enlarged central dome and wings attached to the existing north and south facades and extending eastward both to reduce the apparent length of the extended structure and to minimize the cost of building foundations over the upper of Bulfinch's earth berms on the west side of the Capitol. Under the committee's direction, Mills had with assistance drawn a series of elevations and plans before 7 February 1851, when he signed a detailed estimate totaling $1,291,000, excluding the dome.[152] One of the plans was an isometric rendering for the principal floor, unique in his oeuvre (102a). All the drawings are consistent, with the exception of a sheet of combined plans that shows the retention of the existing House of Representatives. In the two other detailed plans, that chamber is replaced by a broad corridor flanked by rectangular rooms, one of which on the east side was to serve as the House library. The new House conflicted with Mills's views on acoustical design by being rectangular (112 feet by 104 feet), only the Senate (112 feet by 70 feet) having the horseshoe arrangement he preferred.

The plans and elevations naturally betray the compromise between the various entries and the opinions of the individual committee members. It was greatly to Mills's credit that he managed such a successful synthesis. But the proposed elevations, heavily accoutred with columns, had lost the restrained elegance and harmonious blend of new with old that distinguished his 1850 scheme (102b, 102c). This synthetic scheme reaped the inevitable harvest of imposed compromise: division and dispute. Into this impasse stepped President Fillmore, exercising the prerogative granted him by Congress. A Whig Northerner, clothier's apprentice become schoolteacher and lawyer, Fillmore rejected the southern compromise and its Jacksonian architect. Instead, on 10 June he appointed Walter as architect of the Capitol extension and approved his design for two lateral wings fronted on the east by marble steps rising steeply to Corinthian porticoes and an even more flamboyant two-stage drummed dome over the rotunda. Of course, Walter had used features from the Davis–Mills project but had hardened the forms and ornamental dressing, as well as increased the scale, especially of the dome. Consequently Walter's additions dwarf rather than complement the old fabric yet transform the Capitol into a magnificently bold and symbolic edifice, truer to the brash taste of the times and dominance of federal authority hastened by the looming Civil War. How appropriate that the dome, erected from 1855 to 1865 (chiefly under the direction of Walter's assistant A. G. Schoenborn) was the largest cast-iron structure of the period, promise of the coming age of American technology.[153]

Could Mills appreciate how his idea of an American architectural style and of American culture had been overtaken by the more technical, eclectic, and extrovert values exhibited by Walter's Capitol extension? If so, his perception of those changes cannot have been unaffected by memories of Walter's conduct in 1838 and his own pathetic reward for twice obliging Davis's committee, let alone the casting aside of his patently more economical projects. Apparently,

a

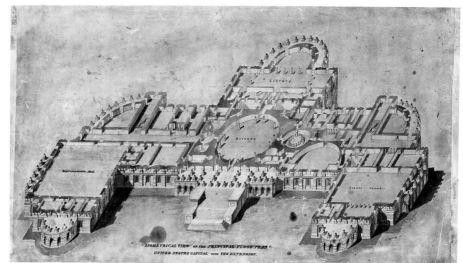

b

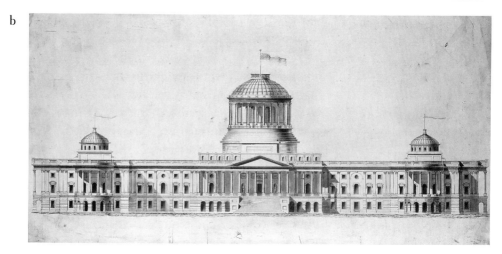

c

102.   Mills and congressional committee, design for extending the Capitol (1851):
(a) isometrical plan, (b) front elevation, and (c) rear elevation.

he mounted one last assault on the commission by once again proposing his east-wing design to Davis and Stanton in mid-June.[154] They could do nothing, hastening Davis's resignation in September to contest the governorship of his native Mississippi. Suffering the misery of shattered expectations, Mills might not have attended the cornerstone ceremony for Walter's wings on 4 July 1851, although it took place not far from his new home.

Unhappily for Mills, the loss coincided with a determined assault on his position as superintendent of the Patent Office wings commission. Six weeks before his 1850 annual report to Commissioner Mudd was printed on 3 March 1851, Mills had been accused of "deceptions, impositions and frauds" by William Archer in a letter of 14 January 1851 to Interior Secretary Stuart.[155] In replying via Mudd on 31 January, Mills countered Archer's "malignant & false aspersions" by pointing out that he had been ordered to face the whole of the courtyard facade, not just the basement, with granite.[156] It was his opinion that Archer, dismissed as architect of the Georgetown Presbyterian Church "because of his perversions," was the "tool of others." Among them, although unrealized by Mills, was quite possibly Captain Easby, one of the unsuccessful contractors for the east wing of the Patent Office and Washington National Monument.[157] They had cooperated on the federal commissions, including repairs to the Potomac Bridge in 1844 and 1847, when Easby's artificers rigged up Crutchett's gas beacon atop the Capitol, and together attended meetings of the National Institution. Indeed, Mills had referred to Easby as "our estimable fellow-citizen" in his 1849 articles on the supply of water to the city of Washington and probably welcomed President Fillmore's decision to appoint him as commissioner after the death of Mudd in March 1851.[158]

Yet within a month of his appointment, Easby began to question Mills's conduct of the commission to supervise the erection of the Patent Office wings. Beginning on 31 March, he directed a barrage of letters to Mills criticizing his handling of the contracts, alteration of the design, and payment of bills. The next month, he asked for the original drawings of the Patent Office, "respectfully" demanded "that you will not purchase articles for the use of the Building without my consent,"[159] and on 24 May informed Stuart, "I therefore deem it my duty most respectfully to recommend his removal from that office."[160] Within two days, he had engaged Walter to investigate Mills's work, subsequently calling in Ammi Young, John Haviland, and the clerk of works, Robert Brown; Haviland, out of friendship, seems to have declined, since he did not sign the joint report handed to Easby on 6 June.[161] Their major finding was "that the strength of the structure is greatly impaired by the introduction of chimney flues behind the marble piers or anta which are designed to support the arches of the third story," which was disputed by Captain F. Smith of the Army Corps of Engineers, but acted on by Secretary Stuart.[162]

From then on, Easby unremittingly harassed Mills. On 16 June he ordered the return of "all the original drawings & working plans for the Capitol furnished by B. H. Latrobe Esq. & now in your possession. Also the original drawings and working plans of The Treasury Building and Patent Office Building."[163] There is no evidence to show that Mills complied or as yet felt threatened, optimistically finalizing a proposal for a magnificent and sanitary new Center Market at Seventh and Ninth streets, a building 560 feet long and 60 feet wide, containing seventy-six butchers' and fifty-six poulterers' stalls with additional commerical space inside a hexastyle Greek Doric temple-fronted superstructure, itself surmounted by a 200-foot clock and fire watcher's tower.[164] On 20 June he took Eliza to a photographer and in their portrait projects an impression of assurance and vigor (frontispiece).[165] Seated by her side, a little stiffly since the process demanded long exposure, he is bright-eyed, the cast of his features suggesting both humor and the determination that had carried him to that professional success denoted by his fashionable double-breasted suit and silk cravat. His hair is quite thick, brushed forward and across his head from the right to give a jaunty air. Eliza appears less vigorous, even weary, her head partly covered by a white lace cap and her handsome surcoat edged with fur. It is a portrait of their marriage: Eliza devoted and enduring, Robert eager and questing.

Within a matter of days, Easby countermanded the contract Mills had drawn up with P. and J. Berry for the granite foundations of the west wing and on 8 July informed Stuart that he would not pay D. Finch for glazing work because he believed that Mills had drawn up an erroneous contract. This was the overture to an investigation of all the contracts in which Easby again consulted Elliot, the quantity surveyor John Harkness, and the stonecutter W. M. Birth. Their terms of reference evidently corresponded with Easby's two most damaging allegations: that Mills had changed the materials and had failed to consistently award contracts to the lowest bidder; his accusation about alterations to the plan was kept in reserve. Required to investigate the agreements but not the reasons for Mills's decisions, their disclosures were damning. Mills had substituted more expensive cube granite and marble work for the 9-inch ashlar; had enlarged the windows, consequently increasing the expenditure on carpentry, painting, and glazing; and, most reprehensible in their judgment, had condoned an adjustment in the bids made by P. and J. Berry for the ashlar and cube stone.[166] The inevitable result was replacement on 29 July 1851 by Walter, assisted by Edward Clark, who subsequently was engaged to complete the west wing.[167]

The sheer relentlessness and spite of Easby's attack evidently confounded Mills, for he made no riposte at this time beyond privately defending his conduct to Stuart.[168] He found solace in his marriage, and that fall composed a poem entitled "The Seasons of Love," dedicated "To My Beloved Wife":

> I will love thee in the Spring-time
> For 'twas Spring when first we met
> All on earth seemed bright around us
> And that brightness lingers yet . . .
> I will love thee in the Summer,
> For, when the Spring was o'er,
> In the summer of thy beauty
> Thou wert fairer than before;
> And now the fruits of Autumn
> Are ripened on the bough,
> And Autumnal days creep o'er us,
> I will love thee dearly now, . . . [169]

Not that Easby relented, on 9 January 1852 demanding the return of equipment he had ordered when superintendent: "Gills Encyclopediae of Architecture $15.75. Set Mathemal. Instruments 8.50. Portfolio 2.50. Knife hone .75. Rose watercolors 6 $. Eraser .37½. Two Engineer's scales $3–$36.87½."[170] Yet Easby's arrogance was beginning to catch up with him, while the opinion of Mills was still respected. For instance, on 9 February 1852, Mills was requested by the House Committee of Inquiry to give evidence on the "subject of the stability of the work on the rotunda of the Capitol," following a recent fire in the Library of Congress.[171] The investigation also examined Walter's design for the dome and in March cast a critical eye over his work on, and Easby's part in, the foundations for the new wings of the extension. Then on 8 April, Easby was arraigned by three powerful politicians—Treasury Secretary Corwin, House Speaker Linn Boyd, and Senator Stanton—for having "threatened the chairman of the Committee on Public Buildings and Grounds with personal violence for having dared to make a very just and true remark concerning said Easby's official conduct."[172] Within two weeks, the government received a petition signed by no fewer than 661 people accusing Easby of signing false vouchers for stone furnished for the Capitol extension, nepotism, and insolence. He weathered that storm but was finally forced to quit his office on 28 February 1853, when Mills had at long last compiled a detailed defense of the discharge of his duties as superintendent of the Patent Office wings.

That small measure of justice was meted out too late for Mills. There would be no proper restitution of the integrity in service and remarkable architecture he had given the federal government and his fellow citizens, not least in the

Capitol extension or Patent Office wing episodes. While his synthetic style lacked the archaeological and symbolic exaggeration and brasher ornament of mid-century American taste, it was actually truer to the historical traditions and democratic aspirations of the nation. It would be entirely comprehensible if at this junction he had written the incomplete draft of his attack on the practice of blessing those holding government office in American churches: "When we indict any of our citizens into office, we regard them, as they are, *our Servants not our Rulers.*"[173]

Tenacious in adversity, Mills drafted his article on "Water Works, Philadelphia," to support his earlier proposal to pump water from the Potomac River to supply the city of Washington.[174] Then in May, prompted by legislation brought before the Senate by William M. Gwin and encouraged by his son-in-law Edward Pendleton, Mills argued for a transcontinental rail line that would begin on the Red River in Arkansas and run into San Diego with another section up the Pacific Coast to Oregon.[175] In a parallel draft directed at Congress, he proposed a more extensive system between Washington, D.C., and the Pacific.[176] Each was boldly conceived, but the first contained his most radical ideas, recommending the utilization of an "improved new Rotary Engine," built with "*not more than 50 pieces*"; one item in the bill he received from Emil Friedrich in July reads "Rotary Engine 6.00 + specifs $1.00 & copies $2.0 $15—$11.19 pd."[177] Rejecting the "*common* construction" of iron rails on wooden ties, he resuscitated a version of his earlier "raised Rail way," which he maintained, despite its costly failure in South Carolina, would be cheaper, capable of surmounting the snowfall in the mountain areas, and permit speeds of 100 miles per hour to be "run in perfect safety, and with the greatest comfort to the passengers." Upon its arcaded understructure, the railroad could "form a *grand object* in the *architectural display*" in towns, "the passengers being landed on the 2d floor of the houses, and thus another street of business would, or might be here brought into profitable use." A startling vision but one that overlooked structural durability, maintenance costs, danger of severe accidents, and, in urban areas, greater noise and smoke pollution. Equally questionable were his total estimate of $18 million, since he envisaged separate tracks for passengers and freight, and idea that it could be financed by private investment supplemented by the "operatives on the Road" paying for the purchase of land "with their labor," entirely forgetting the effort required to establish themselves.

For good measure, he also wrote on 10 May to his friend Senator Solon Borland of Arkansas, the location he had shrewdly chosen as the hub of his railroad.[178] It would enable American merchants to capture the trade between the Far East and Europe by reducing shipping time and cost, and it would strengthen the integrity of the Union. Therefore, he asked Borland, as chairman of the Committee on the Public Lands, to fund four survey parties, which would require about $40,000, a small price to pay for culling a possible yearly trade of at least $250,000. Borland was impressed and encouraged Mills to submit a new memorial, but stripped of his contentious propositions for an elevated track or a rotary steam engine. Thus streamlined, and illustrated by three engravings, it was printed by the Senate with Borland's commendation on 18 August as "Mills's Central Route to the Pacific Ocean."[179] The first engraving carried the prophetic inscription "This Map shews the position of our Continent as compared with Europe and Africa on one side and Asia on the other, placing us in the center of Europe 5,000 [miles] from us, with a population of 250,000,000, and Asia on the other side, about 5,000 miles from us, with a population of more than 700,000,000. The Rail Road across our Continent will make us the center and thoroughfare for both." The second was a map of the United States "shewing the proposed route of a Rail Road from the Mississippi Valley to the ports of San Diego, Monterey & St. Francisco" and connection "with those of the Atlantic States leading West as far as Mississippi," and the third was a "Barometric [topographical] Profile of the route" (103a). Obviously, Mills had spent a good deal of time reading the reports compiled by the army surveyors, particularly those undertaken between 1836 and 1850 by Colonel John C. Frémont, whom he may have met through their mutual patron, Joel Poinsett.[180] The $34 million required to lay the 1,700 miles of railroad could be more than offset by the sale of public lands and would ensure American interests along the west coast and in Pacific commerce. In addition, the rail was "well fitted to receive the [telegraph] wires in the cavity formed underneath—the wire being previously coated with *gutta percha* to check outer metallic influences." But this detail reveals how enthusiasm short-circuited Mills's judgment. He forgot that if the *"lightening speeded agent"* were to become defective, sections of the track would have to be removed for repairs, thus disrupting rail service.

As ever, Mills was juggling with several projects concurrently, his capacity for creative thought always flying ahead of his ability to achieve the means of implementation. Every item on Friedrich's July bill was for ongoing designs, including drawings for the monuments to Jackson, and to Jefferson at the University of Virginia, a "National Theatre," and the customhouse in Norfolk, Virginia, while his memo to Walter requesting the return of his "drawings and papers from the Capitol" seems to have concerned a new try at the troubled extension commission.[181] Not that any of these plans came to fruition, although among Treasury Secretary Corwin's papers is a letter from Mills, dated 5 August 1852, recording his agreement with the Norfolk collector on the "arrangement of the building [customhouse]," tailored to the July appropriation of $100,000.[182] As built between 1853 and 1859 under the direction of Ammi B.

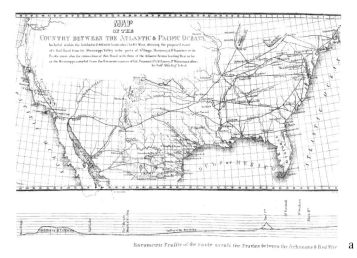

Barometric Profile of the route across the Prairies between the Arkansas & Red Riv.   a

b

103.   Mills, (a) "Central Route to the Pacific Ocean" (1852), and (b) Pacific Express (1853).

Young in his capacity as supervising architect to the Office of Construction of the Treasury, it was a more Italianate version of Mills's Southern Palladian style. Young and his assistant, Captain Alexander Bowman, may have reworked Mills's design, since they had a large number of new commissions during the first year of their duties.[183] They followed Mills in developing a series of design types, but their appointment sounded the death knell of Mills's federal service.

That bleak truth was not yet apparent to Mills, who found a new patron among the congressmen battling for another compromise to preserve the Union. In "July 1852" he prepared a design and estimate for a "country villa [for] Hon. R. Johnson."[184] The brick structure with wooden floors was to be of two stories, the main block measuring 50 feet by 40 feet, fronted by a four-column portico with a service wing measuring 30 feet by 16 feet, and estimated at $4,205.[185] There is no evidence that Johnson proceeded with this pretty Neoclassical interpretation of the villa popularized by Alexander Jackson Downing, although the Washington directories indicate that he had moved from North Maryland Avenue to Vermont Avenue north of H Street before 1863.

During the same month Mills also hurried to prepare a grandiose proposal to erect a national mausoleum, "agreeably" to the "instructions" of Robert Hunter, now chairman of the Senate Committee on Public Buildings. His design now exists only in the form of a draft and more meticulously scribed long-hand paper delivered with a lost "drawing" on 31 July.[186] Probably rendered by Friedrich, its embryo may be a sketch in Mills's notebook showing two rotundas apparently joined by wings to the north and south facades of the Capitol.[187] In his written description, however, two 30-foot-high rotundas, elevated on 35-foot-square bases, were to be linked together by "a spacious elongated gallery" 200 feet long flanked by 150 "catacombs or Niches" for the "reception of the honored dead." Each rotunda would be surmounted by a "superior ornamental structure," a tripod to distinguish the presidents, and a fascial column for members of Congress. The mausoleum would be rendered "fire proof throughout" by hydraulic-brick vaulting, and the exterior would be clothed in white marble with panels for inscriptions. Whether the senators disliked his design or were troubled by his estimate of $160,000, the national mausoleum was interred in congressional opposition to nonfunctional public expenditure.

Mills's attention was quickly engaged by current events. On 6 August he reacted to the recent burning of the steamer *Henry Clay* on the Hudson River and composed an article published fifteen days later in *Scientific American*.[188] To counter the problem of overheated boilers in wooden ships—a particular blight in the competitive Mississippi traffic, as Mark Twain recounted—Mills proposed installing a "*cavity* or flue wall around the heating body, and supplying this *cavity* with a volume of *steam*," a seemingly good theory but in practice compounding the danger with superheated steam, which would be demonstrated by the explosion aboard the leviathan British steamship *Great Eastern* on its trials in the English Channel in September 1859.[189] Other newspaper reports prompted him in August to address "Improvement of the City of New Orleans in the navigation of the Mississippi River at its debouche into the Gulf" to Louisiana senator Pierre Soulé.[190] Mills proposed the construction of breakwaters along the southeast stream, thereby creating stronger currents to prevent silting.[191] Six days later, he wrote from Washington to the governor of South Carolina, John L. Manning, trying to promote a new edition of his *Atlas*, which he airily promised could earn $43,000 profit and "a moiety" for himself.[192] Nothing came of either, so in December, he aimed another equally nugatory memorial at the House and Senate on the Washington water supply currently under consideration. Mills's memorial, printed by Lemuel Towers together with his 1850 articles as *Water Works for the Metropolitan City of Washington*, mixed biblical story, ancient history, and recent American developments to persuade Congress to spend some $550,000 to pump water from Rock Creek into holding reservoirs for piping to the homes of the citizens of Washington.

Almost as the ink dried on his memorial, Mills on 20 December mailed a fascinating letter to Navy Secretary J. P. Kennedy "advising the use of suitable

Balloons" under the direction of the "experienced Aeronaut" John Wise of Philadelphia to locate the British expedition to the Northwest Passage under Admiral Franklin (1845–1846).[193] He reminded Kennedy that Napoleon had made use of balloons for military reconnaissance but, once more revealing his limited technical comprehension, ignored the effects of the severe arctic climate. Kennedy referred him to Dr. Elisha K. Kane, a geographer and arctic explorer also intent on clearing up the mystery surrounding the disappearance of Franklin. Mills corresponded with Kane on 27 December 1852 and again on 7 January 1853, proposing a balloon survey of the elusive Northwest Passage, now the object of his visionary nationalism, since "it is destined for our people, as Americans, to open the Northern passage of the Pacific."

That correspondence brought Mills back to the subject of commercial transportation and his own belief in the potential of the elevated railroad. On 23 March 1853 he wrote to James Lyons, an acquaintance of his "good friend Dr. Duval of Richmond" and one of the commissioners appointed by the Virginia Legislature to build a line from Richmond to the York River.[194] He now proposed suspending the carriages on either side of arcaded masonry piers in order to prevent derailment but still permit speeds of up to 100 miles per hour. His estimate was equally optimistic, a mere $5,000 per mile, but the concept impressed the editor of *Scientific American* who, having accepted his article "Railroads—Their Improvements for Safe Travel" for the 28 May issue, on 5 August published an illustrated report headed by an engraving of his Pacific Express astride the arcaded and elevated rail drawn by a locomotive ornamented with arched moldings (103b).[195] As prophetic but faulty was the proposal for a railway elevated on iron columns 10 feet apart along Broadway that he dispatched in about August 1853 to the New York City Council.[196] At second-floor-window level, a "gallery or walk will be placed to land and receive passengers" from the cars suspended on either side of the "double line of Iron rails" laid some 15 inches apart on wood and iron beams atop the columns. Those were to be reinforced by further iron bars projected halfway down the columns into the abutting buildings—industrial-age flying buttresses. The council welcomed the potential for easing traffic congestion and pedestrian safety, but also anticipated those problems of structural reliability, noise pollution, and vibration that he had entirely ignored. Indeed, he blithely asserted that the railway would raise property values by increasing the business frontage without detriment to either the light or the amenities of the adjoining buildings. Neither, as a discerning journalist commented of his plan for an elevated transcontinental railroad in the *Baltimore American Times* reprinted in the *Charleston Courier* on 8 September 1853, had he accounted for the oscillation of the cars, especially if unevenly loaded. Nor had he accounted for the maintenance costs of the necessarily substantial supports for the rails that, in rural areas, would represent an "inconvenience." Although patronizingly dismissive, that journalist caught the measure of Mills's fecund but unscientific mind: "This is the country for inventions, and this is the age of novelties."

When Mills's "new plan of construction for the Pacific Road" was reported as having engaged the "public mind," Walter floundered as architect of the Capitol extension. A movement that developed into a concerted lobby to reinstate Mills in place of Walter began on 7 February 1853. On that day, President Fillmore received a letter from the controversial former Indiana senator R. S. Thompson, whose "only object" was to "promote the welfare of a friend whom I esteem, and to endeavor to secure him that justice to which he is eminently entitled by his integrity and excellence of character."[197] Mills had "constructed more public buildings than any other man in America, and many other public works exhibiting the highest skill and competency." The Treasury vaults "have not since then sprung or become dislodged to the width of a single hair," whereas the foundations of the Capitol wings had already cost twice the estimate for their execution (one-third of the $3 million required for the entire extension). To seal his case, and possibly using data provided by Mills, Thompson appended a comparative table of the major buildings in the United States, whereon Mills fared best and Walter worst. For good measure, Thompson explained how Mills had provoked Easby's "hatred" by refusing defective shipments of stone intended for the Washington National Monument. Justice demanded the appointment of Mills as architect of the Capitol, there being no "more meritorious man in this country, or one of higher competency in his profession." Fillmore, not surprisingly, since he had selected Walter and was embroiled in the closing phase of the presidential election, did nothing.

Mills, emboldened by Thompson's patronage and the subsequent defeat of Fillmore, petitioned the new Democratic president, Franklin Pierce, for Walter's post on 1 March.[198] A lawyer from New Hampshire, Pierce had risen to the rank of brigadier general during the Mexican War and had become a friend of Jefferson Davis, whom he quickly appointed secretary of war. Hopeful of his support, Mills claimed that the present wings represented "a modification of my original Plan [really the Davis–Mills scheme]," which had been entrusted by Fillmore to the "hands of another Architect to arrange the details." Probably more impressive to a seasoned politician were two letters of "Testimonial," which either accompanied Mills's petition or arrived on the president's desk about the same time. Each is also dated 1 March, one signed by twenty members of the House, and the other by seventeen senators. With two exceptions, all were Democrats, a few espousing the Union or states'-rights wings of the party, and the greater majority from the South or the

West.[199] They attested to Mills's "competency" and "high personal worth," the senators from South Carolina adding, "He is an excellent Architect and a Man of Integrity."

Over the ensuing weeks, Mills solicited other men of influence.[200] He began with Pendleton on 3 March, implying that Fillmore had selected Walter "in order to sustain their [the president's and Easby's] unjust act in removing me from office" as superintendent of the Patent Office wings. The accumulated hurt of the last two years, and indeed of his treatment by successive administrations since 1842, burst forth toward the end of the letter: "And tho' I have dispersed millions of dollars in such constructions, I have to labor still for *my bread*—Had I been unfaithful to my trust I might have been wealthy at this day—in place of not having a dollar to call my own." Likely Mills wrote similarly to J. B. Floyd, since the former governor of Virginia assured the interior secretary on 8 March that Mills had discharged his duties as architect for the Richmond Monument "with facility and skill." Then he petitioned Davis, who as war secretary was responsible for the Capitol extension commission, to revive his plan for the east wing. But before 6 April, when Davis referred him to Captain Meigs, Mills offered a more sensible alternative, accompanied by the drawing that ended up among Walter's papers, "Modification of Design No. 2 Plan R.M." (104).[201] Mills had pasted the main floor plan from his 1847 *Guide to the Capitol* onto the middle of the sheet and added the foundations of Walter's new wings, but introduced six major changes. First, he clothed the whole entrance front with "an open colonnade," which led him to describe the scheme to Meigs on 8 April as his *"Colonnade Plan."* Next, he placed eight-column porticoes, minus steps, on the east end of each wing, directly fronting the new chambers. Both chambers now had semicircular seating, the House within a space 115 feet square and the Senate in a rectangular apartment 115 feet wide by 80 feet deep, and large colonnaded lobbies. Then, on the north and south elevations he inserted single porticoes that imitated the Corinthian order of the original entrance portico. On the west side, he added ranges extending from the existing Library of Congress for additional book stacks and separated by courtyards to provide adequate lighting and fire protection. Last, the new wings and library were to be fronted by porticoes of eight and sixteen columns, respectively. In vain, for Davis, prevailed upon by the ambitious Meigs, rejected Mills's *"Colonnade Plan"* and decided to retain Walter's design, but to replace Walter with Meigs as superintendent.

Undaunted, Mills then wrote to Pierce on 11 April about the Patent Office.[202] Easby, "prejudiced against me," had misrepresented the contentious bid Berry had entered for the granite as 27 cents instead of 55 cents per foot "in its rough [unfinished] state," thus inflating the difference between estimate and cost. On 30 April, he further explained that Commissioner Mudd, a "Me-

EXTENSION OF CAPITOL.

MODIFICATION OF DESIGN Nº 2   PLAN.
2 M.

104.   Mills, "Modified Plan" for extending the Capitol (1853).

chanic," had "made all the contracts" and that the change from ashlar to cube stone had been ordered by Interior Secretary Ewing, who "requested *that the walls of this building should be made as thin as practicable to sustain* the thrust of the arches." Finally on 3 May he submitted a "Synopsis of the Charges Against the Supt. of the Patent Office Buldg. by the Commissioner of Pub. Buildings." Herein he reiterated that all the alterations to the design were officially sanctioned and that all the contracts were awarded by Mudd on the basis of a revised statement of bids that allowed for the intervening official decision to face the front with marble and the rear with granite. Whatever his motive, Pierce forwarded the correspondence to Walter, who returned it to Mills in August (although copies remain to this day in the Office of the Architect of the Capitol). Walter coyly pretended to be unable to comment, since "my natural aversion to meddling with other people's business, led me to avoid entering into the merits of anything said in reference to it." Perhaps prompted by Pierce, who reportedly attended the First Presbyterian Church in Washington, as did Mills, Davis asked Meigs whether Mills could be given "some professional employment."[203] That same day, 12 September, Meigs responded sarcastically, "I have seen some of Mr. Mills's working drawings of the Patent Office & I should not be willing to trust to his assistance in carrying on this work."

The trust Mills had reposed in the new administration for reparation of past injustices was utterly annihilated. Particularly unjust was the fact that he had been berated for overspending on his federal buildings, only to have his cheaper and not aesthetically inferior Capitol extension spurned a second time for a more costly construction. His prospects were bleak indeed, with about as much chance of success as the maintenance of the compromise between North and South. The times seemed to favor the extremist and the bigot, from violent Free-Soilers like John Brown, who were trying to eliminate slavery in Kansas, to George Fitzhugh, who from his bat-ridden Virginia plantation championed a "Free Society" founded on the feudal system with white and black slavery. Observing symptoms of the cancer of libertarian sectionalism destroy the ideal of liberty in his country and robbed of federal employment, Mills must have felt alienated. It is not surprising that his 1853 essay, "Architecture in Virginia," is permeated with retrospection and justification for his own brand of American Classicism—for example, defining the Monumental Church as a development of the innovations in American architecture begun by his mentors Jefferson and Latrobe. Although he missed a typographical error in the dating of Latrobe's Bank of Pennsylvania to 1792 (1799–1800), the essay proves that he was by no means failing mentally.

On 27 January 1854 he drafted yet another memorial, "To the Citizens of Charleston S.C.," proposing the installation of a water supply from the Edisto and Santee rivers, supported by references to systems in other American cities and in London and Paris.[204] The day before, he had sent a letter to Professor John C. S. Salmon endorsing his proposal for pumping water from the Potomac as superior to the more costly aqueduct system that Meigs was constructing from the Great Falls. Although a small consolation, Mills had the satisfaction of seeing Meigs successfully challenged in print when Salmon soon thereafter published his *Plan of Water of Works for the Cities of the District with Explanatory Remarks: also letters from Robert Mills, Esq., Architect and Civil Engineer and Hon. Francis O.J. Smith of Maine.* At the beginning of March, Mills sent Congress a "Plan for conducting the Waters of the Tiber into the Eastern Branch," marking the two feeder lines on the engraving by Hill of Benjamin Ellicot's street map of the District of Columbia.[205] On 15 February, this proposal was referred to the Committee on Public Buildings and Grounds, but was not acted on. Confronting such unrelieved rejection, Mills might at this juncture have begun to compose, with a quavering pen, his incomplete commentary on man's ingratitude toward his Maker, "Creation Its Glories—And Ends."[206] Many of the words cannot be deciphered but the purport is clear from the first sentence, "*Man* in every age of the world has witnessed, and enjoyed the works of *Creation* without a knowledge of their Author and His requirements." Man, he continued, with evident personal allusion, was corrupted by "*Pride, Envy,* and *Malice*" and "self-interest."

His faith may have encouraged him to make one last attempt to brave the callous indifference of politicians and civil servants. Congress at last acknowledged the shortage of space in the Treasury and General Post Office, and the matter had been aired in the press. Upon reading a piece on the Treasury in the 12 March issue of the *Washington Sentinel,* Mills composed a short article, "The Public Buildings," which was printed ten days later, arguing for the addition of his north and south wings. Adroitly he used the fractious political scene (which brought the Republican party into being that year) to dispel fears that the extended complex would intrude upon the President's House: "As long as we are true to our Republican principles, we shall be satisfied that our President will also be, and not object to be in near proximity with his cabinet officers." If the pressure of government business forced the expansion of adjacent public buildings, the executive mansion could be rebuilt on "the *public mall,* where there would be comparative quiet, splendid gardens, *jets d'eaus,* walks and drives."[207]

Congress prevaricated while the Know-Nothing party disrupted the already halting progress on the Washington Monument. Meanwhile, Mills prepared yet another edition of his *Guide to the Capitol,* generously including a passage on the progress of the Capitol extension, which quoted Walter's own description.[208] As further testimony to his objectivity, Mills also printed Walter's commendation of the acoustical advantages of rectangular chambers. However, he did enlarge the comments in the 1847–1848 edition on the superiority of the circular form. Equally mild was his suggestion that the original front colonnade be extended right across the new entrance facade and his regret at the loss of the old Library of Congress, which had been arranged in alcoves following Jefferson's categories of memory, reason, and imagination. He even occasionally attended meetings of the National Institution; his last recorded attendance was on 15 January 1855.

Then at the beginning of March 1855, he learned that he would not be awarded any part in the forthcoming commissions to extend his own Treasury and General Post Office. That shocking news, piled on more than a decade of almost unremitting stress and rebuff, appears to have precipitated a severe stroke. Whatever the precise medical reason, Mills's heart stilled as the frigid light of dawn illuminated the stump of the Washington National Monument and suffused the stonework of his federal edifices.[209] He died at about half past seven on the morning of Saturday, 3 March, tended by his beloved Eliza and daughters Sarah, Jacqueline, and Anna. Before his corpse was prepared for burial, Eliza sent word to the *Evening Star,* and the news was soon registered by other local papers.[210] Under the heading "Distinguished Architect Dead," the editor encapsulated Mills's achievement: "The Treasury Department, Post Office and Patent Office buildings, are monuments of his skill and taste, as is also the Washington Monument." The next column printed Eliza's funeral announcement: "His funeral, to which the friends of the family are respectfully invited, will take place tomorrow (Sunday) at 3 o'clock p.m. from his late residence, No. 553 New Jersey Avenue, corner of B Street South." His body was committed to the earth at the Congressional Cemetery in grave number 111, although unmarked by a headstone until 1937.

One day after his burial, a large group of friends from the National Institution gathered at their quarters in the Patent Office to mourn Mills's passing. Dr. Gale, who in October 1851 had read a favorable analysis on the marble used for the east wing of the Patent Office, expressed their "unfeigned sorrow" and unanimous decision to compose an obituary for publication by the *National Intelligencer*.[211] On 12 March, Mills's "goods, chattels and personal estate," including a "Mantle clock" valued at $30, ten "Hair cloth Parlor Chairs" at $15, a "Refrigerator" at $3, and a "Copper Kettle & Kitchenware" at $17, were appraised at $390.50.[212] The appraisal was finally cleared through the legal processes on 23 February 1856 in the District of Columbia Orphan's Court and finalized on 15 April under a bond of $2,000, probably guaranteed by Eliza's sons-in-law. Meanwhile, she struggled to settle Mills's tax title and debts, apparently together in excess of $1,000, chiefly by the sale of the undeveloped Bath Lands with Alexander Dimitry's sanction to Robert G. Briscoe of Bath and Washington for $2,886.58.[213] Enough remained for Eliza to live out her final ten years at their New Jersey Avenue home overlooking the federal capital, which Mills had so ennobled through the exercise of those qualities celebrated by his peers in the National Institution.

7

Retrospect
"an eminent and useful man"

"In the death of Mr. Mills," the members of the National Institution stated in the obituary they sent to the *National Intelligencer* on 7 March, "our city has lost an eminent and useful man, who for a quarter of a century was connected with many of its greatest improvements." They recognized that he had brought to the District a measure of the architectural distinction of the European capitals, and to the nascent architectural profession greater respect through the quality of his design, concern for efficient structural and contracting systems, and participation in so many aspects of the nation's development. Justly they indicated that his architecture equaled or bettered that of his major competitors.

Mills's creative adaptations of American Palladian and of ancient and modern Classical sources, together with his sure command of composition and proportion, resulted in a style that had attained consistent maturity by the time he moved to Baltimore and in its subsequent evolution can be deemed quite as inventive and relevant as that of his peers. Even in the Gothic, which he pioneered in the South, Mills created convincing effects without elevating archaeological precedent above practical requirement. His architecture, moreover, displayed a broader range of style, scale, and type than did that of most American architects of the period between the Revolution and the Civil War. That is exemplified by the more regional emphasis of his South Carolina architecture of the 1820s and greater monumentality of his federal buildings, no less than by his innovative churches, functional yet dignified courthouses and customhouses, and humanitarian and sanitary prisons and hospitals, built from New England to Alabama. He responded to changes of taste, as in the more insistent Neo-Greek and latterly Italianate emphases of his work in Washington, yet did not alter his fundamental creative conception since it reflected his personal integrity, respect for tradition, and Rationalist approach to design. Consequently, he was opposed to the imitative practice that was nurtured by nineteenth-century archaeology and academism, averse to the greater stress on ornament, polychromy, and complex forms preferred from the mid-1840s, and wary of the metal technologies and more utilitarian values that emerged from the 1850s. Mills was not an innovator; he did not create novel compositional and spatial patterns or radically reinterpret historical stylistic conventions and motif. He was possessed of a notable talent for conceiving formally and aesthetically homogeneous and appropriate design, together with the diligence and determination to realize a remarkable number of projects. His architecture belonged to a passing phase in American and transatlantic taste, nicely defined by the sculptor Horatio Greenough in *Remarks on Art, Design and Architecture* (1851): "The redundant must be pared down, the superfluous dropped, the necessary itself reduced to its simplest expression, and then we shall find, whatever the organization may be, that beauty was waiting for us."

If the members of the National Institution could only indicate Mills's achievement as an architect, they could comment authoritatively on the man. They discerned that his "constant" industry proceeded from "love of his art," much as his "temper" was "serene, gentle, and loving to the whole family of man; guileless and single-minded as a child, yet with an imagination as exhaustless, a power as benevolent, a taste as accurate and practical as is seldom combined in the same individual." They implied that the inventive compass of his mind had been compromised by limited scientific comprehension and technical analysis in commenting that his civil engineering and transportation schemes had "foreshadowed," rather than accomplished, "many of the greatest and most useful of our public improvements." In that respect, they confirmed those characteristics that Latrobe had discerned much earlier—industry, intelligence, idealism, and integrity—but, whether from admiration of Mills's achievements or acquaintance, did not allude to those faults attributed by his chief mentor—intellectual superficiality, religiosity, impetuosity, and opportunism. Mills in their opinion merited "the fame of those who helped to make" society "richer, wiser and better." They had observed Mills's courageous and optimistic response to repeated professional adversity and concluded that he had died "while his intellect was still unclouded, and its natural force unimpaired," and, despite recent reverses, "full of honor."

In fact, Mills's reputation had already waned and would diminish further over the following decades until the gradual reawakening, beginning in the 1930s, of scholarly interest in his career and in Neoclassical design. Shifts in aesthetics would, as has been seen, even threaten the survival of the Washing-

105.   Mills, Washington National Monument (1848–1854, 1880–1884).

ton National Monument, although at his death it was singled out for special praise in the closing, exalted, sentences of the National Institution obituary:

> From the window of his chamber, dying he could look upon the last and greatest monument of his genius, the stupendous pile climbing towards the skies in honor of the father of his Country.

That eulogy would have profoundly satisfied Mills because the architecture he completed, and the engineering and transportation schemes he promoted, were expressions of his intense patriotism. The incomplete obelisk stood as a promise of the survival of the Union through the Civil War. Once finished during the era of Reconstruction, the monument soared as a vital image of the republic, every day the objective of popular pilgrimage and, in the words of the accomplished late-nineteenth-century American architect Ralph Adams Cram, "the noblest architectural structure in the United States" (105).[1]

The monument continues to impart a sense of the transcendent, of the fusion of mortal record with immortal significance, a mystery that fascinated Mills since his thought intermixed theological proposition and secular morality, while his architecture interwove the idealistic and the pragmatic. He was at once dedicated to the hope of eternal salvation and to the aim of material improvement. "My object is to benefit the profession," he had written to General Macomb on 8 November 1827, "and in so doing to advance the good of my country."[2] Mills's Americanism was demonstrated in his adaptive concept of design, the synthetic and flexible character of which matched that of the swiftly expanding and fundamentally egalitarian republic. He tempered the elitist architectural vocabulary to modern requirement, as in the Baptist Church in Baltimore or the General Post Office in Washington. An anonymous contributor to *The Crayon* in June 1856 judged the General Post Office to be "the most *sensible* of the new government buildings," being distinguished by "constructive thought" and "suited to its department in character and importance."

The discerning judgment of the National Institution obituary was confirmed when the Senate of the United States uanimously resolved on the bicentennial of his birth that "Robert Mills was the first American born and trained architect establishing a tradition of outstanding American architecture."[3]

Notes

Books and articles are cited by author's name, and date where necessary, and archival sources are abbreviated, the full citations appearing in the list of abbreviations and Select Bibliography.

Abbreviations

AAA	Archives of American Art, Smithsonian Institution, Washington, D.C.
A. Bull.	*Art Bulletin*
AIA	American Institute of Architects
AL	Avery Library, Columbia University, New York
AP	Athenaeum of Philadelphia
APS	American Philosophical Society, Philadelphia
BCA	Baltimore City Archives
BDAC	*Biographical Dictionary of American Congress*
Burl. Mag.	*Burlington Magazine*
DAB	*Dictionary of American Biography*
FI	Franklin Institute, Philadelphia
GUL	Georgetown University Library, Washington, D.C., Richard X. Evans collection
HABS	Historic American Buildings Survey
HL	Huntington Library
HSP	Historical Society of Pennsylvania
JSAH	*Journal of the Society of Architectural Historians*
JSCMA	*Journal of the South Carolina Medical Association*
LC	Library of Congress, Mills Papers (unless otherwise stated), Washington, D.C.
LHS	Ladies Hermitage Society, Hermitage, Tennessee
MHM	*Maryland Historical Magazine*
MHR	Maryland Hall of Records, Annapolis
MHS	Maryland Historical Society, Baltimore

MHSW	Maryland Historical Society, Washington Monument Papers, MSS 876
MAHS	Massachusetts Historical Society, Boston
MEHS	Maine Historical Society, Portland
MMNY	Metropolitan Museum of Art, New York
NA	U.S. National Archives (Record Group), Washington, D.C.

(with record group number)

RG 21	District of Columbia, Wills
RG 28	Records of the Post Office Department
RG 42	Records of the Commissioner of Public Buildings and Grounds, correspondence (by volume number or letter number), ledger, minute book, and contracts
RG 45	Miscellaneous Letters to the Secretary of the Navy
RG 46	Records of the Senate
RG 48	Records of the Department of the Interior
RG 49	Letters received from Registers and Receivers of the United States Land Offices
RG 56	Correspondence of the Treasury Secretary and Collectors
RG 56f	Treasury Notable Person file 1809
RG 59	Records of the Department of State
RG 77	Records of the Army Corps of Engineers
RG 90	Letters Received on Marine Hospitals
RG 92	Records of the Army Quartermaster General
RG 94	Records of the Army Adjutant General
RG 121	Records of the Public Building Service
RG 136	Records of the West Point Academy
RG 217	Commissioner of Public Buildings and Grounds, payments
RG 233	Records of the House of Representatives
RG 351	Records of the Government of the District of Columbia, Surveyor's Office
NHCHS	New Haven Colony Historical Society
NYHS	New-York Historical Society
OAC	Architect of the Capitol, Washington, D.C.
PM	Peale Museum, Baltimore
PRM	*Papers of Robert Mills,* ed. P. Scott (Scholarly Resources Microfilm ed., 1990)
PH	*Pennsylvania History*
PSA	Pennsylvania State Archives, Harrisburg
RCHS	*Records of the Columbia Historical Society*
SCDAH	South Carolina Department of Archives and History, Columbia
SCHS	South Carolina Historical Society, Charleston
SCH[G]M	*South Carolina Historical [and Genealogical] Magazine*
SCL	South Carolina Library, Columbia
Statistics	Robert Mills, *Statistics of South Carolina including a view of its Natural, Civil, and Military History, General and Particular*
Tulane	Southeastern Architectural Archive, Howard-Tilton Memorial Library, Tulane University, New Orleans, Mills Papers MSS 625
UNC	University of North Carolina, Chapel Hill
UV	University of Virginia, Charlottesville, McCure Papers MSS 6840
USNMB	*United States National Museum Bulletin*
VHS	Virginia Historical Society, Richmond

VMHB	*Virginia Magazine of History and Biography*
VSA	Virginia State Archives, Richmond
VSL	Virginia State Library, Richmond
YU	Yale University, New Haven, Connecticut

Chapter 1

1 Mills to John Vaughan 16 December 1814, APS misc. mss; *PRM*, 0482, adding "which I have ever had."

2 For the family ancestry, see Gallagher, 184–86; for the historical background with reference to Ann, see Haley, esp. 243. See also the family genealogy compiled in about 1850 by Mills, GUL; *PRM*, 2704.

3 Bryan (1989), 4–5.

4 Liscombe (1985), 1; Easterby, 28–29; G. C. Rogers, 294, notes that Mills's name is not listed between 1790 and 1793.

5 B. H. Uhlendorf, *The Seige of Charleston* (Ann Arbor, 1938) 327; for Charleston architecture in the period, see Ravenel; Lane (1984); G. C. Rogers; Mazyck; and Severens.

6 Pierson, 1:121–122; Mazyck, no. 49.

7 *Statistics,* 406 (reprinted *PRM* 5003); of the more sophisticated St. Philip's church, he wrote that it had "more of design in its arrangement than any other of our ancient buildings" (404–5).

8 *Statistics,* 407.

9 Walker, 4; Dunbar.

10 J. A. Cohen, 15–32, discusses the use of books and architectural education during the period.

11 Lane (1984), 69; Rutledge (1980); and Bryan (1989), 10, list other drawing teachers who advertised in the 1780s and 1790s. For the state house, Faut.

12 *Statistics,* 53; Gallagher, opp. 8, reproduces a clumsy drawing of a classical temple as by Mills (actually the base from an anonymous design for the Washington National Monument, [NA RG 42 WMAP]).

13 Dunlap, 2:375, continuing, "Here he prosecuted his studies about two years."

14 "Architecture in Virginia" (1853) 38; *PRM*, 3026.

15 Gallagher, 14, from Frary, 170. For Nourse, see *City of Washington,* 293. *PRM* 0027, is a letter from this period written by Mills describing Georgetown, GUL.

16 LC.

17 *Exemplar,* Library, The Grand Lodge, Pennsylvania; *Grand Lodge 1717–1967* (Philadelphia, 1967); Callahan.

18 Cassia Lodge, number 45, Baltimore, admitted 20 April 1815; membership speculated in Denslow.

19 Quoted in Harvey, 143.

20 Respectively owned by Col. H. Anderson, Columbia, S.C., and SCDAH, MB–17, folder 6; *PRM*, 6070. See also Hollis, vol. 1; Bryan (1976), 19–23, and (1989), 17–19, figs. 1.3, 1.4 (pl. 17); and Rogers, 293.

21 Tulane; *PRM*, 2705.

22 Tulane, reprinted Gallagher, 153–54; *PRM*, 4000.

23 The Tuscan, "according to Vitruvius, . . . is the most simple and plain of all the orders in architecture," (14).

24 Mills, *Guide to the Capitol of the United States* (1834), 58.

25 *Guide,* 58.

26 Charleston Will Deed Book, 1800–1807, vol. 28A, no. 35, Charleston City Archives.

27 *Washington Sentinel*, 22 March 1854.

28 Dunlap, 2:375.

29 LC, Jefferson Papers; *PRM*, 0012.

30 Respectively, YU, dated 18 October 1802, and Gallagher, 8; *PRM*, 0016A, 0014.

31 LC, Jefferson Papers; *PRM*, 0203.

32 Dunlap; also stated in Mills's draft autobiography, SCHS, 11–518–1.

33 Thomas Jefferson Foundation, watermarked "J. RUSE 1800," figs. 1.11, 1.10, in Bryan (1989); *PRM*, 6044, 6040.

34 LC, draft for "Progress of Architecture in Virginia," possibly dating from about 1842, and associated with his projected "Statistical history of the State of Virginia," for which he sought information in a circular dated 28 August 1842 (*PRM*, 2388).

35 "Doctrine of Sounds," SCHS, 11–517–13; *PRM*, 6063.

36 In his *Guide to the Capitol* (1834), 1 n., Mills nevertheless criticized Bulfinch's dome as "so disproportionate to the building: it destroys the beauty of this [east] front."

37 "Progress of Architecture in Virginia," SCHS, 33–22–10; *PRM*, 2706. Jefferson's library was then the largest in the United States, being donated to the Library of Congress in 1815 and matched only by the collection he assembled from 1825 for the University of Virginia (O'Neal [1976]).

38 "Progress"; the drawings are MAHS, K.156, K.155 (Kimball), the elevation of Monticello being fig. 1.6 in Bryan (1989); *PRM*, 6081.

39 SCHS, 33–22–10.

40 Rutledge (1955), 143.

41 "Architectural Works of Robert Mills," Tulane; *PRM*, 2705.

42 LC, Jefferson Papers; *PRM*, 0071.

43 Tulane; *PRM*, 0016B.

44 MAHS; *PRM*, 6098. Lowry (1976), vol. 1, incorrectly associates the design with Jefferson's proposal for the President's House.

45 LC, Jefferson Papers; *PRM*, 0088A.

46 "Architectural Works of Robert Mills," Tulane; *PRM*, 2705.

47 J. A. Cohen, 24.

48 Tulane; reprinted Cohen (1950); *PRM*, 4001.

49 "Autobiography," SCHS, 11–518–1, also in a letter dated 13 June 1808 to Jefferson, LC and *PRM*, 0203.

50 Hamlin (1955), 222.

51 Van Horne and Formwalt, 1:330; *PRM*, 0025.

52 Carter (1976), 174/C1 (illustrated Norton, fig. 34), 174/C9.

53 Carter (1976), 35/G5; *PRM*, 0042, 0036 for Mills's survey notes.

54 LSC mss 195; *PRM*, 6073; Liscombe (1985), 3–5.

55 Unexecuted, but included in his "Designs of Buildings for Virginia," ca. 1798, LC Prints and Drawings, and Hamlin (1964), 116–17; for Latrobe's acoustical theory and its influence on Mills, see Bryan (1989), 20ff.

56 The surviving minutes, SCHS, cease between May 1801 and March 1812; for the later church, see Dalcho, 365.

57 *DAB*, 15:338–39; for his historical writings, see H.C. Hockett *The Critical Method in Historical Research and Writing* (1935, reprinted Westport, Conn. 1977), 202–3 and E. Pinckney, "Robert Y. Hayne and the Sale of David Ramsay's *History of the United States*," SCHM 86 (1985), 72–74; *Statistics*, 141, for his vaccination.

58 Register of the Independent Congregational Church, 1796–1824; D. Ramsay, 10; *PRM*, 6057.

59 Register; Liscombe (1985), 5–7; Severens, 206.

60 Carter (1976), 49/E9; Hamlin (1955), 585–91; *PRM*, 0084.

61 Palladio, trans. I. Ware, *Four Books* (1738), 81–82.

62 Carter (1976), 157/E10; dated ca. 1803 by Van Horne and Formwalt, 400–408.

63 Norton, in his review of Liscombe, *Church Architecture JSAH*, 66 (1987):256, proposes that Latrobe might have told Mills about George Stewart's St. Chad's, Shrewsbury (1790–1793) and the Spa Fields Chapel, London, converted in the late 1770s, from the Pantheon "pleasure palace" (1770).

64 *Statistics*, 414.

65 SCHS, 11–517–13; for the de l'Orme system, illustrated as pl. 26 in Owen Biddle, *Young Carpenter's Assistant* (1805), see Harnsberger and Wiebenson (1973).

66 SCHS, 11–517–13, Thomas's bond for $240.

67 Senate Committee Report 145 (31st Cong., 1st sess.), 1850.

68 SCHS, 11–517–13; *PRM*, 6063, 0028, 0030–0032. See also Williams; and Liscombe (1985), 5.

69 Watson, 101–5.

70 Tulane; *PRM*, 0326.

71 Dunlap, *Rise and Progress*, 2:376.

72 Revenues collected by the federal government from the Charleston district averaged $750,000 between 1804 and 1806 (*Statistics*, 168).

73 Evans; *PRM*, 0021/2/7 (0029, since it describes Charleston, was probably addressed to Sarah Mather).

74 Lane (1984), 87.

75 The survey is at the Hall of Records, Dover, Delaware.

76 Carter (1976), 37/E12.

77 GUL, they corresponded from 18 July 1804 (*PRM*, 0033) until 27 October 1807 (*PRM*, 0154A). The correspondence with "A.M.A." noted below dates between November 1804 and September 1805 (*PRM*, 0040, 0065).

78 For Dorsey, see J. A. Cohen, 39–42.

79 Typescript Academy of Fine Arts; Mease (1824), 314, cites no architect.

80 SCDAH, 1807–50–13, replies 1807–50–21/55/; *PRM*, 0083Cff.

81 SCDAH, 1807–50–61; Bryan (1984), citing all the references in the General Assembly Reports, and Bryan (1989), 28.

82 Carter (1976), 51/D4; *PRM*, 0091.

83 LC; *PRM*, 0096. For the Smith family, see Cartmell, especially 296; Norris, 667–69, and *Genealogies of Virginia*, 4: 463–65; *PRM*, 6087, is a contemporary watercolor view of Hackwood.

84 *Genealogies of Virginia*, 4:465.

85 The rumor, evidently investigated by General Smith, is recounted in Eliza's letter to Mills written in early January 1807 (GUL; *PRM*, 0101); Mills, however, did infer that he had contemplated marriage to another woman about the time their courtship began, in an undated letter (*PRM*, 0077) that casts valuable light on their relationship. "How much am I indebted to you for breaking twice of formality . . . I should, alas!, have plunged into a sea of difficulties, by giving my hand when my heart was another's." Their courtship correspondence is preserved at GUL, LC, and SCHS, and reproduced *PRM*, from 0077–0222.

86 Carter (1976), 54/C2.

87 SCHS, 11–517–1; *PRM*, 0184.

88 Via his brother Thomas, he sold a parcel of land in St. Thomas and St. Denis united parishes for $800; on 28 April a brick house and lot at 31 Eliot Street and a wooden house and lot at 7 Liberty Street for $5,000 were purchased by Thomas (Charleston District Conveyance Book, 1806–1807, respectively, vols. 57, 470–71, and T7, 298–99 [Charleston City Archives]).

89 LC, Mills to the Congressional Committee on Public Buildings and Grounds, 14 March 1838; *PRM*, 1715.

90 Carter (1976), 62/F1/; *PRM*, 0176.

91 Carter (1976), 57/G14/ and 59/F11/; *PRM*, 0146 and 0125.

92 The letter is dated 22 April 1808 (Carter [1976]), 64/D7/; *PRM*, 0195.

93 First Presbyterian Church Archives; Liscombe (1985), 7–9; Bryan (1989), pls. 19–21, fig. 1.19; and *PRM*, 0236, advertisement for building estimates *Augusta Herald*, 1 June 1809, and 6018, drawings.

94 HSP, Bc 615 M657b; *PRM*, 6042. Gallagher, 96, suggests that it was estimated at $30,000 but misdated the drawings as 1842; see also Massey, no. 33 The multilevel plan recalls Latrobe's scheme for the Capt. William Pennock House in Norfolk (1796), in "Designs of Buildings in Virginia," LC.

95 Mount Holly Library, Mount Holly, N.J.; Giger; Bryan (1989), fig. 1.20 and *PRM*, 0233, 6039, drawings.

96 Examined in Braham.

97 LC, Jefferson Papers posted to the president on 16 June 1808, to which he replied on 23 June (*PRM*, 0204). Possibly contemporaneous was his scheme for cutting "two or three large main tunnels from [the Ashley] to [the Cooper] River, along Broad and Boundary Streets [Charleston], crossed by one running along Meeting Street," (*Statistics*, 440 n.).

Chapter 2

1 Their marriage license is dated 15 October 1808 (VSL; *PRM*, 0225).

2 Bryn Mawr College; *PRM*, 6047. Discussed Massey, no. 32; Ames; Tinkcom, and Alexander in Bryan (1989), 41–42, fig. 2.6–2.7 (as built).

3 No. 482, Rutledge (1955), 142.

4 For the history of the commission, see Etting; White ed.; Riley; and J. A. Cohen, 60–62.

5 Elam; in about 1800 Charles Peale had painted Latrobe, pl. 33 in Hamlin (1955).

6 APS, C. W. Peale Letter Books, vol. 10, 103, and vol. 11, 4, reprinted L. B. Miller, IIA/48A8, and 48E1; *PRM*, 0238, also 0246, 0251.

7 APS, vol. 11, 4.

8 He also built a small Federal-style house for Robert Blackwell at 313 Pine Street, now St. Peter's Church House (Tatman and Moss, 542, from Webster, 10–11).

9 No. 15, Rutledge (1955), 143.

10 AP, fig. 2.23, in Bryan (1989); *PRM*, 6048.

11 Finkel, pl. 76.

12 Jackson (1922), 134.

13 SCHS, 11–518–1.

14 Gallagher, 128.

15 HSP, C. W. Unger Collection, aa 17b; for the houses, see Alexander in Bryan (1989), 40, fig. 2.50.

16 Retrospective account in Chew's letter of 31 July 1810 to Mills is in HSP, Chew Papers, box 85; *PRM*, 0253, further correspondence 2059–0261. See also J. A. Cohen, 58–59. Mills's drawings are in box 85a (*PRM*, 6045), including three plans that are much cruder in form and rendering, being arranged across the sheet right to left unlike Mills, discussed by Alexander in Bryan (1989), 36–40, figs. 2.1, 2.2 (as built), 2.3–2.4.

17 Mills wrote in a similar vein to Henry Wise regarding work apparently completed for the Pennsylvania legislature (MHS, C. E. French Collection; *PRM*, 2384), adding, "The expense of educating an Architect is equal to that of any other profession. You, as a lawyer, would think yourself poorly paid by receiving such a fee, for the same amt. of labour mental, and physical."

18 *Charter By-Laws and Standing Resolutions of the Pennsylvania Academy of Fine Arts* (1813), 18; AP, Mills file.

19 LC, Jefferson Papers; documents relating Mills's contribution to the society are *PRM*, beginning from 0254 and continuing to 0415.

20 Alberts.

21 Liscombe (1991).

22 Latrobe accepted on 30 January 1811 (Carter [1976], 83/C10); his address was printed in *Port Folio*, 5 (1811) 4ff. See also Goodyear.

23 LC, Jefferson Papers; Mills had written in a similar vein to Paul Hamilton, at that time secretary of the navy, in 1811 (SCHS, 11–517–8), and the *National Intelligencer*, April 1815, 3–4, would publish "The Art of Painting," *PRM*, 0510.

24 Cummings.

25 State Archives of Philadelphia, William Penn Memorial Museum, 05.87; Liscombe (1985), 9; Alexander in Bryan (1989), 60, fig. 2.20; *PRM*, 6043.

26 He might also have recalled the diagonal arrangement of circular and elliptical spaces created by Ledoux for the Hôtel Montmerency, Paris (1769–1771), illustrated Krafft and Ransonette, *Plans... des plus belles maisons* (1801–1802), pl. 40, owned by Jefferson.

27 Scharf and Westcott, 1:424; Hitchcock and Seale, 59.

28 Cummings and Withey.

29 PSA, RG 2, Dept. of Auditor General, Internal Improvements file, receipt no. 53, 25 September 1811.

30 Tulane; *PRM*, 4000, including sketches for the buildings discussed in this paragraph, and for "Kraumbar's House" on Third and Spruce streets, dated 1810. The circus was opened in 1809 by Victor Pepin and John Brechard and later called the Olympic Theater.

31 Mease, 331–32; for Mease, see Simpson, 689–90.

32 *Port Folio* (February 1811): 125. For Dorsey's Manufactory, see Tatum (1961), 76, 177; and Massey, no. 30; and for *Port Folio*, see Scharf and Westcott, 3:1979–1981.

33 Thomas (1952) and (1957), 658.

34 SCHS, 11–517–8.

35 Lossing, 968.

36 *DAB*, 9:539–40; and Scharf and Westcott, 2:1309–10.

37 Mease, 326–28; Finkel, pl. 69; Liscombe (1985), 9–11; Alexander in Bryan (1989), 54–55, fig. 1.14, illustrating Mill's section and plan of the dome, now with the American Baptist Historical Society; *PRM*, 6051.

38 Illustrated White, pl. 12.

39 Scharf and Westcott, 2:1309–10.

40 NA, RG 42, Committee on Public Buildings and Grounds, no. 2189; for Pettibone, author of *Economy of Fuel* (Philadelphia, 1812), see Bryan (1989), 32 n. 90.

41 MHSW; *PRM*, 1166.

42 HSP, Lancaster-Schuylkill Bridge Records; *PRM*, beginning with 0303 and continuing to 0414; see also Nelson, 159–83, rejecting Mills's claims to its design.

43 *DAB*, 10:pt. 2, 2–3.

44 P. Du Prey, "English Sources for a History of Swiss Wooden Bridges," *Zeitschrift fur Schwergerische Archaëologie und Kunstgesichte* 36 (1979, 56–63).

45 *Rise and Progress,* 2:377; Wernwag's next large bridge at New Hope near Philadelphia was less original, having six 175–foot trusses.

46 Accepted by R. S. Allen, 37.

47 No. 24, Rutledge (1955), 143.

48 *Statistics,* 467 no.

49 HSP, Lancaster-Schuylkill Bridge Records; *PRM,* 0303ff, 0649. See White, 20, pl. 13, and Tatum (1961), pl. 50.

50 SCHS, 11–517–16; Mills had consulted a Dr. Bollman in Philadelphia and Mr. Cloud of the U.S. Mint.

51 LC; *PRM,* 4002.

52 PSA, Mss Group 110, Letter Book 1.

53 These investments, the largest which was on 7 December 1814 for building the three-story brick tenement with Richard Ware, are recorded in the City of Philadelphia, Deed Books, reproduced in *PRM,* 0330, 0432, 0473, 0475 (the tenements), 0484–51, 0580 (the sale of property to William Griffiths on 28 February 1816).

54 Rutledge (1955), 143.

55 Scharf and Westcott, 2:1405.

56 Stillman (1979), 2, fig. 11.

57 SCHS, 33–22–6 on paper watermarked "WHATMAN 1828"; *PRM,* 6050. For the church, see Liscombe (1985), 11, and J. A. Cohen, 62, no. 16, citing Geffen. For Strickland's church, see Gilchrist, 77–78, pl. 23a.

58 Rutledge (1955), 143. Drummond described it as "one of the few Greek Revival [period] churches of originality" (58–59).

59 Pierson, 1:377–86; Mickler; Harnsberger, 33–35; Liscombe (1985), 11–13; and Alexander (1987), 243–47 and in Bryan (1989), 55–56, fig. also 2–13; *PRM* 6084, reproduces illustrative material, mainly from VHS.

60 Carter (1976), 96/B11; *PRM,* 0319.

61 UV; *PRM,* 0291, a series of letters from Smith to Mills is reproduced from 0285, several about "your Temple" (0327, GUL, 30 April 1812).

62 *Richmond portraits in an exhibition of makers of Richmond,* 1737–1860 Valentine Museum, Richmond, VA. 1947: 6–7.

63 Latrobe's reply from Washington to Mills's query is dated 15 September 1812 Carter (1976), 103/A10; *PRM,* 0347.

64 The composition also recalls the so-called Baptisterium of Constantine, actually post-Classical in date, engraved in the sixteenth chapter of the last of Palladio's *Four Books of Architecture;* Ware in his 1738 translation stated that Palladio considered the "Baptisterium" to be "a beautiful invention" (96–87, pl. 42).

65 Draft autobiography, SCHS, 11–518–1; *PRM,* 2706.

66 The detailed dimensions were recorded in 1868 by Colonel J. B. Danforth, printed by Fisher, 38, and Liscombe (1985).

67 Scott and Zimmer.

68 SCHS, 11–517–3; *PRM,* 0353.

69 SCHS, 11–517–15.

70 LC, and SCHS, 11–517–15 (*PRM,* 0677–0678); for Capellano, see Groce and Wallace, 108, and for the monument, see Scott in Bryan (1989), 145–46.

71 Carter (1976), 102/C2; *PRM,* 0474.

72 *Virginia Historical Register,* 39.

73 Kirker (1969), 282–87; William Rhoad's cruder Old Round Church at Richmond, Vermont, of 1813 derived more directly from Gibbs's circular church plans (illustrated Kennedy, 242).

74 Goodfellow.

75 AL, typescript AA 737 R5 R631; Rogers was in Richmond to discuss the design of the projected Exchange Hotel and the coppering of the capitol roof.

76 No. 123, Rutledge (1955), 143.

77 AAA; *PRM,* 0360ff. Further contemporary correspondence remains at the SCHS, also reproduced in *PRM,* 0348ff; in an earlier letter addressed to her sister Anna Smith on 21 March 1809 (*PRM,* 0235), Eliza wrote "must go... Billy awaits me."

78 The Philadelphia tenements are illustrated in Bryan (1989), 42, fig. 2.8.

79 Alexander (1987), 252–53, figs. 12.9–12.11, and in Bryan (1989), 46–50, based on M. W. Scott (1941), 112–14, 119–21, 138–41 (attributing the Hayes–McCance house to Mills), 146–51.

80 Jackson (1922) 125; and *Encyclopedia of Philadelphia* (1933) 4, 1169–1170.

81 White, 24, pl. 16: Alexander in Bryan (1989), 61, figs. 2.24, and 13.

82 Rutledge (1955), 143.

83 Illustrated in Stuart and Revett's *Antiquities of Athens* (1762), vol. 1.

84 The portico corresponds with the scheme for a garden structure in Ware's *Designs of Inigo Jones,* which may have been an inspiration for Claude-Nicolas Ledoux's Hotel Guimard in Paris (1770–1771), itself identified as a source for Latrobe's Center Square Pump House (R. Bornemann, "Some Ledoux-inspired Buildings in America," *JSAH* 13 [1957]: 15–17).

85 Huss, 1:131, stating the purchase price as $20,000 and that they divided the main hall into two rooms and added gaslight; see also J. A. Cohen, 57–58.

86 Pocket memorandum book, 29 October, published with Mills's description in *Port Folio,* series 5 (1817): 164–66, 222–28; illustrated by White, and Tatum (1961), pl. 53; *PRM,* 6053.

87 UV; *PRM,* 0468.

88 SCHS, 11–517–2; *PRM,* 0469. Jefferson's recommendation of 17 February 1814 (LC Jefferson Papers), was in vain, since President Madison appointed Latrobe. About this time, Mills also sent Postmaster General Thomas Monroe a plan for restoring the "Deflagrated Hall [of Representatives]" (NA, RG 42, Letters no. 2172; *PRM,* 0505).

Chapter 3

1 MHSW; *PRM,* 0421ff; Hoyt; Miller, although erroneously attributing to Mills a crude design for a polygonal monument, figs. 4, 5, (also accepted by P. Scott (1985)), and in Bryan (1989), 146–48, pls. 5, 6, 13, fig. 1.8; *PRM,* 0410.

2 No. 252, Rutledge (1955), 143, the description occupied pages 22–24 of the exhibition catalogue.

3 Published in *The Crayon* (1856), quoted Hoyt, 181–82. Mills's submission is MHSW.

4 Addressed to Godefroy on 10 October 1814 (Carter [1976], 102/C2); for the Dublin Nelson Pillar, see Liscombe (1980), 57–58.

5 An indirect inspiration for the galleries might have been the rusticated bands on the shaft of James Gibbs's design for a commemorative column in his *Book of Architecture,* pl. 87, interestingly surmounted by a figure in Roman dress.

6 LC, Jefferson Papers; *PRM,* 0885.

7 MHSW; *PRM,* 0453.

8 AAA.

9 SCHS, 11–517–3.

10 APS, Misc. Mss; *PRM,* 0482.

11 For the New York Academy, Sizer in Cowdray, 11ff.

12 Alexander (1974), 72.

13 Mills to the Building Committee, 11 May 1815, MHSW.; Hoyt, 178, the foundation was dug along Charles Street.

14 Gallagher, 184.

15 MHSW.

16 Miller, 25, fig. 9.

17 Tulane; *PRM*, 0699. For Delaplaine, see Scharf and Westcott, 2:1059.

18 Benjamin in the preface also stressed that European books were not suitable, since "the style of building in this country differs very considerably from that of Great Britain, and other countries in Europe, which is partly in consequence of the more liberal appropriation made for building in those countries, and of the difference of materials used, particularly in the external decoration."

19 Olson; for the ceremony and commission, see Scharf, 3:143ff. Howland and Spencer.

20 *Baltimore, Past and Present,* 286–88; "Famous Baltimore Names: Gilmor," *Baltimore Sun,* 18 July 1979. Robert Gilmor, Jr. (1774–1848), the merchant and art collector, became a frequent correspondent of Mills.

21 Bryan (1989), 72 n. 50; associated documents are reproduced *PRM*, 0741ff, and 6026, an illustration of Courtland Street.

22 *An Authentic Account of . . . Laying of Cornerstone of the Washington Monument,* 22; *PRM*, 0497.

23 Regarding contemporary Baltimore architects, Mills, writing to Gilmor on 24 May 1832 would mourn the death of William Small, trained by Latrobe, as "a young man of talent, and promising in his profession," MHSW; *PRM*, 6023.

24 MHSW; see also Scott in Bryan (1989), 147–48, pl. 2 and fig. 5.6.

25 MHSW; *PRM*, 0729. In his 1818 report, Mills acknowledged that it would be prudent to "pursue the more simple character of a monument" without ornament on the shaft. Nonetheless, in this period Mills drafted a proposal (SCHS, 11–517–19), for placing at each corner of the pedestal "*Colossal Busts*" of the first four presidents or the chief members of Washington's cabinet and for a winged horse carrying a figure of Washington or a "colossal *statue*" of Victory atop the column.

26 MHSW; *PRM*, 1035, 1042.

27 MHSW, some illustrated in Miller, dated 1816 in Bryan (1989), pl. 2, fig. 5.6; *PRM*, 6023. Another signed but undated sheet shows the pedestal unornamented in three elevations and the shaft in two, but in each having Washington in Roman military costume with his right arm extended. Contemporaneously he might also have drawn a framed pen elevation having a simpler pedestal with inscriptions and the figure of Washington with his left arm outstretched; two larger elevations (LC) delineate a plain shaft but allegorical figures on the corner of the pedestal, somewhat akin in style to sketches for trophies in his Washington notebook dateable to 1830.

28 Reiterated in another letter Mills mailed on 22 August 1826 (MHSW; *PRM*, 1043).

29 MHS, also containing the account books. The advertisement is *Weekly Register* 21 (30 September 1826):65.

30 Tulane; *PRM*, 4005; H. Cohen (1951), 219–21.

31 Tulane, entry for 3 December; H. Cohen (1952), 36.

32 MHSW, Mills estimated the decorations plus tripods at $20,000; *PRM*, 1139, 1161.

33 MHSW.

34 MHSW numbered 19; *PRM*, 6023.

35 BCA, RG S1, box 36, no. 744.

36 BCA, box 36, no. 312, James Carroll to the City Commissioners estimating the cost at $3,006.70.

37 Alexander (1983), 181–82; Mills traveled to inspect the castings in December 1836, being reimbursed $65 for expenses.

38 SCHS, 11–5–17–3; other letters are in AAA, including one from Eliza dated only 26 August [1816] accusing slaves of being "without any principles whatever, Fear is their prompter and self-interest their ruling Passion."

39 LC; *PRM*, 4002 reprinted with omissions by Evans (1935).

40 Fort sold Mills a brick house on St. Paul's Lane, agreement dated 27 February 1816 (Baltimore Circuit Court Land Records, MHR, *PRM*, 0578), apparently resold on 18 April 1816, (*PRM*, 0593). Another agreement, dated 24 December 1816, records Mills's sale of property on Mount Royal for $2,750 to Thomas Caldwell (*PRM*, 0628). Further evidence of Mills's property dealings comes in an advertisement for the sale or exchange of two houses in Philadelphia and one in Charleston, currently rented for a total annual income of $1,200, printed on 30 April 1817 in the Baltimore *American and Commercial Daily Advertiser* (*PRM*, 0658B).

41 BCA, RG 4, S2, Tax Assessors Records Tenth Ward, 14; *PRM*, 0632.

42 Liscombe (1985), 13–14; and Alexander in Bryan (1989), 56–58, n. 41 citing contemporary criticism of the acoustics, figs. 2.19–2.20; *PRM*, 0575ff.

43 SCHS, 11–517–17.

44 MHSW, Baptist Church file; Harnsberger, 35–36, figs. 43, 44; also *PRM*, 0577ff, 6028.

45 Scharf, 124.

46 Carter (1976), 139/A8. Mills's Baptist Church possibly encouraged Latrobe to send Jefferson a sketch of a Pantheon-like rotunda for the main building of the University of Virginia in July 1817 (Liscombe (1985), 13; O'Neal [1960], 19).

47 Bryan (1989), 86 and 103, n. 440.

48 Alexander (1987), and in Bryan (1989), 249–50, figs. 12.7–2.8.

49 M. W. Scott (1950), 94, and (1941) 130–31, illustrating the Brander House; also Alexander in Bryan (1989), 47, fig. 2.12; Mills's correspondence with Ambler is VHS, Ambler Papers. *PRM*, 6083 is the 1815 insurance policy for the Ambler House (VSL).

50 SCHS, 11–517–17.

51 LC; further records are VSA, [Richmond City] Council Ordinances, 1804–1821, and Minutes Common Hall, 5.

52 This would have contrasted with the Roman Corinthian portico of Jefferson's capitol and anticipated Mills's remark in his "Architectural Works" that Latrobe had introduced a "better" Neoclassical style into the United States (Gallagher, 169).

53 Stillman (1964), esp. 132–34; Liscombe (1985), 13.

54 Pocket memorandum book, LC, and VSA [Richmond City] Acts of Assembly, 1816, 28, 69; also Alexander (1974), 126–29.

55 Scott (1941), 146–48; Glave, Newman, Anderson Associates; typed report on the fabric by the restoration architects; and Alexander in Bryan (1989), 47–50, figs. 2.13–14.

56 Mills may also have been influenced by the plan of Latrobe's nearly complete Van Ness House (1813–1816) in Washington, D.C.

57 Alexander (1987), 248, 255 fig. 12–6.

58 SCHS, 33–22–3; *PRM*, 6027.

59 Elder, and Alexander (1983), 156, fig. 16, reproducing the 1936 HABS Survey, Md. 7, and in Bryan (1989), 44–46, figs. 2.9–2.11; *PRM*, 6034 (6025 illustrates the Buchanan house).

60 The term appears in Mills's *Waterworks for . . . of Washington* (1853). The entry for 7 August 1816 in his pocket memorandum book reads "President" and gives his salary as $500 per annum; in the resignation announcement printed on 3 October 1817, Mills was described as having been "President and Superintendent," remaining on as "Engineer" at $1,200 per annum.

61 BCA, RG 3, S1, no. 94; and VSA, Bath County Deed Book, vol. 8 (1832–1837), 248–50; *PRM*, 0718, is the deed of purchase for the Bath County property recorded with the Baltimore County Circuit Court (MHR), and *PRM* 0896 is the mortgage Mills assumed on it in 1820.

62 SCHS, 11–518–3.

63 As late as 1847, the Winchester lawyer John J. Jackson assured Mills in a letter of 21 August that the proximity of his Bath lands to Covington, "The future terminus of the James River Canal, will give it a value which it would not otherwise have" (SCHS, 11–518–3).

64 BCA, RG 32, S1, box 3: 1818, no. 704 (*PRM*, 0802), and 1819 no. 526; the mayor's report on the cancellation of the bonds is RG 16, S1, box 22, 1823, no. 316.

65 BCA, RG 41, S1, box 6, 1818, no. 953.

66 In September, Mills, assisted by John Davis, made surveys for the installation of a wood pipe system to improve the supply in the downtown area, for which subscribers paid $10 per annum, noted by Mills in his *Water Works for the Metropolitan City of Washington* (1852), 28. His memorandum book for 24 September states that with Davis he took "the levels of Holliday Center and Bath sts, and surveying the line for the new road to intersect the York turnpike."

67 Griffiths, 250.

68 MHR, Chancery Records, 118 (1821), 512–55, and 123 (1823), 372–410; *PRM*, 0946. Mills was involved contemporaneously in litigation initiated by Thomas McCoy, *PRM*, 0891, 0916.

69 Tulane, the stubs are inscribed "Office of Discount Deposit"; *PRM*, 0716.

70 Recounted in a letter to Eliza dated Fredericksburg, 12 February 1817 (AAA).

71 SCHS, 11–517–4; reprinted Evans (1938), 117–19.

72 By contrast, Alexis de Tocqueville commented in the next decade, "The American of the South is fond of grandeur, luxury, and renown, of gaiety, of pleasure, and above all idleness" (*Democracy in America*, 1:395).

73 Coit, 114–15.

74 PM, MA 3885, reproduced as fig. 3.17 by Bryan (1989), 99–100; *PRM*, 6031.

75 McCauley, no. 120.

76 Carter (1976), 232/Bll; Minute Books, MHS, Mss 80, box 2 and 17; *PRM*, 0671 is Mills's letter to John Hoffman quoted in the text.

77 MHSW; illustrated Harnsberger, fig. 50, 37–38, 120; *PRM*, 6021.

78 Mills recalled entertaining Mrs. Potts in Philadelphia in a letter to Eliza dated 21 September 1813 (SCHS, 11–517–2). In a letter to Mills dated only August 1814 at Hackwood, Eliza referred to a payment for work on the Potts's existing house (AAA, file 1–10).

79 Henry Francis du Pont Winterthur Museum, no. 82.363.4; Alexander, (1983); Bryan (1989), 50–51, figs. 2.15, 2.16; *PRM*, 6035. See also Mathias (1952).

80 Liscombe (1985), and Alexander in Bryan (1989), 59–60.

81 NYHS, Davis Papers, dating from about 1860.

82 On 12 August 1817, Frederick Graff, engineer to the Philadelphia Water Works, replied to Mills's queries about the protection of lock boxes and iron pipes from frost (SCHS, 11–517–8).

83 SCHS, 11–517–4; *PRM*, 0681.

84 BCA, RG 16, Series 1, box 16, no 602; Olson, 50–51, 292; see also *PRM*, 0630ff., Mills's articles are 0692.

85 BCA, box 56, no. 987; *PRM*, 1155.

86 BCA, box 40, no. 801.

87 BCA, box 16, nos. 376, 377; *PRM*, 0768–0769.

88 BCA, box 16, no. 375, Mills to D. J. C. White 30 June 1818, mentioned in his Autobiography; Tulane, reprinted Gallagher, 160. For the contract with Wernwag, see BCA, RG 32, S1, box 3, no. 708, dated 29 September 1818. Mills submitted a separate design for a bridge with stone abutments estimated at $1,600 on 14 October 1818, no. 59, and on 10 November 1818 presented an estimate for a wooden bridge over Tanners' Run with stone abutments 60 feet long and 23 high for $2,085. The Gay Street bridge was not replaced until 1821.

89 Gallagher, 160; *PRM*, 6024, is a photograph of the bridge.

90 On 13 January 1821, Wernwag wrote to Mills of having been forced to "make up the losses that I have sustained at the falls Bridge which I candidly declare to you is to hard for me," totaling $850; he continued, with reference to Mills's appointment on the South Carolina Board of Works, of having "left you in peace, but it is now your time, & it is now in your power to do something for me; remember I have kept it quiet our connection with the falls Bridge, this would be done in future you know me" (AAA; *PRM*, 0909).

91 BCA, RG 16, S1, box 11, nos. 484A, 443; Bryan (1989), 91, *PRM*, 0701.

92 PM, MA 8088, erroneously attributed to Mills by Bryan.

93 BCA, RG 16, S1, box 11, nos. 483A, 424.

94 SCHS, 11–517–20, Huber to Mills from Baltimore 4 January 1818 for a total of $1,275.

95 First Baptist Church, Charleston, Archives; *PRM*, 6062.

96 SCHS, 11–517–4.

97 Cook; for the church, see Treasurer's Accounts, Church Archives; Craven; Liscombe (1985), 14–15; and Alexander in Bryan (1989), 58–59, fig. 2.21.

98 Cook, 34.

99 *Statistics*, 411.

100 BCA, RG 16. SI, box 12, nos. 394, 386.

101 In the *Statistics*, 329ff., Mills reviewed Count Rumford's reports on poverty in Munich and other German cities.

102 BCA, box 12, no. 749.

103 SCHS, 11–517–21; *PRM*, 0743.

104 HSP, Bc615 M657; illustrated Bryan (1989), 65–66, fig. 2.25; *PRM*, 6030.

105 Mills referred to the scheme in his *Statistics*, 332, adding, "A society of gentlemen of the first respectability and standing in that city was soon after formed to carry a similar system into effect on a private scale."

106 Gilchrist, 53–55.

107 LC; *PRM*, 0781, 0785 (31 August).

108 Hamlin (1955), 502.

109 Pierson, for example, entitled the chapter on the Revival in his *American Buildings*, vol. 1, "The National Phase"; apart from its dependence on British publications, archaeological and otherwise, the revival in the United States was popularized by British immigrant architects such as William Nichols and James Gallier, Sr.

110 Tulane; Reiff, 29–31 and 42; *PRM*, 2705.

111 Hitchcock and Seale, 59ff.

112 Cummings, "Pennsylvania's State Houses," *PH*, 20, no. 4.

113 Gilchrist, 49–50.

114 MHSW; *PRM,* 0821.

115 Illustrated with *Analectic Magazine,* ns, no. 2 (July, 1820):42, and by Gallagher, opp. 42, as by Mills.

116 Dunlap, 2:378; see also Scharf, 3:147.

117 AAA; *PRM,* 0657B, reproduces the account book of the Baltimore physicians Darridge and Wright, who billed Mills $43 between November 1818 and June 1819.

118 BCA, RG 3, SI, box 24, no. 540, letter dated 10 November. Mills also apparently acted as assessor on at least two subsequent occasions, in 1822 and 1825 each concerning the grading of East Street; BCA, RG 3, SI, box 28, no. 17, box 32, no. 10.

119 *Analectic Magazine* (April, 1820): 277–93; Gallagher, 217, rejected by Scott in Bryan (1989), 144, as also the Ross monument.

120 *By-Laws . . . First Troop Philadelphia City Cavalry 1774–1815.*

121 *Analectic Magazine,* 321, reproduced Gallagher, opp. 98.

122 Examined in the economic context by Olson, 72, 360; also Bryan (1989), 77.

123 PSA, introductory notes for register of canal records.

124 Mills, *Inland Navigation,* 39; reprinted *PRM,* 5000.

125 Gallatin had sought advice from Latrobe, (Carter [1976], 194/B3, E12, March 1808).

126 Breeden.

127 Griffiths, 251; Olson, 50; Alexander (1983), 157–159, figs. 17, 18; and in Bryan (1989), 52, fig. 2.18; *PRM,* 6029.

128 A similar arrangement was adopted in 1829 by W. F. Small for the entrance of the Bishop's House on North Charles Street.

129 MHSW; *PRM,* 0874.

130 LC, Jefferson Papers; *PRM,* 0885–0886.

131 In October, the managers received an estimate of $30,000 for a statue of Washington from the celebrated British sculptor Richard Westmacott, via Robert Gilmor (MHSW).

132 MHSW; *PRM,* 0900.

133 MHSW

134 Dunlap, 2, 378.

Chapter 4

1 AAA; *PRM,* 0909.

2 For the program, see Waddell and Liscombe, 1ff, and Bryan (1989), 75–79.

3 Graydon, 31–33.

4 Nichols (1976); Lerski, though the account of Jay's work for the state is inaccurate.

5 SCDAH, Misc. Records 4W, 67–68.

6 A marble portrait bust by G. F. Pettrich of 1841 is at the National Museum of American Art, Washington, D.C., No. xx 33; for Poinsett, see Severens, esp. 22–23; 25–41 reviews Mills's work for the state.

7 LC, Poinsett Papers, Mss 1421, 49; *PRM,* 0903, also 0910, 0914.

8 Kohn and Glenn, and Waddell and Liscombe, 21, showing that Leckie designed the locks on the Catawba River formerly attributed to Mills. Related documents are printed in *PRM,* 0921ff., 0949A being a letter of 9 April 1822 from Leckie to Mills.

9 Poinsett Papers, 3.

10 MHSW and SCHS, 11–517–5 (*PRM,* 0912).

11 SCHS, 11–518–9, dated 5 December 1822.

12 SCL, Session Book, 1819–1847; *PRM,* 0934A.

13 SCL, 1, Oob 4281.

14 AAA; *PRM,* 0963.

15 Graydon, 26–28, marked by a small slab; the boy is not mentioned by Gallagher, who, however, states that Mills later adopted a boy who took his name and became a physician (185).

16 In "Do you know your Charleston," *Charleston Courier,* 11 March 1935, T.R.W. proposed that Mills had designed the clumsily proportioned and detailed South Carolina National Bank on Broad Street, actually completed in 1817.

17 Marsh, 94–97, rejected by W. J. Petty when revising the HABS report (1941) in 1961, but accepted in Bryan (1989), 182, dated ca. 1824.

18 G. N. Banks, "Edgewater on the Hudson River," *Antiques,* (June 1982), 1400–1410.

19 Sweet, Smith, and Boykin, 72–73; Camden Historical Society.

20 Bethesda Presbyterian Church; Liscombe (1985), 16.

21 *Statistics,* 259 no.

22 One example is HSP, Bb 63 K14; *PRM,* 6054. The design of the session houses recalls that of Santee Episcopal Church, dating from 1768.

23 *Statistics,* 591–92.

24 SCHS, 33–2–10.

25 Howe, 295.

26 The triple portico began to appear on South Carolinan churches from the mid–1830s, as at the Hopewell Methodist Church near Clinton (1835–1840).

27 Waddell and Liscombe, 2–4; Bryan (1989), 79–83, fig. 3.2. Jay's Sumter and Chester courthouses were already finished, as also his jails for Chester, Sumter, and Pendleton.

28 J. A. Hall, "That onerous task. Jury service in South Carolina during the early 1790s, *SCHM* 87 (1986), 1–13; for Jay's designs, see Waddell and Liscombe, 2–3. For Bulfinch's innovative design, see Kirker (1969), 165–67; and for contemporary courthouse design, see Whiffen.

29 The conjunction of central projection and cornice at Colleton was, perhaps, inspired by Bulfinch's reconstruction of the Boston Theater (1798).

30 In 1822, for example, he inspected work on the Colleton and Fairfield courthouses, making sketches in the bound volume containing his later draft "Manual on Rail Roads" (Tulane; *PRM,* 6076–6077).

31 Poinsett Papers; *PRM,* 0923. That same day, Mills wrote to Poinsett, "Will the unfortunate situation of your health absolutely require you to deny us the aid of your good judgement & zeal in the cause we are engaged in."

32 SCHS, 11–517–5; *PRM,* 0930–0931.

33 Tulane.

34 *Statistics,* 28.

35 Noble, 148, written on 6 July 1835; Mills would describe the vista from Table Rock, north east of Greenville as "one of the richest prospects that can be unfolded to the eye of the beholder" (*Statistics,* 38).

36 SCDAH, Reports ND–104–05; *PRM,* 0938. See also Derrick, 8. SCHS, 11–517–24 (*PRM,* 0905) is Mills's estimate of $295,515 for a canal to Charleston using the Edisto River.

37 SCHS, 11–517–5; *PRM,* 0956.

38 SCHS, 11–518–1, and Gallagher, 161; Poinsett's journal indicates that the daily operations were directed by James Anderson.

39 *Statistics,* 705.

40 This intense interest is exemplified in "Internal Improvements in South Carolina," *North American Review* 4 (July, 1821): 143–54.

41 Lane (1984), 222.

42 Quoted by M. B. Davidson, "Benjamin Henry Latrobe," in J. J. Thorndike ed.
Three Centuries of Notable American Architects, (New York, 1981), 34.

43 An echo of this scheme appeared in Mills's 1822 report as acting commissioner
recommending the continuation of the partially cut canal from Charleston Harbor
northward to the Santee River by a route later to be adopted by the Army Engineers
for the Intracoastal Waterway (Baldwin).

44 *Internal Improvement* is reprinted in *PRM,* 5001; for the Picturesque genre, see
Hayes, 43ff.

45 *Internal Improvement,* 10; 13 no.

46 *Internal Improvement.*

47 Eliza, for example, wrote from Abbeville on 27 November 1829 to Mills in Baltimore concerned about Maryland laws against bringing slaves into the state (Gallagher,
213).

48 LC, Jefferson Papers; *PRM,* 0965, reply 0967 dated 25 September.

49 SCDAH, Treasury Upper Division Ledger, 1821, 91.

50 Toqueville, *Democracy in America,* 1:61.

51 *Statistics,* 631.

52 SCHS, 11–517–34; *PRM,* 1655–1656.

53 SCHS, 11–518–1, printed by Gallagher, 170. *Statistics,* 632.

54 The triple arcade appears on smaller villas designed by Palladio, such as the
Villa Saraceno, the engraving of which in the *Four Books* shows thin horizontal windows in the entablature akin to the slit openings Mills used on this jail type. Sumter
Jail, completed in 1826 but probably to Jay's plan, measured 64 feet by 34 feet with a
rear addition 30 feet by 14 feet.

55 Waddell and Liscombe, 47; Bryan (1989), 84, fig. 3.6.

56 *Internal Improvement,* 36.

57 Waddell and Liscombe, 37.

58 Fortier, 2:300–302, not listed in Bryan (1989).

59 *Rise and Progress,* 2:379; NA, RG 56f; *PRM,* 1529.

60 UV; for the Penitentiary, see Baigell. The other major American system was pioneered at Auburn, New York (1816–1825), where the prisoners slept in separate
cells but worked, ate, and worshiped together in segregated silence.

61 *Rise and Progress,* 2:378–79, outlines Mills's contribution to the state program of
internal improvements.

62 *Statistics,* 772.

63 Guinness and Sadler, 156–59.

64 SCHS, 33–22–1 (*PRM,* 60601), reproduced Liscombe (1985), pl. 84, and Bryan
(1989), pl. 1 and fig. 3.9, plan fig. 3.10, 88–90; for the commission see Waddell
(1979), revising Pierson, 1:386–94.

65 *Statistics,* 168, for the Charleston revenues; Mills's letter is SCHS; *PRM,* 0945.
Mills was paid an additional $500 in January 1823 and $100 on 8 February 1825.

66 Waddell and Liscombe, 41.

67 *Statistics,* 410.

68 For example, William Chambers's Duntish Court, Dorset (1760–1762), illustrated in the second volume of *New Vitruvius Britannicus* (1808), plate 60, having a
raised portico and curving side steps. Mills may well have seen a copy of this book,
plate 60 of which showed the portico that William Wilkins added to Osberton House,

Nottinghamshire (1805), aligning its cornice to that of the house as on the Fireproof Building (Liscombe [1980], 56–57, pl. 20).

69 Writing from Charleston on 21 February 1825 Ithiel Town failed to mention the Fireproof Building, instead remarking the "uncommonly handsome dwelling houses built in a very neat style of Architecture" amid "the appearance of decline of its property" (NHCHS, Town Papers, Mss 105, box 1, folder F).

70 SCDAH, Treasury Upper Division Ledger, 1825–1829; Bryan (1989), 85, noting the revised estimate of $46,500 and final cost of some $91,000.

71 The ceremony was reported in the *Charleston Courier,* 3 August 1822; *PRM,* 0964B.

72 SCHS, 33–22–2; *PRM,* 6066.

73 *Statistics,* 704–5.

74 Bryan and Johnson; Babcock; see also Pevsner (1976), 159–68.

75 Kirker, 307–10.

76 SCDAH, MB–17, folder 10 (*PRM,* 6066), reproduced HABS Survey of South Carolina and Bryan (1989), pls. 7–10, figs. 3.4–3.7. Gray was appointed on 2 March 1827 to complete Mills's design for $9,270 (*Acts and Resolutions of the General Assembly of the State of South Carolina* [1826], 174).

77 *Statistics,* 702–3; for the academy, see Graydon, 104–6.

78 SCDAH, Petition, 1833.

79 Advertisement, SCL, 1 & 0 8612; for Augustine Smith, see Cartmell, 296.

80 Testimony to their enlightened ideas, President James Buchanan was to eulogize their daughter Jacqueline (Gallagher, 188).

81 Waddell and Liscombe; the portico is akin to designs in Chambers's *Treatise on the Decorative part of Civil Architecture* (1792).

82 SCHS, 33–22–5; frontispiece Waddell and Liscombe; Bryan (1989), pl. 22; *PRM,* 6055. For the commission, see Waddell and Liscombe, 7–8, 51–52.

83 *Statistics,* 591.

84 Kimball, 80–81, 192–95, figs. 214–15.

85 Downs, 36, fig. 50b. Niven may have met Mills, having as a young man worked for the New York stonecutting firm of Dick and Waterson in South Carolina; their aquaintance could have been renewed in 1829, when Mills apparently visited Niven's hometown of Newburgh regarding a survey for a railroad into the Pennsylvania coalfield.

86 The courthouse in Camden was closer to the American Greek Revival type, as represented by Strickland's Crawford County Courthouse, Meadville, Pennsylvania (1824–1848) (Gilchrist, 67, pl. 14B).

87 Waddell and Liscombe, 7–8, 33.

88 Incidentally, Hall had apraised the value of land in Columbia that was needed for the canal that Mills oversaw (SCDAH, Superintendent of Public Works Record Book A, 57, 6 August 1822).

89 Graydon, 227; Massey.

90 SCHS, 33–22–4, fig. 2.17; in Bryan (1989), 51–52, described as Mills's design for the first Ainsley Hall House (1817–1818); *PRM,* 6067.

91 SCL, P4505, printed by Massey; *PRM,* 0974A–D, 0980A, 0982B.

92 Hamlin (1955), fig. 25; Waddell (1979 n. 18; Latrobe had also used a similar plan for Senator J. Pope's house in Lexington, Kentucky (1811). An ultimate inspiration were the apsidal rooms Palladio illustrated among the plates of the so-called Temple of the Sun and Moon in book 4.

93 A similar arrangement appears on Sir John Soane's stable at the Royal Hospital Chelsea, London (1813).

94 SCHS, 11–517–9.

95 *Acts and Resolutions* (1822), 95–100.

96 SCDAH, Reports, 1822–109–11F.

97 Waddell and Liscombe, 4, 6, 33–37.

98 *Acts and Resolutions* (1822), 102; N. M. Davis, "Public Powder Magazines at Charleston," in *Year Book of the City of Charleston* (1942), 208; Bryan (1989), 90–91, fig. 3.11; *PRM*, 6060. SCDAH, Records of the State Treasurer, includes agreements dated 1 October 1826 with Thomas Walker for the stonework and 12 December 1827 with J. G. Spidle, J. Horlbeck, and W. Knox for checking the completed work; SCDAH, ND–486–05 is a contract with Johnson dated 1 January 1826 for the metal work in the magazines "now building."

99 *Statistics*, 421–22; a further $2,000 was voted in 1827.

100 Latrobe had also planned a domical vaulted powder magazine for Gosport, Virginia, in July 1809, although octagonal in plan like the brick magazine at Williamsburg (1676).

101 Waddell and Liscombe, 2, no. 33; see also 64 for changes in public policy; Severens, 52, quotes the *Courier* for 27 February 1824 predicting that the "ungrateful treatment towards Mr. Mills" would "injure the tasteful character of our public buildings."

102 *Southern Review* 2 (1828) 470; the article (470–91) states that in 1827 nearly $4.5 million was slated for expenditure north of the Potomac River compared with a mere $77,000 in the South.

103 NA, RG 56f.

104 AAA; the year is omitted from the date on the letter; *PRM*, 0978.

105 SCHS, 11–517–9; she began the letter on 23 January.

106 MHSW; *PRM*, 1002A.

107 Liscombe (1985), 16–18.

108 George Washington Parke Curtis, step-grandson of the first president, rhymed: "And St. Patrick's brave boys Know how to handle those toys Shovel and spade in making railroad or canal" (quoted R. Kennedy [1985] 164).

109 Toker.

110 *Statistics*, 706.

111 Hegarty; *PRM*, 6069.

112 *Statistics*, 164–67 n. For the project, see SCDAH, 1823–8–01; Glenn and Salley, 5; and Meriwether and Wilson, 9:341–42, 571–72.

113 SCHS, 11–517–6; *PRM*, 1012.

114 Cosentino, esp. 38, 57–59, 75–76.

115 Noted in his letter to Eliza from Philadelphia on 11 October 1824 (quoted Gallagher, 32–34); see also *PRM*, 1014A, for subsequent official correspondence.

116 SCHS, 11–517–6; *PRM*, 1011.

117 *Statistics*, 707 and 433 n.

118 Waddell (1980); Bryan (1989), 92–93.

119 Tulane (formerly FI. 621.166 M626, 1813); Bryan (1989) 98, figs. 3.15, 3.16; *PRM*, 4003. On 4 August 1827 Mills wrote to Eliza of experimenting with a model steam engine invented by someone from the "Western Country" (SCHS, 11–517–6; *PRM*, 1081).

120 SCDAH, ND–1269–01.

121 LC, Jefferson Papers, and VHS, MS 2/J1323/a/2 (holograph), *PRM*, 1036; and LC, Jackson Papers; *PRM*, 1080.

122 *Statistics*, 207.

123 *Acts and Resolutions* (1826), 62.

124 On 30 November 1827, he petitioned the South Carolina House of Representatives to discharge his debt of $1,500 to the engraver (his 1828–1830 journal lists Tan-

ner's fee as $3,500 [Tulane, 47v; H. Cohen (1951), 135]). On 8 March 1843, he informed Poinsett that he still owed $300 to Tanner (HSP, Poinsett Papers, vol. 16, folder 15); on 18 August 1852, he warned Governor John L. Manning that he would have to sell the copper plates unless a new edition were printed, for which he predicted $4,300 profit (SCHS, 11–517–11).

125 C. A. Newton, esp. 151, 156; Bryan (1989), 93.

126 *Statistics*, 706–8.

127 *Statistics*, 208.

128 *Statistics*, 163–64.

129 *Statistics*, 400; one of the leading nullifiers, George McDuffie, did not subscribe.

130 *Statistics*, 114.

131 Kennedy (1985), 7, 164.

132 *Statistics*, 197–202, esp. 200.

133 *Statistics*, 339.

134 *Statistics*, 441.

135 Waddell and Liscombe, 8–9, 38; for the jails, 36, 37–38.

136 Carrott; Clayton, esp. 14ff.

137 *Statistics*, 592; incidentally, in about 1819 Bulfinch had installed two Franklin stoves in the (old) Senate, surmounted by small obelisks. See also Bryan (1989), 100, 155.

138 Kirkland and Kennedy, 2:73–74.

139 Quoted Wheildon, 89–90 (*PRM*, 1015A); in it, Mills cited "Kercher" as his source, meaning the seventeenth-century publications of Anastasius Kircher; Bryan (1989), 100, 154–155.

140 Gallagher, 101–2; his letter to the association is 204–7.

141 LC; *PRM*, 6099.

142 Formerly on loan to MHS, illustrated Gallagher, opp. 104.

143 Bryan (1976), 63–71, and (1989), 100, fig. 3.18; *PRM*, 6068.

144 *Statistics*, 701.

145 MHSW, (*PRM*, 1035); noted by Scott in Bryan (1989), 157, that to Kosciuszko being for West Point but awarded to J. H. Latrobe.

146 Severens, 40–41.

147 SCDAH, Md–220–01; SCHS 11–517–24.

148 *Statistics*, 395 n; Glenn and Salley, 16–17.

149 SCDAH, 1825–24–03; see also Bond, and Waddell and Liscombe, n. 41. Severens, 61–63, attributes it entirely to Gadsden.

150 *Statistics*, 421 n.

151 SCDAH, Ledger Upper Division State Treasury, 1825–1829, 249.

152 Glenn and Salley, 10–11. The letter to Gilmor is MHSW; *PRM*, 1042.

153 Respectively dated 5 May 1827 and 31 March 1827; Glenn and Salley, 9–10 and NA, War Dept. Misc. Letters, vol. 3, 384–85 (*PRM*, 1065–1066, 1068).

154 Glenn and Salley, 6–8; *PRM*, 1044–1047.

155 MSHW, the account book lists payments to Mills on 18 May ($50), 7 July ($168.50; including a fee for two plans of Washington [Monument] Place) and 15 September ($100). Presumably these were mainly for "superintendence," the term written alongside the single entry regarding Mills in 1828, on 30 November ($200).

156 HL, HM 823, draft (*PRM*, 1058B); Bryan (1989), 93–94, figs. 3.12, 3.13 (Palmer print), 3.14, a more sophisticated scheme for a steam elevated railroad Mills contributed to *Scientific American*, 6 August 1853 (*PRM*, 3061).

157 HL For McLean, see *BDAC*, 1388; this is the source for biographical information on all U. S. congressmen.

158 Proposed by White, "Railroads: Wood to Burn," in Hindle, *Material Culture*, 188–89.

159 *American Farmer,* 9 (20 July 1827): 141–42; the "Plan" is reproduced *PRM,* 1058A.

160 SCHS, 11–517–6; *PRM,* 1081.

161 *Rise and Progress,* 2:380.

162 AAA, originally enclosing a $2 bill; *PRM,* 1084.

163 SCHS, 11–517–6; *PRM,* 1086. In it, he regretted to "learn how the Committee of the Church [First Presbyterian Church at Columbia?] has served you," not least since "they might have considered the professional services I have rendered in the building of the Parsonage house."

164 Tulane; *PRM,* 4004.

165 Glenn and Salley, 11–13; *PRM,* 1089.

166 SCHS, 11–517–9; *PRM,* 1113. In his 1828–1830 journal, on 3 January 1829 (Tulane; *PRM,* 4005), he noted that he had written to Carey and Lea about his "work on Railways."

167 Gilchrist, 5–7.

168 Derrick, 12n; D. A. Grinde, "Building the South Carolina Railroad," *SCHM* 77 (1976): 2, 84–96.

169 Mills, *Substitute for Railroads and Canals* (1834), 7n. *PRM,* 5004.

170 NA, RG 56f; *PRM,* 1529. The 1828 *Report of the Directors of the Maryland Penitentiary,* 9, reads, "Confiding in the known talents of the architect, Mr. Wm. F. Small, the general arrangement of the building has been submitted to his direction, and the Committee are satisfied that he has rendered entire justice, both in the plan and in his attentions to the labor of the workmen at a cost of $36,806.42."

171 SCHS, 33–22–1/6; *PRM,* 6067, the other drawings, each previously cited, are 6027, 6055, 6066, 6061, 6050.

172 Writing from Savannah on 10 May 1830, Eliza recalled that the family had resided at Abbeville "for the last two years" (SCHS, 11–517–7; *PRM,* 1162). For the judicial commissions, see Waddell and Liscombe, 9, 31, 12, 35.

173 Waddell and Liscombe, 15; E. B. White added the portico in 1850 (Severens, 54–55). The debt is noted in his journal (Tulane); *PRM,* 4005; H. Cohen (1952), 91–92.

174 Waddell and Liscombe, fig. 47B.

175 Tulane; H. Cohen (1951), 133.

176 Tulane; Cohen (1951), 139.

177 Waddell (1979); Severens, 91–94.

178 Tulane; H. Cohen (1951), 218.

179 Tulane, 45v.

180 Hermann; John Wood, in *The Origin of Building* (1741), had argued a divine and biblical origin for architecture (E. Harris, "John Wood's system of architecture," *Burl. Mag.,* 131 [1989]: 101–7).

181 SCHS, 11–517–7; *PRM,* 1147. For the effects of the recession, see T. W. Rogers.

182 Another proposal was for a rail line between Fredericktown and Newcastle (for which he offered his 1805 surveys to General William McDonald on 21 December); writing to Lynde Catlin of Newburgh on 19 February, Mills described a system linking the town with a terminus between Utica and Albany on the Mowhawk in New York State. H. Cohen (1952), 96 n. 41 states, "Mills subsequently made surveys for this railroad." See also Gallagher, 138.

183 Tulane; H. Cohen (1952), 90, 93–94; Liscombe (1985), 18.

184 Tulane; H. Cohen (1952), 95; Liscombe (1985), 18.

185 Kirker, 317, illustrating Alexander Parris's 1823 elevation of the hospital.

186 Tulane, sketches 30, 31. Somewhat similar is a series of sketches on each side of an undated sheet of writing paper depicting a two-story house in which the only pedi-

ments of the four and six columns in antis front and rear porticoes rise over continuous cornices (SCHS 33–22–8; *PRM*, 6090). An alternative plan, having one eight- and
one four-column portico, partially simulates a Palladian proportioned layout and bears
some relationship to The Launch built about 1830 for the Chisholm family (Stoney
[1964]).

187 See n.16; *PRM*, 7001, reproduces his 14 January 1830 proposal for altering the
Hall of Representatives.

188 SCHS, 11–517–7; *PRM*, 1148.

189 AAA; *PRM*, 1151.

190 Waddell and Liscombe, 13–15; for American courthouses, see Paré.

191 SCHS, 11–517–6; *PRM*, 1086.

Chapter 5

1 The addresses at which the Mills family lived from 1830 to 1855 are listed by
Clark, although not all have been verified. *PRM*, 1165 reproduces a bill of sale of fur-
niture Mills entered with the Washington, D.C. Recorder of Deeds on 3 July 1830 toward two promissory notes.

2 First Session Record, First Presbyterian Church, I.

3 On 24 November 1832 the Ordinances of Nullification were to be voted at a
convention in Columbia, causing Jackson to enact the force bill, and in December to
reinforce Forts Moultrie and Sumter. In March 1833 Calhoun returned to Charleston
to join Poinsett in combatting the secession of South Carolina from the Union.

4 LC, Misc. Mss; Senator Hayne's letter is addressed to Judge Daniel Johnson.

5 *Statistics*, 356.

6 Toqueville, *Democracy in America*, 1:203; Dickens was even more acerbic about
Congress in *American Notes*, 118–122.

7 House Report no. 495 (22nd Cong., 1st sess.) 30 June 1832. For the House, see
Frary; Lowry (1976), 2, chap. 1; Brown, 72, 298, states that Mills submitted a memorial to Congress on 26 April 1815 concerning the heating (citing Gallagher, 57). The
poor acoustics had been criticized by S. A. Elliot in *The Washington Guide* (1826), and
attributed to the "prostyle" on the south side of the House.

8 SCHS, 11–517–7; *PRM*, 1147.

9 Mills's 1830 journal contains a sketch of a new semicircular desk (Tulane, 30;
PRM, 4005).

10 *PRM*, 1214, letter of appointment from E. Haywood, commencing March 1831.

11 MHS, Mitchell Papers, Mss 1948, box 4; *PRM*, 1154. See also Harvey, 16–20.

12 "Architecture in Virginia," SCHS, 33–22–10; *PRM*, 2706.

13 NA, RG 200, NN–369–64; *PRM*, 1293.

14 SCHS, 11–517–30, the draft is dated 9 February 1832 and addressed to L.
Maguire; *PRM*, 1296A.

15 SCHS, 11–517–30; *PRM*, 1292.

16 Estimated at approximately $40,000, reprinted in House Report 344 (21st
Cong., 1st sess.), 5 April 1830. Mills corresponded with Verplanck on these projects
on 15 March 1830 (Verplanck Papers, NYHS, box 18, 81; *PRM*, 1153), and further associated correspondence is reproduced 1154 ff. For the history of the Capitol water
supply, see Nicolay, 166.

17 Information kindly supplied by Florian Thayne, formerly head of the Art and
Reference Section, OAC.

18 MHSW.

19 MHSW.; he was still owed $150.

20 NA, RG 233, HR 21A–D4.5 (*PRM*, 1159); Bryan (1989), 162, fig. 5.16.

21 M. W. Fazio, "Benjamin Latrobe's Designs for a Lighthouse at the Mouth of the Mississippi River," *JSAH*, 48 (1989):3, 232–47.

22 MHSW; *PRM*, 1163.

23 MHSW (*PRM*, 1161); OAC.

24 Prucha, 237–42.

25 MHSW; *PRM*, 1166.

26 SCHS, 11–517–28; LC; *PRM*, 1168, 1183–1184.

27 NA, RG 200, NN–396–46; *PRM*, 1212.

28 MHSW; *PRM*, 1191. For Peck and the trial,see *DAB*, 13:379; Haynes, 2:878.

29 NA, RG 217, no. 136316, signed by James Iredell.

30 Rathbun; the *Washington Gazette*, 23 June 1824, noted that the institute met in the Capitol.

31 Record of Proceedings of the Columbian Institute, vol. 1 (1816–1838) 321, LC, Mss 358 (*PRM*, 1182ff.); membership notice, SCHS, 11–518–4, and for a contemporary biography of Elliot, *Washington Directory and Governmental Register*, 1843–1846.

32 Record of Proceedings, 345; Mills's estimate for the brick pilastered greenhouse, having a main building 663 feet long covered by a shingled roof and two shed-roofed wings 440 feet deep, is LC; the property developer Thomas Law presented plans and estimates of a building for the institute to Congress via Judge Cranch in 1830.

33 Eliza advertised her Washington Female Academy in the *National Intelligencer* in the spring of 1832 (*PRM*, 1300A). SCHS, 11–518–8, is Anna's mark sheet dated 26 October 1832. For contemporary schools, see *City of Washington*, 138–39.

34 NA, RG 200, NN–369–46; *PRM*, 1202.

35 *United States Statutes*, 4:462; the proposals are SCHS, 11–517–29, dating from April to November 1831; *PRM*, 1997ff, 6006. See also NA, RG 45, vol. 1829–1831, 384–85.

36 Allen, 1905.

37 NA, RG 200, and contracts SCHS, 11–517–28; *PRM*, 1212.

38 AP, Thomas U. Walter Papers; *PRM*, 6096.

39 LC; *PRM*, 1211.

40 NA, RG 56, and Alder, 33–37 and appendix 83–86; Severens, 68–70, citing criticism in the *Mercury*, 1 September 1831.

41 NA, RG 217, no. 59702; *PRM*, 1240.

42 NA, RG 56f; *PRM*, 1423.

43 LC, Peter Force Papers, Mss Div., Series III–c.

44 NA, RG 351 (LC, Maps); *PRM*, 6013.

45 NA, RG 351; see also *PRM*, 1260B, for the company's minutes.

46 NA, RG 77 Cons. 57–1, 3 (*PRM*, 6078), the former is reproduced in "Unbuilt Bridges of Washington D.C.," *RCHS*, (1973–1974). On 3 November 1823, W. Trumbull wrote to Ithiel Town for an estimate of a "superstructure" wood and iron aqueduct (NHCHS, Town Papers, Mss 105, folder C).

47 GUL, reproduced in Bryan (1989), pls. 13–15, erroneously dated 1852; *PRM*, 6008.

48 House Report 291 (22nd Cong., 1st sess.) 1832, printing Mills's letter dated 13 February 1832; NA, RG includes "1st Estimate of Mr. Dumeste" amounting to $32,298 and a sixth at $43,710. On 11 October 1833, Mills sent plans for supplying water to the President's House and public offices to the commissioner of public buildings via Dickins (NA, RG 42, Letters, no. 2814).

49 Mills's ideas for the entrance and Speaker's chair appear to have been sketched on the back of a note concerning the cost of the alterations (NA, RG 200, NN–369–46; *PRM*, 2485 [placed with material dated 1846]).

50 MMNY, Davis Collection, 24.66; *PRM*, 1308.

51 NA, RG 217, 62791 (*PRM*, 1314A); on 24 May, Mills wrote to Gilmor of having "just finished my work on the lighthouses of the United States" (MHSW; *PRM*, 1304 [see also 1192]).

52 Reports from various lighthouse keepers remain in Mills's papers (LC, box 1); *Guide* is *PRM*, 5009.

53 NA, RG 49, Missisippi, vol. 29, 1822–1833.

54 MHSW; *PRM*, 1324.

55 BCA, RG 16, S1, box 6, no. 740.

56 NA, RG 56f; *PRM*, 1529.

57 Harvey, 21–26, based on the society's records (NA, RG 42); Freeman; Scott in Bryan (1989), 158.

58 MHSW; *PRM*, 1509 (included with material from 1836).

59 In 1800 the British architect George Dance designed a pyramidal monument to Washington at the request of Benjamin West, and the form was proposed by Force in the 1837 competition (Craig, 59; Freeman, fig. 1).

60 Jordy, 282–86.

61 Mills's fee is noted in *Receipts and Expenditures of the U.S.* (1834), 38, and was paid on 2 July (Treasury Warrant 65356 [*PRM*, 1417]); see also Lowry (1976).

62 On 4 May, Mills received instructions from Clark, at Milledgeville, to contract with "Plantt" for the new desks and "Hill" for the alteration of old ones (designed in 1819) "according to your directions"; an eagle and twenty-four stars were to be woven into the new carpet (LC; *PRM*, 1339).

63 Corcoran Gallery, discussed by Staiti and Reynolds, 41–42, fig. 40; Morse had been supported by Poinsett.

64 MHSW; *PRM*, 1399.

65 Remini, 3:55.

66 NA, RG 56f; Mills's plans of the old Treasury are NA, RG 121, illustrated in Lowry (1976), vol. 1, chap. 3, and *PRM*, 6010.

67 NA, RG 56f; *PRM*, 1366.

68 SCHS, 11–517–28 (*PRM*, 1514A); and *A History of Public Buildings*, 94–95.

69 *Rise and Progress*, 2:381.

70 NA, RG 56; NA RG 217, 63165, 63258, 63352, 63478, paid through the summer of 1833; *PRM*, 1343–1346, 1351, 1361. *PRM*, 1341 is Mills's payment of $150 dated 1 June 1833 for checking the estimate of Town and Davis for their design for the New York customhouse design; Mills, writing to Secretary Taney on 31 May 1834 (*PRM*, 1411), claimed to have redesigned the interior, since the drawings by Town and Davis had been destroyed in the Treasury fire of 1833.

71 NA, RG5 6f; *PRM*, 1370.

72 NA, RG 56, 5 and 30 July 1833.

73 NA, RG5 6, Series K; *PRM*, 1356; 1363/5 Duane's instructions to Mills.

74 Cited in *Congressional Globe* (1838), appendix, 419; on 7 May 1834, Mills would write to James K. Polk in his capacity as a member of the House Ways and Means Committee about the appropriation for the Appraisers' Stores (Weaver and Bergeron, 406).

75 NA, RG 56.

76 Gallagher, 185, incorrectly suggesting that Edward was related to a Senator Pendleton; the Pendleton family is examined in *Genealogies of Virginia Families*, vol. 4. For the gift of property, see Clark, 28, and for the Pendleton's married life, see Nicolay, 284–85.

77 *Substitute for Railroads*, 12 (*PRM*, 1446, 1453); the article was commended by the *New Bedford Mercury* but criticized in the *Baltimore Sun*, 6 October 1834.

78 NA, RG 42, Letters, vol. 8, 30–31, 33–34; *PRM,* 1402–1404. See also Evelyn in Bryan (1989), 110ff.

79 For the Town, Davis, and Elliot designs, see Hall (1956), 27–30; Davies (1965), 229–51, and (1967), 71–73; and Lowry (1976).

80 NA, RG 42, Letters, no. 2825; *PRM,* 1407A.

81 NA, RG 42, vol. 8, no. 34; *PRM,* 1408.

82 *Scientific American,* 22 January 1851.

83 Other examples were Dr. J. McHenry, *The Jackson Wreath or National Souvenir* (1829), and J. Elliot, *Historical Sketches of the Ten Mile Square with a Picture of Washington* (1830); in the 1840s W. M. Morrison, G. Watterston, and W. Q. Force published guides, the last also containing a directory of government offices.

84 *Guide to the Capitol,* (*PRM,* 5005 [the later editions are 5007, 5010, 5012]), respectively 46, 8, 9, 13, 58.

85 *Guide,* 30, 45.

86 NA, RG 42, no. 2825; *PRM,* 1425.

87 Goode (1979), 303, incorrectly dated 1836.

88 Reprinted from the *Washington Mirror.*

89 House Document 35 (23rd Cong., 1st. sess.), Noland's report dated 23 December 1834.

90 OAC, Capitol File, Treasury warrant no. 13, 66980; *PRM,* 1475.

91 NA, RG 56f; *PRM,* 1435.

92 SCHS, 11–517–7; *PRM,* 1442.

93 *Receipts and Expenditures of the United States* (1838), 38–39; Mills's letter is NA, RG 56f. See also *A History of Public Buildings,* 60–61 (Middletown), 64–65 (New London), 283–84 (Newburyport), and 280–81 (New Bedford).

94 House Committee on Public Buildings, Report 737, 29 March 1838. Clark, 20–21.

95 Woodbury to Mills, 24 July 1834, NA, RG 56f.

96 SCL, P6003; *PRM,* 1433.

97 SCHS, 11–517–31; *PRM,* 1345, 1357, another version for Newburyport. A similar specification dated 28 August 1834 for New London, of four pages with eight drawings, belongs to the local Maritime Society; *PRM,* 6002.

98 SCHS, 11–517–31; *PRM,* 1459 (incorrectly placed with 1834 correspondence).

99 *A History of Public Buildings,* 254–55; HABS Survey (1933–1936) Md–3; Jones, 34.

100 NA, RG 121.

101 SCHS, 11–517–32; *PRM,* 1178. See also *A History of Public Buildings,* 11.

102 Replaced 1854–1856 by Ammi B. Young, one of forty-six that were completed using nine design types (1853–1856), Lowry (1985), 52–53.

103 House Report 90 (23d Cong., 2d sess.), Lowry (1976), vol. 1, chap. 3.

104 MEHS; *PRM,* 6010.

105 Addressed to M. S. Legaré (SCL, 3335; *PRM,* 1713). Mills, in his letter to the *Washington Sentinel,* 22 March 1854, claimed that he had submitted the scheme to President Jackson shortly after the fire in the Old Treasury. For his part, Elliot had written to Noland on 15 January 1836 that the "principal feature" of his plan for the public offices was the "preservation of the present buildings that are very substantial and well built [those by Hadfield and Hoban]" (NA, RG 42, Letters, 2860).

106 LC; *PRM,* 6092.

107 Gallagher, 23. The *Intelligencer* articles are *PRM,* 1478–1480.

108 NA, RG 56f; *PRM,* 1483.

109 Glenn and Salley, 16; notebook, LC, 40, 47–50 (*PRM,* 4006). See also *PRM,* 1678, Mills to W. C. Johnson regarding a National Foundry (GUL).

110 NA, RG 42, 2935, letter to Noland 10 January 1839.

111 LC, 102–3.

112 Schlesinger, 39; Gallagher.

113 Hall (1956), 30 n. 15; *PRM,* 1531.

114 Barsett, 5:295.

115 LHS, D846.

116 LC, Jackson Papers; *PRM,* 1546.

117 Gallagher, 185.

118 Sarah's son Richard J. Evans wrote on 2 December 1876 to the government architect Edward Clark seeking employment, "I studied architecture under my grandfather *Robert Mills,* (OAC).

119 *Washington Directory,* 1858, gives the Dimitry address as 409 H St., NW and indicates that their son John was a clerk in the attorney general's office. In 1859 Dimitry was appointed minister to Costa Rica and Nicaragua, resigning upon the secession of the southern states to become assistant postmaster of the Confederacy throughout the Civil War. After the war he returned to the outskirts of New York City, collecting some 15,000 books before his death in 1887, about four years before that of Mary.

120 Lane (1985), 167 (*PRM,* 1513); Mills recommended that Paton use zinc.

121 HSP, Poinsett Papers, vol. 7, folder 17, 167 (*PRM,* 1517); Mills also referring to the proposed construction of a railroad from Charleston to Cincinnato; and Glenn and Salley, 16–17; *PRM,* 1518.

122 Tulane; *PRM,* 1496.

123 LC.

124 NA, RG 56f; *PRM,* 1529. Incidentally, among prior attempts to interest Jackson in his favor, Mills had on 5 June 1832 sent the president a paper entitled "Paving the Pennsylvania Avenue" (NA, RG 233, Records of the House of Representatives, HR 28A–15.3; *PRM,* 1310).

125 NA, RG 42, 2874; *PRM,* 1533.

126 The history of the office is outlined in a letter Noland sent to President Jackson on 26 October 1836 (NA, RG 42, Letters, vol. 8, 228–29). It had been created in 1817 by President Madison to undertake those duties formerly performed by the superintendent for the City of Washington between 1802 and 1815 and the three commissioners appointed in 1791.

127 SCHS, 33–22–10; quoted Gallagher, 156.

128 On 2 October 1837, rent of $37.50 was paid to J. R. Hagner (NA, RG 56).

129 NA, RG 42, Letters, 2897.

130 Notebook, LC, 44 (*PRM,* 4006); the books Mills recommended cannot now be traced, since the collection passed with that of the War Department into the Library of Congress before 1944, by which time the original inscriptions had been expunged due to rebinding.

131 MHSW, (*PRM,* 1605); for Pettrich (1798–1872), who had studied under the celebrated Danish Neoclassical artist Bertel Thorwaldsen and been patronized by Pope Pius X before moving to Washington in 1836, see R. L. Stehle, "Ferdinand Pettrich in America," *Pennsylvania History* 33 (1966): 389–411. OAC has a receipt $120 for "sculpturing three of the Caps of the Piers of the West Gate of the Capital," signed by Pettrich on 1 July 1837 and countersigned by Mills.

132 SCL, P371; in 1839 Mills hired Pettrich to cut capitals for the pilasters on the General Post Office and possibly secured him the commission for a bust of Poinsett donated to the National Institution in 1841 (Journal of Proceedings, Smithsonian Institution, 7058, vol. 1.1); the bust is at the Museum of American Art (the former Patent Office built under Mills's supervision) no. XX33.

133 AIA, Gr. 505–(1–10)a; R. C. Long wrote of having "no doubt of enlisting Mills & Elliot in the cause"; *PRM*, 1559, reprints an entry of 2 November 1836 by Walter in the ledger of the institution (AP), indicating that Mills had been solicited.

134 At the Fourth Annual Convention of the American Institute of Architects, the direct successor of the institution, held in November 1870 at Philadelphia, Walter in his vice-presidential address identified one of "the greatest drawbacks to the progress of architecture in this country" as the "want of intercourse between architects" (*AIA Proceedings*, 1:205ff).

135 LC, Jackson Papers; *PRM*, 1546.

136 Remini, 2:55; confirmed in Robert Brown's testimony before Congress in 1838 (NA, RG 233, HR 25A–D20.1 [*PRM*, 1673]).

137 House Report 737 (25th Cong., 2d sess.) 29 March 1838; Lowry (1976), vol. 1, chap. 3.

138 Baird, 2:193–94.

139 *Appropriations and Expenditures in D.C.*, 65; House Document 28 (25th Cong., 2d sess.), 15 December 1837.

140 *Guide*, 65; writing to the Commission on Public Buildings in the spring of 1851, Mills stated that in 1836 he had "had to make new drawings" for the building (NA, RG 42, nos. 3154 to Mudd, and 3183 to Easby).

141 The author of the 22 January and 1 February 1851 articles was probably William Elliot, Jr., since the 1 February article criticized Mills for taking the "liberty to deviate from the plan" in both 1836 and 1849 when supervising the erection of the east wing; for this dispute and the commission, see Evelyn in Bryan (1989), 115–17, 130–32, figs. 4.4, 4.6, 4.13.

142 NA, RG 42, Letters, vol. 9, 293–95; other Patent Office records are NA, RG 48.

143 Notebook, 10–11, 12–13, inscribed "House H. Dening Pittsburg." An earlier inscription reads, "Mon. Recd. for design for Hon. Mr. Denny of Pittsburg $100." Denny owned a large property, Deer Creek, fronting the Allegheny River (A. C. Miller [1927]; Toker, 14); in correspondence, Toker has suggested that Mills might have contributed to the design of Homewood, the house of Judge William Wilkins, for which (without mention of Mills) see Stotz.

144 Notebook, 100, 106–9, 112–13; Mills's submitted plan is at the SCL; *PRM*, 6071. See also Bryan (1976), 87–95, figs. 39–42.

145 Modeled after Bulfinch's Old Congressional Library in the Capitol, perhaps at McDuffie's behest; for the Old Library of Congress (Newton, 1941).

146 Hall (1947).

147 NA, RG 42 for the official records; the Notebook (LC; *PRM*, 4006) measuring approximately 3.5 inches by 6 inches; on 88–89 lists the wages paid to bricklayers, stonecutters, and laborers in Baltimore and Philadelphia: respectively $2 or $1.50, $1.75 or $1.50, and $1.12 or $1.12½.

148 In a letter to Lincoln dated 22 February 1837 (LC; *PRM*, 1586), and to Noland, 1 April 1837 (NA, RG 42, Letters, no. 2897; *PRM*, 1597).

149 SCHS, 11–517–39, undated draft; *PRM*, 2455B.

150 *Appropriations and Expenditures* (1837), 8.

151 *Appropriations and Expenditures* (1837), costing $6,318.75; also *PRM*, 1580.

152 NA, RG 42, no. 2897 (*PRM*, 1576), jottings for this partly realized scheme appear in his notebook, 77, 81–84, while 71 shows a sketch for a small building housing a water spout behind its arched front intended for a location on the Capitol grounds. About this time, he made estimates for a railing around Lafayette Square ranging between some $11,000 and $19,000.

153 Notebook, 79; House Document 28 (25th Cong., 2d sess.), the screen was ornamented with Greek motifs; Harvey, 25–26, based on NA, RG 42; *PRM*, 1610.

154 UV; *PRM,* 1609.

155 Notebook, LC, 18–19 (*PRM,* 4006), shows a design for the tripod based, at Poinsett's suggestion, on published illustrations of antiquities from Herculaneum; he also made models for the trophies with Pettrich using John James Audubon's book on American birds, abandoned because the four bronze castings were estimated at $20,000.

156 Notebook, 30; Scott in Bryan (1989), 158, proposes that Mills also considered a 100-foot robed statue of Washington atop a 100-foot cubical base for catacombs and a three-tier design topped by a version of the Choragic Monument of Lysicrates, here associated with Mills's proposed Jefferson Monument (ca. 1854).

157 Bryan (1989), 157, 176, nn. 43, 44; for further discussion of the impact of Freemasonry on architecture, see Ryckwert.

158 Notebook, 21, 22; Liscombe (1985), 18–20. Unconnected with another sketch (26), showing a rectangular building with a portico of four widely spaced columns carrying a pediment decorated with sculpture and combining Neoclassical and Georgian detailing, inscribed "R. Cath Church Rn Doric covered with zinc," possibly for refurbishing the small brick St. Patrick's Roman Catholic Church in Washington (in use ca. 1810–1872 Liscombe [1985], 21).

159 Mills may have recalled L'Enfant's proposal for a National Church.

160 Pioneered by the British Cambridge Camden Society in 1839, upon which was based the New York Ecclesiological Society, founded in 1846 (Stanton, [1968]; Pierson, 2:149ff., 207ff.

161 Harvey, 28–38.

162 Rooney; Mills had applied to War Secretary Poinsett on 25 March (HSP Poinsett Papers, vol. 8, folder 5, no. 46, and NA, RG 56F).

163 Tulane; *PRM,* 1640. See also Reynolds and Christovich, 228, and Swanson, 112.

164 Notebook, LC, 40, 42.

165 NA, RG 90, Set M, 1839, no. 138; Alder, appendix 87–90, fig. 19.

166 Notebook, LC, 52, 53.

167 Notebook, LC, 114.

168 Notebook, LC, 22, 44, for an 80-foot span bridge of Jones' Falls, Baltimore (see also BCA, RG 16, S1, box 56, no. 990, 1837, and for a Palmetto log pier bridge over the River Ashley at Charleston (see also Mills to Robert M. Allan, 15 August 1837 [LC], estimated at between $46,000 and $70,000 (*PRM,* 1631).

169 Notebook, LC, respectively 44, 42, 116, 117.

170 NA, RG 90, no. 235; Mills's notebook, 43, lists prices at Louisville and New Orleans in "Feby 1838."

171 NA, RG 90, no. 56f.

172 SCHS, 11–517–33; *PRM,* 1654.

173 House Document 3 (25th Cong., 2d sess.) 22 December 1837; a set of the lithographs is NA, RG 77, drawer 162, sheet 1; *PRM,* 6093.

174 House Executive Document 131 (42d Cong., 3d sess.); see also Alder, esp. 15–23.

175 NA, RG 56, Letters, Set K, vol. 2, no. 217; Gallagher, 43, proposes that marine hospitals to Mills's designs were built in St. Louis, Natchez, Napoleon, Paducah, Cleveland, and Wheeling, refuted by reference to the original documents by Alder, 44ff.

176 The Treasury paid two local builders (Alder, 45).

177 Notebook, LC, 45.

178 Notebook, LC, 56–57.

179 Epstein, 597–98.

180 Lowry (1976), vol. 1, chap. I; *City of Washington,* 124–25 Possibly in 1837 he

sketched a plan in his notebook, 89, for merely inserting a new block between the extant War and Navy buildings aligned to their western facades.

181 Copied into Mills's notebook, 58.

182 NA, RG 42, vol. 8, 303.

183 *PRM*, 1823, is the printed constitution of the society, of which Eliza was a manager; 2453 is a petition dated 12 December 1844 to the House of Representatives; and 2710–12 draft in Mills's hand promoting the society.

184 LC; *PRM*, 1683B.

185 Walter was paid on 22 March (NA, RG 42, 174); NA, RG 233, Records of the House of Representatives, includes a letter of 1 May 1838 from Charles Bulfinch declining to judge between Mills and Walter (*PRM*, 1730).

186 NA, RG 42, Letters no. 2905/2 (*PRM*, 1692); the draft is LC, illustrated Gallagher, opp. 180.

187 House Report no. 737 (22d Cong., 2d sess.); also reviewed by Evelyn in Bryan (1989), 117–21.

188 Goode (1979), 195–96; on 8 December 1840 Archer requested the return of his "Plan . . . for the Public Executive Buildings," NA, RG 42, Letters, vol. 8.

189 SCHS, 11–517–28; *PRM*, 1711, 1712, for letter as sent, with the relevant documents continuing after 1715.

190 SCL, P. 3335; *PRM*, 1713.

191 *Congressional Globe* (1838), 274–75; the other debates quoted below are 262–63, 336–41, 410–12, 418–21.

192 *Congressional Globe* (1838), 336–41.

193 NA, RG 42, vol. 8, 151.

194 NA, RG 42, vol. 8, 154–57.

195 *Congressional Globe* (1838), 441.

196 *Congressional Globe* (1838), 419; a somewhat loose allusion since, although Hector as leader of the Trojan forces was defeated by forces in part commanded by two men with the name of Ajax, each came to grief.

197 UV 5796; *PRM*, 1737. Perhaps associated are notes for the "demonstration of the manner that the stones which comprise the vault of arch sustain each other" (SCHS, 11–517–28; *PRM*, 1736).

198 NA, RG 42, vol. 9, 9.

199 MHSW; *PRM*, 1755, 1759, letter of 29 June.

200 SCHS, 11–517–28; *PRM*, 1758.

201 These alterations, finished by 1842 for some $60,000, are illustrated in Bryan (1989), figs. 4.7–4.9.

202 *Congressional Globe* (1838), 482, only opposed by James Garland of Virginia, whose opinion was endorsed by former President John Quincy Adams (*Memoirs* [Philadelphia, 1876], 10:14), describing Mills as a "wretched bungler in architecture" (*PRM*, 1725A).

203 For these commissions, Hamlin (1955), 288, and Hitchcock and Seale, 110–113.

204 NA, RG 42, Letters, no. 2930/6 (*PRM*, 1766); Somerville, 145, illustrating the old Bank.

205 NA, RG 42, NCP–0–29/30; Waddell and Liscombe, 13, figs. 48–49; Bryan (1989), fig. 3.3.

206 NA, RG 42, Letters, vol. 8, 168, dated 25 October 1838, Noland being "decidedly in favor of the plan proposed by Mr. Mills."

207 Noted House Report, 460, 1842 (27th Cong., 2d sess.) 29 March 1842; contract, *PRM*, 1814.

208 House Document 32 (26th Cong., 1st sess.) 30 December 1839.

209 SCHS, 11–517–34 (*PRM*, 1655); Reiff, 28–30, 42–43.

210 Mills fitted two hot-air furnaces, receiving a fee of $20 on 28 February, shortly before their installation for $2,525 (HSP, S. Graz Collection, case 7, box 24); for the payment, NA, RG 217, Treasury Warrant no. 77114 (*PRM*, 1852), noted in Report Senate Committee on Public Buildings and Grounds, 30 December 1839.

211 NA, RG 42, no. 2935; *PRM*, 1829. See also Myers. House Report, 460 (27th Cong., 2nd sess.), 29 March 1842, states that John Haviland also made a design.

212 House Report, 187 (26th Cong., 1st sess.), 26 March 1840, and NA, RG 42, no. 2937, Mills's letter to Lincoln of 21 January (*PRM*, 1837).

213 House Document 129 (25th Cong., 3d sess.), 30 January 1839; *PRM*, 1845, 1830, a letter to Noland of 10 January describing the clock.

214 NA, RG 42, Commissioners Proceedings, vol. 8, 81. On 26 May 1840 Mills asked Poinsett to secure agreement that all except the large windows have angular pediments for aesthetic and economic reasons (RA, RG 28; *PRM*, 2073).

215 Owen, 52; Palladio's career was most closely associated with the city of Vicenza.

216 LC, Corwin Papers.

217 Reiff, 141–42.

218 Strickland's letter of 25 November 1839 is SCHS, 11–517–10.

219 House Report, 40 (27th Cong., 2d sess.), 13 January 1842.

220 Dickens, 122.

221 House Report, 90 (30th Cong., 2d sess.), 13 February, 1848.

222 Tuthill, 267.

223 *The Builder*, no. 9 (1851):262.

224 HSP, Bc 615 M657a; *PRM*, 6014 See also Goode (1979), 304–5; Liscombe (1985), 19.

225 House Document 40, (27th Cong., 2d sess.), 13 January 1842.

226 NA, RG 42, Contracts.

227 The purchases of real estate probably began with lot 3 in square 506 in 1839. This and other lots in squares 453 and 651 are mentioned in deeds mainly concerning the payment of debts to Messrs Middleton and Beall, Briscoe, Carbery, Clarke, and Truman, and including a trust for Eliza set up by Michael Nourse, are reproduced in *PRM*, 1943 (September, 1839); 2064 (May 1840); 2327, 2358, 2391, 2394, 2401 (1842); 2466 (March 1854); 3106, 3110 (November 1854).

228 For the history of the commission, see Boynton, 259–61, and J. A. Cohen, 84–85.

229 AL, typescript, AA 737 R5 R631.

230 NA, RG 77, drawer 32, sheet 13; *PRM*, 6041; see also 1890, 1897, 1907, 2240 for further official correspondence (NA, RG 136).

231 Another version is NA, RG 77, drawer 32, sheet 11 (*PRM*, 6041); illustrated by J. A. Cohen, no. 30, 85.

232 Glenn and Salley, 18–19, said to refer to a design for a barracks; NA, RG 94, record the date of payment as 1 August; *PRM*, 1929.

233 This "Old Observatory" is illustrated in Schaff.

234 NA RG 77, drawer 67, sheet 1.

235 Hafertepe; Rhees.

236 Senate Bill 245 (26th Cong., 2d sess.), 10 February 1841.

237 NA, RG 77, Cons. 90–1; (*PRM*, 6009); also discussed in Lowry (1976), vol. 1, chap. 4, and J. A. Cohen, 87–88, no. 32.

238 NA, RG 77 Cons. 90–4; *PRM*, 6009, including the other related design cited below.

239 NA, RG 77 Cons. 90–2; NA, RG 77 Cons. 90–3.

240 NA, RG 77 Cons. 90–5.

241 NA, RG 77 Cons. 58; *PRM*, 6009.

242 Mills's 1846 letter is SCHS, 11–517–39, reprinted Gallagher, 189–98; for the British Gothicists, see Pevsner (1972).

243 House Document 32 (26th Cong., 1st sess.), 30 December 1839, costing $1,431.

244 NA, RG 42, Letters, no. 2977; *PRM*, 2011.

245 NA, RG 42, vol. 9, 129.

246 14 April 1840 (Schlesinger, 293).

247 House Report 244 (26th Cong., 1st sess.). *Congressional Globe,* (1842), Appendix 48 prints Preston's resolution and opinion that the statue matched "the brightest names of antiquity."

248 House Document 45, (27th Cong., 1st sess.) 1841. For the episode, see Lowry (1976), 2, chap. 1; and related correspondence from NA, RG 59; *PRM*, 2018–2020, 2025, 2028.

249 House Report 244 (26th Cong., 1st sess.), 5 March 1840.

250 House Document 50 (27th Cong., 1st sess.), 4 August 1841; House Report 219 (27th Cong., 3d sess.).

251 OAC.

252 SCHS, 33–22–10; *PRM*, 3026.

253 Printed in House Document 187 (26th Cong., 1st sess.), 26 March 1840.

254 Senate Document (27th Cong., 1st sess.), 28 April 1840, prints Mills's letter of 5 April to Noland (NA, RG 46, Records of the Senate, SEN 26A–D3; *PRM*, 2050). House Report 6 (27th Cong., 1st sess.), 7 August 1841, prints Mills's report on Robert Grant's memorial on lighting with gas, also referring to experiments for obtaining gas by burning bark.

255 HSP, Poinsett Papers, Calendar; *PRM*, 2116.

256 NA, RG 56f–57; *PRM*, 2130.

257 "Journal of Proceedings," Smithsonian Institution, 7058, vol. 1, 166. Other records, including the minutes, exist in the Peter Force Collection, LC, reproduced *PRM*, 2056ff.

258 Tulane; *PRM*, 2274.

259 AAA.

260 House Document 58 (26th Cong., 2d sess.), 13 January 1841.

261 LC, correspondence between Skirving and Mills, 12 February 1841 (*PRM*, 2174, Skirving claiming $991.50 for his work) and 23 March 1841; NA, RG 42, nos. 3035, 3042, 3044 (the two latter *PRM*, 2365, 2385) concerning the House, drawings for which are in the Thomas U. Walters Papers, AP (*PRM*, 6011).

262 Bryan (1989), 121–23, fig. 4.10, a proposal for wings published in Senate Document 123, 11 September 1841, and fig. 4.11.

263 Bryan (1989), 156, fig. 5.9; Morrill, 23–24.

264 NA, RG 77, Cons. 92–2 (*PRM*, 2295); Glenn and Salley, 19–20. See also Lehman (1964), and Lowry (1976), vol. 1, chap. 6.

265 House Reports 460 and 549 respectively (27th Cong., 2d sess.), 29 March and 1 April 1842.

266 NA, RG 42, no. 3039; *PRM*, 2335, related correspondence is reproduced from 2341.

267 House Report 460 (27th Cong., 2d sess), 29 March 1842.

268 LC; *PRM*, 2349.

269 LC; NA, RG 48, entry 472; *PRM*, 6016. For the penitentiary, see Sullivan.

270 NA, RG 42, no. 3041; *PRM*, 2341.

271 *Congressional Globe* (1842), 728–29, opposed by Calhoun on the grounds that it would involve "a large expenditure, to be drawn from the national funds though its character would be purely local."

272 *City of Washington,* 125, 130.

273 LC, (*PRM*, 2359–2360); Liscombe (1985), 20–21.

274 One example is St. Louis Priory, St. Louis, Missouri, designed by Hellmuth, Obata and Kassabaum in 1962 (Kennedy, 62–63).

275 HSP, Poinsett Papers, vol. 16, folder 13, no. 130; *PRM*, 2371; Bryan (1989), fig. 4.11.

276 NA, RG 56f.

277 House Document 54 (27th Cong., 3d sess.), 12 January 1843.

278 House Report 152 (27th Cong., 2d sess.), 6 February 1843; the post of clerk in the commissioner's office was also abolished on 3 March 1843.

279 *PRM*, 2388; the project was mentioned in the letter Mills received on 11 April 1843 (LC, [*PRM*, 2419]).

280 NA, RG 42, no. 3044; *PRM*, 2385.

Chapter 6

1 By comparison, Mills's acquaintance George McDuffie had during a speech in the Senate on 25 January 1843 asked with regard to western expansion, "Who are to go there along the line of military posts, and take possession of the only part of the territory fit to occupy... I would not, for that purpose [agriculture] give a pinch of snuff for the whole territory" (quoted Bergon and Papnikolas, 111).

2 NA, RG 92, received on 21 November; *PRM*, 6089.

3 LC, Corwin Papers, vol. 2, pt. 1, no. 628 (*PRM*, 2790–2791); the method was described in S. W. Johnson, *Rural Economy* (New Brunswick, 1806).

4 LC, (*PRM*, 2299); for Belmas, see *La grande encyclopédia*, vol. 6.

5 House Document 85 (27th Cong., 3d sess.), 25 January 1843. For the history of the commission see Lehman.

6 HSP, Poinsett Papers, vol. 16, folder 15; *PRM*, 2413.

7 W. S. Solomon to Mills, 5 December 1842, requesting payment of annual fees (Tulane [*PRM*, 2405]); the association was later renamed the American Art Union.

8 NA, RG 45, Letters, 1843, no. 94; *PRM*, 2414.

9 NA, RG 56f; *PRM*, 2417, Spencer's reply is 2418. For the commission, see *A History of Public Buildings* 454–55, and Lane (1985), 174, with a review of Norris's work.

10 NA, RG 90, Set M, 1843, no. 66.

11 Executive Document 204 (28th Cong., 2d sess.).

12 House Document 51 and House Report 516 (28th Cong., 1st sess.), 8 January and 24 May 1844; *PRM*, 2439 is Mills's letter to the speaker and members of Congress dated 25 1844 outlining his proposal (NA, RG 77). See also Gilchrist, 101–2.

13 NA, RG 77, Cons. 53–3; *PRM*, 6011.

14 NA, RG 77, Cons. 53–1, no. 1, inscribed in a different hand on the verso, "*Robt. Mills* April 29 1844 referred to Commee on Pub. Buildings Winthrop," and Cons. 53–2; *PRM*, 6011. See also Lowry (1976), vol. 2, chap. 1, and Port.

15 NA, RG 45, no. 32.

16 House Document 85 (28th Cong., 1st sess.),. 1843; Lehman (1964); Gilchrist; Lowry (1976), vol. 1, chap. 1.

17 NA, RG 77, Cons. 92–1/4; *PRM*, 6012.

18 Based on the information in House Document 85 (27th Cong., 3d sess.)

19 Respectively UNC, Dromgoole Papers, no. 230, and LC; *PRM*, 2439, 2449; Mills also wrote to Navy Secretary Henshaw (NA, RG 45); *PRM*, 2433.

20 GUL; *PRM*, 2408A, 2443, the latter was sent with an additional signatory (NA, RG 59, 2444).

21 Senate Bill 334, 1844.

22 House Report 434 (28th Cong., 1st sess.), 12 April 1844.

23 House Report 514 (28th Cong., 1st sess.), 25 May 1844.

24 NA, RG 56f.

25 House Report 20 (28th Cong., 2d sess.), 31 December 1844.

26 House Report 89 (28th Cong., 2d sess.); the design is NA, RG 77, Cons., Drawer 162, sheet 9; illustrated in Lehman, 17.

27 Mills's letter, 20 January 1845 (*PRM*, 2456), is printed in Report 89 and refers to "plan No. 1" and "diagram No. 2," probably corresponding with his plans NA, RG 77, Cons. 92–3/4

28 House Report 185 (28th Cong., 2d sess.).

29 NA, RG 56f; *PRM*, 2465.

30 Published in nine volumes (1834–1867) (*DAB* 1:564–70).

31 NA, RG 45, nos. 151, 192.

32 A *History of Public Buildings*, 86–87; Topham; Reiff, 135, fig. 218.

33 Completed under the supervision of Thomas U. Walter (Tatum, "William Johnston").

34 NA, RG 59.

35 NA, RG 121, box 124 including the drawings and contract with Simontown; *PRM*, 6017, 2451. The specification is SCHS, 11–517–36, dated 1 July.

36 Alder, 91–95, 131–34, fig. 1.

37 E. S. Friedrich billed Mills in about July 1852 for a "Coat of Arms for Texas 1.00" (SCHS, 11–517–42).

38 NA, RG 217, Treasury Warrant no. 89, 93.022 (OAC); NA, RG 42, Contracts.

39 NA, RG 56f; *PRM*, 2462.

40 NA, RG 42; see also *PRM*, 2454, 2476, 2478, the minutes of the society for 20 November 1845 reiterating the decision, setting the budget at $200,000, and awarding Mills a $100 fee.

41 Evelyn in Bryan (1989), 123–24, for Mills's 1846 Patent Office extension proposal, which was, due to variation of grade estimated at $80,000, west, and $70,000, east. Mills's roadway Memorial is House Document 173 (29th Cong., 1st sess.), 18 February, 1846.

42 An accompanying map, dated December 1847, was printed by the Senate as Misc. Report 51 (30th Cong., 1st sess.), 15 February, 1848.

43 Billington, 644.

44 House Report 145 (30th Cong., 1st sess.), dated December 1847 but published in 1848.

45 Coit, 484; the bar was located behind the Senate post office near the Rotunda, measuring a mere 10 feet square and had been opened in 1830.

46 Senate Report 251 (29th Cong., 1st sess.), 25 March 1846; NA, RG 46, 29A–D3, 31A–D1, are Mills's letter of 18 March to Breese, and accompanying two plans and one section; *PRM*, 2486, 6011.

47 NA, RG 217, Treasury Warrant no. 95028 (OAC); *PRM*, 2489B.

48 VSA, Deed book 12, 1858–1874, 74; they also seem to have raised funds by selling a lot, probably in Washington, to their son-in-law Edward Pendleton, Eliza noting on the verso of a letter addressed to Mills by the architect James Renwick dated 27 December 1847 concerning the Smithsonian commission (SCHS, 11–517–29; *PRM*, 2511) that Pendleton offered to "assume [up] to $300, independent of the price of the lot, payable in $30 installments per month."

49 NA, RG 42, Ledger vol. 6, 389–90, and vol. 7, 164–69.

50 NA, RG 45, Misc. Letters 1846, no. 77; *PRM*, 2483A.

51 VHS, Tayloe Mss, T2118, al 1139, (*PRM*, 2489K) asking a fee of $500 with an advance of $25–30; the addition is listed as completed in Bryan (1989), 185.

52 LC, and SCHS, 11–517–37; *PRM*, 2715–2716.

53 Smithsonian Private Fiscal Records, box 10, 110; Mills was paid a premium of $75 for his design on 30 December 1846; *PRM*, 2489H, 88. For Owen, see *DAB*, 8:118–20.

54 Rhees; Reiff, 89ff; Hafertepe.

55 SCHS, 11–517–39; *PRM*, 2455B. *PRM*, 6009 includes a rendering of Mills's 1846 proposal, and 2472 and 2475B include correspondence between Robert Dale Owen and David Owen concerning the revision of Mills's scheme between August and October 1845 (Workingmen's Institution Library, New Harmony, Ind.).

56 Stanton; Pierson, vol. 2; Greiff.

57 AL, typescript AA 737 R5 R631, 548.

58 SCHS, 11–517–39; *PRM*, 2511.

59 AAA; see also *PRM*, 2499.

60 SCHS, 11–517–4; *PRM*, 2507.

61 LC; *PRM*, 2597.

62 Gardner, 2–4; Crane, 169–269.

63 LC, 92, 93, 99, 110; *PRM*, 4006.

64 SCHS, 11–517–42; LC, letter dated 19 July 1852 (*PRM*, 2987).

65 Truett, 251–52, and Goode (1974).

66 Draft SCHS, 11–517–40, with two sketches, fair copy LC; *PRM*, 2502–2506. Mills's fee is noted in Senate Misc. Report 9 (30th Cong., 1st sess.), 16 December 1847.

67 Noted in Senate Misc. Document 7 (30th Cong., 2d sess.), 1848.

68 Douglas warned of the danger of vibration in windy weather and of lightning and criticized the conduct of the contractors in House Exec. Document 61 (30th Cong., 1st sess.), 4 May 1848.

69 Senate Misc. Document 9 (30th Cong., 1st sess.), 16 December 1847; NA, RG 217, Warrant 22, 100.906 (OAC). House Misc. Document 4 (30th Cong., 2d sess.), 18 December 1848, records a payment of $25 on 8 December for another set of plans of the gas system.

70 NA, RG 42, Ledger, vol. 7, 192.

71 UV, Hunter Mss, 10, no. 142; *PRM*, 2539, 2540 official version, NA, RG 233.

72 Commissioner of Public Buildings and Grounds Reports for 1849 and 1850 list expenditures of some $12,500 (House Exec. Documents 34, 30).

73 Tulane (*PRM*, 2705); 2706–2707, are other versions at SCHS and Smithsonian, reprinted Gallagher, 168–71; in the draft, Mills referred to the recent completion of the marine hospital at New Orleans, which would date its inception to 1848 (*PRM*, 2509, Mills's letter of 26 October 1847 to R. J. Walker concerning the use of bricks for the hospital [NA, RG 56]).

74 LC, Corwin Papers, vol. 2, pt. 1, no. 543; *PRM*, 2717.

75 AL, typescript, 4 April 1842.

76 Wilson.

77 Comparable with the letter Thomas U. Walter had addressed on 17 April 1838 to L. C. Loudon, editor of the British *Architectural Review*, quoted in Liscombe (1980), 307.

78 Scott in Bryan (1989), 158–65, figs. 5.10, Mills design (NA, RG, 42, WMAP–16; *PRM*, 6015), and 5.12, based on the official records (NA, RG, 42).

79 Mills's design also compares favorably with the more ornate obelisk scheme that Lafever was to enter in the abortive 1854 competition for a Washington Monument in New York City, which was not executed (Landy, 140–46).

80 Harvey, 26–28; Lowry (1976), vol. 1, chap. 5; Mills's design is illustrated in Gebhard and Nevins, 38, pl. 12.

81 Compare the only other, anonymous, design apparently surviving from the competition (NA, RG 42, WMAP–13), a crudely drawn pen elevation that shows a thick Doric column rising from a row of caryatid figures atop a pedestal fronted by a six-column Doric pedimented portico and supporting a statue of Washington; the portico base was formerly identified as the work of the youthful Mills by Fiske Kimball (Gallagher, illus. opp. 8).

82 Force, *Picture of Washington,* 87ff.

83 The British architect William Wilkins had projected a diminutive version of such top-lighting to illuminate statuary in the base of his unexecuted 1828 design for a monument to the Duke of York (Liscombe [1980], 113, 187).

84 SCHS, 11–517–11; that to Judge Cranch is GUL; *PRM,* 2470. Harvey, 38ff, relates the fund-raising campaign.

85 Harvey, 41–43, for this phase, and Scott in Bryan (1989), 166–71; see also *Riders Washington,* 342–44.

86 A copy is at the HSP, Ba 984 H 672 also illustrated in Craig, 153, and a smaller version in Bryan (1989), fig. 5.19; *PRM,* 6015.

87 Harvey, 43–48, 111–12, for the order of the parade, and 113–43, for the oration, prayer, and address.

88 Two working drawings, probably traced for Mills since the captions differ from his inscription, dated 24 October 1848, are with the Society for the Preservation of New England Antiquities (Bryan [1989], fig. 5.21; *PRM,* 6015). The article is reprinted in House Exec. Document 1, pt. 8 (45th Cong., 2d sess.), 1877, "Report of the Joint Commission . . . Washington Monument."

89 Payments listed House Report 48 (42d Cong., 2d sess.), 19 April 1872, "Report of the Joint Commission . . . Washington Monument."

90 Journal of Proceedings, Smithsonian Institution, 7058, vol. 2, 409–16, including Mills's response; *PRM,* 2630. 2697A is Mills's response of 19 November.

91 Gallagher, 120.

92 Harvey, 50–51, 238.

93 On 23 April, Smith acknowledged receipt of Mills's drawing and that he had "taken some liberties with the Monument" (LC; [*PRM,* 2978, 2980]); reproduced Goode (1979), fig. 170, and Bryan (1989), fig. 5.18.

94 UV; *PRM,* 2954.

95 Goode (1974), 384–85, originally to have been raised on a high, three-tier plinth decorated with reliefs.

96 Harvey, 52–64, for this episode.

97 Craig, 152; the *American Architect and Building News,* 13 May 1876, further stated that Mills's original design had been "made at a very undeveloped period in our architecture, and does not comport, unless by its bigness, with either the dignity of its aim, or the requirements of American architects."

98 House Report 90 (30th Cong., 2d sess.); on 30 April 1849, however, Cluskey would tell Ignatius Mudd that Mills's specification for the Patent Office wing was too imprecise (NA, RG 48, [*PRM,* 2619]). For Cluskey, see Nichols (1976), 58–59, and Lehman (1973).

99 LC; *PRM,* 2597.

100 NA, RG 46, SEN 31A–D1; *PRM,* 6011.

101 NA, RG 42, Letters, no. 3105/7; the government refused to reinstate Mills's former title, D. C. Goddard to I. Mudd, 20 April 1849 (*PRM,* 2616). See also Evelyn in Bryan (1989), 124–25, 132–36, figs. 4.12, 4.15, working drawing for the east facade (AIA [*PRM,* 6007]).

102 1849 Report, House Exec. Document 30 (31st Cong., 1st sess.), 24 January 1850; these cost about $4,700 (NA, RG 42, Ledger, vol. 7, 284–85); Mills was paid

$150 on 26 March 1853 (vol. 8, 422). NA, RG 42, no. 3119, Mills to Mudd 5 July 1850, proposing that water be piped from Rock Creek at a cost of $550,000 (printed in 1853 as *Waterworks for the Metropolitan City of Washington*); see also Evelyn in Bryan (1989), 133–36.

103 House Exec. Document 28 (31st Cong., 1st sess.), 24 January 1850; the 100-foot-square wings scheme was published in House Report 334 (28th Cong., 1st sess.), 12 August 1844.

104 House Exec. Document 28 (31st Cong., 1st sess.), 24 January 1850.

105 NA, RG 42, Contracts.

106 House Exec. Document 28 (31st Cong., 1st sess.), 24 January 1850.

107 NA, RG 42, Letters, no. 3144/1.

108 The twenty articles printed from 3 September to 7 December 1849 are reproduced in *PRM*, 266off. SCHS, 11–517–11, dated 13 August. The monument is cited by Scott in Bryan (1989), 171, noting that Mills was also consulted contemporaneously about the Kentucky War Monument.

109 Nye.

110 VSL, 755. 44/24 folder 5 (*PRM*, 2719–2721), and VHS, Mss 2/M6283/a, possibly drawn by Emil S. Friedrich, whom Mills would hire in 1852; *PRM*, 6085.

111 LC; (*PRM*, 3077) dated ca. 1854 in Bryan (1989), 172.

112 VSA; Brumbaugh; Crane, 341–53.

113 VSA, Washington Monument Vouchers, box 18.

114 Severens, 170.

115 *Report of the Select Committee on the Subject of the Washington Monument* (1852), House of Delegates Report no. 54.

116 Printed House of Delegates Document 53, 9 March 1852; draft, SCHS, 11–517–18.

117 VHS, Robinson Mss, 1 R 5685 b741, Mills's letter of apology to Robinson of 18 March 1852 (*PRM*, 2974); 2997 is Crawford's letter of 12 August to Robinson.

118 Printed as House of Delegates Document 10, "Report on the Statue House"; *PRM*, 2968.

119 VHS; the monument was largely completed in 1854.

120 Tulane (*PRM*, 2738A); the letter is not in Mills's handwriting. Life in contemporary Washington is described in Pryor.

121 *Congressional Globe* (1850), pt. 2, 416.

122 Senate Report 145 (31st Cong., 1st sess.), 28 May 1850.

123 LC, and Davis Papers (*PRM*, 2796C; 2735C is Mills's official letter to Davis of 1 May, NA, RG 46, SEN 31A–D1). Mills would repeat the argument in a letter to Senator Stanton, a draft of which is reprinted, Gallagher, 71–73. See also Eaton, 76–77.

124 Lowry (1985), 30.

125 NA, RG 46, 29A–D3 (1846), accompanied by a "Plan of the Capitol as it now is" (*PRM*, 6011.); the inscription on the letter indicates a date before Davis resigned from the Senate in September 1851.

126 OAC, the location of the other drawings cited below, each reproduced under *PRM*, 6011.

127 Senate Report 145 (31st Cong., 1st sess.), 28 May 1850.

128 Kerr in 1891 edition of Fergusson, 1:357.

129 Respectively, OAC, and AP, Thomas U. Walter Papers; *PRM*, 6011.

130 New York Public Library, Davis Papers, box 1, file 50.

131 The articles are reproduced in *PRM*, 2763Bff. SCHS 11–517–24, is a preliminary estimate of $295,515 for the water supply from the Edisto River.

132 *Statutes at Large of South Carolina*, 12 (1874):279.

133 *Congressional Globe* (1850), 1876.

134 *Congressional Globe* (1850), 1944, 1970–71.

135 LC; *PRM*, 2714.

136 *Scientific American,* 22 January and 1 February 1851, and Mills's reply 23 August 1851; *PRM*, 2818, 2821, 2919.

137 NA, RG 121, box 1422, undated (Treasury extension), and NA, RG 56f, letter dated 21 September; *PRM*, 2784.

138 LC, Corwin Papers, vol. 2, pt. 1, nos. 628 and 629 (*PRM*, 2790–2791); Mills had read Colonel W. H. Emory's "Notes of a . . . Reconnaissance from Fort Leavenworth . . . to San Diego [1846]" published in 1848 as Senate Document (30th Cong., 1st sess.), and Rondelet's *L'Art de bâtir,* and Pliny for pisé.

139 *A History of Public Buildings,* 44–45, undertaken by Ammi B. Young as supervising architect of the treasury.

140 UV, Cabell Family Papers, 38–111, box 38.

141 UV, Minutes of the Rector and Visitors, vol. 3 (typescript), 219ff.; Bruce, 3:21–27, and O'Neal (1976), 53–56, 73–78, 83.

142 The campus plan had been adapted by Latrobe in his 1812 National University project (Woods), probably inspired by William Wilkins's Downing College, Cambridge (1804–1822), for which see Liscombe (1980), 46–49.

143 UV, RG 31/5/1771; *PRM*, 6082, reproduces contemporary illustrations of the extension.

144 SCHS, 11–517–41, includes a contract with Ward and Brown for the brickwork and an estimate dated 9 April 1852 from a Richmond firm for fourteen capitals for the columns at $110 each and two pilaster capitals at $80, each based on the order of the Tower of Winds at Athens, including transport costs by railroad; *PRM*, 2975.

145 UV Bursar's Account Book, 8437 (1851–1854), 59–64.

146 O'Neal (1976), 54.

147 *Virginia Historical Register,* 6:37–42, signed "R.M."; *PRM*, 3026.

148 SCHS, 11–517–38, (*PRM*, 2807), signed "Virginius," stating that "Mr. Mills proposes to erect this *Monumental Structure* in the Campus of that Institution." LC, Notebook 33, has a sketch possibly intended for a National Monument but being capped by a Lysicrates motif; *PRM*, 4006.

149 Yetter.

150 Senate Report 273 (31st Cong., 2d sess.).

151 Lehman (1973).

152 OAC, now comprising elevations of the east and west fronts, and four floor plans; *PRM*, 6011. See also Lowry (1976), vol. 2, chap. 2.

153 It was more advanced than its main inspiration, Auguste Ricard de Montferrand's St. Isaac's Cathedral, St. Petersburg (1818–1858).

154 LC; *PRM*, 2803; Gallagher, 71–73.

155 Mills's Report is House Exec. Document 47 (31st Cong., 2d sess.), 3 March 1851, applying for $20,000 to finish the east wing and $150,000 to forward the west wing of the Patent Office; accusations NA, RG 42, Letters, no. 3152.

156 NA, RG 42, no. 3154; *PRM*, 2815. Archer's letter is NA, RG 42, no. 3152; *PRM*, 2811.

157 Easby-Smith.

158 *Water-Works for the Metropolitan City of Washington* (1853), 30; reprinted *PRM*, 5011.

159 NA, RG 42, Letters, vol. 10, 58, dated 24 April; *PRM*, 2853 (Mills's reply is 2854), and 2855ff.

160 NA, RG 42, 72–74; *PRM*, 2866.

161 NA, RG 42, 84; their joint report is Letters Received no. 3174 (*PRM*, 2878).

162 Mills to Meigs, 9 April 1853 (OAC); *PRM*, 3042.

163 NA, RG 42, Letters, vol. 10, 93.

164 Published in the *National Intelligencer*, 14 July 1851 (*PRM*, 2899), and associated with his undated plan of the market, LC; *PRM*, 6003. On 21 July the *Intelligencer* printed his article, "The Coal Trade and Our City Council"; *PRM*, 2904.

165 *PRM*, 6000. Illustrated Goode (1979), 471, taken by Jesse Whitehurst, possibly at the "Plumbe National Daguerrian Gallery founded 1840 Concert Hall Penn. Ave.," advertised in the 1846 *Washington Directory*.

166 NA, RG 42, 185–87; Easby had first contacted them in April (NA, RG 48 [*PRM*, 2833]).

167 Stuart to Mills, NA, RG 42, Letters, no. 3207; *PRM*, 2906. Earlier, on 23 June, Charles Morehead wrote to President Fillmore that he had received excellent advice about a proposed monument (to Kentuckians killed in the Mexican War) and "rarely met with any one who has made a more favourable impression on me" (NA, RG 48; *PRM*, 2892.

168 Evidence of Mills's contact with Stuart comes in a letter dated 12 December 1851 that Easby sent the secretary stating the Mills's worst offense had been to allow Berry to change his bid in May 1849 (NA, RG 42, 185–87). Earlier, on 2 October, Walter wrote contradicting Easby's accusation that Mills had compensated the carpenter, F. Mohun, for door locks and hinges not included in the contract (NA, RG 42, Letters, no. 3232); *PRM*, 2930.

169 Tulane; *PRM*, 2806.

170 NA, RG 42, Letters, vol. 10, 203; *PRM*, 2957.

171 OAC, and an earlier request of 12 January, SCHS; *PRM*, 2961 (Mills's evidence is *PRM*, 2965B).

172 NA, RG 42, 286; Easby's reply is 299–312.

173 GUL, undated; *PRM*, 0001.

174 SCHS, 11–517–43; *PRM*, 3025. In this period, Mills also presented his scheme for the District water supply to the House and Senate (*PRM*, 2958, 3017).

175 SCHS, 11–517–45; *PRM*, 2949, 2952. In December, Gwin had relayed a resolution from the California Legislature petitioning for a railroad from the Mississippi to the Pacific.

176 LC; *PRM*, 2951.

177 SCHS, 11–517–42; *PRM*, 2986.

178 SCHS, 11–517–45; *PRM*, 2981.

179 House Report 344 (32d Cong., 1st sess.).

180 F. S. Smith.

181 A. P., Thomas U. Walter Papers, memo dated 2 February (*PRM*, 2960), most arrived before 17 March.

182 LC Corwin Papers, vol. 10, no. 4184; (*PRM*, 2994). Authorized in 1849, the customhouse was constructed of granite and cost $203,903.75 (*A History of Public Buildings*); Overby, 464, attributes the building entirely to Young.

183 Lowry (1985), 52–53.

184 SCHS, 33–22–9, dated on the verso.

185 LC; *PRM*, 6091.

186 LC, draft SCHS, 11–517–46; *PRM*, 2991–2992. Mills had submitted a similar scheme to Congress on 22 July 1850 (NA, RG 233, HR 31A–G 17.1 [*PRM*, 2757–2758]), as noted by Scott in Bryan (1989), 166.

187 Notebook, LC, 101; *PRM*, 4006.

188 OAC; clipping SCHS, 11–518–5, (*PRM*, 2995A), and *Scientific American*, 21 August 1852; *PRM*, 3001.

189 Designed by I. K. Brunel (Noble, 244).

190 NA, RG 77, (*PRM*, 2996); Glenn and Salley, 20–22, dated 12 August.

191 Gallagher, 185, proposes that Mills visited New Orleans in this period.

192 SCHS, 11–517–11 (*PRM*, 2999); 11–518–4 is Mills's IOU for $16 to C. Eckloft.

193 APS, E. K. Kane Papers, B. K132; *PRM*, 3020. Mills's correspondence with Kane is *PRM*, 3022A, 3027. For Wise, see *DAB* 20:428–29.

194 HL; *PRM*, 3036B.

195 The articles are reproduced in *PRM*, 3052, 3061 (6 August 1853). A comparable article appeared in the *Charleston Courier*, 8 September 1853, as "Mills's Rail Road Track" (*PRM*, 3067B).

196 LC; *PRM*, 3024.

197 OAC, (*PRM*, 3030). This file contains copies of contemporary official correspondence concerning Easby's attack on Mills's conduct of the Patent Office wing, beginning from 27 March 1851, mainly culled from the Committee on Public Buildings and Grounds records, NA, RG 42; *PRM*, 2833ff for the correspondence examined in this section, including Mills's "Synopsis," also preserved in NA, RG 48; *PRM*, 3003–3004.

198 OAC; *PRM*, 3033.

199 The senators, all Democrats, were D. R. Atchison, Missouri; J. A. Bayard, Delaware; S. Borland, Arkansas; A. P. Butler, South Carolina; J. Clemens, Alabama; A. C. Dodge, Iowa; H. Dodge, Wisconsin; S. A. Douglas, Illinois; S. W. Downs, Louisiana; J. J. Evans, South Carolina; B. Fitzpatrick, Alabama; W. M. Gwin, California; J. M. Mason, Virginia; T. J. Rusk, Texas; W. K. Sebastion, Texas; and J. B. Weller, California. The congressmen, all Democrats unless otherwise indicated, were L. Boyd, Kentucky; J. C. Breckinridge, Kentucky; S. Clemens, Virginia; C. B. Curtis, Pennsylvania; O. B. Ficklin, Illinois; J. Gamble, Pennsylvania; A. Gilmore, Pennsylvania; I. G. Harris, Tennessee; A. Johnson, Tennessee; G. W. Jones, Tennessee; J. Lockhart, Indiana; F. S. Martin, New York (Whig); W. H. Polk, Tennessee; W. A. Richardson, Illinois; R. Scurry, Texas; W. R. Smith, Alabama (Union Whig); W. W. Snow, New York; F. P. Stanton, Tennessee; J. W. Stone, Kentucky; and A. White, Kentucky. The letters, OAC, are reproduced as *PRM*, 3032, 3034 (Senators), respectively.

200 The letters cited in this paragraph are OAC, respectively *PRM*, 3035, 3036A.

201 AP, Thomas U. Walter Papers; *PRM*, 6011. The 1 April letter from Davis to Meigs is OAC; *PRM*, 3040.

202 OAC; *PRM*, 3043ff, for the correspondence discussed below.

203 *PRM*, 3069. On 21 December, Meigs, acceeding to Mills's request for the return of his drawings wrote, "I do not think that any of them will be of use to the U. States." For Pierce's attendance at First Presbyterian Church, see Gallagher, 31.

204 LC; *PRM*, 3081. The letter to Salomon is NA, RG 233, HR 33A–G 5.8; *PRM*, 3080.

205 LC; *PRM*, 3084, 3085, as submitted to Congress.

206 SCHS, 11–518–2; *PRM*, 0005.

207 Reproduced in *PRM*, 3089. Mills's description recalls a rhyme about the Charleston Vaux Hall Pleasure Garden, opened in 1798, "Where the jet d'eau delights the eye" (Rogers [1969], 115). In August 1854 Mills sent a final appeal to Jefferson Davis regarding the expansion of the federal buildings (GUL); *PRM*, 3099.

208 *Guide*, 25–27. In a footnote on page 18, Mills stated that he owned a vase made from an elm that stood near the place where William Penn signed his celebrated treaty with the Indians in 1682.

209 In his 1885 speech (Harvey, 239) Winthrop commented of the monument at this time, "156 [high] . . . with the dismal derrick still standing as in mockery at their summit . . . the subject of pity or derision."

210 Gallagher, 215–16, printing most of the obituaries; *PRM*, 3113–3115, 3117.

On 3 March the *Courier and Enquirer* conjectured, "He thought he had been promised the superintending of them [additions to the General Post Office and Treasury], but learned in a few days since that they were to be placed under the supervision of Capt. Bowman and Capt. Meigs. The disappointment was too much for him. He became deranged and died." Kinder notices appeared in the *Washington Sentinel* on 4 March, and in the *National Intelligencer* on 5 March. Not content with his earlier defamation, Archer wrote to the Secretary of the Treasury on 22 March 1855 that the Treasury had been "located, and directed, by deception, fraud and false declarations of the Architect and Commissioner, avowing that the *President,* had approved of the plan and location, to have a wing on the south end of the present building, for the Post Office Dept., and on the north for Dept. of State, to be all connected" (NA, RG 121, box 1422).

211 Journal of Proceedings, Smithsonian Institution, 7058, vol. 2.

212 NA, RG 21, no. 3577 OS; the appraisers were William H. Winter and Thomas A. Scott (*PRM,* 3118).

213 LC, (*PRM,* 3119), the notes of payment being dated 15 April, 25 June, 23 October, and 26 November, the two last to W. H. Winter for $451 and a Mr. Mclain for $556.75; for the Bath Lands sale, see VSA, Bath County Deed Book, vol. 12, 71–74.

Chapter 7

1 Harvey, 239.

2 NA, RG 77; Glenn and Salley, 11; *PRM,* 1089.

3 Resolution no. 178 (97th Cong., 1st sess.), dated 31 July 1981, moved by Senator Ernest Hollings of South Carolina.

Select Bibliography

Publications by Robert Mills (by date)

"The Art of Painting." *Daily National Intelligencer,* 1 April 1815.

"Report on the Survey of Jones' Falls, accompanied by a Plan for the Improvement of these Waters." *Baltimore American Daily Advertiser,* 3 October 1817.

A Treatise on Inland Navigation accompanied by a Map. Baltimore, 1820.

Inland Navigation. Plan for a Great Canal between Charleston and Columbia and for connecting our waters with those of the Western Country. Columbia, S.C., 1821.

"Description of St. Peter's Church." *Charleston Courier,* 22 September 1824.

Atlas of the State of South Carolina. Columbia, S.C., 1825.

Statistics of South Carolina, including a view of its Natural, Civil, and Military History, General and Particular. Charleston, S.C., 1826.

"Plan of a Rail Road" (1826). *Daily National Intelligencer,* 27 June 1827.

"For the American Farmer Timber Rail-ways." *American Farmer* 9 (20 July 1827): 141–42.

The American Pharos, or Light-House Guide. Washington, D.C., 1832. Reprint (as *The American Light-House Guide*). Washington, D.C., 1845.

Substitute for Railroads and Canals embracing a New Plan of Roadway. Washington, D.C., 1834.

Guide to the Capitol of the United States. Washington, D.C., 1834.

New Guide to the Executive Offices. Washington, D.C., 1841.

Guide to the National Executive Offices and the Capitol of the United States. Washington, D.C., 1842. Reprint. Washington, D.C., 1847–1848, 1854.

"Water Works for the City of Charleston." *Charleston Mercury,* 7 August–12 September 1850.

"Architecture in Virginia." *Virginia Historical Register and Literary Companion* 4 (1853):37–41.

Water Works for the Metropolitan City of Washington. Washington, D.C., 1853.

"The Public Buildings." *Washington Sentinel,* 22 March 1854.

Publications on Robert Mills

Alexander, R. "Robert Mills." In *Macmillan Encyclopedia of Architects,* edited by A. K. Placzek, vol. 3, pp. 33–38. New York, 1982.

Alexander, R. "The Potts House Drawings by Robert Mills." *Winterthur Newsletter* 29, no. 1 (Spring 1983):9–10.

Alexander, R. "The Special Orders of Robert Mills." In *The Documented Image: Visions in Art History,* edited by G. P. Weisberg, L. Dixon, and A. B. Lemke, pp. 243–56. New York, 1987.

Ames, K. "Robert Mills and the Philadelphia Row House." *JSAH* 27, no. 2 (1968): 140–46.

Baldwin, W. P. "Robert Mills's Inland Passage." *Carologue* [SCHS Bulletin] 1 (1986): 3–8.

Bryan, J. M. *Robert Mills Architect, 1781–1855.* Columbia, S.C., 1976.

Bryan, J. M. "Robert Mills, Benjamin Henry Latrobe, Thomas Jefferson and the South Carolina Penitentiary Project, 1804–1808." *SCHM* 85 (1984):1–21.

Bryan, J. M., ed. *Robert Mills, Architect.* With essays by R. Alexander, D. Evelyn, and P. Scott. Washington, D.C., 1989.

Bryan, J. M., and J. M. Johnson. "Robert Mills's Sources for the South Carolina Lunatic Asylum 1822." *Journal of the South Carolina Medical Association* 75, no. 6 (1979):264–68.

Clark, A. C. "Robert Mills, Architect and Engineer." *RCHS* 40–41 (1941):1–32.

Cohen, H. "An Unpublished Diary by Robert Mills 1803." *SCH[G]M* 51, no. 4 (1950):187–94.

Cohen, H. "The Journal of Robert Mills." *SCH[G]M* 52, no. 3 (1951):133–39, no. 4 (1951):218–24; 53, no. 1 (1952):31–36, no. 2 (1952):91–100.

Elder, W. V. *Robert Mills's Waterloo Row, Baltimore 1816.* Baltimore, 1970.

Evans, R. X. "The Daily Journal of Robert Mills, Baltimore 1816." *MHS Journal* 30 (1935):257–71.

Evans, R. X. "Letters from Robert Mills." *SCH[G]M* 39 (1938):110–19.

Evans, R. X. "The Washington Monument in Baltimore." *Federal Architect* (October 1973):38–41.

Gallagher, H. M. P. *Robert Mills, Architect of the Washington Monument, 1781–1855.* New York, 1935.

Glenn, B., and A. S. Salley. *Some Letters of Robert Mills, Engineer and Architect.* Columbia, S.C., 1928.

Hoyt, W. D. "Robert Mills and the Washington Monument in Baltimore." *MHM* 34 (1939):144–60; 35 (1940):178–89.

Kimball, F. "Robert Mills." *DAB.* Vol. 7, pp. 9–13. New York, 1962.

Kohn, D., and B. Glenn. *Internal Improvements in South Carolina, 1817–1828.* Washington, D.C., 1938.

Lane, M. "Robert Mills's First Commission." [U.S.]. *Walpole Society Journal* (1982): 59–63.

Lapham, S. "Architectural Specifications of a Century Ago, Being a Copy, with Commentary, of Documents and Drawings of a Church on St. John's Island, South Carolina, by Robert Mills, Architect." *Architectural Record* 53, no. 294 (1924): 239–44.

Liscombe, R. W. *The Church Architecture of Robert Mills.* Easley, S.C., 1985.

Marsh, B. *Robert Mills, Architect in South Carolina.* Columbia. S.C., 1970.

Massey, J. C. "Robert Mills Documents, 1823: A House for Ainsley Hall in Columbia, South Carolina." *JSAH* 22, no. 4 (1963):228–32.

Pierson, W. H., Jr. "Robert Mills." In *American Buildings and Their Architects: The*

Colonial and Neo-classical Styles, edited by W. H. Pierson, Jr., pp. 373–39, 404–17. New York, 1976.

Ravenel, B. St. J. "Robert Mills." In *Architects of Charleston,* 114–33, Rev. ed. Charleston, S.C., 1964.

Scott, P., ed. *The Papers of Robert Mills.* Washington, D.C., 1990. Microfilm.

Waddell, G. "Robert Mills's Fireproof Buildings." *SCHM* 80 (1979):105–35.

Waddell, G. *Mills's Atlas of the State of South Carolina, 1825.* Easley, S.C., 1980.

Waddell, G., and R. W. Liscombe. *Robert Mills's Courthouses and Jails.* Easley, S.C., 1982.

Williams, G. W. "Robert Mills's Contemplated Additions to St. Michael's Church, Charleston and Doctrine of Sounds." *JSAH* 12 (1953):23–31.

Wilson, C. C. "Robert Mills, Architect." *Bulletin of the University of South Carolina* 77 (1919):5–47.

Publications cited in the text

Adams, W. H., ed. *The Eye of Jefferson.* Washington, D.C., 1976.

Alberts, R. C. *Benjamin West: A Biography.* Boston, 1978.

Alder, G. "Robert Mills and United States Marine Hospitals." M.A. thesis, University of Missouri, 1974.

Alexander, R. *The Architecture of Maximilian Godefroy.* Baltimore, 1974.

Alexander, R. "Neoclassical Wrought Iron in Baltimore." *Winterthur Portfolio* 18 (1983):147–86.

Allen, G. W. *Our Navy and the Barbary Corsairs.* 1905. Reprint. Hamden, Conn., 1965.

Allen, R. S. "Documenting Early American Technology: Covered Bridge." In *Historic America: Buildings, Structures, and Sites,* edited by A. Stamm and C. F. Peatross. Washington, D.C., 1983.

Armstrong, E. C., ed. *History of Public Works in the United States, 1776–1976.* Chicago, 1976.

Babcock, J. W. "State Hospital for the Insane Columbia S.C." In *The Institutional Care of the Insane in the United States and Canada.* N.p., 1916.

Baigell, M. "John Haviland in Philadelphia." *JSAH* 25 (1966):197–208.

Baird, R. *Impressions and Experiences of the West Indies and North America in 1849.* London, 1850.

Baltimore, Past and Present. Baltimore, 1871.

Barsett, J. S., ed. *Correspondence of Andrew Jackson.* 7 vols. Washington, D.C., 1926–1935.

Bénezit, E., ed. *Dictionnaire critique . . . des peintres, sculpteurs . . .* Paris, 1970.

Bergon, F., and Z. Papanikolas, eds. *Looking Far West: The Search for the American West in History, Myth, and Literature.* New York, 1978.

Bethseda Presbyterian Church, Camden, South Carolina, 1805–1955. Camden, S.C., 1955.

Billington, R. A. *Westward Expansion. A History of the American Frontier.* 3d ed. New York, 1967.

Bilodeau, F. W., et al. *Art in South Carolina, 1670–1970.* Charleston S.C., 1970.

Biographical Dictionary of the American Congress, 1774–1971. Washington, D.C., 1971.

Bond, D. J. *The Story of the Citadel.* Richmond, Va., 1936.

Boynton, E. C. *History of West Point.* New York, 1863.

Braham, A. *The Architecture of the French Enlightenment.* London, 1980.

Breeden, R. L., ed. *Those Inventive Americans.* Washington, D.C., 1971.

Brodie, F. M. *Thomas Jefferson: An Intimate History.* New York, 1981.

Brown, G. *History of the United States Capitol.* Washington, D.C., 1900.

Bruce, P. A. *History of the University of Virginia, 1818–1919.* New York, 1921.

Brumbaugh, T. S. "The Evolution of Crawford's 'Washington.'" *VMHB* 70 (1962): 1–18.

Bryan, J. M. *An Architectural History of the South Carolina College, 1801–1855.* Columbia, S.C., 1976.

Bryan, W. B. *A History of the National Capital.* Washington, D.C., 1914–1916.

Caffrey, K. *The Twilight's Last Gleaming: Britain vs. America, 1812–1815.* New York and London, 1977.

Callahan, C. H. *Washington: The Man and the Mason.* Alexandria, Va., 1913.

Carleton, M. T. *Politics and Punishment: The History of the Louisiana State Penal System.* Baton Rouge, La., 1979.

Carrott, R. G. *The Egyptian Revival: Its Sources, Monuments and Meaning, 1808–1858.* Berkeley, Calif., 1978.

Carter, E. C., ed. *The Papers of Benjamin Henry Latrobe.* Clifton, N.J., 1976. Microtext.

Carter, E. C., ed. *Journals of Benjamin Henry Latrobe, 1795–1820.* 3 vols. New Haven, Conn., 1977–1980.

Cartmell, T. K. *Shenandoah Valley Pioneers and Their Descendents.* 1908. Reprint. Berryville, Va., 1963.

Clayton, P. A. *The Rediscovery of Ancient Egypt: Artists and Travellers in the Nineteenth Century.* London, 1982.

Clerk, N. *Palladian Style in Canadian Architecture.* Ottawa, 1984.

Cohen, J. A., J. O'Gorman, G. E. Thomas, and G. H. Perkins. *Drawing Toward Building: Philadelphia Architectural Graphics, 1732–1986.* Philadelphia, 1986.

Coit, M. L. *John C. Calhoun: American Portrait.* Boston, 1950.

Cook, H. T., ed. *A Biography of Richard Furman.* Greenville, S.C., 1913.

Cosentino, A. J. *The Paintings of Charles Bird King, 1785–1862.* Washington, D.C., 1977.

Cowdray, M. B. *American Academy of Fine Arts and American Art Union.* New York, 1953.

Craig, L. *The Federal Presence: Architecture, Politics and Symbols in the United States Government Buildings.* Cambridge, Mass., 1977.

Crane, S. E. *White Silence: Greenough, Powers and Crawford, American Sculptors in Nineteenth Century Italy.* Coral Gables, Fla., 1972.

Craven, P. J. *Adventure in Faith: Three Hundred Years of the First Baptist Church in Charleston.* Nashville, Tenn. 1982.

Dalcho, F. *An Historical Account of the Protestant Episcopal Church in South Carolina.* Charleston, S.C., 1820.

Davies, J. B. "A. J. Davis' Projects for a Patent Office Buildings, 1832–1834." *JSAH* 24, no. 3 (1965):229–51.

Davies, J. B. "Six Letters by William P. Elliott to Alexander Jacks on Davis 1834–1838." *JSAH* 26, no. 2 (1967):171–73.

Denslow, W. R. *Ten Thousand Famous Freemasons.* Clinton, Miss., 1959.

Derrick, S. M. *Centennial History of the South Carolina Railroad.* Columbia, S.C., 1930.

Dickens, C. *American Notes.* London, 1842.

Documentary History of the Construction and Development of the United States Capitol Building and Grounds. Washington, D.C., 1904.

Dohme, A. *Shenandoah: The Valley Story.* Fort Royal, Va., 1973.

Dorsey, J. D., and J. D. Dilts. *A Guide to Baltimore Architecture*. Centreville, Md., 1981.

Downs, A. C. *The Architecture and Life of the Man: Thornton Macness Niven (1806–1895)*. Goshen, N.Y., 1972.

Drummond, A. L. *The Church Architecture of Prostestantism: An Historical and Constructive Study*. Edinburgh, 1934.

Dulaney, P. S. *The Architecture of Historic Richmond*. Charlottesville, Va., 1968.

Dunbar, J. G. *The Historic Architecture of Scotland*. London, 1966.

Dundas, F. de S. *The Calhoun Settlement District of Abbeville, South Carolina*. Staunton, Va., 1949.

Dunlap, W. *History of the Rise and Progress of Art in the United States*. 3 vols. 1834. Reprint. New York, 1965.

Dupuy, R. E., and T. N. Dupuy. *An Outline History of the American Revolution*. New York, 1975.

Easby-Smith, W. *Personal Recollections of Early Washington*. Washington, D.C., 1913.

Easterby, J. H. *A History of the College of Charleston*. Charleston, S.C., 1935.

Eaton, C. *Jefferson Davis*. New York, 1977.

Eberlein, H. D., and C. V. D. Hubbard. *Diary of Independence Hall*. Philadelphia, 1948.

Edwards, G. N. *A History of the Independent, or Congregational Church of Charleston, South Carolina*. Boston, 1947.

Elam, C. H. *The Peale Family: Three Generations of American Artists*. Detroit, 1967.

Ellis, G. E. *Sketches of Bunker Hill Battle and Monument*. Charlestown, Mass., 1843.

Epstein, E. R. "The East and West Wings of the White House." *RCHS* 71–72 (1973):596–617.

Etting, F. W. *An Historical Account of the Old State House of Pennsylvania*. Philadelphia, 1891.

Faut, C. Z. *The State House of South Carolina*. Columbia, S.C., 1970.

Fergusson, J. *The History of the Modern Styles of Architecture*. Edited by R. Kerr. London, 1891.

Finkel, K. *Nineteenth-Century Photography in Philadelphia*. New York, 1980.

Fisher, G. D. *History and Reminiscences of the Monumental Church, Richmond Virginia, from 1814–1878*. Richmond, Va., 1880.

Force, P. Q. *Picture of Washington and its Vicinity*. Washington, D.C., 1848.

Forman, S. *West Point: A History of the U.S. Military Academy*. New York, 1950.

Fortier, A., ed. *Louisiana*. Vol. 2. New Orleans, 1914.

Frary, I. T. *They Built the Capitol*. Richmond, Va., 1940.

Freeman, R. B. "Design Proposals for the Washington National Monument." *RCHS* 73 (1973–1974):151–86.

Froncek, T., ed. *An Illustrated History of the City of Washington*. New York, 1981.

Frothingham, R. *History of the Seige of Boston and of the Battles of Lexington . . . and Bunker Hill*. Boston, 1849.

Gardner, A. T. *American Sculpture: A Catalogue of the Collection of the Metropolitan Museum of Art*. New York, 1965.

Gebhard, D., and D. Nevins. *200 Years of American Architectural Drawings*. New York, 1977.

Geffen, E. M. *Philadelphia Unitarianism, 1796–1861*. Philadelphia, 1961.

Genealogies of Virginia Families. Vol. 4. Baltimore, 1982.

"The Genesis of the National Museum." *Annual Report of the Smithsonian Institution, 1891* (1892):273–380.

George, F. D. *History and Reminiscences of the Monumental Church, Richmond, Virginia, from 1814–1878*. Richmond, Va., 1880.

Gibbs, J. *A Book of Architecture.* London, 1728.
Gibson's Guide and Directory of the State of Louisiana. New Orleans, 1838.
Giger, G. J. *A Model Jail of the Olden Time.* New York, 1928.
Gilchrist, A. A. *William Strickland: Architect and Engineer, 1788–1854.* Philadelphia, 1950.
Goode, G. B. *The Smithsonian Institution, 1846–1896.* Washington, D.C., 1897.
Goode, J. *The Outdoor Sculpture of Washington, D.C.* Washington, D.C., 1974.
Goode, J. *Capitol Losses.* Washington, D.C., 1979.
Goodfellow, G. L. H. "William Jay and the Albion Chapel." *JSAH* 22, no. 3 (1963):225–27.
Goodyear, F. H. *In This Academy: The Pennsylvanaian Academy of the Fine Arts, 1805–1976.* Philadelphia, 1976.
Govan, T. P. *Nicholas Biddle: Nationalist and Public Banker, 1786–1844.* Chicago, 1959.
Graydon, N. S. *Tales of Columbia.* Columbia, S.C., 1964.
Greenough, H. *Remarks on Art, Design, and Architecture: Aesthetics in Washington.* Edited by H. A. Small. 1851. Reprint. Berkeley, Calif., 1957.
Greiff, C. M. *John Notman, Architect.* Philadelphia, 1979.
Griffith, T. W. *Annuals of Baltimore.* Baltimore, 1824.
Groce, G. C., and D. H. Wallace. *The New York Historical Society's Dictionary of Artists in America, 1564–1860.* New Haven, Conn., 1957.
Guiness, D., and J. T. Sadler. *Mr. Jefferson, Architect.* New York, 1973.
Gunnis, R. *Dictionary of British Sculptors, 1660–1851.* London, 1951.
Gwilt, J. *An Encyclopedia of Architecture.* London, 1842.
Hafertepe, K. *America's Castle: The Evolution of the Smithsonian Building and Its Institution, 1840–1878.* Washington, D.C., 1984.
Haley, K. H. D. *The First Earl of Shaftersbury.* Oxford, 1968.
Hall, L. "Mills, Strickland and Walter: Their Adventures in a World of Science." *Magazine of Art* 40 (1947):266–71.
Hall, L. "The Design of the Old Patent Office." *JSAH* 25, no. 1 (1956):27–30.
Hamlin, T. *Greek Revival Architecture in America.* New York, 1944; rev., ed. 1964.
Hamlin, T. "Federal Architecture in Washington: The First Fifty Years." *Magazine of Art* 43 (1950):223–29.
Hamlin, T. *Benjamin Henry Latrobe.* New York, 1955.
Hampton, A. F. *Historic Courthouses of South Carolina: Colleton County.* Columbia, S.C., 1980.
Harnsberger, D. "In Delorme's Manner." M.A. thesis, University of Virginia, 1981.
Harris, J. *Sir William Chambers, Knight of the Polar Star.* London, 1970.
Harris, J. *The Palladians.* New York, 1982.
Harvey, F. L. *History of the Washington National Monument and Washington National Monument Society.* Washington, D.C., 1903.
Hayes, J. *Thomas Gainsborough, 1727–1788.* London, 1975.
Haynes, G. H. *The Senate of the United States: Its History and Practice.* Vol. 2. New York, 1960.
Hegarty, T. P. *Manual and Directory: St. Peter's Catholic Church.* Columbia, S.C., 1901.
Hegarty, T. P. *History of St. Peter's Parish Church, Columbia, S.C.* Columbia, S.C., 1914.
Hennig, H. K. *Columbia: Capital City of South Carolina, 1786–1936.* 1936. Reprint. Columbia, S.C., 1966.
Hermann, W. *Laugier and Eighteenth-Century French Theory.* London, 1962.
A History of Public Buildings Under the Control of the Treasury. Washington, D.C., 1901.

Hindle, B., ed. *Material Culture of the Wooden Age.* Tarrytown, N.Y., 1981.

Hitchcock, H. R., and W. Seale. *Temples of Democracy: State Capitols of the U.S.A.* New York, 1976.

Hollis, D. W. *University of South Carolina.* Vol. 1, *South Carolina College.* Columbia, S.C., 1951.

Howe, G. *History of the Presbyterian Church in South Carolina.* 2 vols. Columbia, S.C., 1870, 1883.

Howland, R. H., and E. P. Spencer. *The Architecture of Baltimore: A Pictorial History.* Baltimore, 1953.

Huss, W. A. *The Master Builders: A History of the Grand Lodge of Accepted Masons of Pennsylvania.* Vol. 1, *1731–1873.* Philadelphia, 1986.

Jackson, J. *Early Philadelphia Architects and Engineers.* Philadelphia, 1922.

Jackson, J. *Encyclopedia of Philadelphia.* Vol. 4. Harrisburg, 1933.

Johnson, M. "Madame Rivardi's Seminary in the Gothic Mansion." *Pennsylvania Magazine of History and Biography* 54, no. 1 (1980):3–38.

Jones, C. *Lost Baltimore Landmarks.* Baltimore, 1982.

Jordy, W. *American Buildings and Their Architects: The Impact of European Modernism in the Mid-Twentieth Century.* New York, 1970.

Julien, C., and D. W. Hollis. *Look to the Rock: One Hundred Antebellum Presbyterian Churches of the South.* Richmond, Va., 1961.

Kennedy, R. "Arlington House: A Mansion That Was a Monument." *Smithsonian* 16, no. 7 (1985):157–66.

Kidder Smith, G. E. *The Architects of the United States.* Vol. 2, *The South and Midwest.* New York, 1981.

Kidney, W. S., and J. R. Morrison. *Winchester: Limestone, Sycamores and Architecture.* Winchester, Va., 1977.

Kimball, F. *Thomas Jefferson, Architect.* Edited by F. D. Nichols. 1916. New York, 1968.

Kirker, H. *The Architecture of Charles Bulfinch.* Cambridge, Mass., 1969.

Kirker, H. "Charles Bulfinch." In *Macmillan Encyclopedia of Architects,* edited by A. K. Placzek. Vol. 1, pp. 321–29. New York, 1982.

Kirkland, T., and R. M. Kennedy. *Historic Camden: Part II, Nineteenth Century.* Columbia, S.C., 1965.

Kohn, H. M. *Great South Carolinians.* Columbia, S.C., 1940.

Kouwenhoven, J. A. *The Columbia Historical Portrait of New York.* New York, 1972.

Landy, J. *The Architecture of Minard Lafever.* New York, 1970.

Lane, M. *Architecture of the Old South: South Carolina.* Savannah, Ga., 1984.

Lane, M. *Architecture of the Old South: North Carolina.* Savannah, Ga., 1985.

Legerton, C. L. *Historic Churches of Charleston.* Edited by E. G. Lilley. Charleston, S.C., 1968.

Lehman, D. J. *Executive Office Building.* General Services Administration, Historical Study No. 3. Washington, D.C., 1964.

Lehman, D. J. *Lucky Landmark: A Study of a Design and Its Survival.* General Services Administration, Historical Study No. 4. Washington, D.C., 1973.

Lerski, H. H. *William Jay: Itinerant English Architect, 1792–1837.* New York, 1983.

Liscombe, R. W. *William Wilkins, 1778–1839.* Cambridge, 1980.

Liscombe, R. W. "T. U. Walter's Gift of Drawings to the Institute of British Architects." *JSAH* 39, no. 4 (1980):307–11.

Liscombe, R. W. "Charles B. Cluskey." In *Macmillan Encyclopedia of Architects,* edited by A. K. Placzek. Vol. 1, p. 427. New York, 1982.

Liscombe, R. W. "A New Era in My Life: Ithiel Town Abroad." *JSAH* 50, no. 1 (1991):5–17.

Lowry, B., ed. *The Architecture of Washington.* 2 vols. Washington, D.C., 1976.

Lowry, B., ed. *Building a National Image: Architectural Drawings for the American Democracy, 1789–1912*. Washington, D.C., 1985.

Lucas, F. *A Picture of Baltimore*. Baltimore, 1832.

McCauley, L. B. *Maryland Historical Points, 1752–1889*. Baltimore, 1975.

Maddex, D. *Historic Buildings of Washington, D.C.* Pittsburgh, 1973.

Marion, J. F. *The Charleston Story*. Harrisburg, Pa., 1978.

Massey, J. C. *Two Centuries of Philadelphia Architectural Drawings*. Philadelphia, 1964.

Mathias, C. M. C. "Court Square, Frederick." *MHM* 47, no. 1 (1952):119–20.

Mayer, A. *The Kings Chapel: The First Century, 1686–1787*. Boston, 1976.

Mazyck, A. *Charleston in 1883*. Edited by G. Waddell. Easley, S.C., 1983.

Mease, J. *A Picture of Philadelphia*. Philadelphia, 1811; rev., ed. 1824.

Mease, J. "Observations on the Present Style of American Architecture, with a Plan for Improvement." In *Archives of Useful Knowledge*. Vol. 3, pp. 82–86. Philadelphia, 1813.

Memorial of the Centennial Anniversary of the First Presbyterian Church, Augusta, Georgia. Augusta, Ga., 1904.

Meriwether, R. L., and C. W. Wilson, eds. *The Papers of John C. Calhoun*. 19 vols. Columbia, S.C., 1959.

Meyers, M. "Architectural History of the P.[ennsylvania] A.[academy of] F.[ine] A.[rts] before 1870." M.A. thesis, University of Pennsylvania, 1958.

Mickler, M. P. "The Monumental Church [Richmond, Va.]." M.A. thesis, University of Virginia, 1980.

Miller, A. C. *Chronicles of Families, Houses and Estates*. Pittsburgh, 1927.

Miller, J. J., II. "The Designs for the Washington Monument in Baltimore." *JSAH* 23, no. 1 (1964):19–28.

Miller, L. *Patrons and Patriotism: The Encouragement of the Fine Arts in the United States, 1790–1860*. Chicago, 1966.

Miller, L. B., ed. *The Collected Papers of Charles Wilson Peale and His Family*. Millwood, N.Y., 1980.

Miller, N. "Philibert Delorme." In *Macmillan Encyclopedia of Architects*, edited by A. K. Placzek. Vol. 1, pp. 542–56. New York, 1982.

Mock, E. B. *The Architecture of Bridges*. New York, 1949.

Moltke-Hansen, D., ed. *Art in the Lives of South Carolinians: Nineteenth-Century Chapters*. Charleston, S.C., 1979.

Morison, S. E. *The Oxford History of the United States, 1783–1917*. Vols. 1, 2. Oxford, 1927.

Morrill, P. *Who Built Alexandria?* Alexandria, Va., 1979.

Morrison, D. B. *Two Hundredth Anniversary of the St. Andrew's Society of the State of New York*. New York, 1956.

Myers, D. P. *Historic Report of the General Post Office Building*. General Services Administration Report. Washington, D.C., 1980.

Nelson, L. H. "Robert Mills, Architect and Engineer, 1781–1855: A Brief Chronology of His Activities While in Philadelphia." Philadelphia, 1962. Typescript.

Nelson, L. H. "The Colossus of Philadelphia." In *Material Culture of the Wooden Age*, edited by B. Hindle. Tarrytown, N.Y., 1981.

Nevins, A., and H. S. Commager. *A Short History of the United States*. New York, 1976.

Newton, C. A. "Three Patterns of Local History: South Carolina Historians." *SCHM* 65 (1964):145–47.

Newton, R. H. "Bulfinch's Design for the Library of Congress." *A. Bull.* 23, no 3. (1941):220–22.

Nichols, F. D. *Thomas Jefferson's Architectural Drawings*. Boston and Charlottesville, Va., 1961.

Nichols, F. D. *The Architecture of Georgia*. Savannah, Ga., 1976.

Nichols, F. D. "Thomas Jefferson." In *Macmillan Encyclopedia of Architects,* edited by A. K. Placzek. Vol 2, pp. 484–93. New York, 1982.

Nicolay, H. *Our Capital on the Potomac*. New York, 1924.

Noble, C. B. *The Brunels: Father and Son*. London, 1938.

Norman, B. M. *Norman's New Orleans*. New Orleans, 1845.

Norris, J. E., ed. *History of the Lower Shenandoah Valley*. Chicago, 1890.

Norton, P. F. *Latrobe, Jefferson, and the National Capitol*. New York, 1977.

Nye, W. A. R. *Historical Account of the Washington Monument in the Capitol Square, Richmond, Virginia*. Richmond, Va., 1869.

Oates, S. B. *With Malice Towards None: The Life of Abraham Lincoln*. New York, 1977.

Olson, S. H. *Baltimore. The Building of an American City*. Baltimore, 1980.

O'Neal, W. B. *Jefferson's Buildings at the University of Virginia: Rotunda*. Charlottesville, Va., 1960.

O'Neal, W. B. *Pictorial History of the University of Virginia*. Charlottesville, Va., 1976.

O'Neal, W. B. *Jefferson's Fine Arts Library: His Selection for the University of Virginia Together with His Own Architectural Books*. Charlottesville, Va., 1976.

Oration, on the laying of the corner stone of the Lunatic Asylum, at Columbia, S.C., July 1822. Charleston, S.C., 1822.

Overby, O. "Ammi B. Young." In *Macmillan Encyclopedia of Architects,* edited by A. K. Placzek. Vol. 4, pp. 463– 64. New York, 1982.

Owen, R. D. *Hints on Public Architecture*. Washington, D.C., 1849.

Palmer, T. *Charles II: Portrait of an Age*. London, 1979.

Paré, R., ed. *Courthouse: A Photographic Document*. New York, 1978.

Park, R. *A Sketch of the History and Topography of West Point and the United States Military Academy*. Philadelphia, 1840.

Peterson, E. "Early Architects of Independence Hall." *JSAH* 2, no. 1 (1952):23–25.

Petty, W. E. "Funding a Restoration." *AIA Journal* (December 1966): 61-62.

Pevsner, N. *Some Architectural Writers of the Nineteenth Century*. Oxford, 1972.

Pevsner, N. *A History of Building Types*. Princeton, N.J., and London, 1976.

Pierson, W. H., Jr. *American Buildings and Their Architects*. Vol. 2, *Technology and the Picturesque: The Corporate and the Early Gothic Styles*. New York, 1978.

Placzek, A. K., ed. *Macmillan Encyclopedia of Architects*. 4 vols. New York, 1982.

Pope, T. H. *The History of Newberry County, South Carolina*. Vol. 1, *1749–1860*. Columbia, S.C., 1973.

Port, M. H., ed. *The Houses of Parliament*. London, 1976.

Preamble and Regulations of the Columbian Society of Artists. Philadelphia, 1813.

Prucha, F. D. *American Indian Policy in the Formative Years: The Indian Trade and Intercourse Acts, 1790–1834*. Cambridge, Mass., 1962.

Pryor, S. A. *Reminiscences of Peace and War*. New York, 1905.

Quarles, G. R. *The Churches of Winchester, Virginia*. Winchester, Va., 1960.

Quinan, J. "Asher Benjamin and American Architecture." *JSAH* 38, no. 3 (1979): 244–62.

"The Railroad Men of America." *Magazine of Western History* (1888):67–75.

Ramsay, D. *Memoirs of the Life of Martha Laurans Ramsay*. Charleston, S.C., 1811.

Ramsay, D. *The History of the Independent Congregational Church in Charleston, South Carolina*. Charleston, S.C., 1815.

Rathbun, R. "The Columbian Institute for the Promotion of Arts and Sciences." *United States National Museum Bulletin* 101 (1917).

Receipts and Expenditures of the United States. Washington, D.C., 1831–1837.

Reiff, D. D. *Washington Architecture, 1791–1861: Problems in Development*. Washington, D.C., 1971.

Remini, R. *Jackson and the Course of American Democracy, 1833–1845.* New York, 1984.

Reynolds, M., and M. L. Christovich. *New Orleans Architecture.* Vol. 2. Gretna, La., 1972.

Rhees, W. H. *The Smithsonian Institution: Documents Relative to Its Origins and History, 1853–1891.* Washington, D.C., 1901.

Rider's Washington: A Guide Book for Travellers. New York, 1922.

Riley, E. M. "The Independence Hall Group." In *Historic Philadelphia from the Founding Until the Early Nineteenth Century,* edited by L. P. Eisenhart. Philadelphia, 1953.

Rogers, G. C. *Charleston in the Age of the Pinckneys.* Norman, Okla., 1969.

Rogers, G. C. "The College of Charleston and the Year 1785." *SCHM* 86 (1985): 282–84.

Rogers, T. W. "The Great Population Exodus from South Carolina, 1850–1860." *SCHM* 68 (1967):16–18.

Rooney, W. E. "Thomas Jeffereson and the New Orleans Marine Hospital." *Journal of Southern History* 22, no. 2 (1956):167–82.

Rosenau, H. *Social Purpose in Architecture.* London, 1970.

Ruch, J. E. "Regency Coade." *Architectural History* 2 (1968):34–46.

Rutledge, A. W. *Cumulative Record of Exhibition Catalogues.* Philadelphia, 1955.

Rutledge, A. W. *Artists in the Life of Charleston.* Columbia, S.C., 1980.

Ryckwert, J. *The First Moderns: The Architects of the Eitheenth Century.* Cambridge, Mass., 1980.

Saunder, F. W. "Equestrian Washington from Rome to Richmond." *Virginia Cavalcade* 25 (1975):5–12.

Schaff, M. *The Spirit of Old West Point, 1858–1862.* Boston, 1907.

Scharf, J. T. *The Chronicles of Baltimore.* 1874. Reprint. New York, 1972.

Scharf, J. T. *History of Maryland.* 1879. Reprint. Baltimore, 1967.

Schlesinger, A. M. *The Age of Jackson.* Boston, 1945.

Scott, M. W. *Houses of Old Richmond.* Richmond, Va., 1941.

Scott, M. W. *Old Richmond Neighbourhoods.* Richmond, Va., 1950.

Scott, P. "Robert Mills's Washington National Monument." M.A. thesis, University of Delaware, 1985.

Scott, P. "This Vast Empire: The Iconography of the Mall, 1791–1848." In *The Mall in Washington 1791–1991,* edited by R. Longstreth. Washington, D.C., 1991.

Scott, P., and A. J. Lee. *Buildings of the District of Columbia.* New York, 1993.

Scott, P., and E. Zimmer. "Alexander Parris, B. Henry Latrobe and the John Wickham House, Richmond, Virginia." *JSAH* 41, no. 3 (1982):202–11.

Scully, A. *James Dakin, Architect: His Career in New York and the South.* Baton Rouge, La., 1973.

Seale, W. *The President's House.* 2 vols. Washington, D.C., 1986.

The Senate Chamber, 1810–1859. Washington, D.C., 1985.

Severens, K. *Charleston Antebellum Architecture and Civic Destiny.* Knoxville, Tenn., 1988.

Simpson. H., ed. *The Lives of Eminent Philadelphians.* Philadelphia, 1859.

Smith, A. R. H., ed. *A Charleston Sketchbook, 1797–1806.* Charleston, S.C., 1959.

Smith, F. S. *Fremont, Soldiers, Explorer, Statesman.* New York, 1966.

Somerville, M. *Washington Walked Here: Alexandria on the Potomac.* 1970. Reprint. Washington, D.C., 1981.

Staiti, P. "The 1823 Exhibition of the South Carolina Academy of Fine Arts." In *Art in the Lives of South Carolinians: Nineteenth-Century Chapters,* edited by D. Moltke-Hansen. Charleston, S.C., 1979.

Staiti, P., and G. A. Reynolds. *Samuel F. B. Morse.* New York, 1982.

Stanendraus, P. "Letters from South Carolina, 1821–1822." *SCHM* 58 (1957):2–12.

Stanton, P. B. *The Gothic Revival and American Church Architecture.* Baltimore, 1968.

Stanton, P. B. "Richard Upjohn." In *Macmillan Encyclopedia of Architects,* edited by A. K. Placzek. Vol. 4, pp. 236–44. New York, 1982.

Stapleton, D. H., ed. *The Engineering Drawings of Benjamin Henry Latrobe.* New Haven, Conn., 1980.

Stillman, D. "New York City Hall: Competition and Execution." *JSAH* 23, no. 3 (1964):129–42.

Stillman, D. "Church Architecture in England." *JSAH* 38, no. 2 (1979):103–19.

Stillman, D. *English Neoclassical Architecture.* 2 vols. London, 1988.

Stoney, S. G. *The Early Architecture of Charleston.* 1927. Revised by A. Simons and S. Lapham. Columbia, S.C., 1970.

Stoney, S. G. *Plantations of the Carolina Low Country.* 1955. Reprint. Charleston, S.C., 1964.

Stotz, C. *Early Architecture of Western Pennsylvania.* New York, 1936.

Stroup, R. E. "The Robert Mills Historic House, Columbia, South Carolina." *Antiques* (December 1981): 1432–33, 1437–39.

Stuart, J., and N. Revett. *The Antiquities of Athens.* 4 vols. London, 1762–1830.

Sullivan, D. K. "Behind Prison Walls: The Operation of the District Penitentiary." *RCHS* 72 (1973):241–66.

Swanson, B. *Historic Jefferson Parish.* Gretna, La., 1975.

Sweet, E. W., R. M. Smith, and H. D. Boykin. *Camden: Houses and Heritage.* Camden, S.C., 1978.

Tanner, H. S. *Memoir on the Recent Surveys, Observations, and Internal Improvements in the United States.* Philadelphia, 1829.

Tatman, S. L., and R. W. Moss. *Biographical Dictionary of Philadelphia Architects, 1700–1930.* Boston, 1985.

Tatum, G. B. *Penn's Great Town.* Philadelphia, 1961.

Tatum, G. B. "John Haviland." In *Macmillan Encyclopedia of Architects,* edited by A. K. Placzek. Vol. 2, pp. 332–36. New York, 1982.

Tatum, G. B. "William Johnston." In *Macmillan Encyclopedia of Architects,* edited by A. K. Placzek. Vol. 2. pp. 502–3. New York, 1982.

Tatum, G. B. "William Strickland." In *Macmillan Encyclopedia of Architects,* edited by A. K. Placzek. Vol. 4, pp. 139–44. New York, 1982.

Thomas, A. S. "The Protestant Episcopal Society for the Advancement of Christianity in South Carolina." *Historical Magazine of the Protestant Episcopal Church* (December 1952):447–60.

Thomas, A. S. *An Historical Account of the Protestant Episcopal Church in South Carolina.* Charleston, S.C., 1957.

Thorndike, J. J., ed. *Three Centuries of Notable American Architects.* New York, 1981.

Three Centuries of Custom Houses. Washington, D.C., 1972.

Tinkcom, M. B. "Urban Reflections in a Trans-Atlantic Mirror." *Pennsylvania Magazine of History and Biography* 100, no. 3 (1976):309.

Tocqueville, A. de. *Democracy in America.* 1835. Translated by Henry Reeve. Revised by Francis Bowen. 2 vols. New York, 1956.

Toker, F. K. *Pittsburgh: An Urban Portrait.* Pittsburgh, 1985.

Topham, W. "The Winder Building." *RCHS* 37–38 (1973):169–72.

Toro, L. P. "The Latrobe Survey of New Castle, 1804–1805." M.A. thesis, University of Delaware, 1971.

Truett, R. B., ed. *Washington D.C.: A Guide to the Nation's Capital.* 1942. Reprint. New York, 1968.

Tuthill, L. *History of Architecture from the Earliest Time: Its Present Condition in Europe and the United States.* Philadelphia, 1848.

United States Copyrights, 1794–1858. Washington, D.C., 1925.

Van Horne, J. C., and L. W. Formwalt, eds. *The Correspondence and Miscellaneous Papers of Benjamin Henry Latrobe.* 3 vols. New Haven, Conn., 1984–1986.

Varle, C. *A Complete View of Baltimore.* Baltimore, 1833.

Waddell, G. "The Introduction of Greek Revival Architecture to Charleston." In *Art in the Lives of South Carolinians: Nineteenth-Century Chapters*, edited by D. Moltke-Hansen. Charleston, S.C., 1979.

Wainwright, N. B. "Andalusia: County Seat of the Craig Family and of Nicholas Biddle and His Descendants." *Pennsylvania Magazine* 101, no. 1 (1977):1.

Wallace, D. D. *The History of South Carolina.* New York, 1934.

Walker, D. M. *Architects and Architecture in Dundee, 1770–1914.* London, 1955.

Ware, I. *Designs of Inigo Jones.* London, 1733.

Ware, I. *A Complete Body of Architecture Adorned.* London, 1756.

Watson, H. L. *An Independent People: The Way We Lived in North Carolina, 1770–1820.* Chapel Hill, N.C., 1983.

Weaver, H., and P. H. Bergeron. *Correspondence of James K. Polk.* Nashville, Tenn., 1972.

Webster, R. *Philadelphia Preserved.* Philadelphia, 1976.

Weidner, T. R. "The Journal of John Blake White." *SCHM* 43, no. 3 (1942):162–65.

Weishampel, J. F. *The Stranger in Baltimore.* Baltimore, 1872.

Wheildon, W. W. *Memoirs of Solomon Willard: Architect and Superintendent of the Bunker Hill Monument.* Boston, 1865.

Whiffen, M. "The Early Courthouses of Virginia." *JSAH* 8, no. 1 (1959):2–10.

White, T. B., ed. *Philadelphia Architecture in the Nineteenth Century.* Philadelphia, 1953.

Whitehall, W. M. *Destroyed Boston Buildings.* Boston, 1965.

Wiebenson, D. "Two Domes of the Halles aux blés in Paris." *A. Bull.* 55 (1973): 262–69.

Wiebenson, D. *Sources of Greek Revival Architecture.* London, 1969.

Wilmerding, J., ed. *The Genius of American Painting.* New York, 1973.

Wilson, R. G. "American Architecture and the Search for a National Style in the 1870's." *Nineteenth Century* 3, no. 3 (1977):76.

Whithey, H. F., and E. R. Whithey. *Biographical Dictionary of American Architects.* Los Angeles, 1970.

Woods, M. N. "Thomas Jefferson and the University of Virginia: Planning the Academic Village." *JSAH* 44, no. 3 (1985):266–83.

Yeadon, R. *History of the Circular Church, Its Origin, Building, Rebuilding and Recent Ornamental Renovation.* Charleston, S.C., 1853.

Yetter, G. H. "Stanford White at the University of Virginia: Some New Light on an Old Question." *JSAH* 40, no. 4 (1981):320–25.

Map of South Carolina, from Mills's *Atlas of the State of South Carolina* (1825).

Photographic Credits

The following individuals and institutions have given their gracious permission to reproduce the illustrations as listed below, together with books (cited in full in the Select Bibliography) containing historic photographs:

Architect of the Capitol	85a, 85b, 98, 102a, 102c
The Athenaeum of Philadelphia	16, 59, 99, 104
Charleston in 1883	36, 37, 46
Early Architecture of Charleston	1a
First Baptist Church, Charleston	35
First Presbyterian Church, Augusta	11a, 11b, 12a, 12b
Historical Society of Pennsylvania	13, 17, 19a, 20, 38, 40, 86b
A History of Public Buildings	62, 63a, 63b, 65, 91
Thomas Jefferson Memorial Foundation	5a, 5b
Library of Congress, Historic American Buildings Survey	33b, 65b
Library of Congress, Manuscripts Division	29b, 30, 55a, 55b, 66b, 73a, 73b, 74a, 74b, 74c, 74d, 75a, 75b, 77, 93a, 93b
Library of Congress, Prints and Photographs Division	8a, 64, 68, 70, 72a, 72b, 79, 80a
Maine Historical Society	66a
Manual and Directory of St. Peter's Church, Columbia	53a, 53b
Maryland Historical Society	26, 28a, 28b, 29a, 33, 34a, 34b, 39a
Massachusetts Historical Society	6b
Mount Holly, N.J., Library	14a, 14b
National Archives, Manuscript Division	57b, 6ab, 87, 92, 100

Index

CAREER: Public Patronage
United States Marine Band, 264
United States Naval Academy (Annapolis, Md.), 163
University of Maryland, 50
University of Virginia, 115, 282. *See also* Jefferson, Thomas: ARCHITECTURE; Mills, Robert: ARCHITECTURE
Upjohn, Richard, 257
Upshur, Abel P., 243, 247
U.S.S. *Princeton*, 247

Van Buren, Martin, 204, 210, 216, 228
Vaughan, John, 66
Vaux, Calvert, 260
Verplanck, Guilian C., 158

Wallack, Richard, 140
Walter, Thomas U., 56, 149, 174, 176, 189, 192, 195, 208, 209, 211, 212, 219, 257, 277–85, 288, 295, 296, 297, 299
  ARCHITECTURE: *Charleston, S.C.:* Hibernian Hall, 149; *Philadelphia:* Girard College, 198, 212; *Washington, D.C.:* Capitol extension, 277, 284, 285, 287, 289; Patent Office extension, 195; Treasury extension, 192
Ware, Isaac: *A Complete Body of Architecture*, 9, 13; (trans.) Palladio, *Four Books of Architecture*, 6, 10, 19
Warren Henry, 67, 267
Warren, Russell, 180
Washington, D.C., 7, 8, 133, 155–56
  ARCHITECTURE: Bridge Street Church, 210; Congressional Cemetery, 159; Corcoran Building, 249; Executive Office Building, 251; First Presbyterian Church, 155, 197; Lincoln Memorial, 166; Long Bridge, 169; Navy Yard, 23, 133, 163; Potomac Bridge, 169, 287; President's House, 8, 23, 208, 209; St. Elizabeth's Hospital, 177; Second Presbyterian Church, 155; Smithsonian Institution, 162; State Department, *190*, 199, 283; Treasury Department, 171–72. *See also* Bulfinch, Charles: ARCHITECTURE; Hadfield, George: ARCHITECTURE; Latrobe, Benjamin Henry: ARCHITECTURE; Mills, Robert: ARCHITECTURE; Renwick, James: ARCHITECTURE; Walter, Thomas U.: ARCHITECTURE
  BUILDING TRADE: 199, 218–19, 234, 276
  GUIDEBOOKS: 172
  MILLS'S VIEWS ON: 8, 153, 155

TOPOGRAPHY: 16, 155, 158, 162, 163, 166–67, 183
Washington, George, 11, 37, 59, 61, 63, 70, 73, 80, 110, 158, 159, 170, 264, 269, 272
Washington Benevolent Society of Pennsylvania, 59
Washington Canal Company, 146, 166
Washington Female Academy, 162, 222
Washington Female Benevolent Society, 207
Washington National Monument Society, 201, 225, 265
Washington Teetotal Abstinence Society, 247
Watterston, George, 170, 253
Webster, Daniel, 231
Wernwag, Lewis, 47–48, 49, 88, 89, 96, 103
West, Benjamin, 41
Whig party, 263
White, Edward B., 131, 154, 272
White, John C., 88
Whittlesley, Elisha, 263
Wilkins, William, 65
Willard, Solomon, 141
Willcocks, Richard, 39
Williams, Amos, 72
Williams, Charles, 83
Williams, James, 69
Williamsburg, Va.: asylum, 119
Williamson, David, 84
Wilson, John, 135
Wilson, T.: *A Picture of Philadelphia*, 51
Wilson, William, 73, 75
Winchester, David, 69, 76, 84, 85
Winchester, Va., 25. *See also* Mills, Robert: ARCHITECTURE
Winckelmann, J. J., 190
Winder, Levin, 69
Winder, William H., 69, 249
Winthrop, Robert C., 247, 264–65, 268
Wise, John, 294
Woodbridge, William, 251
Woodbury, Levi, 177, 184, 212, 230
Woods, John, 36
Woodside, James D., 71
Woodward, Benjamin, 278
Wren Sir Christopher, 65
Wright, Frank Lloyd, 171

Yell, Archibald, 211
Young, Ammi B., 192, 209, 230, 257, 287, 291–92
  ARCHITECTURE: *Boston:* customhouse, 209; *Norfolk, Va.:* customhouse, 292

Zane, Sarah, 61